THE RED FOG
OVER
AMERICA

by

WILLIAM GUY CARR, R.D.
Commander R.C.N. (R) Ret'd

Previous Books by the Same Author

By Guess and By God	*Hell's Angels of the Deep*
High and Dry	*Good Hunting*
Checkmate in the North	*Out of the Mists*
Brass Hats and Bell Bottomed Trousers	*Pawns in the Game*

Copyright 2018

ISBN: 978-1-893157-28-6

Published By: Bridger House Publishers, Inc.
PO Box 599, Hayden ID, USA 83835
1-800-729-4131   www.nohoax.com   Published in the United States

CONTENTS

Foreword

"The Red Fog Over America" is published because the Publications Committee of the N.F.C.L. are convinced that an international conspiracy is in operation for the purpose of destroying our national and religious institutions in America. The evidence obtained by Commander Carr, as the result of thirty five years of investigations, is submitted. We ask our fellow Christian Laymen to study that document and then give us their verdict.

Many honest people support the idea of a One World Government because they have been convinced, by propaganda, that it is the ONLY solution to our economic, political, and religious differences. They fail to realize that ALL organizations with international aspirations have been organized, financed, directed and controlled by the Illuminati since 1786. They secretly intend to usurp the powers of whatever kind of One World Government is first established and then impose the Luciferian totalitarian dictatorship upon those who survive the final social cataclysm. The only solution to our present problems is for the people to insist that their elected representatives establish God's plan for the rule of Creation, as explained to us by His Prophets, and Jesus Christ, and put it into effect in order that His Will may be done here as it is in Heaven.

The Constitutions of both Britain and the U.S.A. state clearly that the WILL of the people shall always be SUPREME. We therefore ask all those who become convinced that an international conspiracy does exist to join with us and take constitutional action to confound the conspirators. We must insist that our properly constituted lawful authorities deal with ALL subversives in accordance with our laws passed to protect the public against such conspirators. They must be dealt with firmly and as they so richly deserve regardless of what their position in government or society may be.

We regret to inform our readers that we have been notified that ALL the books published by Commander Carr previous to 'Pawns In The Game' have been allowed to go out of print.

A. HERRIDGE, N.F.C.L.

GLOSSARY of TERMS & PHRASES

Agentur : Well bred exceptionally clever minded individuals whom the Illuminati select in early youth, educate, and then indoctrinate into the ideology of secular materialism. They are then trained and made capable to act as experts and specialists behind the scenes of ALL governments. The Illuminati thus obtain control AT THE TOP of all legitimate and subversive movements, as well as all levels of politics, economics, finance, industry, the social sciences, and religion. By exercising this control they can persuade, or force, executives to adopt policies which further their own secret plans to bring about a One World Government the powers of which they are organized, and ready to usurp.

Anarchists : Are people who believe a person has the "Right" to do as he or she pleases without restraint. They claim there should be no government, police force, or code of law. Their motto is "The less government the better".

"Apparatus" : Code name for the National organization of the Communist Party.

Asdic : All manner and types of anti-submarine detection devices and weapons.

Auto-da-fe : The extreme torture of the inquisitors.

Baby Markets : A tightly controlled organization which takes unwanted babies from unmarried mothers and sells them to foster-parents for as much as $5,000.

Black Book : A book in which the directors of the international conspiracy kept a record of the private lives of influential people with a detailed report of their characteristics, faults, and failings. The information is used to "Persuade" people into doing the bidding of the Conspirators either because of fear of exposure or for the sake of obtaining more luxury and material rewards.

Black Markets : The markets in the underground and underworld organizations in all large centres of population where smuggled and stolen goods are disposed of. The "Black Markets" are the biggest single cause of bankruptcy and business failures.

Black Nazism : The hard core of Aryan War Lords who believe in the Deity of Man. They dont believe in God or a Supreme Being. They believe the State should be all-powerfull; that only men of Aryan blood should rule; and that all others should be forced to serve the State.

Blood-lust : The last degree of fanaticism when blood only will satisfy the sadistic desires of men and women who have already satiated their animal passions. It is a condition deliberately aroused in "The Mob" by revolutionary leaders as a prelude to introducing their "Reign of Terror".

Bolsheviks : Followers of Lenin : the revolutionary party which overthrew the Soviet formed by the Menshevists, and the republican government formed by Kerensky, in Russia the early half of 1917. The Bolsheviks brought about the Dictatorship of the Proletariat which Lenin promptly turned into a Luciferian dictatorship. Most of the Menshevists and Bolsheviks were liquidated after they had served their purpose.

"Brain washing" : A combination of scientifically applied mental anguish and physical torture used in conjunction with hypnotism, drugs and psychiatrical treatments to induce a person to give up certain beliefs and accept others. It is the exact opposite of God's gift of a "Free Will" to human beings. A common term for Psychopolitics as developed into a science by Sigmund Freud.

Cabala : Originates back in antiquity and has to do with Black Magic and Devil Worship. A modern version was announced in the 10th century as a mysterious Hebrew or Jewish theosophy. It was carried to great excesses as Cabalists among the Rabbis claimed they could explain the hidden meanings of the Sacred Scriptures pretending to read signs, letters, forms, and numbers. It is still practised today in a combination of pagan and heathen rituals used in "The Black Mass" by those who practice Satanism. It is used in the ritual of Illuminism also.

Capitalism : The word is generally used to indicate or identify selfish and greedy men who use ruthless means to obtain more wealth and greater power regardless of who they crush or brush aside. Capitalism is one half of the international conspiracy the other half being international Communism. International Capitalism destroys private responsible enterprise. The international Capitalists use combines and cartels and finance the illegal traffic trade, (used by Communists and other subversives) to put legitimate business and private enterprise into bankruptcy.

Cartels : International agreements between those who produce certain commodities which ensure all those concerned a profit regardless of circumstances or world conditions.

Classicism : Old fashioned ideas "whereof the memory of man runneth not to the contrary" : Ancient and antiquated ideas. Wrong ideas generally accepted as sound.

Combines : National and international agreements entered into by industrialists and financiers by which they control production, distribution, and price of commodities and restrict trade for their own benefit and detrimental to the public welfare and interests.

Cominform : Top-level officials organized to take over the duties of plotting and planning popular world revolution after Stalin dissolved the Comintern in 1944 as a pretended gesture of good-will towards the Western Powers.

Comintern : The Communist Executive Committee which, prior to 1944, was charged with the responsibility of plotting, planning and directing world revolution.

Communist "Cells" : Groups of three to five people who put into effect the subversive orders issued by the Central Committee of the Communist Party in the country in which they reside.

Council of thirteen : The supreme executive of the Illuminati.

Darwinism : The theory that man evolved from the Ape species and was not created by God in his own image and likeness i.e. with a soul, intellect, and free will.

Fascism : The original organization was formed in 1919 in Italy to counteract International and Atheistic Communism. It did a tremendous amount of good for the Italian people until the Agentur of the Illuminati obtained control AT THE TOP, and gradually changed the policies of the leaders until they were led into the various conspiracies which enabled the Illuminati to throw the British and French, German and Italian people at each others throats again in 1939.

Forces of Evil : Every person who thinks and acts contrary to the Commandments of God, and the teachings of His Divine Son Jesus Christ. As Christ said : "He who is not with me, is against me". There can be no compromise between "Good" and "Evil" forces.

Genocide : The practice of destroying a whole race of people to obtain control over their domains. The U-boat blockade of Britain was an act of genocide which just failed in its purpose.

Gestapo : A secret police force controlled by Dictators who have usurped the powers of government.

Glass Club : A luxurious den of iniquity used as an espionage centre controlled by agents of the Illuminati in London, England, 1914-1918.

God : The Supreme Being-Creator of Heaven and earth.

Goyim : A contemptuous term meaning "Human cattle". Some claim it is the term used by Jewish internationalists to refer to Gentiles. The author believes it is the term used by the Illuminati to refer to all those who are marked down for subjection regardless of Race or Creed.

Heaven : Wherever the Rule of Almighty God prevails. There could be heaven on earth as well as in heaven if we so desire.

Hell : Wherever the Rule of Satan prevails. There is Hell on earth everywhere the powers of Satan have been permitted to prevail.

Illegal Traffic and Trade : All business transactions, and professional practices, which are outside the law. People who engage in unlawful practices constitute the subversive "Underground", and are members of the "Underworld".

Illuminati : Members of Grand Orient Lodges who have been initiated into "The Order and Sect of the Illuminati". They are a small but powerful group which include international-minded bankers, industrialists, scientists, military and political leaders, educationalists, economists, etc, etc. They are men who have accepted the Luciferian plan for the rule of Creation as being preferable to that of Almighty God. They worship Lucifer as required by Weishaupt in his book "Morals and Dogmas". They acknowledge the authority of no mortal except their leader. They give loyalty to no nation. They direct the CONTINUING LUCIFERIAN CONSPIRACY to prevent God's plan, for the rule of Creation, being put into practice; they plot to obtain absolute control of this world and everything in it. They use ALL subversive movements to divide masses of the people into opposing camps on political, social, racial, economic, and religious issues, then arm them, and make them fight and destroy each other. They hope to make humanity follow this process of self-destruction until all existing political and religious institutions have been eliminated. They then plan to crown THEIR leader King-despot of the entire world and enforce the Luciferian dictatorship with Satanic despotism.

Internationalists : All who advocate doing away with National Sovereignty and favor a One World Government. They include "WORLD FEDE-RALISTS".

Illuminism : Is the name given the special rites as written by Professor Adam Weishaupt of Frankfort, Germany, at the instigation of the men who in 1773 constituted the High Priests of Satanism. The ritual of the

Illuminati was introduced into the Bavarian Grand Lodge in 1776 as a preliminary step towards infiltrating Grand Orient Lodges into French Freemasonry for the purpose of furthering the plans for 'The Great French Revolution' which was scheduled to take place in 1789.* A modern version of "The Black Mass" was introduced by Gen. Albert Pike 1871.

International Money-lenders : The Illuminati and their agentur who by reason of their cartels and combines and the use of usury have obtained control of the monetary systems and economy of the so called "Free Nations". They lead the people of those Nations slowly into economic bondage so they can ultimately enslave them body, mind, and soul.

Jews : The word is used in its generally accepted sense. The majority of those who control the wealth and power in this world use Jews and Gentiles alike to further their evil secret plans and ambitions.

Joint Stock Company principle : An organization in which the identity of the real directors is never made known to the public. It means "Secret government".

Junkers : Young German nobles who followed military careers out of a sense of National pride and duty. They are not to be confused with the "Black Nazi".

Lesser Brethren : All Jews who are under the Evil control of the False Priests and Elders in their communities. They differ in no way from the masses of the Gentiles who have been led into revolutions and wars by the same "Evil Experts" and "Advisers" who usurped control of our governments.

L'Infamie : The practice of character assassination. The use of calumny, detraction, lies, and slanders to ruin those who try to make God's will and the TRUTH known. Commonly known as "The Smear".

Luxury : Comfort, belongings, extravagances, and possessions purchased beyond a person's ordinary needs. Things bought with money which should be used to benefit others less fortunate than themselves. Luxury is the opposite of Charity.

Mammon : The God of Gold and Evil Power : Materialism.

Marajuana : A drug derived from Indian Flax, generally used in cigarettes to bring about artificial stimulation of the animal instincts in human beings and used to deaden the finer susceptibilities in young people and remove restraints and inhibitions.

May Laws : Severe laws passed by the Russian Government restricting the lives and activities of the Jews in retaliation for terrorism practiced by Jewish revolutionaries.

Materialism : Consideration only for this world's goods and pleasures. The disbelief in all spiritual values.

Miscegenation : Calculated results of indiscriminate intermarriage between white and coloured people.

---

* While this book was in galley proof stage Mr. Ron Gostick, editor of Canadian Intelligence Service, was so impressed by the fact that my independent research reached the same conclusions as Mrs Nesta Webster in "Secret Societies and Subversive Movements", a book I had not read, that he made arrangements to obtain some copies from England. He gave me a copy and turning to Weishaupt on pages 255-257. I find that this modern historian agrees with what I say in this regard.

Mont-Tremblant, P. Q. : A luxurious place of ill-fame similar to the Club Glass in London, Eng. An espionage centre in Canada.

Modern Schools : Those in which Secularism is taught, teaches that our human interests should be limited to the concerns of the present life.

National debts : The accumulation of principal and interest on loans forced on nations to fight wars which were fomented by the people who had the money to lend. National debts were instituted by the International Bankers for the purpose of leading the masses of the people into economic bondage in order that they could then tell them how they must live, what they must think and do, and when they must die.

National Socialist : The opposite to International Socialists.

Nationalist : A person who believes in National autonomy and the right of the people to elect and direct the policy of their government.

Nazi : The extreme "Right" of the Nationalist Party, the same as the Illuminati are the extreme "Left" of the Internationalist groups.

Nihilists : The executioners used by all conspirators who aspire to control of a world dictatorship. History reveals these assassins are to be found in all classes of society. They try if possible to make the murders they commit look like accidents, suicides or natural deaths.

Obscene Movies : These are "Black Market" films. They illustrate the acts described in the very worst of pornographic literature and give full length films showing every type of subversion and perversion. They are owned and controlled in Canada by the agentur of the Illuminati rather than by Communist "Cells". Two distributors are top-level business executives.

Premier-Dictators : The Prime Ministers and Presidents of so-called democratic Nations who Rule by "Orders-in-Council" and decide their governments' policies in accordance with the "Advice" (orders) given them by "The Illuminati" through their "Experts", "Specialists", and "Advisers" with which they have been surrounded. They do not ask for plebiscites.

Protocols : Are the original written record of the conspiracy by which the Illuminati intend to use internationalists of all kinds to further their secret ambitions to form a World Dictatorship.

Psychological Warfare : The war for the minds of men. Those who put it into practice try to make others believe what they tell them to believe regardless of whether it is true of false; good or evil. It is hooked up with propaganda. Every negative thing we see or hear is propaganda for the forces of Evil.

Racketeers : All those who engage in illegal traffic and trade and prostitute their professional knowledge and skills regardless of their race or creed or standing in society.

Reign of Terror : The period in every revolution when the directors stir up blood-lust in "The Mob" and turn them loose on the public so that the vast majority will be reduced to one common level by degradation, physical suffering, and mental anguish. The Illuminati consider it the quickest and cheapest way to subjugate the people, and make them obedient to their edicts.

Satan : Lucifer's Prime Minister; an actual supernatural being with great powers for everything Evil. He is determined to win the souls of men away from Almighty God. Satanists claim he is the elder son of God the Father, and that Christ was the younger son of God. Satanism teaches that Satan was in the RIGHT when he quarreled with Christ.

Sea-lawyer : Seamen who have the gift of the gab and try to convince their shipmates that they know everything.

Secularism : Teaches that we should only concern ourselves with the matters of this life.

Subversion : Every act, every word, and every deed which is against the Commandments of God and subversive to our lawfully constituted government. Every book and picture, every spoken word, which leads persons to believe they are entitled to use force to achieve any desired goal.

Theism : Belief in a personal Deity.

Tyburn Hill : a place which was used for public executions in London, England, until the practice was abolished.

U-boats : German submarines.

Underworld : The place where anti-social people live and where illegal traffic and trade flourishes. A secret subversive empire within the State.

Underground : The revolutionary 5th Column and subversive organizations planned to overthrow the existing government.

Zombies : A name given to men conscripted for military service in Canada during World War Two who refused to be sent overseas as reinforcements for volunteers on active service.

LIST OF ABBREVIATIONS

A.F.L. — American Federation of Labour

A.M.A. — American Medical Association

A.S.D.I.C. — Anti-Submarine Detection Investigation Committee

B.B.C. — British Broadcasting Corporation

B.M.A. — British Medical Association

C.B.C. — Canadian Broadcasting Corporation

C.C.F. — Cooperative Commonwealth Federation (Canadian Socialists)

C.C.L. — Canadian Congress of Labour

C.C.M.C.O. — Council of Clergy and Ministers for Common Ownership

C.I.O. — Congress of Industrial Organizations

C.I.I.A. — Canadian Institute of International Affairs

C.P.R. — Canadian Pacific Railway

C.M.A. — Canadian Medical Association

C.N.R. — Canadian National Railway

D.S.C.R. — Department of Soldiers Civil Re-establishment

D.V.A. — Department of Veteran Affairs (Canada)

E.D.C. — European Defence Council

F.B.I. — Federal Bureau of Investigation (U.S.A.)

G.P.S. — General Political Strike

I.P.R. — Institute of Pacific Relations

I.G.P.S. — International General Political Strike

L.I.D. — League for Industrial Relations

N.A.T.O. — North Atlantic Treaty Organization

N.F.C.L. — National Federation of Christian Laymen

N.S.H.Q. — Naval Service Headquarters (Ottawa)

P.E.A. — Progressive Educational Association

P.Q. — Province of Quebec

R.C.M.P. — Royal Canadian Mounted Police

R.C.N. — Royal Canadian Navy

U.T.G. — Spanish Labour Organization

U.N.O. — United Nations Organization

U.S.S.R. — The so-called Union of Soviet Socialist Republics

W.R.M. — World Revolutionary Movement

CHAPTER I

The International Conspiracy

The Protocols or Scheme explained

INTERNATIONALISM, regardless of whether it be Communistic or Capitalistic is diametrically opposed to God's plan of creation. God, the Creator, quite obviously intended that the world should be broken up into many nationalities. He made the people of the various nationalities speak different languages. God evidently planned·that races and nationalities should enjoy autonomy and should remain separate, except that all members of the human race should be united as brethren under the benevolence of God the Father. Christ made this intention of God's quite clear when he told his disciples ''Go ye, and teach all nations, baptising them in the name of God the Father, God the Son, and God the Holy Ghost''. The Holy Ghost made it possible for the disciples to carry out this mandate by giving them ''The Power of Tongues''. At Pentecost, the ignorant fishermen, and peasants, who had become followers of Christ, were suddenly and miraculously transformed into linguists and scholars. Then they set out to preach the Fatherhood of God and told of the love Christ had for *all* people who would serve and worship Almighty God. — The **FATHER**.

If unity of *all* people under the Fatherhood of God is the plan and purpose of the Creator then it is obviously the plan of Satan to prevent the Rule on earth of Christ as King. This being pure logic, it is obvious that the Devil inspired his agents on this earth to work to establish Internationalism as opposed to Nationalism; The Devil's agents advocate dictatorships as opposed to constitutional governments. That the Illuminati conceived the Long Range Plan for ultimate world domination, and put it into effect, is proved by the number of times it is referred to in the Protocols. Their diabolical scheme was designed for the specific purpose of defeating God's plan for creation and setting up the despotism, and tyranny, of Satan to take its place.

In order to prove this contention the document published as ''The Protocols of the learned Elders of Zion'' must be studied carefully, keeping in mind that despite all arguments regarding their source and origin, they are undoubtedly and indisputably, ''The Scheme'', ''the Long Range Plan'', ''The Plot'', ''The Conspiracy'', whatever you may wish to call it, by which a comparatively small group of men, who are immensely wealthy; extremely cunning; and exceedingly influential, use **GOLD**, lies, and deceits to subvert, and pervert, the human race. They used the promise of wealth, luxury, and carnal pleasures to lure·human beings away from God in order to subjugate them to the will·of Satan.

To support the contention that the materialism of GOLD was used, long before the Christian Era, to subvert human beings away from the worship of God we have the Biblical story of the Golden Calf. To prove how successful the lure of Gold has been we have the fact that today, more millions worship the "Almighty Dollar" and the "Golden Sovereign", than thousands worshipped the Golden Calf in days of old.

In addition to cornering the "Gold" of the world, in order that it could be used to bribe and corrupt those the conspirators wished to destroy, the directors of the international conspiracy caused those they plotted to subjugate to first of all break, and afterwards ridicule and defy, the laws of God. To do this they teach the inversion of the Commandments and they introduce a wide variety of creeds and denominations of religion, including atheistic-materialism as expounded by Karl Marx in his "Communist Manifesto" in 1848. They did this to enable them to move their conspiracy towards the final goal. The men who conceived the diabolical conspiracy, as set forth in "The Protocols", were not atheists. They worshiped Mammon and Satan.

The Protocols — or "The Scheme" by which the Illuminati intend to win ultimate World Domination were broken up by Victor Marsden into Articles and Paragraphs, as a matter of convenience for the student who wished to use the excellent index to be found at the end of the book. The documents which "fell" into the hands of Professor S. Nilus of Russia in 1901 comprised a series of lectures which a member of the Illuminati, or their agentur, had delivered to a selected group of highest degree Grand Orient Masons. These lectures were delivered at a convention reported to have been held in 1900 in the headquarters of Grand Orient Masonry on the Rue Cadet, Paris. Another well informed person claimed the lectures were delivered at the "Clarte Lodge" in Paris. It is quite possible the lectures were delivered in both places, and others also. The only fact which concerns us is the manner in which the substance of these lectures became known. Professor Nilus, who first published the documents in 1905, told friends of mine that he had obtained the original papers from a friend. The friend claimed the papers were obtained from a woman of easy virtue in Paris, France, in 1900. The woman claimed she had picked them up off the bedroom floor after a wealthy and influential Jew, who was a high degree Grand Orient Mason, had spent the night in her apartment. These details are really immaterial. A friend of mine, who knew Professor Nilus intimately, stated that he would vouch for his honesty, his truthfulness, and his integrity. This same friend however told me that despite his opinion, his investigations forced him to conclude Nilus was in error in regard to the source, (beginning) of the documents, and also his interpretation of the word "Goyim" which is so often used.

My friend is an experienced research man. He has conducted many top-secret missions for the British and Allied Governments. He knows international intrigue in all its aspects. He has been an Intelligence Officer in many countries including France, Russia, and Germany. He is an accomplished linguist. I have known him forty-one years and I have never known him to give me a misstatement of fact.

He provided me with many "leads" which enabled me to dig up the information I published in "Pawns in the Game". I mention these facts to justify my belief that he is right, and the better known authorities are wrong, regarding the source and origin of the documents which were published by Professor Sergyi Nilus in Russia in 1905 under the title "The Jewish Peril"; and by Victor E. Marsden, and the Britons Publishing Society, in London, England, in 1921 under the title "The Protocols of the Learned Elders of Zion". Short title — "The Protocols of Zion".

Both Nilus and Marsden, and the vast majority of people who have read the Russian and English translations of the original documents, (which were written in French) honestly believe the protocols, or scheme, disclose the plot by which the International Conspirators plan to destroy all forms of nationalism, and Christianity, in order to ultimately obtain undisputed control of the wealth, natural resources, and man-power of the entire world, and bring about their Messianic Age.

On the other hand International Jewry have persistently claimed the Protocols are a forgery. My friend investigated the claims and denials and reached the following conclusions, with which I agree.

1.) The Protocols as published are not a forgery because to commit a forgery the perpetrator must have an original to copy. My friend convinced himself that the documents translated by Professor Nilus were drafts of a series of lectures delivered over a period of several days.

2.) My friend says he is satisfied that the documents translated by Professor Nilus contain the original plan of the Illuminati, by which the directors hope to achieve ultimate world domination. He says this plan dates back to the earliest days of the human race. It is, as the word Illuminati implies, "The Plan of Lucifer", or those who believe him to be the highest, most intelligent, and the most brilliant of the angels or supernatural beings, who oppose Jehovah, the benevolent God of Justice.

3.) He contends that the directors of the Illuminati were worried in the 1890's because historians like Mrs. Nesta Webster had been studying the plot leading up to the French Revolution which took place in 1789, and particularly that phase of it which indicated that the members of the Illuminati (who had their headquarters in Frankfort, Germany, under Weishaupt, at that time) had directed the World Revolutionary Movement. The very fact that the papers found on the body of the courier of the Illuminati, who was killed by lightning in 1785 while riding through Ratisbon, proved conclusively their connection with the international plot. This, according to my friend gave the Illuminati considerable concern.

4.) Because the policy of the directors had always been to work behind the scenes, and never to allow their identity or their connection with the revolutionary forces to be known, it was decided that a new document should be made available to the historians. The new document was written in such a way that suspicion was turned away from the directors of the Illuminati and directed towards the leaders of the

Jewish revolutionary movement in Russia. Those charged with preparing the hoax used the plan found on the courier's body, but they changed certain words and phrases to make those who read the "New" document believe it was the Jewish plot to obtain world domination in accordance with the policy of Political Zionism as advocated by Herzl in 1897.

5.) The reason the Jews were picked to be the scape-goats was because the directors of the Illuminati had met in 1893 and planned the Spanish American War, 1898, to give them control of the Cuban sugar industry; and the Boer War, 1899, to give them control of the African Diamond Mines and gold fields; The Russian Japanese War of 1904 in order to weaken the Russian government and economy so it might be overthrown by the revolution planned for 1905.

6.) By having the Jews blamed as the authors, and perpetrators, of the international conspiracy the Illuminati felt certain there would be such a wave of anti-semitism created in Russia and France that they, the directors of the Illuminati, could proceed with the rest of the plans for revolutions and wars without being suspected.

7.) In 1900 the Illuminati arranged that the original plan, found in Ratisbon in 1785, be altered to serve their purpose. The conspirators decided the altered plans should be placed in the hands of an outstanding Russian whose character and reputation were above reproach. The man chosen to be their unsuspecting accomplice was Professor S. Nilus. He checked and believed the documents placed in his hands were genuine as in actual fact they really were. By publishing them as "The Jewish Peril" he played right into the hands of the Illuminati conspirators. The revolution broke out in 1905 as planned.

8.) The allegation that the documents were stolen by a prostitute from an international Jew, who was a high degree Grand Orient Mason, caused anti-semitism to break out again in France in 1905. The previous wave of anti-semitism, created by the same Illuminati, had died down by 1905. It will be recalled that it was anti-semitism which caused the Jewish Colonel, Alfred Dreyfus, to be charged with treason in 1894. He was sentenced to life in prison on Devil's Island for crimes he had never committed. He was completely exonerated in 1906. This illustrates most clearly how the conspirators use anti-movements and emotionalism to serve their devilish purpose.

9.) I had conversations in Europe in 1930 with other well-informed people, some of whom had defected from Grand Orient Free-masonry because they had become aware of its treasonable nature. I was given the names of men in various countries who were alleged to be the members of the Council of Thirty-Three. This Council is the executive committee of the Grand Orient Lodges of Freemasonry. From these thirty three men are chosen thirteen members who are the Supreme Council or the Illuminati. The Chairman of this Supreme Council is literally "God" to all members of the Grand Orient Masonry. I was informed that during the initiation ceremonies all reference to God as "The Grand Architect of the Universe" is omitted. Grand Orient Masons swear allegiance to the head of the Council of Thirty Three. They swear to acknowledge no mortal as above him.

10.). The Council of Thirty Three is comprised of Capitalists, Industrialists, and scientists of many countries. I was surprised to hear several Canadians named as top-level Agentur of the Illuminati. I did not accept this information as true at the time even after my experience with the Royal Commission in Canada 1925-1929.

After I returned from Europe I continued my investigations into the organization and ramifications of the internationalists. Canada proved an ideal country in which to conduct such an investigation because the territory is large and the population comparatively small. Knowing what I did it was easy to identify Canadian agentur of the Illuminati who worked in the top-levels of Government, Finance, Industry, and Commerce. They knowingly or unknowingly worked to bring about a One World Government. Men who are knowingly furthering the cause of internationalism invariably lead others to believe that Communism is our real danger while all the time they know that Communism is their instrument of action which they use to destroy men, institutions, and organizations which stand in their way. These men know that they, and their affiliates, have always controlled the Communist revolutionary forces in countries subjugated to date. The French revolutions between 1789 and 1889 and the Russian revolutions of 1905 and 1917 are the best examples of their modus operandi. This has been fully explained in "Pawns in the Game".

Among the Internationals named were the following :

England — The Rothschilds and all their associates and affiliates.

The United States—The Rockefellers and the Schiffs and all their associates and affiliates, headed by Bernard Baruch.

Japan — The Mitsuis and all their associates and affiliates.

Germany — The Warburgs and all their associates and affiliates.

Russia — The Ginsbergs and all their associates and affiliates.

France — The Rothschild family and their affiliates.

These money barons have their agentur in every country in the world. The agentur consist of men and women of *all* nationalities. They work to bring about a One World Government either because they believe in it as the only solution to the present political, social, and economic problems, or because of the rewards they receive for serving the Illuminati. These rewards consist of :

1. Funds and influence to obtain leadership in politics, commerce, or industry.
2. Rapid promotions in the Government's services — the Civil Service — Diplomatic Service — the Armed Forces, etc., etc.
3. Publicity, prestige, and honours in the Social Sciences.
4. Wealth and social security in the luxury class.

It is frankly admitted that many outstanding citizens who have been made into Agentur by the directors of the Illuminati are blissfully ignorant that they are serving the cause of Satan. They have simply been sold on the idea for a One World Super-government. They have not delved into what is behind the promotion of such an idea. It is for the information of such men that "The Red Fog" is written. After reading the evidence in this book they will no longer be able to say, "I did not realize what I was doing".

11.) As my friend pointed out the members of the Illuminati are *all* internationalists, pure and simple. They give allegiance to no ruler except the head of the Illuminati. They worship no other God than Mammon. They accept Satan as the connecting link between them and their God, Mammon, exactly as we believe Christ was made man so he could be the connecting link, the mediator, between our God Jehovah and ourselves. They give loyalty to no nation or government. They have one goal. They intend to obtain absolute control of the wealth, natural resources, and man-power of the entire world. In order to reach that goal they divide people of different racial groups, nationalities, anl religions against each other. They make them fight and weaken each other so they will subsequently be easy to subjugate. Then, when the time arrives for the Illuminati to come out into the open, the conspirators will enforce their Satanic form of Despotism upon the people of the entire world. It will be shown in another chapter how such an oustanding Canadian as W. L. Mackenzie King knowingly or unknowingly, played into the hands of the internationalist conspirators.

But to return to the "Protocols" or "Scheme". My friend pointed out that the documents alleged to have been stolen by the prostitute from an unknown international Jewish Grand Orient Mason, were not minutes of a meeting or a report. The documents were obviously a series of lectures given by a man who was undoubtedly a very high executive of the Illuminati. Statements in the documents make it clear that it required several days to deliver the lectures. It would be unreasonable to suppose that such a high dignitary would be left at such a loose end between lectures that he would have to resort to spending the night with a prostitute in order to have female companionship.

My friend also pointed out how very unlikely it would be for a highly responsible executive of the Illuminati or the Grand Orient Lodge, to carry documents of such secrecy and importance around on his person. It is most unlikely a responsible person would take documents supposed to be kept secret, into a house of prostitution if he did not want them to be picked up or stolen.

The Intelligence Officer with whom I discussed this matter pointed out that if the documents had been lost or stolen every agent of the conspirators would have been detailed to the task of recovering them. My friend couldn't believe it was just an accident which directed the man who gave the documents to Professor Nilus into that particular house of prostitution, and to that particular woman. My friend believes that the man Professor Nilus considered his friend was an agent of the Illuminati.

He also reasoned that the lectures as published, could possibly have been given to a specially selected group of Zionists who were also Grand Orient Masons. As political leaders of the Zionist movement they were probably convinced that in working for Zionism they were putting into effect the intentions of "their" God, who they believed intended that they, as his chosen people, would ultimately inherit and rule the earth.

My friend pointed out that the substance of the plot was the same as that discovered at Ratisbon in 1786 but that the documents handed Professor Nilus had additions which would appeal to Zionists. My friend added, with a smile "If Satan is a Jew — then the documents we are discussing are definitely the substance of a Jewish conspiracy". They are in actual fact the details of the diabolical conspiracy — The proof that the plot was inspired by a supernatural agency, is to be found in the fact that it is flawless and it has had a continuity of action which nothing natural or human could have had. The documents are undoubtedly the conspiracy by which Satan plans to bring about his kingdom on this earth. If it succeeds Christians and Jews; black men and white; Aryans and Semites; Communists and Nazi; Socialist and Capitalist; will all have to fall down on their knees and adore his Satanic Majesty We will have "Peace" and "Security" from the cradle to the grave — but will we enjoy it ? The most important lesson to learn, by studying the details of the plan word by word, and phrase by phrase, is the fact that the directors of the plan admit that they will use anti-semitism to serve their purpose. They blithely mention that they will sacrifice as many of the lesser Jews as is necessary to serve their purpose. The directors of the conspiracy play no favourites as far as race or nationalities are concerned. They sacrifice Jews and Gentiles alike. They acknowledge that they have, since 1773, used Darwinism, Communism, and Zionism to further their secret and selfish ambitions. They boast that they will sit back behind the scenes and use their agentur, trained from birth, to act as "Advisers" and "Specialists" to do their bidding. The history of the past two hundred years shows that the "Specialists" and "Advisers" of the Illuminati have been clever "ill-advisers". They have succeeded in dividing the human race against each other so they could wend *their* way peacefully towards the day when they will come from under cover and say with certainty "No earthly power or cunning can now prevent us putting our King upon his throne and introducing the rule of Satan".

12.) The other point on which my friend thinks Professor Nilus and Victor Marsden were both in error is on their definition of the word "Goyim". Both these men claimed the word "Goyim" was used to indicate Gentiles or non-Jews. My friend says his interpretation of the word actually means "Cattle" and is used in a slurring manner to indicate *all* people of *all races* and *all creeds* who are not educated and trained members of the Illuminati's agentur. With this opinion I agree.

13.) The word agentur is defined by Mr. Marsden as "a word adopted from the original and it means the whole body of agents and agencies made use of by the Elders (of Zion), whether members of their tribe or their Gentile tools". My friend and I agree with this definition if the word "Elders" is changed to read "Illuminati".

14.) With Mr. Marsden's interpretation of the words "The Political", we both agree. The words quite evidently mean "not only the "body politic" but the entire machinery of politics at all levels of government.

After Professor Nilus published "The Jewish Peril" in 1905 the Jews in every country of the world flooded the press with angry protests and denials. No other book has caused such an international uproar. The fact that the book exposed the actual diabolical international plot intended to enable a few intellectual capitalists to subjugate the whole human race and impose their will, and the rule of Satan, on all peoples regardless of colour, race, or creed seems to have been completely lost sight of in the arguments, discussions and lawsuits launched to decide whether the Protocols were, or were not, the Jewish "Scheme" to obtain ultimate world domination.

In Russia the directors of the plot against the Jews made "the Lesser Brethren" increase the hatred of non-Jews by making the Jews take possession of every copy of Professor Nilus's book they came across regardless of whether they bought them or stole them from their owners. One Russian officer, now resident in Canada, refused to sell his copy at any price. Those Jews who wanted to purchase his copy were so persistent that they attacked him and he had to defend himself with his sword.

If a Jew saw a copy of "The Jewish Peril" in the hands of a non-Jew he would follow that person for blocks and offer to buy it from him at his own price. The book only cost the equivalent of a few cents American money but I know of instances in which $100.00 was offered for a copy of the book. Where did the "Lesser Jews" obtain this kind of money to throw away on a dime book? One can only conclude it was all part of the publicity campaign embarked on by the agentur of the Illuminati to arouse hatred of the Russian Gentiles against the Jews and to inflame the Jews with the spirit of revenge against non-Jews so they would revolt and introduce the reign of terror. Copies of "The Jewish Peril" were stolen from houses and apartments wherever spies reported them to be. Copies which were owned by members of the Czar's Household disappeared mysteriously from the bedrooms and apartments.

My friend and I first met in October 1914. We served together in two wars. We have been friends ever since. I visited him recently in his hide-away. I asked his permission to tell the public some of the services he has rendered his King, his country, and the human race — but he asked me to keep his identity secret. — So be it.

This man of whom I speak has often come in contact with the "Specialists" and "Advisers" of the Illuminati. I know of several instances in which the advice he gave our government was not accepted. Subsequent events proved his advice had been sound, while the advice given by other "specialists" led our government agencies into serious error. Sometimes these errors were accompanied by heavy loss of life and costly equipment. In "The Red Fog" the information regarding the Illuminati's conspiracy will be called "The Protocols", "The Scheme", or "The Long Range Plan". All will mean the same thing.

Article IX, Paragraph 2, supports my friend's theory that the Illuminati, or whoever conceived the conspiracy published as the

"Protocols", does create and use anti-semitism to serve their diabolical purpose. It says "*Nowadays if any States raise a protest against us it is only pro forma at our discretion, and by our direction, for their anti-semitism is indispensable to us for the management of our lesser brethren — I will not enter into further explanation for this matter has formed the subject of repeated discussions amongst us*".

Then again — Article II, Paragraph 5, says : "*Through the Press we have gained the power to influence while remaining ourselves in the shade; thanks to the Press we have the GOLD in our hands notwithstanding that we have had to gather it out of oceans of blood and tears (wars and revolutions). But it has paid us, though we have sacrificed many of our people. Each victim on our side is worth, in the sight of God, a thousand Goyim*". God can mean Mammon or Satan.

I have explained in "Pawns in the Game" how Lenin liquidated all the members of the Communist International after they had served the purpose of the Capitalist conspirators. The reader must remember that the majority of those people who were liquidated after Lenin consolidated the Dictatorship for his Capitalistic Masters were Jews. The Jews who were allowed to live were undoubtedly agentur of the Illuminati.

There can be no question of doubt that the Grand Orient Lodges were formed to infiltrate into Masonry. Some Masons undoubtedly are serving the Internationalist Cause. In order that they may know the fate in store for them Article XI, Paragraph 7, is quoted : "*It is this which has served as a basis for our organization of Secret Masonry which is not known to, and aims which are not even so much as suspected by, these Goy cattle, attracted to us into the "show" army of Masonic lodges in order to throw dust in the eyes of their fellows*".

Article XV, Paragraph 1, then continues : "*When we at last definitely come into our kingdom by the aid of coups d'etat prepared everywhere for one and the same day, after the worthlessness of all existing forms of government has been definitely acknowledged — we shall make it our task to see that against us such things as plots shall no longer exist. With this purpose we shall slay without mercy all who take arms (in hand) to oppose our coming into our kingdom. Every kind of new institution of anything like a secret society will also be punished by death; those of them which are now in existence, are known to us, serve us and have served us, we shall disband and send into exile to continents far removed from Europe. In this way we shall proceed with those Goy Masons who know too much. Such of these as we may for some reason spare will be kept in constant exile. We shall promulgate a law making all former members of secret societies liable to exile from Europe as the centre of our rule*".

There are three other paragraphs detailing how the conspirators intend to use gentile Masons like they have used the Lesser Jews and then Article XV, Par. 9, has this to say in conclusion : "*Death is the inevitable end for all. It is better to bring that end nearer to those who hinder our affairs than to ourselves, to the founders of this affair. We execute Masons in such wise that none save the Brotherhood can ever have a suspicion of it; not even the victims themselves, of our*

— 9 —

death sentence — they all die when required as if from a normal kind of illness. Knowing this even the Brotherhood in its turn dare not protest. By such methods we have plucked out of the midst of Masonry the very root of protest against our disposition. While preaching "Liberalism" to the Goyim we at the same time keep our own people and our agents in a state of unquestioning submission".

In order to understand how the revolutionary movement has been developed in Canada and the United States since 1920 the reader must first realize that the World Revolutionary Movement (W.R.M.) has, for hundreds of years, been organized, financed, and directed in all countries by a small group of Internationalists which includes Bankers, Industrialists, Medical men, Scientists, Professors of Political Economy, and others who were experts in political and economic affairs.

Until 1945 the Illuminati had as rivals for World domination an International group of Militarists who were determined to obtain by Military force what the others were plotting to obtain by cunning and guile. The leaders of the World Revolutionary Movement were dominated by International Bankers. The leaders of the rival party were War Lords. The leaders of the W.R.M. organized International Communism to destroy their opponents* and further their secret plans and ambitions. The War Lords organized Naziism to counteract their moves. The International Bankers were referred to as "Semites". The War Lords boasted they were of "Aryan" descent.

The leaders of both internationally minded groups had many things in common. They kept secret the details of their respective "LONG RANGE PLANS", for ultimate world domination. The Directors of both movements shunned publicity and tried to keep their identity hidden. Both Directorates operated on the Joint Stock Company principle. They organized the subversive movements; they financed and directed the operations; they decided matters of policy, but they put their plans into motion through agents whom they placed behind the scenes of governments in the capacity of "Specialists" and "Advisers". The Protocols Article II, Par. 2, has this to say regarding "Advisers".

"The administrators whom we will choose from among the public, with strict regard to their capacities for servile obedience, will not be persons trained in the arts of government, and will therefore easily become pawns in our game in the hands of men of learning and genius who will be their advisers, specialists bred and reared from early childhood to rule the affairs of the whole world. As is well known to you, these specialists of ours have been drawing, to fit them for rule, the information they need from our political plans, from the lessons of history, from observations made of the events of every moment as it passes. The Goyim are not guided by practical use of unprejudiced historical information, but by theoretical routine without any critical regard for consequential results. We need not, therefore, take any account of them — let them amuse themselves until the hour strikes, or live on hopes of new forms of enterprising pastime, or on the memories of all they have enjoyed. For them let that play the principal

* See page 118 of The Mystery of Freemasony Unvailed" by Cardinal Rodriguez of Chile.

part which we have persuaded them to accept as the dictates of science (theory). It is with this object in view that we are constantly, by means of the press, arousing a blind confidence in these theories. The intellectuals of the goyim will puff themselves up with their knowledges and, without any logical verification of them, will put into effect all the information available from science, which our agentur specialists have cunningly pieced together for the purpose of educating their minds in the direction we want."

The Aryan leaders gathered all groups and organizations "RIGHT" of centre, under their wings. The Semites gathered all groups, and organizations, "LEFT" of centre, under their wings. Thus the people of the world were divided into two hostile camps.

The despots who financed, directed, and controlled the "Right" and the "Left" movements knew that they had to destroy ALL forms of NATIONAL governments and existing religions before they would have undisputed control of the wealth, natural resources, and manpower of the entire world.

To further their plans the propaganda machines of both parties were put into operation at full capacity. People with inclinations to the "Left" of centre were made to believe that it was their DUTY to fight and destroy Fascism and National-Socialism. People inclined to the "Right" were made to believe it was their DUTY to fight and destroy Communism and International Socialism. The conspirators set up Marxian Atheism to oppose Christianity. Thus the people of the world were divided on matters of politics and religion.

"Pawns In The Game" revealed historical facts which prove that the Directors of the International Conspiracy not only fomented wars and revolutions to further their diabolical conspiracy but, in addition to making the people fight their wars, they made them pay for the waste and carnage also. While the rest of the people were at each others throats, the conspirators, and their immediate friends, sat back in luxury; they demanded, and were granted, many special concessions and privileges. They were decorated and honoured by the governments engaged in the wars simply because they provided the necessary funds to prosecute the wars. The above statement is justified because Article II, Par. 1, of the Protocols says most clearly : "It is indispensible for our purpose that wars, so far as possible, should not result in territorial gains. war will thus be brought on the economic ground, where the nations will not fail to perceive in the assistance we give the strength of our predominance, and this state of things will put both sides at the mercy of our international agentur; which possesses millions of eyes ever on the watch and unhampered by any limitations whatsoever. OUR INTERNATIONAL RIGHTS WILL THEN WIPE OUT NATIONAL RIGHTS, IN THE PROPER SENSE OF RIGHT, AND WILL RULE THE NATIONS PRECISELY AS THE CIVIL LAW OF STATES RULES THE RELATIONS OF THEIR SUBJECTS AMONG THEMSELVES".

In order to understand the true meaning of the above quotation the definition of "RIGHT" must be known. Article I, Par. 12, of the Protocols says : "Our "Right" lies in force. The word "Right" is an

*abstract thought and proves nothing. The word means no more than :
— Give me what I want in order that thereby I may have a proof that
I am stronger than you".*

Paragraph 13 asks *"Where does "Right" begin ? Where does
it end ?"*

Paragraph 14 gives the answer *"In any State in which there is
a bad organization of authority; an impersonality of laws and of the
rulers who have lost their personality amid a flood of "Rights" ever
multiplying out of liberalism, I find a new "Right"... to attack by the
"Right" of the strong, and to scatter to the winds all existing forces
of order and regulation; to reconstruct all institutions, and to become
the sovereign lord of those who have left to us the "Rights" of their
power by laying them down voluntarily in their liberalism."*

"Pawns in the Game" explains in detail how the Directors of
the International Conspiracy obtained control of the British economy
in 1694. The author tells how for a *loan* of £1,250,000 the International Bankers were allowed to consolidate the National Debt and had
the payments of principal and interest guaranteed by taxation of the
people. Once the economic controls had been acquired the International Conspirators launched Britain into a series of wars and by
1815 they had succeeded in increasing the National Debt to
£885,000,000.

In 1945 the British National Debt had increased to £22,398,-
000,000. The annual charges amounted to £445,000,000. The National
Debt is divided into "funded" and "unfunded" debt. In the case of
the "funded" debt the date of repayment is remote and it takes the
form of Consols and debts due the Bank of England. The name Bank of
England deceives most people into believing that the British Government owns the Bank of England. It doesn't. The Bank of England is
owned and controlled by the International Bankers and, by reason of
the fact that the British people now owe them so much money, the
International Bankers now control the British Government. The President of the Bank of England has in recent years dictated its policy
both as regards its domestic and foreign affairs. The "unfunded"
part of the National Debt consists of Government short loans redeem-
able at a fixed date. Today, 1955, every man, woman and child in
Britain has to contribute almost £100 a year each in order to meet the
demands of the International Bankers in regard to the "funded"
loan alone.

What is true of Britain's economic bondage to the International
Bankers is equally true of every other SO CALLED Democratic
nation. The only difference between Britain and other "Free" democracies is the degree of economic bondage the International Bankers
have been able to impose. In the United States the degree of economic
bondage imposed on the tax-payers is actually higher. In other
countries it is somewhat less. In *all* cases the rapid increase in the
National Debt is due to the fact that the nations have been FORCED
into wars fomented by the International Bankers for the purpose of
weakening national governments so they can ultimately be easily
destroyed by Communist revolutions or FORCED into accepting the
Internationalists ideas for a ONE WORLD GOVERNMENT.

Germany was in very bad financial shape when Hitler came to power in 1934. No unbiased person can deny that, despite the conditions, and restrictions, imposed on Germany by the Treaty of Versailles, Hitler's financial policy and economic system brought about an era of prosperity in Germany that had never been experienced in any country since the International Moneylenders started doing business at the Government level.

Hitler and Mussolini did in 1934 what Abraham Lincoln had promised to do, if re-elected president of the United States, in 1864. Lincoln exposed the intrigue used by the agentur of the International Bankers to obtain economic control of the United States. He publicly announced that, if re-elected, he would put an end to their usury, curb their political power, and eradicate their evil influence. Lincoln had promised to put back into effect. Article 1, Section 8, Par. 5, of the Constitution which reads "Congress shall have the power to coin money and regulate the value thereof; and of foreign coin". Lincoln knew that Rothschild had said : "Give me the "Right" to make and issue the money of any nation and control its value, and I care not who makes the laws". Acting on this fundamental principle the International Bankers had, by 1865, usurped the monetary rights of most of the governments of Europe and the Americas.

Because President Lincoln was determined to end usury he was assassinated. Since 1865 the International Bankers increased the National Debt of the United States until in 1945 it reached $247,000,-000,000. They used the simple expedient of financing the elections of Presidents they could control. They then forced them to lead the United States into wars.

Because Kings were born to rule by hereditary "right", and were generally accepted as "The Anointed of God", kings and kingdoms had to be destroyed by the conspirators, and replaced by republics governed by presidents, before the International Conspirators could put into effect Article X, Par. 13 of the Protocols which says : "*In order that our scheme may produce results we shall arrange elections in favour of such presidents as have in their past some dark, undiscovered stain... then they will be trustworthy agents for the accomplishments of our plans out of fear of revelations... we shall invest the president with the right of declaring a "state of war". We shall justify this last "Right" on the ground that the President, as chief of the whole army of the country, must have it at his disposal, in case of need for the defence of the new republican constitution... etc.*"

The intentions of the International Conspirators to use wars to serve their purpose is proved by Article VII, Par. 3 of the Protocols, which says : "*We must be in a position to respond to every act of opposition by WAR with the neighbours of that country which dares to oppose us : but if these neighbours should also venture to stand collectively together against us, then we must offer resistance by a universal war*".

The International Bankers in every country in the world completed their amalgamations by 1907. The passing of the Federal Reserve banking legislation was the last act necessary to give the International Conspirators control over the economy of the U.S.A. as they controlled European economy. Two World Wars have increased all national debts until now in 1955 the people of the so called "free" nations are actually slaves of the International Bankers.[1]

Since 1789, when the Geat French Revolution took place, crowned heads have fallen like ripe fruit. Article III, Par. 14 of the Protocols says : *"Remember the French Revolution, to which it was we who gave the name "GREAT"; the secrets of its preparations are well known to us for it was wholly the works of our hands"*.

Wars and revolutions have since broken out everywhere. Just as soon as one ended in one part of the world another started somewhere else.

World War One was said to have been fought to end all wars. In actual fact it was fomented by the directors of BOTH international groups for the purpose of destroying as many Empires as possible. The Russian Empire was totally destroyed and the U.S.S.R's. set up in its place. As long as Lenin lived he remained loyal to the International Conspirators who had financed him and helped him in other ways to overthrow Kerensky's Provisional Government and turn Russia into an absolute dictatorship where the International Conspirators could experiment with their ideas for an international dictatorship.

The International Bankers had their agents attend the negotiations in Paris prior to the signing of the Treaty of Versailles as "Advisers" and imposed penalties and restrictions upon Germany which they calculated would force the German Government to borrow from them to aid with the nations economic recovery. Their scheme worked until General Paul Von Hindenberg was replaced by Hitler. Hitler immediately placed his theories for a new economy into effect and Germany began to enjoy an era of full employment and great national prosperity.

This caused great annoyance to those who were directing the international conspiracy. If every nation decided to follow the example of Germany their long range plan for ultimate world domination was defeated. By 1936 the International Conspirators had decided that the Aryan War Lords; Hitler, and his National Socialist Party, had to be destroyed. World War Two became a certainty. The International Bankers financed Britain and America to fight their war to liquidate their rivals the Aryan War Lords and Fascism. They also sank all the remaining democracies deeper than ever into their debt while they made astronomical profits by supplying the munitions of war. In keeping with their long range plan all nations engaged in the war emerged weakened in man-power, wealth, and in national independence.

As it turned out the Axis Powers suffered a military defeat. When the fighting was over the International Bankers arranged matters so that the "Aryan War Lords" were liquidated. The fact that the "Advisers" of the Allied Governments insisted that the Aryan War Lords be tried as war criminals proves they were *agentur* of the Inter-

---

[1] For further particulars read "The Federal Reserve Conspiracy" by Eustace Mullins.

national Illuminati or Capitalists, because Article 1, Par. 24 of the Protocols distinctly says : "*Our State, marching along the path of peaceful conquest has the right to replace the horrors of war by less noticeable and more satisfactory sentences of death necessary to maintain the terror which tends to produce blind submission*".

The Nuremberg Trials removed the Aryan War Lords who had planned to dispute ultimate world domination with the International Capitalists. After the last of the war "criminals" had died at the end of a hangman's rope, the International Bankers heaved a big sigh of relief. At last they were in the driver's seat... or so they thought... But they were sadly mistaken.

Stalin succeeded Lenin. He first indicated he intended to throw off the yoke of the International Bankers when he purged the Soviets of all those denounced as Trotskytes. There can be no questioning of the fact that in 1935 and 1936 Stalin played around with the idea of developing his own economy in Russia along the same lines Hitler was doing in Germany.

"Pawns in the Game" tells of the skulldugery which went on behind the scenes of international affairs from 1936 to the declaration of World War Two in 1939. All the overtures the agents of the International Bankers made to Stalin between 1938 and 1941 failed to move him. He was determined to stay neutral until Britain and Germany had fought themselves to a stand-still. When the big capitalistic nations had bl..d themselves white, Stalin intended to put into effect his modernized plan for world revolution.

The modernized version included the use of the **INTERNATIONAL GENERAL POLITICAL STRIKE** to paralyze the life of nations about to be subjugated. As early as 1936 Stalin was considering the feasibility of using the Cominform to take the place of the Comintern. Stalin's slogan was to be "The revolution to end all wars".

Knowing Stalin's intentions, Hitler attacked him in 1941. Stalin then pretended to go back into the fold of the International Bankers. As a reward the directors of the International Conspiracy "advised" Roosevelt and Churchill to give Stalin everything he asked. They considered no price too high if they could only keep him on their side until they were ready to dispose of him. The Directors of the International Conspiracy wanted Eastern Communism to be kept alive until they were ready to use it to destroy the remaining National Governments.

Stalin's supposedly friendly relations with the Western Powers puzzled many of the Soviet leaders so much so that Stalin had to take them into his confidence. On February 16th, 1943 Stalin addressed a secret memorandum to his military leaders and top-level political henchmen. It read as follows :

"*The Bourgeois Governments of the Western Democracies, with whom we have entered into an alliance, may believe that we consider it our sole task to throw the Fascists out of our land. We Bolsheviks, and with us the Bolsheviks of the whole world, know that our real task will only begin after the second phase of the war is ended. Then will begin for us the third phase which for us is the last and the decisive one... the phase of the destruction of World Capitalism. OUR SOLE GOAL IS, AND IT REMAINS, THE WORLD REVOLU-TION : THE DICTATORSHIP OF THE PROLETARIAT. We have engaged in alliances becauses this was necessary to reach the third phase, BUT OUR WAYS PART WHERE OUR PRESENT ALLIES WILL STAND IN OUR WAY IN THE ACHIEVE-MENT OF OUR ULTIMATE AIM."*

Stalin disbanded the Comintern in 1944 in order to deceive the International Capitalists, into believing that he had abandoned his plan to destroy the remaining NATIONALISTS governments by revolutions. The Comintern was the top-level committee of the Communist International which until 1944, had plotted and planned, and then directed, revolutions in nations which still remained to be subjugated.

The people of the Western World seem to have failed to realize that when Stalin dissolved the Comintern he replaced it with the Cominform and Profintern. The Profintern is designed to control the International Labour organization which now controls 75,000,000 organized workers throughout the whole world. The duty of the Cominform and Profintern is to organize within the ranks of the International Labour Organization the machinery for an INTERNATIONAL GENERAL POLITICAL STRIKE to be used as the prelude to revolution on an International scale. The old pattern of piecemeal revolution knocked off one country at a time. The new pattern could be used to bring about revolution in all the remaining, so-called, "Free" nations at one and the same time.

Another thing the Western World seems to have overlooked is the important fact that Tito, who has always been tied tight to the International Bankers apron-strings, fell out with Stalin over the Cominform issue. That breach with the Soviet leaders was only healed when the Soviet Communist Leader Nikita Khrushchev and his Premier Bulganin, visited the Yugoslav leader in May 1955.

After the Potsdam meeting Stalin showed that he had not been deceived by the overtures of the Western Internationalists, when they suggested peaceful co-existence between the Communist East and the Capitalist West.

Stalin, as right hand man to Lenin, and close associate of Molotov, knew better than any other man on earth that, in the final stage of the "Long Range" plan, the International Bankers intended to use the strength of the Western Powers to destroy International Communism in order that they might impose their own ideas for a ONE WORLD GOVERNMENT. Stalin knew that the Illuminati did not dare tangle with Communism in a Third World War until after they were absolutely certain that their plans had developed to the stage referred to in Article 1, Par. 15 of the Protocols which says : *"Our power in the present tottering condition of all forms of power will be more invincible than any other because it will remain invisible until the moment when it has gained such strength that no cunning can any longer undermine it".*

The ability of the Illuminati to keep the details of their diabolical plot secret until they have gained such economic strength that no power or cunning can undermine or overthrow their organization, is referred to in Article IV, Par. 2 of the Protocols which reads : "*Who or what is in a position to overthrow an invisible force? And this is precisely what our force is. Gentile masonry blindly serves as a screen for us and our objects, but the plan of action of our force, even its very abiding-place, remains for the whole people an unknown mystery*".

The only reason the details of the Illuminati's plot remain generally unknown is because the general public have persistently refused to heed the warnings given them. The Bavarian Police, revealed the details of the conspiracy to their government after they found a copy of the plan on the body of the Illuminati's Courier killed at Ratisbon in 1785. The Emperor Frances of Austria, knew of the plot because his daughter Marie Antoinette was warned by her sister that the Illuminati planned to overthrow the French Government and murder her and her husband Louis XVI; Sir Walter Scott wrote many volumes on the subject; Napoleon, was betrayed, defeated, and exiled because he dared to denounce the International Bankers as the Illuminati or "Secret Power" which fomented all wars and revolutions for the purpose of furthering their own secret plans and selfish ambitions; Professor Nilus, of Russia, in 1901 obtained a report on the development of the Conspiracy from 1773 to 1900; Victor E. Marsden translated the text of the Russian publication and published it in English in 1921; Top-level officials of the British and American intelligence services have repeatedly warned their governments of the existence of the plan; Henry Ford, in an interview published in the New York World February 17th, 1921, said : "The only statement I care to make about the Protocols is that they fit in with what is going on. They are sixteen years old, and they have fitted the world situation up to this time. They fit it now".

Lord Sydenham studied the Protocols seriously. On August 27th, 1921 the "Spectator" published a letter Lord Sydenham wrote concerning them. He pointed out that regardless of the controversy going on regarding the origin and authenticity of the documents, no person reading them could deny the deadly accuracy of the forecasts they made His Lordship stated "most of the forecasts had since been fulfilled to the letter".

"The Red Fog" is published to prove that the "Long Range" plan, disclosed in the Protocols, predicted with absolute accuracy the development of the International Conspiracy from 1773 to the very end. The fact that Stalin tried to break away from the International Capitalistic Conspirators only delayed their plans, it did not prevent them entering the final stage of their revolutionary programme.

After Stalin's secret memorandum, to his top-level military leaders and political henchmen became known, the tension between the Communist Dictators and the International Capitalists grew until the agents of the Illuminati, in their capacity as "Advisers" to the Western Powers, advised them to strengthen N.A.T.O. and adopt the policy to re-arm Western Germany.

American statesmen woke up too late to prevent Communist "Cells", also working as "Advisers" within the governments of the

Western Powers, from turning China over to the Communists. To offset their mistake the United States had to again back Chiang Kai Shek and defend Formosa.

Stalin finally died. The Western Capitalists then enlisted the aid of Molotov. He is married to the daughter of Sam Carp, of Bridgeport, Conn., who is one of them. The directors of the international capitalistic conspiracy, and their top-level agents, have always arranged matters so their children inter-marry. That has been common practice since the House of Rothschild was formed in the 18th century.

Molotov got rid of Malenkov who succeeded Stalin. Tension lessened somewhat after Bulganin became Premier of the so-called Soviets. The meeting of the top-level administrators of the Big Four Nations in Geneva, July 1955, was arranged so those present could judge for themselves how sincere or how gullible the top-level executives, who now have the responsibility of government, really are. That is why the ''Press'' of the entire world commented upon the fact that so many people attended the Big Four Conference. As was explained in ''Pawns in the Game'', the vast majority of people attending International Conferences are secret agents belonging to International Communism or International Capitalism. At Geneva the ''Agents'', the ''Cells'', the ''Agentur'', the ''Specialists'', and the ''Advisers'' were all there in full strength. They were sizing each other up as well as gathering information for their Masters.

The Communist Dictators know that in the *final analysis* the Long Range plan of the International Bankers requires that there shall be only one government in the entire world and that they intend to control it. Article 1, Par. 24, already quoted, contains this additional statement... ''*for the sake of victory we must keep to the programme of violence and make-believe.*' *The doctrine of squaring accounts is precisely as strong as the means of which it makes use. Therefore, it is not so much the means themselves, as by the doctrine of severity that we shall triumph and bring all governments into subjection to our super-government. It is enough for them to know that we are merciless for all disobedience to cease''.*

The reader should pause and consider for a moment exactly how merciless the directors of the international conspiracy have been during the last forty-one years. Since 1914 we have suffered two world wars and dozens of revolutions. The Communists and the Nazis have persecuted and murdered millions in order to subjugate other millions of human beings. The International Bankers, or the Illuminati, through their agents, fomented the Two World Wars and sacrificed tens of millions of human beings as cannon fodder, in order to weaken opposition to the FINAL STAGES of their ''Long Range'' plan, and to increase their wealth and strengthen their power. Think of America's atom bombs exploded over Hiroshima and Nagasaki, not to force Japan into submission, (her government had already indicated its desire to surrender) but to illustrate to Stalin what could, and would, happen if he persisted opposing the Illuminati.

The Protocols mention the possibility of a ''newcomer'' challenging the supremacy of the Head of the Illuminati. Article V, Par.

6, says : "*It is through me that Kings reign*"... "*Were genius in the opposite camp it would struggle against us, but even so a newcomer is no match for the old-established settler : the struggle would be merciless between us, such a fight as the world has never yet seen. Aye, and the genius on their side would have arrived too late. All the wheels of the machinery of all States go by the force of the engine, which is in our hands, and that engine of the machinery of States is — GOLD. The science of political economy invented by our learned leaders has for long past been giving royal prestige to capital*".

When Benjamin Franklin made the American Colonies prosperous by issuing Script money in proper proportion to the demands of trade and industry, the European Bankers demanded that Script money be abolished and that their money be used in its stead. They made their demand under the threat of war and did not hesitate to involve the Colonies in war when their demands were not acceded to immediately. When President Lincoln declared he intended to challenge their power he was assassinated. When Hitler and Mussolini challenged their power World War Two was fomented to destroy them. When Stalin challenged them we nearly had World War III.

Radio and T.V. commentators announced wonderment at the number of reporters, specialists, advisers, etc., who attended the meeting of the "Summit" leaders of the Big Four at Geneva. They wouldn't have had to express wonderment if they had read Article V, Par. 10 of the Protocols, which says : "*In order to put public opinion in our hands we must bring it into a state of bewilderment by giving expression from all sides to many contradictory opinions and for such length of time as will suffice to make the GOYIM lose their heads in the labyrinth and come to see that the best thing is to have no opinion of any kind in matters political, which it is not given to the public to understand, because they are understood only by him who guides the public. This is the first secret*".

Par. 11 continues — "*The second secret requisite for the success of our government is comprised in the following : To multiply to such an extent national failings, habits, passions, and conditions of civil life, that it will be impossible for anyone to know where he is in the resulting chaos, so that the people in consequence will fail to understand one another. This measure will also serve us in another way, namely to sow discord in all parties, to dislocate collective forces, which are still unwilling to submit to us, and to discourage any kind of personal initiative which might in any way hinder our affair. There is nothing more dangerous (to our cause) than personal initiative; if it has genius behind it, such initiative can do more harm than can be done by millions of people among whom we have sown discord*".

"*We must so direct the education of the GOYIM communities that whenever they come upon a matter requiring initiative, they may drop their hands in despairing impotence. The strain which results from freedom of action saps the forces when it meets with freedom of another. From this collision arises grave moral shocks, disenchantments, failures. BY ALL THESE MEANS WE SHALL SO WEAR DOWN THE GOYIM THAT THEY WILL BE COMPELLED TO OFFER US INTERNATIONAL POWER OF*

*A NATURE THAT BY ITS POSITION WILL ENABLE US
WITHOUT ANY VIOLENCE GRADUALLY TO ABSORB
ALL STATE FORCES OF THE WORLD AND FORM A
SUPER-GOVERNMENT.* In the place of the rulers of today we
shall set up a bogey which will be called the Super-Government Administration". Its hands will reach out in all directions like nippers
and its organizations will be of such colossal dimensions that it cannot
fail to subdue all the nations of the world".[2]

The above knowledge is available to all commentators and reporters. If they don't know the TRUTH about international intrigue
they are not competent to be commentators or reporters. If they do
write the TRUTH then it has not been published and that fact proves
the International Bankers, through their agents, control the so-called
"Free" Press. It is unfortunately true that many commentators and
reporters deliberately slant and distort the news in order to bring
about the state of bewilderment in the minds of the public that the
directors of the international conspirators consider necessary for the
success of their plans for World Domination. The C.B.C. is undoubtedly one of the worst offenders in this regard. C.B.C. broadcasts and
programmes sponsor the idea that a SUPER-GOVERNMENT is the
only solution to our political and economic problems.[3]

The Protocols have more to say about the "Bogey" of a Super-
Government the conspirators intend to set up. Article VI, Par. 3
says : *"In every possible way we must develop the significance of our
Super-government by representing it as the protector and benefactor
of all who voluntarily submit to us."*

Then again in article IX, Par. 3, it is said : *"For us there are no
checks to limit the range of our activity. Our Super-government
subsists in extra-legal conditions which are described in the accepted
terminology by the energetic and forcible word — DICTATOR-
SHIP. I am in a position to tell you, with a clear conscience, that at
the proper time we, the law-givers, shall execute judgment and sentence; we shall slay and we shall spare; we, as head of all our troops,
are mounted on the steed of the leader. We rule by force of will,
because in our hands are the remnants of a once powerful party now
vanquished by us. AND THE WEAPONS IN OUR HANDS ARE
LIMITLESS AMBITIONS, BURNING GREEDINESS, MER-
CILESS VENGEANCE, HATREDS AND MALICE".*

Par. 4, continues : *"It is from us that the ALL-ENGULFING
TERROR PROCEEDS. WE HAVE IN OUR SERVICE PER-
SONS OF ALL OPINIONS, OF ALL DOCTRINES, RESTOR-
ING MONARCHISTS, DEMAGOGUES, SOCIALISTS, COM-
MUNISTS, AND UTOPIAN DREAMERS OF EVERY KIND.
We have harnessed them all to the task; each one of them on his own
account is boring away at the last remnants of authority, is striving*

---

[2] For further particulars read "The Menace of World Government" by Empire Loyalists London.

[3] The C.B.C. had a great deal to do with having Drs Jessup and Keenleyside
accepted as guest speakers at the Couchiching Conference in August 1955. Both
men presented the internationalist propaganda regarding a One World Government.

to overthrow all established form of order. By these acts all STATES are in torture; they who exhort to tranquillity, are ready to sacrifice everything for peace; but we shall not give them peace until they openly acknowledge our International Super-government... and with submissiveness".

Could anything written so many years ago so clearly portray the conditions that exist to-day unless it was written by the men who conceived the Master plan and intended that their progeny would carry it to its conclusion ?

The most important TRUTH to remember is this : STALIN KNEW THAT THE DIRECTORS OF THE INTERNATIONAL CONSPIRACY NEVER INTENDED THAT THE COMMUNIST HALF OF THE WORLD; AND THE HALF DOMINATED BY INTERNATIONAL CAPITALISM SHOULD LIVE FOR LONG IN PEACEFUL COEXISTENCE. HE WAS AWARE THAT THE LEADERS OF THE INTERNATIONAL CAPITALIST GROUPS WERE ALL WORSHIPERS OF SATAN. THEY WERE THE HEAD OF THE ILLUMINATI. Stalin knew that the Illuminati which controlled the capitalist International conspirators had only promoted the Atheistic-materialism of Karl Marx in order that it would help them achieve their own final goal.

The Communist leaders are now busily engaged "Brainwashing" all the people they have subjugated in order to turn them into Atheistic-materialists. But the *agentur* of the Illuminati believe in the supernatural. They know they must destroy Christianity before the way is clear for Satan to rule this earth. That is why the International Conspiracy is a devilish and diabolical conspiracy.

The Directors of the Illuminati base their beliefs on the Cabalistic rites of Satanism. If they do happen to obtain *absolute* and *undisputed* control of the *material* assets of the whole world, as promised to them by Satan, then they will organize the systematic and scientific brainwashing of the human race in order to erase all knowledge of Almighty God, His plan for Creation, and His plan to reward His Faithful Followers with Eternal Life. The logic, and practicability, of this diabolical plot is apparent when we realise that no soul can go to Heaven if its mortal body has not loved and served Almighty God.

I can imagine some people will say : "What utter nonsense".

Let me remind those people that systematic and scientifically applied brainwashing has been experimented with by specialists who belong to the Illuminati in Nazi and Communist countries, for several years. Every person who has undergone brainwashing, admits that its results are judged by the ability of those who apply the treatment to erase the knowledge of the Power and the Glory of Almighty God from the minds of their victims.

Cardinals and bishops of the Catholic Church, and ministers of other Christian denominations have been systematically and scientifically brain-washed by Illuminati scientists in Nazi and Communist controlled countries in order to determine exactly how long the best informed, and strongest willed, people can resist such diabolical treatment.

Article IV, Par. 3, of the Protocols gives this reason for brainwashing. It says : *"But even freedom might be harmless and have its place in the State economy without injury to the wellbeing of the people if it rested upon the foundation of faith in God, upon the brotherhood of humanity, unconnected with the conception of equality, which is negatived by the very laws of creation. With such a faith as this a people might be governed by a wardship of parishes, and would walk contentedly and humbly under the guiding hand of its spiritual pastor submitting to the dispositions of God upon earth. This is the reason why it is indispensable for us to undermine all faith, to tear out of the minds of the GOYIM the very principle of Godhead and the Spirit, and put in its place arithmetical calculations and material needs".*

How well the conspirators have succeeded in their diabolical conspiracy can be gauged by the fact that there are millions of people today who are reconciled to their impending fate. The Red Fog of propaganda has made many people think, and often say hopelessly, "Well, there is nothing we can do about it... matters have gone too far". Other people with deep religious convictions, sit back and say, "My only concern is to save my soul". How wrong... how stupid, can people be? God will not do our work for us. He has told us in no uncertain language that we are on this earth to **WORK** out our own salvation. Doing nothing to stop the agents of Satan isn't going to save one's soul. Shivering in fear, and being ready for meek surrender isn't going to qualify us for our eternal reward.

CHAPTER II

How I came to Canada ... and why

A FTER studying the world revolutionary movement in Mexico, China, and most European countries for many years I decided, in 1919, to investigate Communist infiltration into the United States. I was demobilized from the British submarine service in February 1919. I had served as navigating officer in British Submarines since 1916. Knowing how Communist "Cells" were placed aboard the merchant ships of all nations, and being in possession of a master mariner's certificate of competency, I decided I would óbtain employment with the United States Shipping Board and try to pick up contacts aboard the ship to which I was appointed.

I was appointed chief officer of the *S. S. Lake Fouch* and, in December 1919, sailed from Galveston, Texas, with a cargo of grain for Cette in the south of France.

During the voyage from Newport News, Virginia, where we called for fuel, I made contact with three Communists. My experiences with them, and other members of the Communist Party to whom I was introduced in France and Spain, have been told in a book I wrote entitled "High and Dry". It is sufficient to say that while in Cette a Communist "Cell" working in the office of either the British or American Consulate reported that I was a Bourgeois spy and two attempts were made on my life in less than a week.

I had the opportunity of learning, at first hand, how Communists make the liquidation of a traitor or a spy look as if the victim had met with an accident. The first attempt to kill me was made in Cette. The crew were cleaning shifting boards and dunnage out of the hold, preparatory to taking on board a cargo of ore in Huelva, Spain. One of the Commies aboard the "Lake Fouch" was working the winch used for lifting the heavy slings of lumber out of the holds.

I was walking along the for'ard deck on a tour of inspection. Paddy, my faithful dog, was right at my heels. A sling of lumber had been hoisted out of the hold. The guy ropes had just begun to swing the derrick over so the load could be deposited on the wharf. As I walked under it. I happened to look at McLean, the Commie, who was working the winch. I noticed his hand let go the hoisting lever. I jumped forward like a jack-rabbit. I escaped by such a narrow margin that my dog was crushed to death under the load. I was absolutely sure that McLean's hand hadn't slipped accidentally, but it was another matter to prove that he had made an attempt on my life.

I was so convinced that the incident was no accident that I became certain the Commies, must, in some mysterious manner, have found out that I was only seeking information and was not sincerely interested in furthering the world revolutionary movement, although I had offered to co-operate with the Communist leaders by smuggling some of Moscow's agents into Spain from France. Because the only people I had taken into my confidence were the British and American consuls I knew the "leak" must have originated in one or the other of the consulates.

This made a very complicated situation. I knew there were three Communists amongst my crew. One of them, McLean, had made an attempt on my life. It stood to reason that if I sailed with them aboard they would kill me and toss my body overboard during the voyage back to America. The problem was how to prevent them sailing aboard the "Lake Fouch". Every time I went ashore after the unpleasant experience just related, I carried my revolver with me.

The ship had arrived in Cette just before Christmas. She was due to sail January 3rd. for Huelva in Spain. I was nearly killed December 28th. On the 29th I went ashore during daylight and discussed the matter with the consuls and the chief of police. It was decided that if the three Commies aboard the "Lake Fouch" got drunk during the New Year's celebrations the police would pick them up and keep them in jail until after the ship sailed. It was more than likely they would get drunk because they had been drunk all the time th. ship had been in the Azores, and for most of the time they had been in Cette. With this matter settled, all I had to do was look around for three seamen to replace them. I found three seamen aboard a sailing ship which had just arrived in Cette after a voyage around the world lasting nearly two years. These three men were anxious to get back to the United States. I told them three of my crew were missing. I offered to "sign them on" in their place.

December 30th, I went ashore and while passing through the piles of lumber in the poorly lighted dock area I was waylaid by two men who were armed with knives. Fortunately my previous experience was still very fresh in my mind. I was on the alert and whipped my revolver out of the side pocket of my great-coat. I had them covered before they could do me any harm. They threw their knives away and ran like two deer. I could have shot them before they started to run. The fact that I didn't shoot them probably decided them to make a break for liberty. After they started running there was no sense in shooting. If I had hit them I would have had a tough time explaining to the police WHY I had shot at two men who were running away even if I could have proved they were armed when they first tried to attack me.

As predicted, the three Commies did get really soaked. Police agents, working in plain clothes, picked a quarrel with them in a cafe and started a fight. The fight was cleverly developed into a "rough house". Tables were over-turned and chairs were broken, most of them over people's heads. The "rough house" was enlarged into a street brawl. The street brawl was developed into a near riot. This provided the opportunity for the gendarmes to act with force. My crewmen were amongst those arrested. They all needed medical treatment. We had played the Communists at their own game and beaten them — but only for the time being.

When I arrived back in New York I was tipped off by Federal Agents that word had been received in New York regarding what had happened in Cette. I was told that orders had been given that I was to meet with another accident. This time it had to be fatal. I received my pay and announced to all and sundry that I was leaving immediately for New Orleans to join another ship as chief officer. To make that bluff look good I had the steward address my sea-chest to a ship I knew was loading cargo in New Orleans.

When I got to the station I tore off the label and substituted another addressed to Hartland, New Brunswick, Canada. I had an Uncle living in Hartland. I thought it would be a mighty good idea to visit him because Hartland was a small place of less than one thousand population. When a person is being hunted by people outside the law a small place is the ideal place in which to reside because everyone in a small place knows everybody's business.

A stranger arriving unexpectedly stands out like a sore thumb. People in small places have a habit of asking very blunt and personal questions as I found out on arrival.

I hadn't been in Hartland a week when I knew everyone. I answered hundreds of questions. The main question seemed to be

WHY I had come to visit my Uncle? I told the curious that after ten years of wars and revolutions I felt I was entitled to a holiday. I explained that I had picked Hartland because it was peaceful and quiet and in the heart of the hunting and fishing district of the Maritimes. I told them I was seriously thinking of "swallowing the anchor". By this expression a seaman means giving up the sea.

I arrived in Hartland on June 2nd, 1920. It was my twenty-fifth birthday. I was married. My wife was tired of my wandering all around the world. She had been living in England. She had been visiting me in Cette when the attempts had been made on my life. She had seen the dog killed right at my heels. She wrote telling me she wanted me to give up the sea. When I agreed she broke up her home in England and joined me in Hartland. She brought our two children, Peggy and Bill, with her.

Knowing the directors of both international conspiracies intended that Canada should play a most important part in the third, and last, stage of their Long Range Plans for ultimate World domination, I decided to remain in Canada. I made up my mind to pick up the threads of the conspiracy in Canada and keep myself informed so that I could acquaint the proper authorities with the nature of the conspiracies and their ramifications.

I knew that the international bankers had organized, financed, and directed the last stage of the Russian Revolution in 1917. I knew that without their aid and their influence in very high places in the British, German, American, and Russian governments, Lenin and Trotsky could never have overthrown the provisional government set up by Kerensky and turned the Soviet Republic into a totalitarian dictatorship. I had found it extremely difficult to make even intelligent people understand that international Communism, although avowedly anti-capitalistic, was, in actual fact, the capitalist conspirators "manual of action". It is difficult for the average person to understand that the international Capitalists use international Communism to remove individuals, organizations, and governments which obstructed the development of their secret plans to effect one world government. I was determined I would obtain enough evidence in Canada to make honest government officials see the TRUTH.

Since June 1920 I have worked persistently to keep myself fully informed regarding the international conspiracies. All my investigations have been conducted by myself and at my own expense.

I first accepted employment as a rigger with the New Brunswick Building and Construction Co. I helped build the famous covered bridge in Hartland. It is the longest covered bridge in the world.

Another attempt was made on my life in 1922. This time a man who had been involved in bootlegging, smuggling, and forging of liquor labels was told I had informed the police regarding the illegal activities of the gang to which he belonged. This incident will be dealt with in another chapter.

In 1923 I decided I would join the investigation department of the Canadian Pacific Railway because it would give me the rights and powers and privileges of a police officer in addition to providing me with the facilities for investigating the revolutionary movement in many parts of Canada. It was while I was serving with the C. P. R. police that I obtained the evidence that was given before the Stevens Royal Commission into the Canadian Customs service in 1926-1927.

Having given evidence before the Commission, I left the C. P. R. Police and accepted the position of secretary to the Christie Street Hospital Branch of the Legion. This provided me with a wonderful opportunity to learn at first hand Communist methods of infiltration into Veteran organizations.

In 1928 I joined the staff of the Toronto Daily Star. As a newspaper man I investigated the underground of the Communist party and the underworld. I investigated the methods of smuggling, and the wholesale evasion of excise tax by the agentur of the international capitalists who made new millionnaires as outlined in Article VII, Par. 1 of the Protocols, which says : *"What we have to get at is that there should be in all States of the World, besides ourselves, only masses of the proletariat, a few millionaires devoted to our interests, police and soldiers"*. Then again, Article VIII, Par. 2, reads : *"Around us again will be a whole constellation of bankers, industrialists, capitalists, and... the main thing... millionaires, because in substance everything will be settle by the question of figures"*.[1]

Another reason I wanted experience with the Press was because Article II, Par. 5 of the Protocols states most definitely : *"In the hands of the states of to-day there is a great Force that creates the movement of thought in the people, and that is the Press. The part played by the Press is to keep pointing out requirements supposed to be indispensable, to give voice to the complaints of the people, to express and create discontent. It is in the Press that the triumph of freedom of speech finds its incarnation. But the Goyim States have not known how to make use of this force : and it has fallen into our hands. Through the Press we have gained the power to influence while remaining ourselves in the shade : thanks to the Press we have the GOLD in our hands, notwithstanding that we have had to gather it out of oceans of blood and tears. But it has paid us, though we have sacrificed many of our people"*.

I became a "Free Lance Journalist" in 1930. I was more successful than many "Free Lance Journalists" because between 1930 and 1939 I wrote, and published, six books which helped me provide for my growing family and finance my investigations.

Then in 1939 came the war. As an officer in the executive branch of the Royal Canadian Navy (Reserve) I found the opportunity to study subversive infiltration into the Armed Forces and various departments of government. Having persistently placed the information I obtained regarding all the angles, and ramifications, of the world revolutionary movement and the international conspiracy, in the hands of the proper governmental authorities without getting acknowledgment, recognition, or action; in 1955 I decided to place my evidence before the court of public opinion. The people must weigh the evidence and decide if I have made out a clear case against the various conspirators. The public must decide if the evidence of

---

[1] The words "around us" can only mean The Illuminati.

conspiracy is beyond any reasonable doubt. If I satisfy my readers that a conspiracy does exist, then the public must take immediate action to end the conspiracy before it is too late.

Due to the confusion and doubt created purposely by "The Red Fog" of subversive propaganda which originates from many sources but is in reality controlled only by those who organize, finance, and direct the "long range" plan for bringing into being their idea of a super-government or International Dictatorship, it took me forty years to fathom out the many apparent contradictions and arrive at the TRUTHS as they are recorded in this book. In order that the reader may be better able to understand the revelations I make in regard to the development of the international conspiracy in Canada and the United States during the past 35 years I ask them to study what I have to say in relation to the following TRUTHS.

One :   The real issue at stake is whether Christ or Satan will ultimately reign as King upon this earth.

Two :   The supreme directors of the Satanic conspiracy are a small group of men who believe in the supernatural but who deliberately organize Atheistic-materialism to lure human beings away from Almighty God. The Devil, their Master, wins every soul who has denied the existence of God and refused to love, serve, and obey Him.

Three : The fundamental principle of the Satanic Illuminati is to divide different races, religions, political groups, social classes, and nationalities, etc., and make them fight each other so they become weak in manpower and ruined economically. This plot leads them towards internationalism.

Four :   In the 20th Century there have been five fields of thought trying to influence the course of world events.

(A) *Christianity.* Which teaches that Jesus Christ is the Son of God and that he will some day come back on earth in majesty and glory, to restore the law and order of Almighty God.

(B) *International Communism.* Which teaches Atheistic-materialism and claims that everything starts from MATTER (energy) and returns to MATTER. Its leaders work to bring about an International Atheistic dictatorship.

(C) The Illuminati who used all other to reach their goal to establish the Despotism of Satan upon this earth.

(D) Political Zionism which aimed at control by the Jews.

(E) *International Nazism.* Which taught the deity of man and that the STATE is ALL SUPREME. The leaders sought to impose their ideas for a militarist dictatorship upon the people.

CHAPTER III

How various kinds of subversion grew in Canada

WHEN Jensen, Freina, and Katayama, three Communist-missionaries arrived in Canada the latter part of 1919 or early in 1920, there were just a few people who believed that reform could only be brought about speedily by revolutionary action.

Twenty-four years later, in 1944, Pat Sullivan was delegated by the Central Executive Committee of the Communist Party in Canada to memorize a report and tell the Communist delegates, attending the World Labour Congress in London, England, that the strength of the Communist Party in Canada was 28,000 card bearing members with 560,000 fellow travellers. Mr. Sullivan has since defected from the Communist Party.

It is only fair to say that since 1946 the Communist Party, both in the United States and Canada, has dwindled. The number of card bearing members is now about two-thirds what it was in 1945. The number of Fellow Travellers has also decreased from a ratio of 20 to 1, to 10 to 1.

It is very important to remember, however, that the reduction in actual numbers has been more than offset by increased efficiency. This statement is proved true by the fact that the heads of the R.C.M.P. in Canada, and the F.B.I. in the United States, have both announced in recent years that the Communist conspiracy has gone so far underground since 1946 that it now requires six under-cover agents to do the work one did in 1945.

While working on the construction of the covered bridge in Hartland I became acquainted, through my uncle, with a business man who I afterwards found out was the "King-Pin" with whom international financiers were doing business in Eastern Canada. He was the "brain" behind the agricultural and chemical combines which had been organized by United States and British interests, in the Maritime Provinces in Canada.

I decided to investigate and find out how this combine operated and what the extent of its ramifications might be. I lived in Hartland, N.B. for two years until I had completed this task, and I got to know intimately most of the people involved. The man who organized the Canadian ramifications of this international cartel had been born without a cent to his name. When he grew up he bought and sold skins. In this way he first contacted men who controlled the Canadian Fur trade. Fur prices are manipulated in exactly the same way the international minded "capitalist's" control every other commodity including stocks, and bonds, and money.

Not being adverse to a shady deal the Canadian prospered. I knew him exceedingly well from 1920 to 1923. By then he was very wealthy. He was kind and exceedingly generous to needy individuals in his community. He didn't consider a shady deal crooked or criminal. To him putting it over the other guy was simply smart business.

Men who engage in "smart" business make it their business to have friends in "high" places. One way the man I refer to obtained friends was to pay $5.00 to everyone, who promised to vote for the man he wanted to be elected. He also provided those who accepted the money with all the liquor they wished to drink *after* they had voted.

The men who formed this international combine controlled the marketing of all agricultural products in the Maritimes; the sea-bordering States in the U.S.A.; and the West Indies. They also controlled the fertilizer business, which is part of the International Chemical Combine. I had samples of the fertilizer analyzed. They were proved to contain a considerable percentage of foreign material which could have been road-sweepings. The quantity of lead found in the fertilizer was sufficient to cause one warehouse man to comment — "The Fritzes must have ground up all the animals killed during the war and made fertilizer out of them".

In 1920 the international bankers ordered their agents in all parts of the world to take money out of circulation, restrict credits, and call in notes. The Maritimes combine did exactly as they were told. The Canadians received their instructions from men who came from New York and Boston to enjoy a hunting trip. But they didn't go into the woods until after all details of the conspiracy had been fully worked out. I know, because I took them. Records will show that as the result of this conspiracy the price of potatoes dropped from $10.00 a barrel to less than $1.00. The markets in the States, Great Britain, and the West Indies were closed even to seed potatoes. Over 50,000 bags of the finest New Brunswick potatoes were dumped into the St. John River.[1]

Because the price of potatoes had been $10 a barrel in the winter of 1920-1921, farmers needed very little urging to buy sufficient fertilizer and plant selected seed to ensure bumper crops in 1922. The price of fertilizer was high; the price of seed potatoes was high.

In order to obtain credit, with which to purchase seed, fertilizer, and farm machinery, the farmers mortgaged their farms and their crops. When the bottom fell out of the market in 1921 many of the farmers lost everything they had. There was such a wave of resentment that if arms had been available there could easily have been a civil war. It is a strange thing that the resentment of the people was directed mostly against the Federal and Provincial Governments, and not against those who had manipulated the setting up of the phoney prosperity and the subsequent crash.

---

[1] For further details read "The World Food Shortage a Communist-Zionist Conspiracy, by B. Jensen. I disagree with the title but endorse every thing else the author has to say.

When the bottom was due to fall out of the potato market the men who comprised the combine had a considerable quantity of potatoes on hand in their warehouses but they had instructions from those higher up that they were not to ship them to the usual American markets. It was decided to sell these potatoes to the railway. They were shipped in box-cars and billed to a destination in the U.S.A. but, with the help of a railway official, the cars were mis-routed and the fires in the stoves, which kept the potatoes from freezing, went out. This caused the potatoes to become a dead loss. The combine claimed the loss. The claim was paid. The combine made profit and kept faith with their fellow conspirators.

This was really a very "smart" piece of business. The Powers behind the scenes of the international conspiracy decided that they must have the "brains" of the Maritime branch elected to the Canadian House of Commons. This was soon accomplished. One of the men named as guilty under the Anti-combines law was elected to parliament at the next Federal Elections. He didn't represent the people who elected him. He was there to do the bidding of his bosses who directed the international aspects of the capitalist conspiracy.

Few people realize how cleverly such conditions are used by Communists and their Fellow Travellers when they preach class hatred and advocate class warfare.

For a time I was puzzled to know WHY the directors of the international conspiracy knocked the bottom out of the markets of the world in 1921. Further investigation revealed the truth. The conspirators had to create conditions of unemployment and want before they could lead citizens of the countries they were plotting to subjugate into lives of sin and crime. As Lenin so truly said, "*The best revolutionary is a young person without morals*".

The agricultural and chemical combine's actions fitted in with the over-all plan of the directors of the international conspiracy because Article II, Par. 2, of the Protocols says : "*The administrators whom we shall choose from among the public with strict regard to their capacities for servile obedience, will not be persons trained in the arts of government, and will, therefore, easily become pawns in our game in the hands of men of learning and genius who will be their advisors, specialists bred and reared from early childhood to rule the affairs of the whole world*".

When Jensen, Freina, and Katayama arrived in Canada they were supplied with $75,000. How much was real money and how much counterfeit is questionable. I have explained in "Pawns in the Game" how both the directors of the Communist conspiracy and the directors of the capitalist conspiracy finance their subversive activities. I have told how they provide arms and ammunition for the revolutions and wars they foment to serve their secret purposes and selfish ambitions.

Jensen remained in Canada. Freina and Katayama moved on into the United States.

While I was investigating the international combine I came in contact with Jensen, previously referred to. He had been educated in the Lenin Institute in Moscow. The meeting came about in the following manner.

I prospered greatly while I was friendly with those who conducted the combine. My wife joined me. I built a home for her and my children. Everything looked rosy. It was not until I refused to become involved in the election rackets that my popularity began to wane. Then some "spy" reported that I had supplied the evidence which caused the Federal Government to investigate the combine. I was ignorant of the fact that I was suspected as being a Government agent, which I wasn't.

When I first went into business for myself I was literally showered with contracts. In some mysterious manner Jensen worked his way into my employ. Then everything went wrong. Jobs were messed up. Materials were spoiled, and those with whom I had contracts refused to pay their debts. It took me quite awhile to realize that Jensen, a Communist, had been worked into my employ by those who conducted the Canadian part of the international combine. Even after I discovered Jensen was a Communist I couldn't for the life of me understand how a Communist could possibly have contacts with the international capitalists.

It wasn't long before I couldn't get work of any kind. The depression was blamed, but I knew forces were at work that I couldn't understand. When I was almost desperate for need of money I was introduced by Jensen, to certain men who were organizing the illegal manufacture of "Moonshine" liquor in New Brunswick.

I was offered good money to become a member of the bootlegging and smuggling fraternity. At about the same time I met business men in St. John who were members of the Commercial Protective Association. This association had been formed to collect evidence which would force Parliament to conduct an investigation into illegal traffic and trade which was causing such havoc among legitimate merchants and manufacturers. I decided I would work under-cover for the Commercial Protective Association. Mr. R. P. Sparks was at that time national secretary. He worked in close co-operation with the Hon. H. H. Stevens, who ultimately had a Royal Commission appointed to investigate the Customs and Excise Service in Canada. I agreed to help these public spirited citizens obtain the evidence they required.

I contacted and cultivated the frienship of a French-Canadian named Theo. When he first started bootlegging and smuggling he had no more idea that he was helping the 5th Columnists in Canada than thousands of others who unknowingly serve them and their purpose.

Theo was married with a large growing family. His business was fast going into bankruptcy. He was one of the most skilled mechanics I ever met. He could repair a car or a watch efficiently. He was sitting in his workshop looking the picture of despair one day when I called on him.

"What's the matter, Theo ?", I asked sympathetically.

"The beeg trouble ees everybody undersells me... I know damn well they sell smuggled goods and by gar I'm going to do the same... The bank she no more give me credit... I go bankrupt pretty damn soon... Dat no good for wife and kids... Eh ?"

I had to admit it wasn't. Wishing to obtain first-hand knowledge of the bootlegging and smuggling, I tagged along with Theo.

His first "Job" was to take a truck load of liquor to the States and return with dutiable goods, amongst which were cartons containing American-made flavourings which the "Big Shots" used when manufacturing moonshine into, what they sold for, the very best brands of imported liquors.

Theo, like so many others, waded deeper and deeper into the mire of illegal transactions until he was completely bogged down. He found himself bound solidly to the men who were the enemies of his religion as well as of his country. He got involved so deeply he couldn't have backed out without incurring the vengeance of those who had elected themselves his masters.

After the racketeers had involved Theo deep enough to ensure his silence and obedience, they paid him to convert ordinary five gallon copper wash-boilers into efficient portable stills. All Theo altered was the lid so that a removable copper coil could be attached where the knob is located for lifting the cover off and on. This was an ingenious arrangement and very simple to make.

The manufacture of moonshine grew into a tremendous business. One yard stick by which the illicit making of liquor can be measured, is the quantity of crude molasses which was shipped by the wholesale dealers in Halifax, N.S. and St. John, N.B. to small villages throughout the Provinces. I checked some of those shipments. If the molasses shipped, during a single summer, had only been used for baking beans, spreading on bread, or for making molasses cookies, the quantities delivered to some small villages, of less than five hundred inhabitants, would have supplied those families for a hundred years.

The "brew" was made by fermenting crude molasses. It was then simmered in the boilers on top of an ordinary oil burning stove. These stoves are standard equipment in the summer kitchens of most country homes. The alcoholic fumes passed up into the copper pipe and down into the coil or "worm" submerged in running cold water. The fumes were condensed and the alcohol dripped into a container placed beneath the outlet. The rate of evaporation, and condensation, could be regulated accurately by lowering or raising the wick in the oil burner.

I obtained evidence to prove that car-loads of empty bottles, and thousands of gallons of alcohol, were delivered to one warehouse in a border town where the moonshine was "fixed up", flavoured rebottled, and sold to the United States market as genuine imported liquor. This particular racketeer, whom we will call Benny, owned a hotel. The basement of his hotel was connected by a tunnel with a warehouse on a railway siding. This tunnel was used to move shipments of alcohol and bottles back and forth between the hotel basement and the warehouse, unseen by people on the streets. It also provided a means of escape should the hotel be raided by police who really meant business. On one occasion, several barrels of alcohol were seized in that basement. The basement was sealed and guarded by police. While the police were making arrangements to remove the seized liquor to the Government bonded warehouse at Fredericton, the barrels of liquor were removed via the tunnel and barrels of water substituted. I can prove by newspaper reports, and court records, that this racketeer took legal action against the police. He claimed he had a right to possess that alcohol. He won his case on a technicality. The court ordered the liquor to be returned to him but he refused to accept the barrels until the contents had been analyzed by a Government appraiser. The contents of the barrels were proved to be water and the Government had to refund that gangster the value of the liquor the police *thought* they had seized.

Before these racketeers suspected my true purpose, I stayed at his hotel. I was in the basement, and saw the equipment used for transforming moonshine into cases of the most popular brands of imported whisky, rum and gin. Theo obtained the plates and stamps used to reproduce the labels, and the metal caps which fit over the bottle tops. Any British distillery, which exported to Canada between the years 1921 and 1925, will bear me out when I say that the quantities of synthetic spirits sold by racketeers as the genuine goods were so great that the White Horse, and other Scottish distilleries, had to change the type of bottles they used, and have the new bottles fitted with non-refillable necks. Other exporters affixed to their bottles cards which advised their patrons to break the bottles as soon as they were empty so as to prevent them being re-filled again by bootleggers. The legitimate export trade of the British Isles was seriously affected by these illegal operations and the Governments of Canada and the U.S.A. were robbed of many millions of dollars in revenue.

The Prohibition Officer who tried to clean up this particular gang bungled his job badly. He was an ex-clergyman and a rabid prohibitionist. He was not qualified for such a job. Once he brought condemnation upon himself for using a revolver when he had no legal right. He, like a fool, rushed in where experienced investigators would fear to tread. The up-shot of the whole thing was that he soon gave himself away. Once his identify was known, the mobsters took him to a log cabin located away back in the woods. There they amused themselves frightening the poor devil half out of his wits. They threatened him with every form of torture and death. Knowing he was an abstainer they forcibly made him drink raw rum until he was drunk. Then they stripped the victim of his clothing, tarred and feathered him, and turned him loose on the main street of the village just as the workmen were leaving their homes to go to work. The poor enforcement officer was so drunk he kept falling down as he staggered along. The ridicule he was subjected to afterwards caused him to resign and go into retirement. The incident caused such a commotion that hardly a citizen in this Rum Ring's home town failed see the sad spectacle. Those citizens, who had ever dared to voice their objection to "mob Rule", were reminded what could happen to them if they did not mind their own business.

In certain border points, the gangsters controlled the whole town. Because the Mounted Police, and prohibition officers, had made several seizures in the locality of which I write, the local gangster had issued orders that if the street lights went out after dark everyone was to stay indoors and keep the blinds down... or else.

A young telephone exchange operator saw the lights go out, one night. She also saw trucks loaded with men drive into the railway yard. The men proceed to unload a box-car. She telephoned the police. The trucks had pulled away with their loads before either the Customs Officer or the Police arrived. The body of that young, innocent girl was found several weeks later. She had been stripped of her clothing and raped. She was left dying on the banks of the river. On the ground amongst her clothing was a broken Rosary. On her blood-stained chemise was sewn a Scapular of the Sacred Heart. The pirates and buccaneers who ravaged the seas off the American coast a hundred years ago and more, were gentlemen compared with the commercial pirates and 5th Columnists with whom we have to deal to-day.

These events are not fiction. They happened in Canada only a few years ago. The same kind of lawlessness is going on to-day. This statement is proved by the many unsolved murders which are undoubtedly committed by gangsters or their hired killers. Goods in transit are still being stolen in wholesale quantities. The black markets and vice rackets are operating on a larger scale than ever before.

If an investigator makes a mistake, his first is sometimes his last. That very nearly happened to me. I had worked my way so deeply into the activities of this gang that I spent many an hour in the bar of the hotel owned by the leader of the gang, and listened to them tell of their many and varied adventures. They owned the town, and when I say "owned" it, I use the word literally.

Benny and his gang had forced the town fathers to appoint his nephew as the town constable. The Canadian Customs Officer had made so much money that he owned one of the finest homes in the town. He had enough money invested on which to retire. The gangsters had the local magistrate scared half to death; they bribed politicians. Mr. Robinson, Chief of the Canadian Government's Preventive Service in the Maritimes, knew all that was going on. Benny ran his bar and his hotel wide open. He was a "Big Shot". He openly boasted that one of his friends drove around Ottawa in a car worth thousands of dollars which had been stolen in the States, and smuggled into Canada.[2] Benny actually believed he was away above the law. At that time he had every reason to be self-opinionated.[3]

Shortly after the Prohibition Officer had been ridiculed I nearly lost my life. The communists who had landed in St. John in 1920 and started the underground and 5th Column activities in the Maritimes, finally got wise to my identity. They learned about my anti-communist activities in 1919-20 in the South of France and Spain, while on the S. S. Lake Fouch.

The higher-ups who wanted me out of the way didn't believe in getting involved personally with the police if they could help it. To prove how utterly unscrupulous they are, they had the police informed regarding some of Theo's illegal activities. He was arrested when

---

[2] This statement was given as evidence to the Royal Commission which investigated the Customs Service in 1926.

[3] Automobile smuggling is still a major business as is proved by arrests and newspaper reports of convictions in Canadian Courts in 1955.

collecting moonshine for delivery to the warehouse I have described. After his arrest, Theo was convinced that *I was the person who had reported him to the police.* He was warned that if I wasn't put out of the way it wouldn't be long before I had enough evidence to put the whole gang in prison for the rest of their lives. Theo paid a fine.

Theo was a hard-boiled, excitable, French-Canadian. He was very angry when informed of my alleged perfidy; but I didn't know what was the matter at the time. He invited me to go hunting with him. When there are only two men in a hunting party and one says he shot the other by mistake for a deer, it is hard to prove him a liar. The fact that Theo's family and mine had been friendly for more than a year, would have supported his statement that the fatality was an accident. After all, hunting accidents are quite common. Some seasons as many as 200 men have been mistaken for moose, deer, or bears, and shot in the woods both sides of the American border.

We were still-hunting back in the woods near Pole Hill, Carleton County, N.B. I spotted a deer standing concealed behind a windfall. It was so completely hidden that I had to look for a considerable time before I could make out for certain that whatever had attracted my attention was a deer. My companion was on the top of a ridge. I was about halfway down. We were walking slowly along when my eye caught a slight movement in the wind-fall at the bottom of the ridge. I froze and kept my eyes glued to the spot. Finally I could discern the white flash on the back of the front legs below the trunk of the tree. Then I made out the outline of the back of the deer. It was protruding just about three inches above the trunk of the wind-fall. I could not locate the head or the antlers. This was the last day of the season and we needed meat. As it was legal to kill both bucks and does I decided I would aim at the spine just about a foot behind where I judged the deer's shoulder blades would be.

I was standing on a steep slope on newly fallen snow which covered deeper snow on which an icy crust had formed during a previous blizzard. This made walking slippery and dangerous. After I had stopped I didn't dare move again without looking where I intended to set my feet. Once my attention was fixed on the deer I just stayed still and didn't move again until I raised my rifle to aim at the deer. I was using a .303 converted army rifle. It was deadly accurate.

I didn't have much of a target to shoot at. The back of the deer was just about the same colour as the bark of the fallen tree. I aimed so the bullet would pass just above the tree trunk. I figured, as I was standing halfway up the ridge above the deer, the bullet would break the spine as it travelled in a slightly downward direction. In New Brunswick a person who messed up the meat of a deer by shooting it through the paunch or rear-end was considered with much the same disdain as an Englishman considers a man who shoots at sitting hare or partridge.

When I squeezed the trigger I saw the deer go down and start to thrash about. I was so intent watching the deer that I stepped towards it without looking where I was stepping. I slipped and fell. It was a good thing I did because if I hadn't I would have been shot through the head. When I turned to see WHY my companion had fired, I saw his rifle was pointing straight at me. I rolled sideways and placed a tree between me and my murderous companion. I felt sure of his guilt. The bullet that missed me wasn't travelling in the direction of the deer. I was convinced Theo had tried to murder me when he stuttered an explanation that he had fired to finish off the deer with a head shot. I knew him to be one of the best rifle-shots in New Brunswick. I asked him to explain how, if he had shot at the head of the deer, he had missed it. He made no serious objection when I took his rifle and shells. I made him gut the deer and then drag it to the camp on Pole Hill.

To have taken the matter to Court was worse than useless. It would simply have been his word against mine, so I came from under cover and joined the C.P.R. Police.

The story of Theo is typical of hundreds, if not thousands, of citizens who were literally forced into the smuggling and bootlegging business by the men who plot various aspects of the international conspiracy. Clever financial manipulations, combined with control of commerce through combines and cartels, enable the archconspirators to bring about unemployment and depressions. When a man's family is faced with serious discomfort and want he will turn to anything, even crime, to earn a dollar. Smuggling and bootlegging is generally considered as less serious than crime but those who direct the conspiracy use illegal traffic and trade to kill the economy of Nations they plan to subjugate.

CHAPTER IV

The conspiracy and the Communist Underground

ONCE I started my duties with the C.P.R. police, I operated on the principle that an ounce of prevention is worth a pound of cure. I made it my business to get to know as many of the underworld characters as possible. I told them quite frankly what I had learned of the various phases of the world revolutionary movement and the international conspiracy. I explained that the adverse conditions, for which they blamed their own government, were the evil machinations and manipulations of a gang of international gangsters. I pointed out that the Communists were instruments in the hands of the international capitalists.

I was surprised how many underworld characters were adverse to allowing themselves to be used as "tools" or "stooges" by foreigners.

It wasn't long before I had an efficient and reliable information service organized. I promised, and I kept my word, that I would never divulge the identity of any person who gave me information. Using these tactics I obtained information which enabled me to record the following facts.

The first fruits of Jensen's labours were the serious riots in St. John in 1921. Sergeant Lucas of the R.C.M.P. nearly lost his life. As is customary, the Communists gathered tinder, built up the pile, started the blaze, and then left others to clash with the police and take the blame and punishment. Jensen afterwards moved to Montreal and changed his name to Davis.

The missionaries, who had the money, concentrated on obtaining "Fellow Travellers". They accepted any person who was disgruntled, dissatisfied and anti-social, provided he or she subscribed to the principle that only by revolutionary action can reforms be brought about speedily.

Once a number of "Fellow Travellers" had been recruited they were put to work. That is one of the great secrets of Communists' success. They insist that every "Fellow Traveller" works and performs the tasks given to them with speed, accuracy, and efficiency. Some "Fellow Travellers" devote every waking hour, and 10% of their earnings, to the Communist causes and never ask to be admitted to membership.

The first task given a "Fellow Traveller" is that of obtaining information considered as valuable by the members of the excutive council. This is real detective work. The would be reformer is made to believe that gathering information about the private lives and business affairs of influential people in every political party, every religious denomination, every division of industry; every level of government; every Branch of the armed forces; every class of society; every department of education; and every section of the civil service; is essential to the success of the Communist cause, as in fact it really is. The Communist leaders make their stooges believe they are working for a political and economic reform movement. It is explained that, in order to bring about reforms speedily they must know every detail about the lives of persons who are enemies of the people and traitors to the State.

In no time at all the Communist executive had a host of spies working for them. These spies were broken down into FIVE groups.

(A) Military Intelligence : This includes all branches of the armed forces and the departments of government concerned with the internal and external security of the country. It also includes infiltration of "Cell's" into departments of supply, transportation, communications, and intelligence, etc.

(B) National economy : This includes all branches of Trade and Commerce; the Customs and Revenue Services; the taxation departments; and everything, both legal and illegal, which affects the economy of the country.

(C) Industry and Research : This includes every division of industry and science.

(D) Political affairs in all levels of government : This branch includes "Labour" organizations. It is considered the most important of the spy-rings because Lenin said "All revolutions must start within the ranks of labour".

(E) Social Sciences and propaganda : These include education, religion, social welfare, crime and criminals, recreation projects, health and mass medication, and public information outlets such as the Press, Radio, T-V, etc.

The amateur spies were made to think they were real cloak-and-dagger operators. They worked with enthusiasm. In no time at all the Communist Leaders were obtaining information about the private lives and business practices of hundreds of people they consider could be made to further the Communist Conspiracy. Communist leaders do not hesitate to blackmail men and women if they have evidence to prove they have committed some serious moral or social error, or departed from honest procedure in their business and professional activities. The information obtained by the spy rings, once headed by Sam Carr, was used as a two-edged sword. It was used to "FORCE" influential people to work subversively behind the scenes, and it was used to render inactive those who were supposed to combat Communism.

In Canada the Communist "underground" was first established in the underworld of our sea-ports. From the sea-ports they branch out into the underworlds of all large cities. There, amongst misery, ill-health, oppression, injustice, racial hatreds, religious bigotry, and organized crime, they plant more "Cells". Communism is conceived in the gutters; born amidst filth and misery; and it grows strong by sucking the moral and economic life-blood from the veins of the nation it plans to subjugate.

The "Cells" grow and multiply because opportunities are provided, and conditions are created, by greedy capitalists and unscrupulous politicians, which are favourable to the subversive activities and arguments of the Communist leaders.

The Red Cells, injected by the Communist organizers into the life-blood of the nation, find their way into every part of the body-politic and finally erupt in the form of a bloody revolution.

One of the tenets of the Communists Creed is this : "With the basis of the economic interpretation of the revolution well established, the next step in the country chosen for subjugation is the demoralization of the populace in the name of the proletarian revolution. Humanity has to be reduced to its lowest common denominator. The main axiom of Lenin's theory of terrorism is that anything sufficiently debased can always be turned to the good of the cause. The basis for the instruments is bestiality".

The first step the subversive leaders take is to cause disgust in the minds of the people by informing them of the graft and corruption unearthed by their army of Spies. They next inject the feeling of despair into the hearts of the people by convincing them that Evil has prospered so far that nothing but revolutionary action can correct the situation. Carefully controlled negative propaganda is put out by the

Agenturs of the capitalistic conspirators which increases the hopeless feelings of the public and makes them think : "that any change must be for the best". The sensational heading of stories in the Press dealing with crime, rape, abduction, and serious accidents is all part of this phase of the Conspiracy.

The subversives then use their cells and Agentur to kill the individual conscience. No less than nine Articles and fifteen paragraphs are devoted in the Protocols to the duties of the agentur. Article I, Par. 22 says : "*Behold the alcoholised animals, bemused with drink, the right to an immoderate use of which comes along with freedom. It is not for us and ours to walk that road. The people of the Goyim are bemused with alcoholic liquors; their youth has grown stupid on Classicism (meaning obsolete, senile, and antiquated teachings) and from early immorality, into which it has been inducted by our special agents... by tutors, lackeys, governesses in the houses of the wealthy, by clerks and others, by our women in the places of dissipation frequented by the Goyim. In the number of these last I count also the so-called "Society Ladies", voluntary followers of the others in corruption and luxury*".

The next step by the conspirators is to direct their attack against the rallying points of the nation whose government they plot to overthrow, i.e. The King — The Flag — The Constitution or government. They criticize the government and expose anything detrimental of which their spies can get hold. They attack the churches as having become commercialized. They do everything in their power to remove Christian teaching and influence in the schools and they create economic conditions which keep parents so busy earning a living that both are fully occupied. Children are left to the care of baby-sitters or attendants of one kind or another.[1] Religion in the home becomes a thing of the past. The purpose is to break down all respect for parental and lawful authority.

Subversive agents work on the theory that twigs are easily broken one by one. One bad apple placed in a barrel will soon affect the lot. Calumny, detraction, and character assassination are used to discredit all those who try to expose their devilish activities. If "L'Infamie" doesn't silence their opponents effectively, strong-arm methods are often used. Threats are often made against the wives and children of those who actively oppose the conspirators.

Once the people have been brainwashed by propaganda until they think "Any change must be for the best", then any racial hatred, religious difference, regional separatist movement, industrial dispute, and class envy, is worked for all it is worth by the subversives. First bemused and finally terrorised, like sheep without a shepherd, the people turn and look for salvation to the ignoble creatures who plotted their undoing.

---

[1] The best illustration of this comes from Southport, England, where a woman employed to look after a childrens clinic objected to paying the fee of six shillings and three pence a day for her own two children who she had to take to the clinic in order that she could hold down her job, and bring the total family income up to £13-0-0 a week.

The Communist Missionaries who arrived in Canada in 1920 explained that it was a fundamental principle of their creed that all their 5th Columnists must learn to live off the people they plan to subjugate. The top level within the government services; the bottom level in the underworld. Once the Communist "Cells" infiltrated into the ranks of the dock-workers and railways employees they taught them it was no sin to steal from any capitalist owned industry, because the capitalists had usurped their wealth and power by defrauding the common people. On this ground subversives claim it is perfectly right to steal back from them as much as possible. The Communist "Cells" always added jokingly "The only sin, when stealing from a Capitalist, or defrauding the government, is the sin of being caught".

Communist missionaries explain to Fellow Travellers that the men who direct the capitalist conspiracy were first of all gold and silversmiths; then money-lenders; and afterwards bankers. The subversives prove by reference to history that the bankers usurped the rights of the people when they forced national governments to give them the right to make, and issue, and control the country's money.

The subversives point out that every citizen, in every so-called "free-nation", is in economic bondage by reason of the ever increasing national debts, the payments on which are guaranteed by the right to tax the people directly.

The Communist "Cells" then slyly mention the fact that the only people who do not pay tribute to the international bankers are the members of the underground. They live in the underworld and make their living in the black market and by engaging in illegal traffic and trade. It is pointed out that the members of the 5th. Column do not keep books. They don't pay taxes. They only deal in cash transactions. They don't pay duty on goods they import or excise on goods they export.

The most extraordinary feature of the international conspiracy is the fact that the public purse is robbed to provide funds for those who plot to subjugate the people and yet the vast majority of the people just sit back indifferently and do absolutely nothing at all to stop this national and international banditry.

In a report of the British Home Office it is stated that "In one year £27,000 was paid to the Communist Party of Great Britain of which at least £10,300 was in forged £5 Bank of England notes made in Moscow". It was further charged in a House of Commons Debate in 1928 that M. Shannin, attache to the Soviet Embassy in London, brought over £27,000 in English notes for use of the Communist Party in Great Britain.

The financial reports of the Communist international for 1931 show that over a million dollars was provided by Moscow to help the revolutionaries in Spain. At about the same time agentur of the international capitalists deposited in Spanish banks, a million pesos to the credit of each of twenty-one generals, so they would support the republican cause. Franco was one general the conspirators couldn't bribe.[2]

2 Read chapters 13-14 and 15 of "Pawns In The Game".

All students of international affairs know about the wholesale use
of home made money to upset the national economy of countries engaged in fighting each other in World Wars One and Two. When
bankers print money they are in reality counterfeiting, because
morally and legally, only the government elected by popular vote of
the people has the right to make money. If this statement were not
true then why did the Founders of America make the matter of
coining, issuing, and controlling the value of money, a right and duty
of government, Article I, section 8 of the American Constitution.

Communism and international Capitalism seem strange bed-
fellows but it is time the public knew that international Capitalism
organized, financed, and directed, international Communism from 1773
to 1936. The international capitalists used international Communism
to destroy their enemies and overthrow National forms of government.

The majority of the Canadian people had been badly hit financially by the international racketeers who had master-minded the reces-
sion of the early 1920s. Those who lived in the Maritimes and on the
Pacific coast suffered more than the others. When a great number
of people are on the verge of financial ruin they are ripe fruit for those
who tempt them into illegal traffic and trade in order to recuperate
their financial losses.

In 1922 New Brunswick was under the Scott Act. Both Communist subversives, and the agentur of the capitalist conspirators have
always used prohibitory laws to their own advantage. Under the Scott
Act the Provincial Government had *sole* control of the purchase and
sale of liquors. The provincial government appointed the proprietors
of drug stores as the only legal retail outlets. According to the Scott
Act the only legal way to obtain liquor was to get a fully qualified
medical man to prescribe that you drink liquor as medicine.

Such ridiculous laws play right into the hands of the directors of
the international conspiracy. The prohibitory laws enabled those who
organized smuggling on an international scale to make billions and at
the same time break down public respect for law and order. The
profits were so great that the agentur of the international financiers
were able to corrupt by bribery, Customs and Excise officials, from
the bottom right to the top-level of the administration, so that they
compromised cabinet ministers and the head of the Civil Service Commission into doing their will.

The important fact to remember is that illegal liquor moves only
one way. Because rum-runners are in the business to make money
they insist on being provided with return loads. The result is that
millions of dollars worth of dutiable goods cross the border in the
other direction.

The 5th Columnists' job is to bring about *general* dissatisfaction
and unrest amongst *all* classes of the communities. In order to do this,
they organize an economic war, calculated to achieve three purposes :
(a) Bankrupt as many business men as possible. (b) Corrupt officials in the police forces, Customs Service and Inland Revenue Preventive Services. (c) Bring the various levels of Government into
disrepute.

How can an honest store-keeper hope to stay in business if he has to compete with others who handle smuggled goods and arrange a fire sale every now and again ? The unscrupulous business man sells to the Insurance Companies what the public won't buy. Statistics prove that fires became so frequent in the 1920's that insurance rates had to be increased in 1923. I investigated one case in which the party concerned had had three profitable fires in three years. He had the effrontery to use the city transportation service to advertise his fire sales. Statistics also prove that bankruptcies and business failures in the Maritimes reached an all time high in the middle 1920's. The Royal Commission into the Customs Service proved the conditions I investigated in the Maritimes from 1920 to 1923 were prevalent throughout the whole Dominion by 1925-26. The black market and illicit trade increased in both Canada and the United States since then. One of the chief objectives of this economic war is to force business and professional men to abandon their ethics and resort to illegal practices to stay in business. If they don't become subversive they are usually forced to sell out to some chain-store or combine. The extent of illicit trade, and its ramifications, were first proved to me by two orthodox Jews. Both were veterans of World War One. They were two of the most patriotic and most principled citizens it has been my pleasure to meet.

Many farmers located near the borders made more money smuggling, or by renting their barns to smugglers than they ever made from the crops they grew on their farms.

What were the forces of law and order doing all this time ? Frankly, they were doing nothing at all. It seemed utterly useless to try to convince those in authority that the illegal traffic going on was planned economic war, calculated to bring the Dominion to ultimate ruin.

Investigation showed how the conspirators worked to further the plans of their masters. Carloads of ale made in breweries, owned by prominent people with great political influence, were shipped to drug stores which had been granted a government license to sell Beer and Spirits for *medicinal purposes*. In one report I made to high officials I pointed out that the quantity of ale that had been shipped to one drug store in a village of 900 population in *one* month was sufficient to supply every man, woman, and child with 50 gallons each. In other words, 45,000 gallons were shipped in a short period of time. This was enough in which to drown the whole population. The beer was kept in the railways box-cars, on a siding near the border, until the bootleggers in the States were ready to receive it. Railway police were detailed to guard these shipments to the border points and make sure they were not hijacked.

The Volstead Act in the States made millionaires by the dozens and law-breakers by the millions. Some doctors made more money prescribing liquor as medicine for people who didn't need it than they made attending patients who really needed their care.

The 5th Columnists brought the doctors, who valued money more than the ethics of their profession, into contact with bootleggers, owners of sporting clubs, and keepers of bawdy houses.

I discovered one doctor in St. John, N.B. who had been inveigled into working with the international drug ring. He was shipping to Toronto, narcotic drugs which arrived on ships from Antwerp and Hamburg.

Agents of the dope ring in Antwerp and Hamburg contacted British and American seamen who bought the "dope" at a price which assured them 200% profit. After the Customs had inspected the ship on arrival the seamen involved turned over the drugs to the steward in charge of the ship's Sick Bay, and received their pay.

When the Medical Officer of Health for that port went on board he visited the ship's hospital and carried the drugs ashore in his "little black bag". He made as many trips as necessary.[3]

The man who was to accompany the shipment to Toronto obtained the drugs from the doctor and took them to the railway station. He had checks for luggage which had been inspected and passed by the Customs. On the excuse that he wished to get something *out* of the trunk, which he said he needed for his journey, he placed the drugs *in* them.

Spies kept the drug trafficker informed as to whether the shipment was "Hot" or "Cold". If "Cold", the luggage was sent to a room in a good hotel in Toronto. Records will prove that as much as $200,000. worth of "dope" have been seized by the R.C.M.P. in raids on down town hotels in Toronto.[4]

After investigating the matter very thoroughly, I reported my findings to Sergeant Lucas of the R.C.M.P. I was with him the evening he tried to arrest the doctor as he left a C.P.R. Liner. This was one case in which the Mountie didn't get his man. To catch the Doctor "red-handed", Lucas decided to wait until he had left the ship and had the drugs actually in his car. He tried to stop him as he drove slowly along the narrow wharf between the dock-side and the freight sheds. Box cars loading freight from the ship were spotted on the tracks outside the sheds.

We saw the doctor get into his car and we took up our position and flagged him to stop. Instead of stopping, he stepped on the gas and tried to run us down. We had to jump to save our lives. The doctor kept going until he crossed the border. As far as I know, he never returned to Canada. He realized the game was up as far as he was concerned.

Those of us who have investigated the international ramifications of illegal traffic and trade know that the "big interests" who control the Drug Markets, the White Slave traffic, and the International Smuggling rackets, have their headquarters in Switzerland.

---

[3] "The agentur of the international conspirators make every effort possible to bring Medical Officers of Health under their control so they can rely on receiving their support when they advocate mass medications such as fluoridation.

[4] Newspaper reports for 1955 prove the same conditions are prevalent only on a much bigger scale. The R.C.M.P. claim that in November 1955 they found heroin valued at several million dollars aboard the S.S. St. Marlo. She had sailed from Antwerp to Montreal.

They control the drug trade just as they control any of their other cartels. They control all drugs from the growing of the plants from which they are derived to the drug stores from which they are dispensed or the dope peddlers who supply the illegal traffic. As in the case of liquor, there would be no large profit in handling drugs, if the use of them wasn't prohibited by law. We must recognize as a fact that no person has ever been legislated into heaven and no one ever will be.

The agentur of the Directors of the conspiracy arrange for an annual crop of young girls for the White Slave trade just like they arrange for the annual crop of drugs. Not only do they arrange for the systematic seduction of teen-age girls, but they have turned the traffic in their babies into a million dollar business in Montreal alone. It takes a tremendous number of seductions to enable Madames to have from 300 to 500 teen-age "call girls" in their "stables", and to produce enough illegitimate children to supply the baby market.

What is true of liquor, drugs, and prostitution is equally true of all phases of illegal traffic and trade. It is organized, financed, directed and controlled by those at the very top of the international conspiracy... the Illuminati... The agenturs of the Illuminati organize illegal business so it finances the underground of the various subversive movements, and in this way the agentur of the Illuminati control the leaders of the subversive movements and all those who made their fortunes by illegal traffic and trade as long as they live. It is through the men they made wealthy that they control national and provincial, and even municipal administrators.

The Directors of the World Revolutionary Movement have their agents involve citizens of all classes in illegal traffic and trade. Many become very wealthy and form the new aristocracy. By reason of their wealth they are accepted into society and become respectable. It isn't long before they are exerting their influence in municipal, provincial, and federal politics. That they must do the will of those who made them rich is proved by Article I, Par. 26-27-28 of the Protocols which read in part : "*On the ruins of the natural and genealogical aristocracy of the Goyim we have set up the aristocracy of our educated class headed by the aristocracy of money. The qualifications for this aristocracy we have established in wealth, which is dependent on us, and in knowledge, for which our learned elders provide the motive force*".

While the agentur of the Capitalist conspirators concentrate on ruining the national economy the Communist "Cells" infiltrate into all levels of government and classes of society innoculating the body politic with the disease of corruption and graft.

To indicate how well they succeeded upsetting the economy of the Maritime provinces, (and they were doing exactly the same sort of thing in all the other provinces). I will quote from the Toronto Evening Telegram of Sept. 30th. 1925. Head line "NOVA SCOTIA ALL OF $2,000,000 ON WRONG SIDE". Auditors working on the accounts the past two months expect there will be a deficit of $2,000,000 for the fiscal year... and a gross debt of $38,000,000 at the same time".

Premier Baxter of New Brunswick speaking for the Press at the same time announced that the Veniot Government (which was defeated in August 1925) had increased the debt of the province to over $34,000,000. Mr. Baxter noted that the Veniot government had spent $750,000 on road improvements in one year and had thus added $100,000 to the interest and sinking fund costs. He forgot to add that the expenditure on roads was for the benefit of smugglers. Exactly the same kind of maladministration was going on in Saskatchewan where Mr. Gardiner, the present Minister of Agriculture, was proved to have spent similar amounts on provincial highways which benefitted those who were bleeding Canada white by engaging in all kinds of illegal traffic and trade. But perhaps the most glaring case of all was the amount of money spent on highways in Nova Scotia. As any native living on one of the many ocean inlets will confirm the provincial highways were extended to the shore line of nearly all the coves so the smugglers could unload their boats on to big motor transports which could not have travelled the old reads along the coast.

Scandal after scandal appeared in the newspapers. Rumours were circulated which hinted at corruption and graft in high places. The people became suspicious, discontented, and disgusted. The only way they could express their feelings was by registering a "negative" vote at the polls. During the elections in the early 1920s it was not uncommon to see a complete change-over in the government from liberal to conservative and vice versa. If only the people had kept up a continuing interest and insisted that the men they elected cleaned up the mess all might have been well, but once the elections were over the public went to sleep again and the conspirators went ahead with their plans unmolested.

To take full advantage of public discontent the conspirators sent a young man to Canada who had graduated from the Lenin Institute in Moscow. His name was Schmil Kogan. He was born at Tomachpol, Russian Ukraine, on July 7th. 1906. He arrived in Canada August 29th. 1924. He afterwards changed his name to Sam Cohen, and later still to Sam Carr. His job was to teach mob psychology and demonstrate how to use it to the advantage of the subversive movement.

I watched this subversive at work on the "harvest specials" which took disgruntled unemployed from the eastern provinces to the western provinces to help with the harvest. He was only 18 years of age at the time but he could develop a grouch into an argument, and develop the argument into a fight, and the fight into a riot, with the greatest efficiency it is possible to imagine. After instigating the trouble he would withdraw gracefully and leave some poor fellow to shoulder the blame. He was working in accordance with what is laid down in Article I, Par. 18, of the Protocols which says *"In order to elaborate satisfactory forms of action it is necessary to have regard to the rascality, the slackness, and the instability of the mob, its lack of capacity to understand and respect the conditions of its own life, or its own welfare. It must be understood that the might of a mob is blind, senseless, and unreasoning force ever at the mercy of a suggestion from any side... consequently members of the mob, upstarts from the people, even though they should be as a genius for wisdom, yet having no understanding of the political cannot come forward as leaders of the mob without bringing the whole nation to ruin"*.

Illegal traffic and trade are deliberately used, as part of the international conspiracy, by the agents of the Communist Party working at the "bottom", and the agents of the international-minded Capitalists working at the "top", to cause discontent among the working people; disrespect for government and law and order among the electorate; and to ruin honest business men; by corrupting government administrators and public servants. Article V, Par. 1 of the Protocols says so : *"What form of administrative rule can be given to communities where riches are attained only by the clever surprise tactics of semi-swindling tricks; where looseness reigns; where morality is maintained by penal measures and harsh laws but not by voluntary accepted principles; where the feelings towards faith and country are obliterated by cosmopolitan convictions ? What form of government is to be given to these communities if not that despotism which I shall describe to you later ?"*

While the international conspirators were building up their illegal traffic and trade, until it became second only to the grain trade in volume and value, Maritime manufacturers dropped their production from $160,000,000 in 1920 to $23,000,000 in 1925. Business failures in Canada reached their peak about this time. As will be proved in the next chapter those directing this economic war corrupted government administrators and public servants from the lowly Customs officer, and policeman, right up the ladder to Cabinet ministers. Public spirited men worked hard, and risked their lives, in order that the public might know how the conspirators were ruining the national economy in order to force Canadians into accepting their proposals for a One World Government at a later date. That day has now arrived.

CHAPTER V

How the conspirators use illegal traffic and trade

"THE Communist party leaders must learn to unite systematically legal and illegal work, but all legal work must be performed under direct control of the illegal party... The task of the proletariat is to blow up the whole system and machinery of the bourgeoisie, to destroy them and all parliamentary institutions with them. This must be done irrespective of whether or not they be *republican or constitutional monarchial"*.

(Extracts from the Theses and Statutes of the
Communist International)

The international conspirators consider the underground, and black market, operations as of the utmost importance to their plans because, by means of wholesale bootlegging and smuggling, the government they seek to destroy is defrauded of millions upon millions of dollars annually, and the burden on the tax-payer is increased proportionately. By means of corruption, graft, and blackmail, the conspirators can place their agentur in position to control officials in the Customs, Police, and various government departments from the lowest to the top-levels.

The majority of railway employees, dock-workers, and labourers are honest, hard working men, but the 5th Columnists who work with them are always preaching their doctrine of class hatred and trying to involve them in crime. They point out for instance how the C.P.R. brought out immigrants under government sponsorship and used them as labourers on road-bed maintenance work at 25¢ an hour, *when they worked.* There isn't a single item of social injustice with which the leaders of 5th Columns are not fully familiar. The typical Communist agitator invariably winds up his arguments along these lines : "Hell ! It ain't no crime to rob the C.P.R., or any of those other capitalistic combines, you are only getting back a little of what you rightly have coming to you".

The result was that thefts and damage of goods in transit amounted to millions of dollars annually.

There would be no point in stealing millions of dollars worth of goods if they couldn't dispose of what they steal in the black markets. The illegal markets should be called "Red" not "Black". Personal investigation proved that more than 75% of "black market operators" are people with foreign names. I regret to say that more and more Anglo-Saxons are becoming involved with each passing year. The black market transactions have increased to such an extent that today they threaten the existence of every honest business man while at the same time small privately owned enterprises are being forced to amalgamate or sell out to "big business" or go bankrupt. These conditions, if permitted to continue can only result in the national economy being controlled by the internationalists who are the enemies of society.

A man who was a clerk in a liquor store in Toronto before Ontario went dry became a millionaire by 1928. He was ultimately accepted into the best of society. He became director of several large companies most of which are connected with the manufacture and distribution of alcoholic beverages.

When I knew him in St. John in 1924 he chartered schooners, and loaded them with liquor from the bonded warehouse. They sailed for the West Indies in the afternoon but returned at dark and unloaded at Long Wharf, St. John, the same night. The same schooner would be back alongside the bonded warehouse ready to load another cargo for Bermuda the next day.

This liquor, upon which no duty was paid, was hauled to various storage warehouses. It was distributed to local drug stores which enjoyed Government licenses. Huge quantities were shipped by freight to the central provinces but most of it was smuggled over the border into the United States.

In 1923-24, the head of the St. John city detective department owned two drug stores. Both of them were licensed to "dispense" liquor. Many such stores replenished the stocks they purchased from the Government legally with stocks they obtained from the smugglers illegally. They paid the smugglers only a fraction of what they had to pay the government. Raids proved there was more liquor of certain brands in stock than had originally been purchased from the government.

The same procedure was being carried out in border cities in the Niagara Peninsula. Row boats cleared the Canadian Customs at Fort Erie for Bermuda, unloaded their cargoes of liquor on the American side and returned immediately for another load.

This short circuiting of liquor involved many Federal officials who knew that no schooner could clear for the West Indies from St. John and Fort Erie one evening and be back again the next day for another full cargo. When two honest Customs Officers in St. John seized one schooner, and sequestered the bond, they were ordered by the Federal Minister of Customs to release the schooner and return the bond. This outrageous state of affairs was proved by evidence given before the Royal Commission by the customs officers concerned. I knew both of them personally.

Such reprehensible conduct on the part of high officials caused almost complete break-down in the morale of the forces of law and order. Police officials, customs officers, and officers attached to the preventive service, knew that the racketeers had grown so powerful, and had involved so many higher-ups, that to step on their toes was to invite dismissal and a prolonged period of unemployment.

Those who shipped contraband from the East and West coasts to Ontario under false consignment paid hundreds of thousands of dollars in freight charges to both the C.P.R. and C.N.R. annually. The policy of the railway management was to mind their own business and ask no questions. The railway police were instructed to look after the interests of the railways and the goods of the patrons who shipped over their lines. There was a mutual understanding that the racketeers would never try to ship liquor under the guise of any commodity that travelled at less *than first-class rates*. Some "cheap-skates" did try hiding consignments of liquor in car-loads of freight which moved under special low rates, but such shipments were usually seized by the prohibition officers, or the provincial police, when they reached their destination.

One consignment of very special liquor was shipped inside a casket as a "corpse". In some inexplicable manner, the "corpse" sprang a leak. One of the baggage attendants said to the "Mourner", who was accompanying his departed relative on his last journey, "Say, Boss... Are you sure he's really dead... Looks as if his kidneys and bladder are working... But what I smell ain't ammonia."

The criminal element which aids the conspiracy in Canada and the United States have another advantage, due to the fact there are so many different forces. In Canada there are over 1,200 separate police forces. Each force is jealous of its territorial rights. Full co-operation between federal, provincial, railroad and municipal police, is rarely experienced. The following case will illustrate what I mean.

On the night of June 13th, 1925, Sergeant Lucas of the R.C.M.P. received a code message from Ottawa saying the schooner "Evelyn B. Miller" was expected to land a cargo of contraband on the coast near St. John. He took some men along and left by car. As he neared the spot, he saw another car parked without headlights. Thinking this car might contain people who were going to receive the contraband, he closed in to investigate. To his great surprise, he saw Customs Officer Lyons sitting calmly smoking in the other car. Lyons claimed he had been tipped off by Ottawa also. But Ottawa didn't tell Lyons that Lucas was on the job, nor did Lucas know Lyons was on the job. To make matters more interesting, Constable Crawford of the local prohibition force drifted onto the scene. He didn't know the other police officials were already on the job, and a gun battle was narrowly averted. But this wasn't the end. Having straightened matters out, the three officers, and their assistants, settled down to wait for the schooner to show up. Suddenly they heard another car approaching without lights.

"This", they told each other, "must be those for whom we are waiting". They crouched down and waited until the car arrived and then pounced upon the new arrivals, but it turned out to be Preventive Officer Dawes. *The only thing that didn't turn up that night was the schooner "Evelyn B. Miller."*

The fact that *all* these officers were notified by code, from Ottawa, that the vessel was due at a certain place, at a definite time, on a definite date, was to my mind suspicious in itself. The fact that *none* of the officers in charge of the four different outfits knew that their confreres had also been notified confirmed my suspicions. Only by having *all* representatives of law and order gathered in one place could the smugglers be sure it was absolutely safe to unload a really big and valuable cargo at some other cove along the coast. Investigation proved how it was done. With two companions I went on a fishing trip into the wilds of New Brunswick.

We followed the old adage, "If in doubt ask a policeman." The man we figured would be best able to inform us from whom we could get really good imported whisky was the preventive officer for that district, so we decided to fish in his locality. He was a dear *old* man.

After he became acquainted he informed us that he was ninety years of age when he received his appointment as Preventive Officer for that district. He didn't know I was investigating the ramifications of illegal traffic and trade. Like so many others he was making money boot-legging and my companions and I became pretty steady customers We drank, played cards, and listened to the old man's tales of smuggling and hi-jacking.

From what he let slip and from observations we made it soon became apparent that a man named Moses Aziz was the King-pin of the conspiracy in that particular area. Because the old Preventive Officer could neither read or write Moses Aziz was considerate enough to write his reports for him. The old man didn't know what Moses wrote to officials in Ottawa and he cared less.

Moses Aziz was the liaison man between the "top" conspirators and the "Bottom". He was the connecting link between corrupt officials in Ottawa and the smugglers and the local police. Evidence given before the Royal Commission (which afterwards investigated the Customs and Excise Service) proved that Moses Aziz was the political campaign manager for a certain member of parliament who was also connected with the illegal traffic and trade. He would notify them when a schooner load of liquor was due from St. Pierre and Miquelon and they would then see to it that the law enforcement officers were drawn away from the spot chosen to unload the contraband cargo. If any questions were asked the officials in Ottawa could always clear themselves by saying they had acted on information received from the old preventive officer.

Even when this man's criminal activities were finally exposed to the Royal Commissioners and his arrest was ordered, it took considerable time to have the order for his arrest executed. This delay was not caused by Moses running away. He stayed right at home and brazened the whole thing out. He practically defied the forces of law and order to arrest him and openly boasted that if he was put behind bars he would tell all he knew and involve men in the highest levels of the government. Finally Moses was persuaded that no good purpose would be served if he exposed the conspiracy. It is presumed he was well paid while he did a ridiculously short term for his numerous crimes. Whatever terms were arranged, Ottawa officials announced on April 30th 1926 that Moses Aziz had at last been arrested. Moses Aziz lived at Caraquet, N.B. and he was jailed in Bathurst. The full account of this man's activities in connection with boot-legging and smuggling would fill a book. It takes up many pages of the evidence given before the Royal Commissioners. His arrest was reported in the newspapers all over the country. But he, like many others, turned out to be a nine day wonder and then the public forgot all about him and the politicians with whom he was associated.

The laws of Canada require that all Civil Service appointments must be decided by *examinations* and the appointments given on *merit* with preference being given to veterans, but, under the political patronage system, the laws of Canada don't mean very much, particularly as far as veterans' preference is concerned. Political Patronage as practiced in Canada means that every member of the party in power, in either the federal or provincial governments, have a certain number of jobs which they can give to their political henchmen even if it means kicking some more efficient person out if he wears another political stripe.

If readers think this case is unique, and dismiss it as happening over thirty years ago, let me remind them that as recently as 1946 when the question of the "Problem of the Older Veterans" and "The Veterans of Two Wars" were being discussed by delegates of one hundred and sixty citizens' rehabilitation committees located in Ontario, statements repeatedly made by delegates went to prove that men of seventy-two and seventy-five years of age, *who were of independent means,* had been appointed to posts in the Ontario Civil Service, while 25,000 Veterans, averaging fifty-six years of age, who had served Canada faithfully in both wars, were unemployed and couldn't get jobs.

Communist organizers don't fail to exploit this kind of thing to the limit.

The feeling of insecurity of citizens employed under the party patronage system is responsible more than anything else for them "making hay while their political sun shines."

In Canada we have the R.C.M.P.; we have provincial police; we have country police; municipal police C.P.R. police; and C.N.R. police. In addition we had in 1923-25 special police and inspectors engaged to enforce the liquor laws etc., etc. The Federal government would be well advised to follow the system now in operation in Great Britain and Western Germany by which the efficiency, and co-operation, of all the forces of law and order are assured. This kind of co-ordination would give the 5th Columnists something to worry about.

Uniting all police into a national force is NOT the answer. Such a force becomes nothing more nor less than a private army under the command of one man, and history proves that only too often that one man has been an agent of one or another revolutionary group and the national police have been used to seize political and economic power. The system used in England and West Germany, while the latter country was under Allied control, was that the National Government subsidized the cost of maintaining Municipal police, but in order to qualify for this financial aid the various police forces had to have the members graduate from a central police school. They had to maintain a high standard of character, physical fitness, and police efficiency. They had to be ready at all times to co-operate fully with the Federal and adjacent police. But most important of all was the manner in which the chief of local police forces was chosen. The local authorities were required to submit the names of at least three men they considered capable of filling the position of chief. The Federal authorities had the right to select from those named the man they thought was the best qualified. Under this system local autonomy was preserved, co-operation between various units was assured, and a high standard of efficiency maintained. The directors of the international conspiracy who work to bring about a one world super-government invariably try to amalgamate a nation's police forces so that, when the time comes, their agentur may control them. The agentur of the international conspirators are even now paving the way for the acceptance of their idea for an INTERNATIONAL POLICE FORCE. Under their plan it would be set up presumably to maintain peace in all countries.

My understanding of the purpose of an international police force is entirely different. It has been suggested that all members of the United Nations would contribute to this international police force numbers pro rata to population. If for instance each member nation was required to supply one policeman for every 10,000 of population that would mean Canada would supply 1,500 men, the United States 14,000, Britain 6,000, the Soviets 60,000, India 60,000 etc., etc. If and when China and Africa and other nations were admitted to sharing responsibility for preservation of the internal security of the member nations it would not be long before the coloured races would outnumber the white police many times over. But the real nigger in their *particular* wood-pile is the intention, rarely mentioned, that no police group would be permitted to serve in the country in which the members of the force originate. In other words Indians might police Canada, Chinese the United States, while Canadians might be detailed to Korea and Americans to Africa, etc., etc. In theory this idea is to ensure that the police would act in a fair and unbiased manner and would not be vulnerable to corruption and graft. Internationalization of police duties is just another of those things our representatives in the U.N.O. need to watch carefully.

In Canada the R.C.M.P., under the direction of the Minister of Justice, is responsible for the dominion's internal security. In July 1955 Mr. Garson, the Minister of Justice, asked Parliament to grant him more money than ever before to enable him to increase the numbers of the R.C.M.P. He explained that he needed more men because his present force spent so much of their time conducting investigations into subversive activities that they could not carry out their ordinary police duties properly.

Mr. John Blackmore, member for Lethbridge, asked the Minister why he permitted Communists to operate schools in every town and city in which children of tender years were taught subversion and the Atheistic-materialistic ideology of Marx? He also asked why the C.B.C. was permitted to hire artists and speakers whose purpose in life was to further the plans and increase the strength of the Communist Party? Mr. Garson replied that the government's policy in regard to internal security was not to interfere with the Communists at the present time.

History teaches us how the men who direct the capitalist conspiracy have used Communism as their manual of action. Therefore it is not unreasonable to assume that their agentur have had a great deal to do with forming our present government's policy as far as our internal security is concerned. The Honourable, the Minister of Justice, admitted he knew that Communist schools are educating our children so that when they reach teen-age they will join the Young Communist Party. He admits that the C.B.C. is issuing propaganda calculated to recruit "Fellow Travellers" for the party. He asks for more police so he can keep proper tab on Communists, their organization, and their activities and yet he states it is the policy of the government to leave them unmolested. What conclusion can one reach other than that the government's policy fits in with the "long range" plans of the international conspirators? I do not suggest that all members of the government are *knowingly* playing into the hands of the conspirators, but those who are not should study history and they will see how essential it is for them to revise their present policy. Otherwise the Communists will be left alone until they are ready to bring about the revolution. Then the agenturs of the international capitalists will take over the direction of our political and economic affairs as they did following the revolutions which took place in France; in America; Russia; Mexico and China.

It must be remembered that the only times their ability to accomplish this fact has ever been challenged was by Hitler and Stalin. Hitler challenged their power in 1936. Stalin challenged them again

in 1946. But since Hitler's defeat and Stalin's death there have been rapid developments. Sometimes it happens that leaders of governments were too much of the gentleman to believe that such a diabolical conspiracy could exist. Mr. Chamberlain was a typical example of what I mean : Then again others were kept in a blissful state of coma by agentur of the conspirators. History reveals that without exception the agentur appointed as "experts" and "advisers" led their nations to the brink of the precipice of destruction over which the revolutionary mob pushed them. History also reveals that those who directed the conspiracy were never harmed by the revolutionary mob.

The Rothschild Mansion, and the Rothschild family, were not molested during the French revolution. The top-level conspirators within the Russian government escaped the fate of the other members. That this policy of protecting capitalist conspirators is common practice is proved by the fact that revolutionary leaders are ordered to arrest the capitalist conspirators in order that their treachery may not be suspected. It is a fact that they are amply rewarded after law and order has been restored. This policy is clearly indicated in Paragraphs 14 and 15 of the instructions issued to revolutionary leaders in Spain in 1936. The instructions read : "Uniformed groups shall also arrest and detain important capitalists whose names appear in appendix "B" of Circular No. 32. Violence shall not be used against these capitalists unless they resist etc., etc.

In 1924 I was given the opportunity to take a personal part in one of the biggest boot-legging and smuggling schemes ever attempted in Canada.

After the treaty of Versailles had been signed, imposing such unjust economic restrictions upon the German people, I was amazed to learn that millions of dollars had been loaned to Germans, hooked up in the international chemical combine, by British and American bankers to build huge distilleries. Officially these distilleries were designed to make synthetic motor fuel... a substitute for gasoline. Propaganda said the fuel was similar to wood alcohol and was distilled after waste wood had been treated by chemical action.

As a matter of fact these distilleries manufactured vast amounts of pure alcohol from grain and potatoes which was smuggled into the United States and Canada by the ship load. It was usually entered on the manifest as "Wood alcohol" or "Denatured alcohol". As such it was subject to very little duty because industrial alcohol is poisonous and is used in the manufacture of anti-freeze; boot-polish, inks, canned heat, perfumes etc., etc. There were a few barrels of industrial alcohol in every cargo and it was from these barrels customs officials were bribed to take their samples. There were several large seizures of pure grain alcohol but when the matter had blown over the alcohol was sold back to the smugglers at .35 a gallon, which is considerably less than the amount they would have had to pay as duty. The grain alcohol smuggled into America from Germany was cut in strength three times, coloured, and flavoured, and sold as genuine imported Scotch whiskey in bottles, on which forged labels and caps had been fixed.

I was investigating a case for the C.P.R. in the vicinity of St. Leonard N.B. where the gang, with which Theo worked, had a warehouse. Theo's boss was also a French-Canadian. He was considered "The King of Bootleggers" in that particular area. We will call him Benny.

Benny wasn't satisfied with the "cut" he was getting from his bosses which he told me, when I arrested him, included high officials in the Customs Service and government administrators in Ottawa and Fredericton. He decided he would double-cross the Big Brass and make himself a fortune.

In the Fall of 1924 Benny received orders to proceed to a town in Maine. He was supplied with credentials and the money with which to purchase a railway carload of alcohol which had been smuggled into the United States from Germany. He had instructions to ship this alcohol to St. Leonard's. He consigned it to the St. Stephen's Bottling Works, St. Leonard's. There was no such firm. The alcohol was intended to go into Benny's warehouse and made into Scotch whiskey like so many other shipments. Benny's plan to double-cross his Bosses was simple and clever. He would undoubtedly have got away with it if he hadn't tried to beat the C.P.R. for the money owing as freight. The fact that he tried to gyp the company for about $300 brought me into the picture to Benny's great regret.

Benny's plan was simple in the extreme. After he had shipped the alcohol to St. Leonards as instructed he arranged with his gang to hi-jack the alcohol the night after it arrived in St. Leonards.

So he would have a perfect alibi he proceeded to get drunk in Van Buren, Maine. He made such a disturbance that he was arrested and thrown into the local jail. He timed everything so that he could prove he was locked up in the United States jail when the hi-jackers swooped down on the railway siding in St. Leonards and made off with the half million dollar cargo.

The car of alcohol arrived in St. Leonards and because there was no such firm as the St. Stephen's Bottling Works, the railway agent went to Benny, who of course, wasn't at home and none of his "gang" would admit that he knew anything about the alcohol or its ownership.

The Station Agent became suspicious. He phoned the Inspector in charge of the investigation department in St. John, N.B. Because I was the investigator nearest to St. Leonards at the time I was told to proceed there. My orders were not to permit the alcohol to be unloaded until ownership had been established and the freight paid."

Even before it got dark I had obtained the following information.

(A) All the barrels except one contained pure grain alcohol.

(B) Benny was actually in jail in Van Buren, just across the river.

(C) Orders had been received by the "gang" to be on hand to steal the alcohol at 1.30 a.m.

I told Benny's gang-leader that I wouldn't let anyone take the alcohol until AFTER the freight had been paid. I ordered the station agent to have the car moved from the siding where it had been spotted outside Benny's warehouse and placed in front of the railway station under the glare of lights. As matters had become complicated the gang-leader drove over to Van Buren to consult with Benny. I was told afterward that Benny demanded he be released from jail. This was arranged after he put up bond.

I was sitting in the Station Agent's office watching the car when Benny's gang arrived with five big trucks. As none of the gang had produced arms I called out to the leader and told him I thought he was foolish to get himself involved in a series of major crimes when all that was necessary to get legal delivery of the alcohol was for Benny to admit ownership and pay the amount of freight which was owing. He consulted with the rest of his gang and then they climbed into the trucks and left the railway property.

About 2 o'clock Benny came stamping to the station platform. He walked right to the office door and walked in. He was fuming with rage. He was an ugly sight.

He told me I was a damn fool. He suggested that if I would go to the hotel and get some sleep he would give me $2,000. As soon as he made this offer I knew the alcohol did not belong to him and that it was his intention to hi-jack the load. If the alcohol had belonged to him all he would have had to do was prove ownership and pay $325.

I told him no dice.

He raised his offer to $5,000.

I asked him why he offered me $5,000 to clear out, when all he had to do was admit ownership, and pay $325 freight?

Benny cursed and told me it was none of my damned business why he was willing to pay $5,000. It was up to me to accept his offer or else.

I told Benny I wouldn't let the alcohol go until he proved ownership and paid the freight charges. Benny lost his temper completely. He told me he was going to order his men to unload the car. He threatened I'd get all that was coming to me if I tried to prevent them doing so.

I was in a rather ticklish spot. I knew my position wouldn't be improved if I let Benny rejoin his gang so I told him he was under arrest. Benny gave a scornful laugh and started for the door.

I placed myself between Benny and the door and drew my revolver. He walked right onto the muzzle and said : "Out of my way, copper; You don't dare use that gun". I stood my ground and said, "Benny, don't be a fool. I've had to shoot *men* before this. I won't hesitate to shoot a skunk".

I saw uncertainty in his eyes and took advantage of it. I clamped one handcuff on his right wrist and locked the other on my left wrist. I made him sit down as I telephoned the inspector in St. John and told him what had happened. The Inspector told me help would be sent by car immediately.

Having finished the telephone conversation I told Benny I thought a little fresh air would do us both good. I walked him out to the station platform and informed the gang that Benny was under arrest.

I took Benny back into the station office. He immediately tried to talk me into going along with him. When I refused he admitted the alcohol didn't actually belong to him. He claimed he was only acting as the agent for people higher up. He hinted that a Senator and a federal minister were both interested in this deal. He promised that if I would play along with him I would be "Cut in".

It wasn't long before I had a visit from Robinson, the chief preventive officer for the Province of New Brunswick. He confirmed what Benny told me. He frankly admitted that Benny was working under the orders, and protection, of a senator and other high officials in the Government. He evidently did not know Benny had intended to high-jack the load. I knew Robinson was armed and I said to him, "Robinson, it is your duty to help me now". Robinson pulled out his revolver, broke the breech, and threw the shells out of the rear window. He said, "Don't look to me for help. You're getting yourself involved in a lot of trouble". He walked out the door and away from the station.

My next visitor was Benny's wife. She begged me to let him go. She was followed by the town constable named White. He evidently did not know that I knew Benny was his uncle because he very kindly offered to lock Benny up in the local jail so I could get a little sleep.

I informed White that I had found Benny such delightful company I had decided to keep him with me so we could have breakfast together before we paid an official visit to the local magistrate.

I hung on to Benny all night. When I walked him from the station to the hotel about 8 a.m. next morning the citizens of St. Leonards couldn't believe that the notorious Benny was actually under arrest.

After breakfast, I took Benny before the local magistrate and charged him with trespassing on C.P.R. property after dark; conspiring to steal the carload of alcohol; common assault, and attempted bribery.

Never, before or since, have I seen such a disgraceful scenes in a British Court of Justice. The magistrate didn't try Benny... Benny told him. He told him in no uncertain terms, what would happen to him, his home, and his family, if he dared convict and sentence him.

Having worked himself into a terrific rage, Benny dashed out of the court and jumped into a car driven by a nephew who raced toward the American border. I telephoned the border authorities and they closed the gates. Benny doubled back and, like a fox, dived for cover.. He hid in his cellar. I was satisfied. I stood guard where I could watch the car of alcohol and the warehouse.

Early in the afternoon a lawyer, who was high up in political matters in the Province, arrived. He consulted with Benny and then came and asked me if I was ready to proceed with the case. I said I was. We proceeded to the court house. The lawyer spent some time with the Magistrate. He then telephoned Benny and he came to court. He pleaded "guilty" to the charge of trespassing on railway property but "Not Guilty" to conspiracy to steal the carload of liquor and the technical charge of assault, attempted bribery, etc., etc. The magistrate fined him $10.00 and costs on the trespassing charge. He dismissed the other charges "because of insufficient evidence".

Immediately after Benny was released an engine arrived to remove the carload of alcohol from St. Leonard to St. John. I received instructions to ride with the car and give it protection while in transit. Before we pulled out Benny rounded up his gang and headed for a junction point where the engine was supposed to stop. I consulted with railway officials by telephone and arranged for the engine, car and caboose to go roaring through the junction without any stop.

When the alcohol finally reached St. John it was turned over to the agents of the higher-ups who Benny had tried to double-cross.

This incident was the beginning of the end for Benny. Once he had tried to double-cross the higher-ups and failed, he was hounded to death. The R.C.M.P. arrested him for illegal activities in Canada. The American police stopped him entering the States. When he tried to handle consignments of liquor they were invariably seized. The last time I saw Benny he didn't look like the tough, hard-boiled French-Canadian who had once boasted he could beat his weight in wild-cats. He didn't look as if he could jump six feet in the air and kick in a man's face before his feet hit the ground again.

Such instances of maladministration demoralize less experienced constables. It shakes the confidence of the public. It encourages class hatreds. It plays right into the hands of leaders of the revolutionary party because the leaders claim that once they obtain political power they will ruthlessly liquidate all criminals, grafters, corrupt politicians, and the capitalists who make millions at the expense of the government and the people.

Revolutionaries, when planning to take over whole communities with comparatively small numbers of helpers, consider a loyal police force and an efficient fire department as their greatest enemies. Because of this fact they do everything in their power to shake the public confidence in the police force. They do everything they can to destroy the respect of the rank and file for their superiors.

Study of the activities of those engaged in criminal pursuits, and illegal traffic and trade in the United States and Canada, brought to light a most important, and very interesting fact. The Federal Bureau of Investigation in the U.S.A. and the R.C.M.P. in Canada estimate that about one million people in the states and three hundred thousand in Canada are engaged in crime or illegal traffic and trade. It may be pure coincidence but the number of Communists and Fellow Travellers in Canada and the United States is almost identical with the number of people engaged in the various rackets, illegal traffic and trade, and criminal pursuits.

But why should the ordinary man-in-the-street be expected to understand the moral and economic importance of these underground activities in relation to our national life if the Government they elect to look after their interests doesn't seem able to realize the danger? They will have no excuse after reading this book.

Every dollar of revenue the government loses, must be made up out of the pockets of the tax-payer. Those who run rackets and operate the black market rarely, if ever, pay income tax because, as we pointed out previously, all of their transactions are cash-on-the-line. Any bank in the United States and Canada will admit that more paper currency in denominations of $100 to $1,000 is being used today than ever before in the history of the two countries. Why[1]? Because large sums can be carried in a bill fold and used for cash transactions of which no record is kept. Large denominational bills are also easier to trace and identify in case of theft. Cash transactions enable unscrupulous citizens to evade paying income tax.

Racketeers keep no books, or if they do they are phoney. How can legitimate business men hope to compete with this kind of illegal competition ?

I can remember the time when there wasn't a train pulling out of St. John without every drawing-room being occupied by big-time bootleggers and dope smugglers. What could the police do except mind their own business ? To do otherwise, was simply to invite a prolonged period of unemployment. I was one of the few who refused to give up the fight against these racketeers, but the further one delved the more one became convinced that some of the men who sat on many directorates were the ones who directed the activities of the underworld without ever coming into the lime-light themselves.

I recall one case in which we followed dope smugglers right to the end of the line. The consignment of dope was left by a coloured man at the home of one of the biggest business tycoons in Canada. Some of the scandal sheets mentioned the fact that it was suspected "Dope parties" were held amongst this man's friends. I waited many years but in 1943 I was able to prove that this man's personal friends ran a "Club" for officers just outside Montreal which was an exact replica of the "Glass Club" which I revealed had been operated in London during World War One. When guests of this kind of host one could get anything he wanted from dope to pretty women. One never had to worry about gasoline or liquor or food being rationed. The war-time restrictions levelled upon the common people meant nothing at all to them. I reported these things as I unearthed them, but the reader must remember that the officer who actually digs up a criminal case is very rarely allowed to proceed with the investigations and carry them through to the end. The usual procedure is to be asked to turn over everything you have found out to a senior officer. If you so far forget yourself as to inquire how the case worked out the usual answer is "Do the job given to you and mind your own business". The ordinary police-officer, even the members of the Royal Canadian Mounted Police, cannot institute legal action against the enemies of our Dominion without the consent of their superior officers and they must obtain permission from the Minister of the department concerned.

---

[1] When I was working for the C.P.R. in 1924 I was approached by a man who came into the yards at 4 o'clock in the morning and asked me to give him protection. He stayed with me until the banks opened and then deposited two hundred one thousand dollar notes. All of them had been torn in halves and had to be joined together.

— 58 —

CHAPTER VI

The conspirators and the White Slave and Drug Rackets

How young Communists are made. Lenin said : "The best revolutionary is a youth without morals". This chapter tells how the White Slave racket is organized and so directed that it furthers the plan of those who direct the international aspects of the World Revolution.

Early in my career I learned to probe deeply in order to find the "cause" which produced any given "effect". I was interested in finding out why so many *ordinary* people departed from our moral code and often took to a life of crime. My investigations proved that those connected with the "conspiracy" never hesitate to use illegal means to further the "cause" of revolution. Knowledge of how they use all the ramifications of the White Slave racket to destroy the authority of parents, break up homes, and spread venereal disease is of vital importance to all married couples. Without this special knowledge they cannot hope to protect their children from the dangers to which they will be exposed.

To spare the feelings of people who were the innocent victims of the conspirators, actual names are omitted, but I can prove every statement I make, and I will prove that the conditions I discovered, prevail today on an ever increasing scale in all larger centres of population.[1]

As a police officer, and chairman of the local welfare committee, I was asked to investigate and report upon juvenile delinquency in an Eastern city. This is what I found. There had been a steady upsurge in juvenile delinquency for about five years. There had been a sudden increase during the two years before I started my investigations in 1924.

Public opinion had forced the police to close down the "Red Light district" in 1919. The doors and windows of bawdy houses had been boarded up. All the inmates had been thrown out on the street. Those who lived off the avails of prostitution had money, but the unfortunate girls themselves had little or none. They were picked up on the streets by local police, accused of vagrancy or street-walking, and thrown into jail. When they were released they were ordered to leave town... They received exactly the same treatment in each

---

[1] The recent exposure of vice conditions in Toronto, Vancouver, and Montreal prove how well the "real" directors of the subversive movements hide their identity.

town they visited. These unfortunate girls were driven from pillar to post. Even those who were suffering from venereal disease could not be detained in prison beyond the period of their sentence. They were turned loose to earn a living by selling their bodies and spreading disease.

I found that many of these unfortunate girls had been accepting the friendship and aid extended to them by subversive agents who frequent the police courts on the look-out for men and women who have become anti-social, because such people can be made useful to the conspirators.

Those plotting a revolution use all the vices to break down the moral structure and to destroy the self respect in the people they plan to subjugate. They teach not only subversion and the atheistic ideology of Marx but they develop an annual group of promising prospects for their revolutionary party by teaching young children the inversion of the Commandments of God, History teaches that revolutionary organizers used even degenerates to further their plans. They liquidate them when they have served their purpose. To-day, investigations have proved there are thousands of homosexuals in the Civil Service in both the U.S.A. and Canada.[*]

I do not recommend legalized prostitution as the answer to preventing the spread of immorality amongst our children. What I wish to point out is the fact that it is poor policy to lock up bawdy houses, without any provision having been made to look after the inmates. This policy plays right into the hands of those who direct the revolutionary plot in this country. The high authorities who have ordered the closing down of Red Light districts were not ignorant or inexperienced men. The action they took had exactly the same effect on their communities as if firemen threw dynamite on a fire instead of water. After the negative action was taken, there were many houses of assignation instead of a few. Girls taken into custody on moral charges should not be given their liberty until they have reformed otherwise they infect others.

Because *all* these unfortunate girls are victims of one phase or another of the White Slave traffic, they should be given every consideration. After they have been convinced of the TRUTH of how they were led to shame, they should be given every assistance in rehabilitating themselves. The Homes of the Good Shepherd have the right idea, but the education they give the girls is incomplete and their training program does not go far enough. There are few if any similar non-catholic institutions.

The laws of supply and demand operate in the White Slave market as they do in legal business. The demand for ''Young Party Girls'' often exceeds the available supply. An illustration of how teen-aged girls are obtained to supply this market should help parents to protect their daughters against the danger.

---

[*] In 1929 the author was informed by an official of the Civil Service Commission that it was useless to make application for any positions advertised by the Civil Service Commission. This was apparently because of the part I had played in the two royal commissions. Crooks and perverts apparently receive preferred treatment. Honest citizens are barred.

The fact that a gang of boys broke into a warehouse on C.P.R. property and stole cooked meats, butter, cheese etc. to provide food for a beach party gave me the opportunity to learn how teen-aged girls are made into Party-girls and Call-girls. My investigation brought to light the following facts :

The gang was dominated by a youth who was a member of the Young Communist League. The stolen goods were to be used at a beach party to be held the following night in a secluded bay near a girl's summer camp on the St. John river. Because it would have been impossible to prove that the food stuffs the boys were taking with them were stolen from the warehouse, I decided to follow the gang-leader in the hope that something might happen which would give me more authority for action.

The boys reached the camp by jumping a freight that left the city limits about 10 P.M. They broke the seals and opened the doors of box-cars containing special freight. The act of breaking the seals of the freight cars involved a maximum penalty of fourteen years imprisonment.

While in transit, the boys stole such things as toilet articles, hair brushes, boxes of deluxe chocolates, perfumes, ladies underwear, etc.

Upon arrival at a point near the girls camp, the train slowed on an up-grade and the boys jumped off. They took their "presents" to the sheltered cove about a quarter mile from the camp. They told the girls the "gang" had arrived. The chaperons were fast asleep. It was the month of August. I watched the party from concealment. A fire was lighted. The whole party enjoyed hot-dogs, toasted marshmallows, sandwiches, cheese and crackers, and chocolates for dessert. Then they drank liquor and those present bathed in the nude. The party continued until nearing daylight. I waited until the last boy had left his girl in her tent or quarters. I arrested the young men as they waited for the east bound freight train to take them back into the city again. I knew most of the boys by sight, some of them by name. They realized it was no use trying to escape. I convinced them it would be better for themselves the fewer people, either civilians or police, who knew the details of their escapades. They seemed to appreciate this advice and offered no trouble.

Next day, the boys came up before the magistrate in a special court. So well was the secret kept there were no morbid spectators. All the boys pleaded guilty to the charges. Because the boys were all first offenders, the Magistrate allowed them to go on suspended sentence.

As can well be imagined, most of the boys were full of gratitude for the way I had helped them to escape publicity and obtain such lenient treatment. As the father of a large family I was very interested in studying the *causes* which led young people into crime. I had several heart to heart talks with some of the boys afterwards. The talks usually took place in my own home.

All of them admitted the member of the Young Communist League was as capable of leading young people into mischief and crime, as a Y.M.C.A. superintendent is in doing youth welfare work.

It was my parting remark to one youth which exposed the most sordid happenings. I said : "Remember, son, the price one pays for promiscuous living is shame and venereal disease. We cannot break the natural, civil and Divine Laws without sooner or later paying the full penalty".

The youth to whom I addressed these remarks hesitated for a moment and finally blurted out the fear that he had contracted venereal disease. I realized that if he was infected, most of the other girls and boys involved in the case must be infected also. It was common practice to "Swap partners" on different nights and even during the course of a single party.

I took the boy with me and explained the whole circumstances to the Medical Officer of Health for the city. He was an exceptionally fine man. He worked quietly and without publicity. As the result of our dual investigations, it was found that fourteen high school girls were diseased and four of those diseased were pregnant.

Further questioning disclosed the fact that when a girl became diseased or pregnant they went to certain women for advice. These women were nearly all ex-madames from the "Red Light" districts. They arranged matters so the girls were "cured" of venereal disease and relieved of their pregnancy. They then became "Party Girls".

Just prior to one big convention I was shown a telegram which was addressed to a woman we knew was an ex-madame from the recently closed "Red Light" district. It read : "Require twenty four birds and forty-eight bottles for convention May 24th".

I determined to find out how Madame could at such short notice provide so many girls who could be relied upon not to disappoint their male partners after such short acquaintance. Investigation disclosed the following facts.

She first enticed teen-age boys to her apartment on the pretense she wanted them to run an errand or perform some simple task. The boys were seduced by young "Party Girls" she had in her "stable".

Following their seduction the boys were shown how they could make pocket-money by selling doped cigarettes, drugs, indecent pictures, obscene playing cards, and pornographic literature to their school companions. These boys graduate into "pushers" of pornography and drugs in our cities. They become "promoters" who supply "circuses" for stage parties, and obscene movie shows, and distributors of indecent pictures. In 1955 investigations by the committee in the United States showed this kind of racket grossed the promoters over $350,000,000 a year.

Girls and boys who "fell" for this kind of filth were invited to selected homes for "parties". The ruin of the girls, who ranged in age from twelve to fourteen, was gradual and unlike the stories of seduction one reads about in pornographic literature. The master minds are too smart to let their intended victims know their modus operandi

Usually, when the boys and girls arrive for the party, the adults leave. This is to prevent them being charged with contributing to juvenile delinquency, if the police should happen to raid the house when the party was in full swing.

Boys and girls who had already thrown off all moral restraints would set the pace. They would produce liquor. Those who didn't want to drink were accused of being "chicken". Marajuana cigarettes would be passed around without the more innocent knowing what they were smoking. Drugs were often introduced. These parties were usually staged at week-ends. Those who wouldn't follow the leaders were "Chicken". It was only a matter of time before all the girls had been seduced. The adults always arrived back unexpectedly and "caught" the boys and girls when they were paired up and in the advanced stages of their dissipation.

The man invariably pretended to be angry. He raised a big fuss and threatened the youngsters that he had a good mind to inform their parents how they had taken advantage of his hospitality, stolen and drank his liquor etc., etc. The woman waited until her "husband" had run out of steam, and then she played the role of being kind, and understanding. She took the attitude : "Boys will be boys... and girls will be girls". She showed the girls sympathy and understanding and became their "friend".

From this point on the downfall of the girls was rapid. They were always getting into hot water at home because of their bad behaviour. Always the female procurer is their friend and confidante. Once the girls had become sophisticated she hinted that they were wasting their time running around with a gang of young "punks" who take all and give nothing in return.

Once a girl has been seduced it is not difficult for a madame to persuade her to sell her favours instead of giving them away. Thus she increases her "stable" of party girls. The reason they are known as "stables" is because the Madames keep a complete record of each girl : her age, height, weight, and other physical features; her abilities as an entertainer; her general education; and her bedroom behaviour. Once the teen-aged girls have accepted money for their favours, the majority are doomed to live a life of shame. A remarkable fact is that very few "party girls" get pregnant until after the bloom of early youth has worn off and they reach their middle twenties. It is uncommon to find a Madame's list which contains the names of girls over twenty-five. Investigation into this angle of the conspiracy showed that most of the girls when they turned twenty-four, unexpectedly found they were pregnant. Their stories are so similar that it seems impossible that their conception wasn't the result of deliberate planning.

The men responsible for the girls' condition invariably offer to pay all expenses so the girls can go to a city where they are not known. There they receive medical attention and free board and lodging until after the babies are born. In return for the sympathy and generous treatment they receive from the fathers of their babies, most girls readily agree that the baby should be adopted. This is arranged by the people who run the million dollar baby rackets.

Most of the girls interviewed claimed they had conceived when the only means of prevention available was that provided by their male companions. The vast majority of the girls claimed the prophylactics used must have been defective.

Because the men, who made the girls pregnant, knew they had been promiscuous, the laying of paternity charges was out of the question.

These unfortunate girls in Eastern Canada were sent to Montreal. Their babies helped support the million dollar racket which has been going on continually since 1924. Contrary to general belief the identity of the male parent is definitely known. The babies are adopted by couples of the same race and creed. In cases in which there is any doubt regarding the male parentage the mother is left to her own devices and usually ends up a prostitute.

The women, whose babies are adopted, are usually found employment. The most amazing thing about this aspect of the racket is that they usually obtained employment with big corporations. Their life of sin is not yet ended. A careful record of these girls, who have been mothers, is kept by those who run the racket. They are still "call-girls", but they are reserved for elderly and sedate business men who could not afford to ruin their reputations by engaging in the riotous parties indulged in by the younger fry. The middle-aged, and elderly, rogues who seek adventure are usually told "I know a smart, young widow, or divorcee. She works for so-and-so. Just call her and mention my name... What happens is YOUR business... She's as safe as the bank".

Investigations conducted since 1950 in many cities in the United States and Canada, where juvenile delinquency has become a serious problem, proves that the systematic seduction of young girls is on the increase. It would be a comparatively simple matter to stop it at the source, but it would appear that the same "Secret Powers" which permit Communist schools to teach our children under teen-age, subversion and the inversion of the Commandments of God, also intend that all aspects of the White Slave traffic shall continue to flourish.

In Western Canada evidence was obtained to prove that one Madame, when she decided to turn respectable, showed her appreciation for several of her "best" girls by introducing them to society. Over drinks one night she confided to an investigator that the best joke she ever played in her life was when she married one of them off to the head of the homicide squad in a big western city; and another to a top-level executive of one of the biggest corporations in the west. Investigation proved that what she said is true. A taxi driver, who had worked with the woman when she was in "business" said he knew both the girls in question when they were "party girls". He said he had actually visited them at their homes since they had married.

Investigation into juvenile delinquency proves that in the very first instance many boys and girls who are used to provide the annual crop of "Party girls" and "Call girls" for the White Slave traffic have been students in Communist schools. That these schools are organized for this purpose I proved in the chapters on Spain, in "Pawns in the Game". Article I, Par. 22 of the Protocols confirms what I say. It reads : *Their youth has grown stupid on classicism and from early immorality into which it has been inducted by our special agents... by tutors, lackeys, governesses in the houses of the wealthy, by clerks and others, by our women in the places of dissipation frequented by the goyim. In the number of these last I also count the so-called "society ladies", voluntary followers of the others in corruption and luxury".*

The subject of the existence of these schools was brought up on the floor of the Canadian Parliament July 8th, 1955, by Mr. John Blackmore, member for Lethbridge, Alberta. During the debate on the budget for the R.C.M.P. he asked the Honourable, the Minister of Justice, Mr. Garson, if he knew such schools were in existence, and if so why the R.C.M.P. permitted them to operate. Mr. Blackmore suggested that if the Communist schools were closed and communist propaganda was not permitted over the C.B.C. the strength and activities of the Communist party might dwindle instead of increase. According to Hansard, Vol. 97, No. 24, page 5884 and on, Mr. Garson replied, "Rightly or wrongly... we think rightly... we have come to the decision, and it is not a snap decision, but one reached after the most careful consideration, and that is, from a security standpoint alone, apart from any other consideration, we believe the practices we have been following are the ones which are in the best interests of the country. If one leaves out of account, as being of no worth at all, any question of freedom of speech and such considerations, and study the whole matter from a purely security standpoint, we are better off as we are than in most other countries where very rigorous anti-communist programs have been developed, in most cases without as good results as we get in Canada".

The reader must agree that it is not government policy, but lack of policy, which allows Communist subversive activities to proceed unchecked in special schools, in our public schools, in our universities, over our radio and television sets, and then asks for an increase in the strength of the R.C.M.P. to try to keep check on the increased number of Communists who carry out the Long Range Plans of the international conspirators, unchecked.

It is a most perverted idea of "FREEDOM" which permits an openly avowed Atheistic revolutionary body to systematically undermine the faith our Canadian citizens are supposed to have for the Christian religion and their Democratic form of Government. Communism is not a political party, it is not a reform movement. It is, as Lenin so clearly stated, a MANUAL OF ACTION. It is being used by the supreme directorate of the international conspirators to bring their idea for a super or one world government into being. That appears to be the reason why Communism in Canada and the United States is permitted to grow unrestricted. When the time is ripe it is to be used to overthrow constitutional government and institutions. Then the Mob will be given FREE REIN for a limited period of time as is distinctly laid down in Article I, Pars. 20 and 21 of the Protocols. After that the agenturs of the international conspirators will take over.

Article III, Par. 7 of the Protocols distinctly says : *"We appear on the scene as alleged saviours of the workers, from the oppression, when we proposed to him to enter the ranks of our fighting forces... Socialists, Anarchists, Communists—to whom we always give support, in accordance with an alleged brotherly rule, (of the solidarity of all humanity) of our social masonry".*

To give another specific illustration of how far and how wide this systematic destruction of youth and morals can spread, I took three citizens I was trying to educate regarding the ramifications of the conspiracy out to a summer cottage where a "party" was being held in "honour" of a well known international sportsman who had recently returned home after covering himself with glory.

It was well after midnight when we arrived at the palatial summer home. We looked through the windows. The scene which met our gaze was worse than the description given of any orgy carried on by a tribe in darkest Africa. All those present were drunk. They were dancing around in front of an open fire Indian fashion. Ribbons and labels from whisky and beer bottles decorated their naked bodies. To climax the whole disgusting display, two of the girls were twin sisters, the daughters of a civic official who had been mainly instrumental in clearing out the "Red Light" district a few years before. I have documentary evidence to prove that when the party broke up, one car full of people crashed into a telephone pole, with fatal injuries to one person and serious injuries to others. The details of this fatal accident were never made public. The Civic official whose daughters were involved, committed suicide shortly afterwards.

As the result of subversive activities there was a complete breakdown of law and order; and as the result of city police becoming involved in the rackets three murders remain unpunished to this day. One murder was committed by the father of a young girl who was turned into a party girl as I describe. The trouble in this case was that he murdered an innocent taxi driver he thought was responsible for his daughter's downfall. Another murder was committed by teenagers who had developed into the hard-boiled revolutionary type. They killed an old woman for her savings and the thrill of doing the deed. The other involved the rape and murder of a young girl. All the information which came into my hands was placed at the disposal of the police, but it was claimed by the heads of the department that they couldn't obtain enough evidence THEY considered would stand up in court.

CHAPTER VII

How the conspirators infiltrate society and corrupt officials

WHITE SLAVERS, and those who live off the avails of vice, are now located in most residential streets, and in many large apartment houses in all big cities. Hotels and motels have taken the place of brothels. By scattering the brands of prostitution far and wide, members of the world's oldest profession have been brought into contact with respectable people.

No matter where our sons and daughters go... to school... to public entertainment... or for recreation and sports... they can't help but come in contact with people who are connected with one or another phase of the White Slave Traffic. At the annual policemen's ball held in a large Canadian city a woman who ran a "stable" of at least 200 call-girls was present as an invited guest. Before the night was over she was in a private bed-sitting room drinking with some of the city's highest officials. She finally planted herself on the knees of the chief of police and twiddled his thinning hair with her fingers. She told him how she admired him for the way he was stamping out gambling and vice.

Not one person in a million would have suspected that her function at that ball was to provide female partners for visiting police and firemen.

The catechism of all Christian denominations teach that we are all born with original sin upon our souls. In other words, we are particularly susceptible to sins of the flesh. Those who direct the Satanic conspiracy know how true this is and they deliberately plan the seduction of children as young as eight years so they may be developed into experienced "Call girls" by the time they reach sixteen years of age.

By scattering the brands of vice broadcast all over the cities we have enabled the White Slave racketeers to take advantage of the fact that children under the age of fourteen (who have already been seduced and corrupted) go into our public schools and, like bad apples, begin to contaminate others. Those who think that the impropriety, which from time to time is publicly exposed as going on in our schools, "just happens", are very badly mistaken. The seeds of immorality are very skillfully planted in our schools and their growth is carefully watched.

Children who tend towards youthful delinquency are carefully watched and cultivated. The Vice-Lords know, that in order to stay in business and reap millions in profits, they must have a big crop of girls come under their control each year. One case of many will illustrate what I mean.

A woman was widowed and left with three sons aged 10, 12 and 14. To support her family she had to go to work cleaning office buildings. She worked from 7 o'clock at night until about the same hour in the morning. She arranged with a neighbour to look after her children until they went to bed at night. She gave her children their suppers before she left for work and their breakfast after she returned home. She never suspected that the woman who looked after her children while she was away rented her rooms more than once each night. The boys mixed with "party girls" and their boy friends. It was proved that they made pocket money by taking tea and toast to the over-night guests before the latter got up in the morning.

These facts came to light when the two older brothers were caught in the act of having sexual relations with a twelve year old girl. They were found in an empty box-car in which there was some straw, by a railway constable while making his rounds. The girl had been stripped of her clothes and was entertaining the two boys.

Under questioning the boys blurted out the fact that they had been mixed up with the inmates of the bawdy house for several months. The case was discussed with a city detective who was efficient and whose character was above reproach. He said : "You know the chief's son supplies that house with liquor. The madame pays protection. If I planned a raid the chances are she would be tipped off".

I suggested to the detective that he arrange a raid and that I would enter the house that night in order to find out how the tip-off was given. He agreed.

On the night in question my companion and I obtained admission to the house by saying we were officers of the S. S. Montcalm. The ship was in port at that time. While we were there quite a number of men entered and sat around drinking and fooling with the girls. Some took girls upstairs while others waited their turns.

I asked one of the girls if there was any danger of the police raiding the place. She informed me that I had no need to worry. She explained that if the morality squad planned a raid Gerty, the Madame, always got warning so the inmates could "scram".

The raid was planned for midnight. At 11.30 o'clock the fire-engines went past on a "dummy run". Gerty immediately burst into the rooms and shouted "Everybody scram... The police will be here in a few minutes". She rushed upstairs to warn others. When the police arrived all the "birds" had flown.

In this particular city the police and fire departments worked together. If the police wanted the underworld warned of a pending raid in a certain section of the city the fire department made a "practice" run.

Investigation showed how subversive elements work their way into police and fire departments in order to corrupt and demoralize the decent members. The directors of the conspiracy consider this work of the utmost importance. Loyal and efficient police and fire departments are considered the revolutionaries worst enemies.

In this particular sea-port a volunteer salvage corps was attached to each fire-hall. The members were warned by a long blast on a powerful siren, followed by a number of short blasts to indicate the district. Young subversives worked themselves into this volunteer salvage corps. They soon had the morale so low that a public scandal followed.

There was a fire in the premises of a large wholesale firm which sold farm implements, cars, and auto accessories. While the firemen were extinguishing the fire, the Salvage Corps, with the co-operation of the city police, stole several thousand dollars worth of tires and automobile accessories. The stolen goods were hidden under the floor of a fire hall and in the attic of a police station.

I passed this information along to the detective previously referred to. Most of the stolen goods were recovered. The police commissioner persuaded the owner of the goods not to prosecute in order to avoid a scandal. It was proved shortly afterwards that the commissioner for public safety had accepted bribes. He had used his influence to place orders for fire-engines and other equipment with the firm whose representative had given him the money.

To illustrate just how completely the morale of a police or fire department can break down under the strain of subversive action the following case is submitted.

A ship was unloading a cargo of imported liquor at a certain wharf. The freight sheds were patrolled by special police. Just after the last sling of cargo was hoisted from the hold of the ship, a gang-foreman rushed to the policeman on duty and told him there had been a serious accident down in number three hold. He asked the policeman to telephone for the ambulance.

The police patrol wagon, and the ambulance, arrived in short order. The injured man, heavily wrapped in blankets, was hoisted out of the hold on a stretcher. With the greatest show of sympathy and care he was carried to the waiting ambulance. While the special policeman was busily engaged obtaining all the particulars necessary for his report, many cases of the finest brands of imported spirits were loaded into the city police patrol wagon and the ambulance. The "accident" victim was a dummy. The men involved in the hoax and theft were not the regular longshoremen who had worked in that particular hold until it was empty. They were off-duty police and firemen.

How can law and order be enforced in such a community when every crook in the city knows the members of the police and fire departments are so deeply involved in graft and crime ?

Another case involved the theft of thousands of dollars worth of expensive blankets, sheets, and table linens from passenger ships in port.

Investigation indicated the head of a local cartage firm as the "brains". He worked in conjunction with the head of a local firm who had the contract for doing the ship's laundry. These two crooks split profits with the stewards who were responsible for the ship's laundry and linen.

Obtaining evidence in this case was very difficult. We had to be very careful because prominent citizens were involved. The ring leader was a relative of the magistrate before whom the case would have to be tried. In time we had enough evidence to prove :

1. The laundry was hauled from the ships to the laundry in trucks owned by suspect No. 1.

2. While the blankets, sheets and table linen were in the laundry the most worn pieces were torn into two. One blanket, one bed-spread, one sheet or one piece of table linen, which was practically new, was stolen for each article which had been torn in two.

3. The linen-steward, working in collusion with the heads of the laundry, and cartage company, counted the articles which had been torn in two as two whole pieces. Thus the tally sheets showed no losses.

4. The thefts were not suspected until there was a sudden increase in the operating costs for the replacement of table and bed-linen, and blankets.

Having obtained this information the question was how to make a charge against those involved stand up in court ? Suddenly I had a brain-wave. I told my fellow investigators about my idea. They thought it worth a try. We waited until the following Monday because Monday is usually wash day. Then we toured the back lanes of the city and jotted down the numbers of the houses, on the clothes-lines of which we found linen and blankets belonging to the steamship company. Such goods are easy to identify. They have a special pattern or special markings woven into the fabric. Using the city directory we checked the addresses to find out the names of the occupants. We then took out search warrants.

We started to make the raids about six o'clock at night so that the husbands would be home. Dozens of families were involved. We knew they weren't all criminals in the ordinary sense of the word. Moral turpitude had become so general that few housewives thought it very wrong to buy the very choicest of bed linen and table cloths for about half their value.

We searched the house of the man we knew had organized the wholesale thefts, and disposed of the stolen goods at a handsome profit. Five beds in his four bedrooms were made up with blankets, sheets, and pillow-slips he had stolen. Everything on the dinner table, including the silver; the carpet on the living room floor, and the clock on the mantel had been taken off ships.

We recovered stolen linen and blankets from a hotel; a big boarding house, several better class homes, and two bawdy houses which operated under the protection of the chief of detectives. He was so angry because we hadn't taken him into our confidence before taking out the search warrants, that he tipped off one bawdy house before we got there. However we recovered enough stolen property to justify our search.

Leading citizens, and members of the underworld, were equally involved. A steamship company and railway system must rely upon good will of the public in order to obtain business. Those connected with the investigation were relieved when the head of the trucking firm made a clean confession and offered to take the full blame.

He appeared before the Magistrate and pleaded guilty. Instead of receiving punishment to fit the crime he was given two years suspended sentence... After all he was related to the magistrate. He was a prominent member of a secret order.[1]

Early in 1925 I decided to make one final effort to impress top-level administrators in both Church and State with the seriousness of the situation. In "Pawns in the Game" I tell how agenturs of the Illuminati infiltrated into the Masonic Order. Just to prove they play no favourites I now disclose how they infiltrated into the Knights of Columbus. I was up for my 3rd. Degree. Amongst the members present were men high in politics and religion, as well as prominent lawyers, business executives, and professional men.

To my intense surprise I noticed that there were also present men and police officials I knew were intimately connected with the vice rackets, as well as with bootlegging and smuggling on the international

---

[1] Communist leaders use incidents like this to convince those they wish to recruit into the Party that in Canada and the U.S.A. there is one law for the rich and another for the poor.

level. I knew that one man present had been involved in a case of piracy.

The S. S. Britannia had sailed from St. John with a cargo of liquor. Her captain had been given seven hundred halves of thousand dollar bills. He had instructions to deliver the cargo to people who would identify themselves by producing the other halves. But the captain of the Britannia was double-crossed. Two men boarded his ship just as she was ready to sail. They produced credentials to show they were representatives of the people who owned the cargo. They had instructions to sail with the ship. The Britannia failed to return. The two men who joined her at the last minute came from Toronto. They were connected with international racketeers in the States. Neither the Britannia or her crew were ever heard of again. It is quite evident that she was boarded when she reached her rendez-vous. The captain and crew were murdered with the aid of the strangers. The pirates obtained both the cargo and the money. They then scuttled the ship, leaving no trace of their crime. How do I know these facts ? Well, my wife and I were staying with Captain Anderson and his wife when this major crime was committed. We did our best to comfort Mrs. Anderson. I carried my investigations as far I could go.

I located in Toronto the women who were married to the two men who sailed with Captain Anderson. I noticed they hadn't gone into mourning. I investigated this angle of the crime. It was evident that the two strangers from Toronto did not meet the same fate as Captain Anderson and his crew. When I informed the police officials regarding my suspicions, the two women moved from Toronto and went over to the United States. Their friends gave them a big party before they left. The police claimed they could not obtain any real evidence that would permit them to lay charges. That may be so, but I am convinced I could have solved the crime if given the necessary authority.

But to get back to the initiation meeting.

When I was asked "Why do you seek admission into the 3rd. Degree ?" I replied. "Because I have been deeply impressed by the by-laws and constitution of this order, and by the ideals all members swear to uphold both in regard to our duty as loyal citizens, of our country, and members of the Christian Faith. I wish to enter the higher degree so that I may help promote all those fine ideals for which this order stands".

My reply was greeted by considerable applause.

When I held up my hand for silence and said I was amazed to see present men I knew were leaders in the smuggling and bootlegging rackets, and police and other civic and provincial administrators I could prove were corrupt, a pin could have been heard to drop. I then disclosed the facts set forth in this book.

In the secrecy of those four walls I appealed for united action on the part of all those who were honestly interested in promoting the good of the order. I asked them first to put their own house in order and then elect, to the civic and provincial administrations, men they could trust to halt the progress of the international conspiracy. The meeting closed without comment as soon as I finished what I had to say.

A young clergyman, who is now an Archbishop, congratulated me afterwards on what he called my courage. He promised he would make a full report to his bishop. I know he made his report because the bishop showed his displeasure at the conditions existing within the order by refusing to allow the members, to take part as a body in any church service, or function, organized under the auspices of the Church. They could attend services, and approach the sacraments as individuals, if their conscience permitted.

My effort resulted in absolute failure. I only mention this fact to prove that the leaders of all Christian denominations must become outspoken leaders of the people if they wish to halt the Satanic conspiracy. I fully realize that any Christian clergyman who dares to invite action rather than prayer to defeat the plans of Satan is going to get really rough treatment. Any man who has the moral courage to fight the conspiracy will find his credits cut off and he will be vulnerable to every form of attack. Such men will be accused of this and that; they will be subjected to slander and abuse. Everything they do will be misconstrued. Those who direct the modern version of L'Infamie will manufacture evidence against them out of whole-cloth. But they must be prepared to take all those things in their stride.

In my humble opinion the only justification for prayer is to ask God for the spiritual strength to put into ACTION the measures which were proposed by the founders of our constitution for no other purpose than to try to protect us from slipping into the conditions in which we find ourselves today. Prayer without good works will avail us nothing. Prayer is the most powerful weapon we possess against the devil, but prayers must be backed up by aggressive action.

I have letters from the leading citizens of this city to prove that I did everything that was humanly possible to clean up the situation. I believed in the honesty of high ranking officials and was firmly convinced at first that they allowed these subversive activities to go on out of ignorance of the facts. I told the proper authorities frankly what I found out thinking I was doing them and the community a service. I soon found out how wrong I could be.

Those who controlled the illegal traffic and trade had such wealth and influence in high places that after they had failed to have me bumped off, they demanded that I be dimissed from the C.P.R. If this had happened while I was still actively involved in the fight against the subversive elements in the Maritimes it might have caused sufficient reaction to have aroused public opinion and created a great deal of unfavourable publicity. It was therefore arranged that I be transferred with my family to Toronto.

CHAPTER VIII

The investigation into the customs service

IN 1924 I explained to people in high authority that the directors of the international conspiracy would ultimately bring about the ruin of nationalism in Canada, and the U.S.A., if they were allowed to continue to use international smuggling and bootlegging and the subversive elements in both countries. I impressed them to the extent that they introduced me to Mr. R. P. Sparks, National president of the Commercial Protective Association. At his request I gave him all the evidence I was able to obtain regarding illegal traffic and trade going on in the eastern Maritimes. I also provided him with information regarding the connection between the directors of the international conspiracy and the underworld.

In 1925, Mr. Sparks asked me to cooperate with Sergeant Lucas of the R.C.M.P. and help him to round up witnesses in New Brunswick to support evidence we had obtained for the newly appointed royal commission. The duty of this commission was to investigate the Canadian Customs and Excise Service, and the ramifications of illegal traffic and trade, throughout the Dominion. Mr. H. H. Stevens, Member of Parliament for Vancouver, had been active in having the commission appointed. To use his own words, spoken in the House of Commons : "Robbery of Customs dues amount in value to nearly one hundred million dollars annually".

The investigators employed to obtain evidence for the royal commissioner were highly qualified, and fully trustworthy. They were picked from the R.C.M.P., the City of Toronto and Ottawa police, the C.P.R. police, and other independent investigating organizations. They produced evidence that connected International conspirators and smugglers with Government officials of all levels *even to Cabinet Ministers*. Members of both Communist and Nazi ideologies were proven to be friendly with high officials in the police forces and with the heads of the Dominion preventive services. The evidence also connected some of the top-level officials of the Dominion's biggest breweries and distilleries, with the underworld both in Canada and the United States. When a member of the underworld ran foul of the law it was usually because he had tried to double cross someone higher up and had been ordered to be "thrown to the wolves". Disputes between gangs were often settled with guns.

Smuggling across the borders on the Niagara Peninsula alone has, over a period of years, resulted in hundreds of murders. More than a score of teen-aged boys were swept over the Falls while rowing boatloads of liquor from the Canadian side to the American side, and bringing dutiable goods back into Canada as return loads.[1]

The Stevens enquiry of 1924-27 also proved that the smuggling racket grew until silks, cotton-goods, and suitings, auto parts, and stolen cars were smuggled into Canada in such quantities that many of the oldest and best established firms were forced to go out of business. This left the field clear for those who had used smuggled goods.

The evidence given before the Royal Commission proved that in 1922 international conspirators used their influence with corrupt politicians to have the R.C.M.P. *removed from the Province of Quebec,* in order to facilitate their illegal activities. It was also proved that the gang I have made reference to in previous chapters, used Rock Island as a wide open crossing point for smuggled goods moving in both directions.

I told how Robinson, the Chief Preventive Officer for New Brunswick, took absolutely no action to enforce the Federal Laws and advised me to mind my own business because "Benny" was well in with those higher up. J.-E. Bisaillon was Robinson's boss. He was at the time chief preventive officer for the Canadian Customs. His salary was only $2,500 a year but in the five years he held office, from 1921 to 1925 inclusive, he managed to build a palatial city residence. He bought a farm for $5,000 near the border; he built a very nice summer home, and he became owner of a private yacht. To make sure he was always in a *liquid* position, - in more ways than one, - he carried a credit balance of $60,000 in the bank.

During the enquiry, Inspector Duncan, one of the special investigators, gave evidence regarding Bisaillon's nefarious practices and said :

'What he did could only have been done with the knowledge and consent of his superiors.''

It was proved to the commissioner that he had deliberately allowed two women to escape with $35,000 worth of narcotics after they had been seized by other officers. He was responsible for selling millions of dollars of seized alcohol to notorious bootleggers at prices as low as .35¢ per gallon. One witness, who admitted purchasing large quantities of seized alcohol from the Chief Preventive Officer, said his transactions amounted to about $1,500,000 in two years.

Evidence also proved that R.C.M.P. officers had made seizures of large quantities of contraband, but they had no power, or authority, to lay charges against those guilty unless authorized to do so by the Minister of Customs. General E.-D. Panet resigned as head of the Quebec provincial police because he was obstructed at every turn when he tried to enforce the law. General Panet was appointed head of the C.P.R. Police in 1926.

Investigation went to show that after "Benny" began to use counterfeit labels and bottle caps, and sold alcohol, flavoured and

---

[1] I investigated the illegal traffic and trade going on along the Niagara border in 1929 for the Toronto Daily Star and disclosed that many teen-aged boys mixed up in the rackets had lost their lives when swept over the Falls.

diluted, as the genuine imported products, monied men stepped in and used a double barrelled gun to bring down stacks of dollars. To give one illustration : Mr. W. J. Huston, of Montreal, engaged in the hay and feed business, but he was also a big shareholder in Dominion Distilleries. Mr. Huston was a close friend of the then Minister of Customs, The Honourable George Boivin. Mr. Gregory George was Vice-President and General Manager of the Dominion Distilleries located at 1185 St. James St., Montreal. Incidentally, Mr. Huston's office for his Hay and Feed business was 1195 St. James, Montreal. They were pretty close neighbours. St. James Street, Montreal, is the "Wall Street" of Canada.[2]

Mr. George was also connected in a very big way with the firm he had christened, the St. George Import and Export Company of St. Pierre. St. Pierre is an island, owned by France, in the mouth of the St. Lawrence. It was the headquarters from which bootleggers and smugglers operated all along the east coast of America. He was also connected with The George Company Limited. This is the gentleman who had offices in the New Brunswick Warehouse and Cold Storage Company, located at the end of Long Wharf.

Investigation proved that 16,000 gallons of alcohol seized on the barge, *Tremblay,* in the River St. Lawrence, and another seizure of between 9,000 and 10,000 gallons, made about this time, were stored in the Custom Warehouse, Montreal. After these seizures had been made, Mr. Huston, who had been Member of Parliament for St. Antoine Division, was able to have the Minister of Customs meet him in Montreal. He made a deal with the Minister by which the Dominion Distilleries bought back the seized alcohol *legally* from the Dominion Government for .36¢ a proof gallon. Just to make sure Dominion Distilleries got good value for their money, *an extra 400 gallons was thrown in for good measure.*

Let us just analyze this little deal, for it was small in comparison with others I heard about, but about which I couldn't obtain first-hand knowledge. A total of approximately 25,000 gallons were involved which at .36¢ cost the Dominion Distilleries $9,000. After this alcohol had been flavoured and reduced to the legal strength for selling as a beverage it would make approximately 75,000 gallons. This equalled approximately 450,000 bottles which would wholesale to those who intended to smuggle it across to the United States for over $1,000,000. This is how some of our big monied men of today got their early start.[3] Mr. George found it necessary to leave Canada on urgent business, and was not available as a witness, when the Royal Commission held its investigation.

Mr. R. P. Sparks of the Commercial Protective Association produced evidence to prove that approximately $5,000,000 worth of silk had been smuggled into Canada annually for a period of five years. Mr. Sparks told how the ex-minister of Customs, Mr. Bureau, had failed to

---

[2] A story which appeared in the Globe and Mail dated Feb. 4th 1954 concerns this very incident. The Bronfmans were mixed up in the liquor deals also.

[3] This is a perfect illustration of what is referred to in Article I, Par. 26 of the Protocols.

prosecute in several cases even after such prosecutions had been recommended by Mr. Farrow, the deputy minister. Mr. Sparks explained how Mr. Duncan, and Mr. Knox (two of the special investigators) had worked to obtain some concrete evidence and had finally got the goods on one big-time smuggler who admitted having defrauded the Government of $100,000 in duty alone. He was allowed to settle his case out of court for $15,000. Why? Does this not indicate the directors of the conspiracy controlled both the Minister of Customs and the Minister of Justice?

Evidence was obtained by other investigators which proved that hundreds of thousands of dollars worth of cotton goods, such as working-mens overalls and shirts, were smuggled into Canada from the United States. The extent of this illegal traffic was so great that it seriously affected employment in Canadian cotton mills. Great quantities of the smuggled goods were prison made garments from the U.S.A. The firms involved in this million dollar racket simply substituted the original labels with others bearing highly patriotic names such as "Empire Overalls".

Other evidence proved that customs officers, who had been proved guilty of accepting bribes and other crimes, were "let out" of the service by being pensioned off long before their time. They knew too much.

One of the worst things exposed by the enquiry was the fact that nine filing cabinets containing dozens of files, containing thousands of documents of an incriminating nature, were secretly removed from the Government Offices and taken to the home of a certain ex-minister and there destroyed.*

Mr. Stevens charged : "The vortex of the customs irregularities is not confined to one spot in Canada. Its fringe was in Prince Rupert, B.C., but its centre, "a veritable cesspool", is in Montreal. "The moving spirit of the Montreal Ring is this man Bisaillon", Mr. Stevens then said, "I could not adequately describe Bisaillon. The worst of crooks, he is the intimate of Cabinet Ministers, and the petted favourite of this government. He rolled in opulence while he debauched officials." These corrupt practices are still going on today.

The nine volumes of evidence given before the Royal Commission prove that the corruption and graft I mention, and the illegal traffic and trade extended right across the Dominion of Canada and involved high officials who at that time were engaged in both federal and provincial affairs. Several of the provincial officials involved are today Federal Officials. One member of the government spent millions of dollars providing the smugglers and racketeers with well paved strategic highways which enabled them to move liquor into the United States and smuggle dutiable goods back into Canada. These highways were connected with secondary roads which enabled racketeers to evade law enforcement officers who tried to intercept them.

The public keep re-electing these men to office. They don't have to. All the money in the world couldn't elect a single individual if the

* Hansard, evidence given before the Royal Commissioners, and newspaper reports all confirm the truth of this statement.

public had not been innoculated with the virus of political inertia and the virus which kills within the individual real patriotic fervour. I repeat again. It is no use winning global wars, if we are going to permit our countries to be subjugated by a mere handful of international conspirators who use well placed agentur and Communist 5th Columnists to further their long range secret plans and ambitions.

The evidence given before the Royal Commission proves that those who directed the conspiracy achieved the following objectives, as far as furthering their Long Range Plans to ultimately destroy Canada and the United States as nations, is concerned.

(A) They seriously affected the national economics by robbing the National treasury departments of hundreds of millions of dollars.

(B) They corrupted government officials to the highest levels and thus obtained control of the two main political parties.

(c) They established a new society in which the wealthiest members had made their money by illegal methods and were thus forever beholden to those who had made their successful operations possible. The majority of the newly rich can't help but carry out the "request" of those who made them rich because those who made them millionaires almost overnight, can reduce them to poverty just as quickly if they so much as even hesitate to do their bidding.

(D) They obtained such a control of high level government officials that they had to adopt a policy regarding international security which permits the Communist Party in both Canada and the United States to perfect quietly their revolutionary plans and await the day when the international conspirators give the order to revolt.

(E) They saw to it that just enough evidence appeared in the public "free press" to disgust the public. It gave the public the feeling that our governments have been proved so rotten and than *any* change must be for the best. But the news reports did not disclose any connection between the international capitalists, who organized the gigantic conspiracy, and the subversives in the underworld who put their plans into effect.

Some of the recommendations made by the accountancy firm of Clarkson, Gordon and Dilworth, respecting the reorganization of the department of Customs and Excise were put into effect. No big heads were lopped off. No international criminals were brought to trial. A Minister, a deputy minister and the Civil Service Commissioner resigned. An ocean going coast guard fleet was ordered for the "marine section" of the R.C.M.P. but those responsible for bringing into being this anti-smuggling fleet saw to it that the vessels supplied to the R.C.M.P. were still slower than those owned by the international smugglers. The marine section of the R.C.M.P. continued to be subjected to political interference.

Few Canadians know why the Hon. H. H. Stevens broke with R. B. Bennett. The truth is that right up until nearly the end of the investigation the evidence had incriminated mostly "Liberal" politicians. Then just as H. H. Stevens and R. P. Sparks were ready to produce evidence that proved that the big financial interests involved in the International racket had contributed heavily to the political campaign funds of the Liberal Party. The inquiry ended with the consent of R. B. Bennett and a general election was called.

The only thing that could explain this unexpected turn of events must have been the fact that the Liberal leaders had evidence to prove that the Conservative party had also received financial support from the same sources. Anyway the Royal Commission fell flat as a pancake. Whitewash was applied in such liberal quantities that a national shortage of lime threatened. The investigation collapsed like a punctured balloon. The electorate was asked to choose between the Liberal and Conservative, but they were not allowed to know the TRUE nature of the evidence. All the public knew was what they read in the Press.

The Hon. H. H. Stevens didn't like what had happened. He broke from R. B. Bennett, who had trained him to succeed him as leader of the Conservative party, and formed the Conservative Reconstruction Party.

Had all the facts, produced as evidence before the Royal Commission, been made public, the electors would undoubtedly have registered their displeasure at the polls by electing the Stevens supporters, but the TRUTH was suppressed by mutual consent of the leaders of both the Liberal and the Conservative parties. The result was that when the votes were counted only the Hon. H. H. Stevens had been elected on his political reform platform. All the men who had supported him went down to political defeat.

A Royal Commission is appointed to investigate charges made in parliament against the administration of a department, or agency, of the government. A Royal Commission is intended to protect the public interest and welfare. I was one of the investigators who produced the evidence which brought about both the Royal Commission into the Customs Service and I also investigated maladministration within the Department of Soldiers Civil Re-establishment, which led up to another Royal Commission in 1928. I say without fear of contradiction that neither commission served the purpose intended. I was so disgusted at the means used to defeat the ends of justice that after the Royal Commission into D.S.C.R. ended I made up my mind to continue my investigations but to keep my information to myself until my task was finished and then make my report to the people themselves.

It is usual for the King's Printer to publish at a nominal charge the evidence given before a Royal Commission in order that the public may study the facts for themselves. They could then instruct their elected representatives what they wished done to correct maladministration. But the evidence given before the Royal Commission into the Customs Service has never been published.

The people were kept in ignorance for fear they might have become sufficiently aroused to have acted in accordance with the constitution. Under our British Constitutional Monarchy the absolute and final authority and sanction for all that is done by Parliaments, as well as local Councils, rests with the electors. EVEN THE KING MUST BOW TO THE WISHES OF HIS PEOPLE. The law is quite clearly stated by the Rt. Hon. Dr. H. V. Evatt K.C. in "The King and his Dominion Governors". Dr. Frank Louat, expert on Constitutional Authority says, "The function of Parliament is to make laws in accordance with the wishes of the people". If it is the duty of Parliament to make laws it is the duty of parliament to see such laws are enforced without fear or favour to anyone.

Dicey in his most famous work "Study of the Law of the Constitution" repeatedly points out "The Will' of the electors is supreme over Parliament and Parliament must obey that WILL or suffer the penalty."

The electors have the constitutional "RIGHT" at any time, not just at election time, to express clearly their WILL to Parliament on ANY matter, and on ANY issue, and Parliament MUST OBEY the WILL of the people. The King, the Governor-General, and Governors, as the case may be, are constitutionally bound, by their oath of office, to carry out the WILL of the people.

The WILL of the people can be properly conveyed to Parliament by the Parliamentary representatives, and IT IS THE LEGAL RIGHT AND OBLIGATION OF THE ELECTORS TO INSTRUCT THEIR PARLIAMENTARY REPRESENTATIVES ON WHAT IS THEIR WILL. If a member so instructed by his electorate refused to do as his electors tell him, then the electors can again petition the King, the Governor-General, or the Governor — as the case may be — to remove him from Parliament because every member of parliament, clearly and definitely, by his Oath of Allegiance to the King, is bound by the King's, or Queen's Coronation Oath to observe the LIBERTIES; FREEDOMS; AND FREE CUSTOMS; AND VESTED RIGHTS OF THE PEOPLE.

THE PEOPLE HAVE *NOT* THE RIGHT TO REVOLT. THERE IS *NO* NEED TO REVOLT. REVOLUTION PLAYS RIGHT INTO THE HANDS OF THE INTERNATIONAL CAPITALISTS AND THEIR MANUAL OF ACTION, WHICH IS THE COMMUNIST PARTY. ALL THE CITIZENS OF ANY BRITISH DOMINION NEED TO DO IS TO PETITION THE KING, OR THE QUEEN, THE GOVERNOR-GENERAL, OR THE GOVERNOR, AS THE CASE MAY BE ... TO DISSOLVE PARLIAMENT SO THE ELECTORS MAY ELECT NEW MEMBERS WHO PROMISE TO CARRY OUT THEIR WISHES.

The reader may stop and ponder the answer to the question : "Why are the children of British subjects not taught the truths regarding their political rights and privileges so that they would know how to take an active, continuing, and intelligent interest in the affairs of their country when they grow old enough to vote?"

All the electors need do to put an end to the plots of both groups of international conspirators is to demand that their elected representatives take action to oust the "Specialists" and "Advisers" the Illuminati have placed behind the scenes of government. It should not be difficult to identify them because they all advocate a One World Super-government.

These agents of the devil didn't overlook a single point. Article VIII Par. 1, of the Protocols says *"Our directorate ... will surround itself with publicists, practical jurists, and administrators, diplomats and, finally, with persons prepared by a special super-educational training in our special schools ... Needless to say that the talented assistants of authority, of whom I speak, will be taken NOT from among the Goyim, who are accustomed to perform their administrative work without giving themselves the trouble to think what its aim is, and never consider what it is needed for. The administrators of the Goyim sign papers without reading them, and they serve either for mercenary reasons of from ambition."*

That the Illuminati fear personal initiative is proved by what they say in Article V, Par. 11 of the "Scheme" : *"There is nothing more dangerous than personal initiative; if it has genius behind it such initiative can do more than can be done by millions of people among whom we have sown discord. We must so direct the education of the Goyim communities that whenever they come upon a matter requiring initiative they may drop their hands in despairing impotence".*

Article IX Par. 9 has this to say. *"In order not to annihilate the institutions of the Goyim before it is time we have touched them with craft and have taken hold of the ends of the springs which move their mechanism.* THESE SPRINGS LAY IN A STRICT BUT JUST SENSE OF ORDER : WE HAVE REPLACED THEM BY THE CHAOTIC LICENSE OF LIBERALISM. *We have got our hands into the administration of the law, into the conduct of elections, into the press, into liberty of the person, but principally into education and training as being the corner-stones of a free existence."*

Paragraph 11 of the same article boasts of what their plan, in regard to existing laws, had accomplished by 1900. It says. *"Above the existing laws without substantially altering them, and merely by twisting them into contradictions of interpretations, we have erected something grandiose in the way of results. These results found expression first in the fact that the interpretations masked the laws. Afterwards they entirely hid them from the eyes of the governments owing to the impossibility of making anything out of the tangled web of legislation".* Then the speaker explains, *"This is* THE ORIGIN OF THE THEORY, OF COURSE, OF ARBITRATION."

A study of all sections of the "Long Range" plan regarding laws reveals that the ultimate objective is to make arbitration replace law. A typical example of the application of this theory was given when the big powers arbitrated such matters that gave Communism control of so much territory, and so many people, at Yalta, Tehran, and Potsdam. The latest example of arbitration taking the place of international law, is the meeting of United Nations Officials with the Chinese Communist Leaders at Geneva August 1st, 1955 when millions

---

* "Pawns In The Game" tells how the legislation which gave the international bankers control over the American economy was pushed through both legislative bodies without question when the sponsors said it was just a routine matter to improve minting of certain coin. The President also admitted he had signed the bill without reading it or having it thoroughly explained to him by competent authority.

of Christians, natives of Indo-China, were arbitrarily placed under the domination of Communist leaders. That, (as Henry Ford remarked so many years ago), is the amazing thing about the Protocols; no person who has studied them can deny that the conspiracy has developed exactly as those who conceived the original plans intended. One clergyman with whom I discussed this matter remarked, "Nothing *human* could have been so absolutely correct and so. perfect in regard to timing and purpose. You have convinced me that the international conspiracy is the conspiracy of Satan". The reader must remember another great TRUTH. I believe it was Edmund Burke who said "All that is necessary for the triumph of EVIL is that GOOD men sit back and do nothing".

CHAPTER IX

Subversion in Veteran Affairs and the Armed Forces

As a result of my investigations, which had required me to be out for days and nights at a time in all kinds of weather, in 1925 I had a return of rheumatism which had originated while serving in H. M. Submarines 1916-1919.

Dr. Beatty, a brother of the President of the C.P.R. advised me to go into Christie Street Hospital. After admittance I found out that instead of being treated for rheumatism I was being examined by various Psychiatric "Specialists". What amazed me most of all was the fact that the doctors who examined me seemed fully familiar with many things I had written in confidential reports I had submitted to the C.P.R. and government officials.

In 1925 I was still convinced the vast majority of people who had become involved in the Communist or Capitalist angles of the international conspiracy had been deceived into believing things that were not true. I expected they would listen to reason. Because of these convictions I was open and frank when answering questions or expressing opinions. I was to find out afterwards that I had committed a serious mistake. Today I have no regrets because I have found out since, that in order to learn the TRUTH regarding all aspects of the international conspiracy, one must of necessity learn from bitter experience.

I was asked if I honestly believed in the existence of God, Satan, Heaven and Hell? When I answered in the affirmative I saw my questioners look at each other as much as to say, "Another misguided boob who has been drugged by religion, the opium of the people."

When I was asked if I honestly believed I could improve or correct the conditions my investigations had proved to exist, I again replied in the affirmative. One doctor then tried to persuade me that my thinking was all wrong. He told me I was simply beating my head against a brick wall. He sneeringly asked me if I thought I could accomplish what Christ had failed to do ? I asked him what he meant. He replied : "Christ tried to reform the people of this world and all he accomplished was his own destruction."

This kind of questioning went on for hours. I found out afterwards that these "specialists" were paid by contributions from wealthy and influential Canadian business men under the pretense that they were helping the Department of Soldiers Civil Re-establishment (D.S.C.R.) to rehabilitate ex-service men. In actual fact they were finding out, by a secret and underhand manner, what ex-service men would serve their purpose best before placing them in key positions. This I will prove.

One day a Mr. N..., who was at that time head of the Veterans Rehabilitation Committee, called to see my wife. I was still in hospital. He opened the conversation by saying that he was amazed to learn of my wide experience and varied career. He told my wife that he had arrived at the decision that I would make an excellent executive. He could obtain a position for me in the Government Civil Service or some Canadian industry, at not less than $4,000 a year. He said "It all depends on you. Can you persuade him to listen to reason and accept the advice his "specialists" are offering him ?"

My wife asked him to explain *exactly* what he meant.

Mr. N... replied "Your husband has one fault. He has the idea that it is his duty to try and reform the human race. For the past seven years he has been investigating this and investigating that. Some people consider what he has been doing as just meddling in other people's business"

My wife flared up and retorted, "My husband has only done what he considered to be his duty".

Mr N ... got up and said "Very well. If you don't persuade him to listen to reason he will find Canada too small to hold him. He won't be able to find employment ... and you, and your five children, will end up in the gutter."

My wife showed Mr. N ... the door. She told him that as I had proved capable of caring for my family in the past she would trust me to take care of their future.

I decided to talk the matter over with a wealthy business man who I knew was a good Christian and loyal citizen. As the result of several conversations he asked me to become Secretary of the newly-formed Christie Street Hospital of the Canadian Legion. This suited me down to the ground.

Because subversive leaders know that the vast majority of ex-service men and women are Christian in their faith, and loyal in their hearts to their Ruler and Country, a special effort is made to infiltrate subversive agents into Veteran organizations of all kinds. The communist "cells" are set to work at the "bottom" with instructions to keep the various organizations divided. They are told to obtain control or wreck the organizations from within. The agents of the Capitalist conspirators work at the "top", to prevent unity or amalgamation regardless of what they may pretend to do. All political parties seem agreed upon one point and that is to prevent ex-service men forming one united national organization. For the purpose of finding out how the subversive elements infiltrated into Veteran movements I accepted the position of Secretary of Christie Street Hospital Branch of the Canadian Legion in November 1926.

What I discovered during the next two years was sufficient to bring about another Royal Commission. Subversives within the Department of Disabled Soldiers Civil Re-establishment, (D.S.C.R.) seemed to have such control that they pensioned those who they figured could be used to serve their purposes and refused to pension those who were considered "reactionaries". That the whole administration was rotten is proved by the fact that in two years I was able to obtain nearly $200,000 in retroactive pensions for men who had been refused what they were entitled to receive under the government's legislation.

At first I did not suspect this wholesale cheating of deserving ex-service men was a carefully designed plot, but as time went on I began to see the light. Subversive elements within the department were deliberately antagonizing Veterans in such a way that they first of all became frustrated, then disgruntled, and finally hostile to the government.

I first realized the truth regarding what was going on when I was repeatedly told by government officials "We'd like to do more for your client but the regulations won't permit"

As I got more experience in handling men's cases, and acting as their official advocate before the government officials concerned, I began to see that putting the blame on the government's legislation was a lame excuse for either gross inefficiency or deliberate maladministration. As I studied the various acts of Parliament covering Veterans rights to medical treatment; rehabilitation; and pensions for incurable disabilities, I came to the conclusion that Canada had been more considerate and generous to her ex-service men than any other country in the world. It was not the fault of the legislation that was causing so much resentment amongst ex-service men, and their dependents, it was the fault of the administration. Investigation showed that the subversives intended to use disgruntled veterans to bring the government into disrepute. It showed how newspaper reports revealing cases of gross injustice perpetrated against Veterans, and their dependents, were being used to disgust the general public and arouse public sympathy for the more aggressive of the abused ex-service men. The conspirators knew that another depression was on the way. These tactics all played into the hands of Communist agitators.

The international-minded Capitalist conspirators had planned to manipulate money values, withdraw currency, tighten up credits and *call* loans. They intended to end the boom period, which had followed the depression of the early 1920's by causing the collapse of the stock-markets and creating industrial chaos and wide-spread unemployment.

These conditions, brought about by the conspirators at the "top", would be ideal for the Communists working at the "bottom" to demand demonstrations, organize riots, and advocate their slogan : "that only by revolutionary action can much needed reforms be brought about speedily". It was essential to the success of such a diabolical plot that the veterans in Canada, and the United States, be kept disorganized, divided, and dissatisfied with the government and its policies.

I reported my findings, with supporting evidence, to the Chief of Police and high legion officials. I have copies of letters written towards the end of 1927 and during 1928 warning the proper authorities that it was essential that provision be made at once to correct the conditions I was ready to prove existed within the D.S.C.R. I urged the authorities to prepare to take care of the mass unemployment I foretold was due to affect the workers of Canada and the United States.

I explained to officials how the Conspiracy worked. I convinced such men as General D. C. Draper, Chief of Police, Toronto; Colonel Le Grand Reed; Canon H. C. Hedley; Dr. Abbott; General J. Langton; who was Harbour Commissioner, and several other influential people. I am sorry to say that the vast majority of Government officials I tried to convince of the seriousness of the situation claimed I was crazy. They contended I was suffering from a Spy Mania. They said I had conspiracy on the brain. They tried to make out that I was negative minded and a pessimist. To those who did believe in me they always said "It's too bad. Carr has plenty of brains and ability, but he's developed a neurosis as the result of his lengthy service in submarines".

I decided to carry on with my work in Christie Street Hospital. I was determined I would expose those officials at the "top" who were deliberately working to create hardship and suffering amongst veterans for the purpose of breaking down their loyalty and driving them into the Communist Party. With the co-operation of the daily Press I exposed case after case of gross injustice. Weight of public opinion didn't make the "top" level administrators budge an inch until the Prime Minister himself gave orders for them to reverse their decisions. When the officials were forced to reverse earlier decisions they glossed matters over by admitting that an error had been made. They would say "All human beings are liable to commit an error. Doctors are not perfect".

I obtained evidence that the *same* doctors and officials were involved in most of the cases of gross injustice originating in the *same* hospitals. I reasoned that the number of cases in which similar methods had been used to perpetrate similar injustices proved the action to have been deliberate and not due to error. I proved that mis-diagnosis had been used to rob veterans and their dependents of pensions; I obtained the statements of outstanding pathologists, and other medical experts, to say that there was no excuse for such wrongful diagnosis in view of the knowledge and facilities available to medical men at that time. Even with statements signed by the men considered absolutely the "top" of the medical profession it proved impossible to bring to justice men who had committed such heinous offenses.

I wish to state that the majority of the doctors and nurses and orderlies employed by the D.V.A. are capable and honest. They would be glad to see the conditions I expose cleaned up. If they did not disapprove of what is going on I could not possibly have obtained the information revealed in this chapter.

I dug up several of cases where men had been allowed to die simply because they were not told the true medical findings in regard to their conditions. There were cases in which outstanding medical consultants had correctly diagnosed the man's case and recommended the treatment required to effect a cure and the advice had been ignored. I will cite just a few cases :

1. A man was found to be suffering from suspected cancer of the stomach by the medical department who recommended an exploratory operation and treatment. The Pensions board told the man he had been awarded 5% pension for ARTHRITIS aggravated by Service.
2. A man admitted to hospital for general examination was found to be suffering from diabetes. The Pension Board concealed this fact and the man was involved in a serious highway accident when he fell into a coma. To make matters worse the Veteran was charged with drunken driving and it was only by an accident that a medical-legal expert stepped in and prvented a serious miscarriage of justice.
3. One of Canada's outstanding heart specialists examined an officer who had been discharged. He said the man's condition was so bad that it would undoubtedly terminate in a thrombosis. The Pension's Board informed the officer he had no disability of assessable degree. He went home and helped his wife move some furniture and died of a heart attack.

On the other hand I dug up plenty of cases in which men, I knew were connected with the subversive movement, were granted pensions to which they were not entitled. These included men and women who also held down good government positions.

Persistent efforts brought about the appointment of the Royal Commission under Colonel A. T. Hunter to investigate the conditions I describe. Its scope was so limited however, that it was impossible to bring before it much of the evidence which had been obtained. The enquiry was limited to proving the practice of political partisanship within the department. The Royal Commission was turned into a political football which enabled the Liberal party to kick out those they didn't want. It was turned into a farce.

Colonel A. T. Hunter was fully acquainted with the corruption and graft going on within the department *before* he was appointed to the hearings. I had given him the information. When the Commission decided to hear only what it wanted to hear, and suppressed what the Government didn't want the public to know, I refused to give evidence. I was threatened by the Counsel for the Commission with being "In contempt of court" but the Commissioner ruled that I be excused. He passed the remark that if I was forced to give evidence I might tell things which would wreck the government.

Among the things about which I had informed him were :

(A) That special very expensive drugs had been imported from abroad at the public's expense and instead of being used in the hospitals they had been used by doctors employed by the D.S.C.R. in private practice. Doctors employed by the Government were not supposed to engage in private practice.

(B) That two top-level officials had entered into a conspiracy with private industry to use public funds to manufacture goods in the Vet-Craft Shops, promote the sale of these special lines throughout the Dominion, and then arrange to discontinue the manufacture of this line of goods in the Vet-Craft Shops so the commercial companies could take over an established business without cost. This conspiracy had deprived dozens of disabled Veterans of their jobs. When one of the officials concerned heard that evidence of his perfidy was to be given before the Commission, he blew his brains out. He acted prematurely.

(C) That there was collusion between certain Pensions Advocates and doctors employed by the Board of Pension Commissioners which resulted in pensions being granted to people who were not entitled to them. Specific cases were cited :

1. That of a University Professor who had suffered a spinal deformity since youth. He had spent less than two months in France where he had gone to inspect sanitary arrangements behind the lines. He was granted 100% disability pension at the rate paid a Colonel, and still held down his job at the University. He taught the Marxian Theories cleverly disguised as modern education.

2. That a man employed as a doctor, and paid as such by the D.S.C.R., had no medical degree. He also drew pension for diabetes although he had never been on active Service.

3. That in one particular case the Pensions Advocate referred to had obtained a pension for a widow of an ex-service man whose claim was exceedingly doubtful as far as its legal merits were concerned. This woman alleged that after she had received back payments, amounting to several thousand dollars, the Advocate accepted payment to which he was not entitled and then seduced her.

4. That investigation would show that several doctors on the Hospital staffs, and some of their wives, were drawing pensions to which they were not legally entitled.

5. That several men known to belong to subversive organizations had been given 100% disability pensions to which they were not entitled. This enabled them to carry on their subversive activities without cost to the Party.

6. That Anti-Communists had been refused pensions to which they were fully entitled.

(D) That several men had been diagnosed incorrectly as insane, for the purpose of depriving them of pensions to which they were entitled.

1. A Lieutenant who was actually suffering from Parkinson disease.
2. A Private who was suffering from pain in the head resulting from gun-shot wounds, but not insanity.

Other cases too numerous to mention.

In the case of (2) the man was committed to prison on false evidence supplied to the arresting officer by hospital officials. He was afterwards transferred to an insane asylum and detained for two years until I heard about the case. After a hard struggle I obtained his release.

(E) That ex-service men had been wrongly diagnosed as syphilitic to deprive them, and their families, of their pensions. I produced evidence from outstanding medical men to prove that in one case in order to make the false accusations stick the true reports of laboratory tests showing "negatives" had been removed from a man's file and replaced by false reports which showed "positive". This man became anti-social. I proved that in this case alone the man, his wife, and his family had been deprived of pension, pay and allowances amounting to nearly $4,000. They were reduced to such straightened circumstances that it had hastened the man's death.

(F) That a few female employees of the D.S.C.R. were having "affairs" with certain doctors on the hospital premises as well as outside. This caused a breakdown in discipline in the hospital. One girl had drawn her sick leave pay on several occasions when she had become pregnant. It was common knowledge among the hospital staff that through some oversight the reason for this "secretary's" absence from work had been put down as "Sick for Tonsillectomy". The question naturally arose "Just how many sets of tonsils could a girl grow ?"

(G) The administration of the relief department was shocking. Deserving cases got the run-around while men engaged as trouble makers within the Veteran organizations seemed to get all they asked for.

After the evidence had been obtained someone divulged that I had been working undercover.

I had served in the British Navy in World War One and I came under the British authorities as far as hospital treatment and allowances were concerned. When it leaked out that I had gathered sufficient evidence to justify asking for a Royal Commission there was the dickens to pay. The most amusing thing was the attempt by one doctor to make me violent. He succeeded only too well. He then cabled the British Ministry of Pensions and told them I had developed into a dangerous neurasthenic. He recommended that I be detained in hospital for treatment. This would have been the first step on the road to an insane asylum.

Fortunately friends on the inside tipped me off. I went to private doctors I knew I could trust. I took examinations which vouched for my mental health in every way. I had the certificate signed and dated. Then I waited for the other people to act.

When it was all over they looked like a bunch of chumps. One doctor went so far that he got others to recommend to the British Ministry that I be pensioned for neurasthenia. All they wanted to do was convince people that the evidence I had dug up, and the statements I made, were not reliable.

Next thing that happened was this. A man who was a high official in the Legion, and a prominent lawyer, informed a private meeting of business men and government officials that he had heard on *reliable authority* that I was flying under false colours. He said he had it on the authority of General E. D. Panet, head of the Investigation Department of the C.P.R. Police, that "I was a Bolshevik by inclination, unamenable to discipline and a danger to any organization to which I might belong". I was not present at the meeting.

This man was considered a great hero, a patriot, and a gentleman. He must have been ordered to put into effect the·threat made to my wife by Mr. N..... : Fortunately I had frienas at that meeting. They told me what had happened. The Rev. Canon Hedley, an ex-Army Padre accompanied me to this lawyer's office the next morning. I'll never forget what happened.

The good Canon politely but firmly invited the Colonel-lawyer to repeat to my face what he had said behind my back. When the gallant Colonel continued to sit in cowardly silence the ex-army Padre did the task for him. Before that meeting was over the Colonel was begging that I would not carry out my threat to prosecute him for slander. I told him that before I made any concessions I wanted to know why it was he had attacked my character ? I said to him "I insist un knowing on whose instructions you attack me at the "top" while every Commie rat in town is attacking me from the "bottom". I demand to know if you and they are "Comrades". You lied — and you know you lied. General Panet would never say such things about me".[1]

He hung his head and remained silent. I got angry. I shouted at him : "Tell me why cowards and traitors are being advanced in the Legion and in the government service while honest men who are patriotic citizens are being subjected to l'infamie such as you committed last night ?"

This alleged hero burst into tears. He actually grovelled on his knees and begged for mercy. I was disgusted — I fired another question at him. I asked, "Were you forced to say what you said ? If so who forced you ? Was it the Communists or was it the men within the Government ?"

He stuttered that he did not understand me.

I told him plainly, "The Communist rumour-mongers claim they have you under their control because you were caught by their spies committing acts of sexual perversion when attending college and again since you left the Army. Did they blackmail you into saying what you did ?"

---

[1] I have preserved the correspondence which passed between me and the principals in the case.

He just sat sobbing like a girl. I said, "If you wish I will name your traducers and give evidence against them if you will lay a charge". He just sat there and blubbered. I made one final effort to get him to speak. I said, "if the pressure wasn't from below I take it your orders came from Ottawa. I'll sue you for everything you've got. I'll expose you for the fake you are".

The gallant ex-Colonel then put on such an exhibition of abject cowardice that Canon Hedley called, "Come on, Carr — let's get out of here — I can't stand it any longer". We left.

Within twenty four hours, influential men, many I believed to be my friends and supporters, began trying to persuade me not to prosecute Colonel M..... They said truthfully that the Legion, and Veterans Affairs, were in a sorry mess. They argued that airing my personal wrongs wouldn't help strengthen the Legion, and clean up the mess. I refused to budge until approached by Colonel Le Grand Reed and Mr. John A. Tory. I admired both these men. They reasoned with me. They asked me not to seek personal revenge. They said the Colonel in question would apologise. They said that to make sure no harm would be done to my character he had agreed to nominate me for membership in the Club in which he had made the statements.

They told me the Colonel was willing to tell those who had heard the derogatory remarks that he had been misinformed. That it was all a mistake.

I pointed out the fact that the Colonel in question had stated definitely that "He had been informed by General Panet, my former employer, that I was a Bolshevik by inclination, unamenable to discipline, and a danger to any organization to which I might belong".

Because I needed the support of these two influential citizens I agreed to follow their advice.

I was provided with an application for membership form. I filled it in and the Colonel signed it. Somebody paid the initial fee. I know I didn't. I was made a member of the club.

In 1928 I was asked by the same Colonel to call and see him. He asked me to bring my wife as what he had to say concerned her also. He asked me if I was willing to resign from Christie Street Hospital Branch of the Legion, and would agree to merge the hospital magazine "Carry On", which I edited, with "the Legionary", in order to accept the position as Provincial Secretary?

I asked him what assurance I had that I would get the position. He said I was the popular choice. He promised me his support. I did as he requested and he double-crossed me and my wife. My sixth child had just been born. He evidently thought I couldn't get another job unless I knuckled under and did as I was told.

He sent for me a few days later. He claimed that delegates from out of town had nominated another member for the position and outnumbered my friends in the final vote. I learned afterwards that the Colonel actually nominated the man who got the position. On the pretense that he wished to make up to me for losing my position he introduced me to his law partner who offered me a job in the Rouen Mining District. I listened to the proposition. It was as crooked as a dog's hind leg. I rejected the offer.

I had grown cagey by this time. I had not been deceived by the Colonel. I did not resign from Christie St. Hospital Branch of the Legion until I had been assured of a good position with a local newspaper.

The man who took the job he offered me landed in jail. Another prominent Colonel got badly entangled in the resulting mess. It cost him a fortune and his reputation. The law partner took all the blame and was disbarred. The gallant Colonel continued merrily on his way to fame and fortune.

Police records will show that although the ex-Colonel-lawyer was not what is generally called "A Criminal Lawyer", he did defend men who were accused of crimes which brought the name "Veteran" and their organizations into disrepute. General Draper, at my request, announced in the Press that these frauds totalled as much as $60,000. a year in Toronto alone. While I co-operated with the police, and brought some of these disreputable creatures to the bar of justice, the gallant Colonel was usually on hand to defend them. If found "guilty" they invariably got lenient sentences. Why ?

Having dealt with the D.S.C.R. we will now look into subversive infiltration into Veteran organizations themselves.

I obtained evidence to prove that Communist "Cells" falsified books and accounts in order to have an anti-red secretary removed from his position in a Provincial Command of the Legion. Another very influential man was forced out of active participation in Veteran affairs, and public life, because a Communist publicity agent persuaded him to use Poppy Day Campaign for private publicity purposes. The agent suggested that it would be a good publicity stunt to have the Press photograph the man in the act of placing his Firm's cheque for $1,000. in the Tag Box of a pretty Society girl in front of the Cenotaph. The business man said, "But we can't afford to give a thousand dollars". The Press agent replied, "I know. But it will be an easy matter to have the box in which you deposit the cheque placed in your office. You can then replace the original cheque with one for a smaller amount. The idea is to set an example. Then others will donate generously also".

The business man swallowed the bait. From then on he was no longer a free man. He did as he was "advised" to do. He said publicly what he was "advised" to say ! He set up one of his tormentors on a farm. Another got a well paid position in his firm.

At one Provincial convention an ex-officer so far forgot the rules of morality that he seduced the wife of the man who invited him into his home as his guest. Letters written by the woman afterward said she no longer loved her husband and intended to obtain a divorce so they could marry. These fell into the hands of a Communist Spy. The letter was used to make the man concerned withdraw his name when nominated for office at the next election. The Communists put into office one of their Party.

Everyone connected with Veteran affairs knew I was anti-Red. It wasn't long before I was under the guns. Communist agents did everything they could to end my career as Secretary of the Hospital Branch. So others may be on their guard I'll mention a few of the things that happened to me. The same tactics are used in the Unions also.

1. I was approached by a "Comrade" who was very anxious to help an "Old Pal". The daughter of the "Old Pal" had got into trouble. Could I help by putting them in touch with a doctor who would perform an abortion? When I said "No", they departed only to return in two days. This time they said they had found a person who would perform the operation. Would I lend them $100.00 to pay the doctor's fee? Again I said "No". After that I was subjected to "The Smear". Without giving the facts every "Red" in Toronto whispered it around that I was autocratic — unsympathetic, — Fascist etc. They said I was in the job for what I could make out of it.*

2. My secretary's husband was a prospector. He was often away from home. Due to the many applications for assistance from ex-service men, who claimed they had been "gypped" out of their just deserts, regarding hospital treatment and pension, we had to work a great deal of over-time. I obtained considerable voluntary help. My wife was among those who worked the hardest. The "Reds" circulated the rumour that I was having an "affair" with my Secretary. They claimed working late was only an excuse to provide the opportunities. This kind of Character assassination was carried to the point where agents whispered the scandal to City Fathers, and influential citizens. Finally, the Secretary's husband was informed. I heard what was going on and wrote and told him all about it. I told him if he cared to investigate matters when he returned he would find that when the office was used at night either my wife, or other volunteer helpers, were always present. It is surprising how many people believe untruths without speaking to the victim of the slander.

Spies in the Executive of the Branch broke open the safe. They tried to foul up the money and the accounts. All they found in the safe was a note saying I was wise to their game. This made them furious.

On another occasion money from one of the Branch's many activities was deposited to my personal account instead of the special account opened for the purpose. I noticed my balance was more than it should have been. I discussed the matter with the Bank Manager. He found out that the man who had made the deposit was one of the members working as a volunteer on a project to raise funds for the Branch. When making the deposit he told the teller I had requested him to make it because I was too busy. I supposed they thought I would keep the extra money and say nothing about it. They were very surprised when I informed the Chairman of the Executive Committee what had happened.

I would like to inform the public who were involved in these sordid facts but the law does not permit it. It would seem that

---

* On Nov. 14th 1955 the police officer who was charged with misappropriating the funds belonging to the York Township Police explained that he had been led into trouble in much the same manner. He had first given money to procure an abortion and then been blackmailed for so doing.

the law now protects the criminals and the subversives and makes it impossible for honest patriotic citizens to expose them without being subject to libel. It would seem that telling the honest and unvarnished truth is no longer of any importance because now-a-days the greater the TRUTH the greater the libel. I mention this once again to emphasize how necessary it is for the electorate to insist that their members of Parliament bring up these matters on the floor of the house. The board of pension commissioners have despotic powers. When they say a case is closed all the evidence in the world can't force them to re-open it. The machinery of the department is such that the veteran is placed in the position of having to make officials of the department admit they are in error. The victim of injustice has to beg those who inflicted the injustice to admit they did it. The Government Advocates, who are paid to advise Veterans, and help them prepare and plead their cases before the tribunals set up by the Pensions Board, are paid by the Department of Pensions to appeal against the decisions made by their own superiors. Could anything be more ridiculous ?

A non-partisan Parliamentary Committee dealing with Veteran affairs is necessary to bring into the open the tactics being used to subvert our veterans. Parliament must make it possible for a veteran to appeal to an authority other than the Pension board itself. In the interest of justice the Veteran should be allowed to see, and read, and study the documents on his own file in order that he can deny false statements and point out where documents have been removed or substituted by others.

When the Legion was first organized in 1926 there was as usual a shortage of money. Certain "Brass Hats" sought office and were elected because their agents convinced a majority of the members that they :

   (A) Were in a position to raise the funds required to put the Legion on its feet financially.

   (B) That they had the welfare of ex-service men and their dependents at heart.

The way some of these "Brass Hats" undertook to finance the Legion was to turn a gang of professional sharks and confidence men loose on the public. They could only have introduced such a policy to bring the Legion into disrepute, and then having chased honest men out they got control into the hands of the men they placed in office. In the Legion, like in the A.M.A. and other organizations, the presidents don't run the Legion it is the paid officials.

I have the written statement of the reputable auditing firm of Oscar Hudson & Co. to prove this charge is true. The investigators proved that the "Big Brass" had engaged Charity Racketeers to raise funds for the Legion and that these racketeers kept 60% of all contributions received. This shameful policy affected both the general funds, and the Service Bureau Funds : The Publications Account of the "Legionary" was also involved in dishonesty.

Just before writing this chapter I decided to find out what had happened to the men who had supported the subversives against the anti-subversives.

One is in the top-level of our diplomatic service abroad. Another is a Judge. Still another — the lawyer who was disbarred, holds an executive position in the Pensions Department of the D.V.A. One of the Commies who was gunning for me is with him. The business man who used Poppy Tag Day to advertise his firm, and then replaced the cheque for $1,000. with one for $10.00 is dead.

Of the lesser fry who worked at the "bottom" — One is retired and living on full pension in England, although his war service was confined to helping in an officer's mess. This man was allegedly pensioned for a very bad ulcerated stomach. Be that as it may I saw him with my own eyes eating fried chicken and chip potatoes and drinking whisky and milk only a few weeks after he was supposed to have had half his stomach removed. The man who took money and seduced the widow for whom he obtained a pension now holds a top-level position in the Pensions Department of the D.V.A. The black-mailers own farms and cars.

Stranger still, those who tried to buck the conspiracy didn't do nearly so well. Three died accidentally under what I consider were suspicious circumstances. Others are still denied the pensions, to which they are unquestionably entitled. None of them obtained a position within the Civil Service. None of them hold positions within the Canadian Legion. One man who has engaged in anti-Communist activities all his life, and once had a price of 50,000 rubles placed on his head while acting as our counter-revolutionary agent in Russia is now broke, and crippled with arthritis. His physical ailments are aggravated by financial worries because he has been refused pension. Another who espoused the Communist Cause since 1924 enjoys a full disability pension and lives in affluence on a farm bought under the V.L.A. He devotes all his spare time working for the Labour-Progressive Party. He ran for Parliament under the L.P.P. banner in 1953. Add these things up and what is the answer ? The time of emergency is very, very near. We may well sing "O, Canada", while the words Royal Mail are removed from our mail boxes, and the name King, or Queen, from our highways.

SUBVERSIVES IN ARMED FORCES

From the day I was appointed to the Naval Control Service in 1940 I was always on the alert looking for Communist "Cells" within the Naval personnel, the Customs Service, and the staff who handled the private telephone system which reported the movement of ships up and down the St. Lawrence. This was only natural because I had obtained copies of the minutes of a meeting held by the Executive of the Communist Party. The meeting had been held at 300 Bathurst Street, Toronto, August 18th. 1934. J. Pacino was in the "Chair". N. Tofan of Hamilton was Secretary, and J. Dolyinsky of Port Arthur assisted. The record of the discussion regarding Communist policy and the Armed Forces read, — I quote : "The military and naval barracks must not be neglected if we are to paralyze the transportation of war materials (during a revolution, to support an attack from without, or to slow up the war effort should war break out). Not only the women but also the children must be got into our organization. Schools must be formed in which children must be taught their duty to the Soviet... They are our hope to start the revolution when they grow up. *"The question of splitting the ranks within the armed forces is the main concern of our activities amongst members of the armed forces. As far as Canada is concerned very little headway has been made to date... Our task must consist in linking up the struggles of the workers in our factories, in the bush, in the mines; the struggles of the workers on the farms, with our activities in the Army and Navy"*.

The government and police authorities were in possession of this information long before World War Two broke out and yet international subversives were funnelled into key positions in all three branches of the Armed Forces.

My five years service in the R.C.N. gave me the opportunitely to investigate subversive infiltration into the Armed Forces. I will list some of the facts I came across.

1. Wholesale corruption in the Royal Canadian Ordinance Corps. Particularly in connection with the disposal of shell casings and other salvagable materials, and the theft and sale of goods from stores. I obtained definite evidence sufficient to convict the persons involved in 1939 and submitted it to the responsible authorities. No action resulted so I concluded that the senior officers to whom I reported the facts must have been involved also. During, and since, the end of the war, news items in the Press prove that similar corruption has been found to exist in army training centres in Ontario, Manitoba, British Columbia, and the Maritimes. The news items stated that officers were nearly always involved. Few people realize the seriousness of this dishonesty. It is used to force the officers involved to aid the subversives. It enables those who direct the conspiracy at the "top" and "bottom" to place their agents within the armed services so they can be worked into key positions. In Petawawa car loads of materials were involved. The reprehensible thing is that while full investigation is always promised by the Minister, the findings and punishment handed out rarely becomes known. It is the duty of the electors to insist that their parliamentary representatives do not allow matters of this kind to die natural deaths. I know of many other cases far more serious. In one case a non-commissioned officer took the blame when theft of thousands of dollars worth of goods was disclosed by people outside the service. This N.C.O. was promoted immediately after he had finished his period of detention. It can be assumed he was well paid by those he shielded while doing detention.

There is an old expression "An officer and a gentleman". It was considered until 1914 that any person given a commission must of necessity be a gentleman in every sense of the word. He was required to be temperate, truthful, honest, courageous, loyal and above committing any act which would besmirch his character or the reputation of the military unit to which he might belong. I was perturbed in 1939-45 to find men with the following records had been awarded commissions in the Armed Forces of Canada. I was further surprised when informed that those who had insisted upon these men being accepted into the service knew of their previous records. In other words the orders to grant them commissions came from the heads of government departments.

Case One : An ex-Imperial officer who had served in World War I. This man became head of the international smugglers communications department after he was discharged from the British Navy. He was an expert in signals and communications. It was reported to me that he was actually in jail in the U.S.A. when war was declared in 1939. Canadian authorities obtained his release. He was immediately commissioned. He was rapidly promoted until he was finally in charge of his department. He was foul mouthed and almost habitually drunk. He hated ministers of religion and openly insulted them before others if he met them in the Mess. On one occasion a Padre hit him and knocked him out because he had called him "A black-robed B..." I investigated some of this man's activities and I am convinced he was a leader in the Pro-Soviet movement. He and others in his group wore their handkerchiefs in the breast pockets of their uniforms so arranged that SIX points were visible. To check my suspicions I arranged my handkerchief to show FIVE points. I hadn't been in the Mess ten minutes when the officer to whom I refer came to me and said, "If you were one of us, a REAL Officer, you would fix your handkerchief better than that". He pulled the handkerchief out of my breast pocket pretended to show me how to fold it properly and dropped it on the floor. He must have been afraid his "friends" might not have been so observant.

Case Two. Another ex-imperial officer, was known to his associates to be a "radical" from 1930 onwards. When in his cups he openly denounced corruption and graft within the government and hooked up his denouncement with praise for Communist leaders. He was given senior rank in the R.C.N. immediately after war was declared. As early as 1941 officers, who had known this man since World War One, mentioned their suspicions to the proper senior authorities. They were concerned because this man had been appointed as head of one or the training departments of the Navy.

This man was alleged to have been involved in the Tim Buck riots when the Communist leader was in Kingston Penitentiary during the early 1930s. I tried to press this case because this man could, if he wished, infiltrate party members into the service and train them how to sabotage the machinery of naval vessels without arousing suspicion. I was asked "Can you prove he is a Communist?" I couldn't prove he was. It wasn't my duty to do so. It was my duty to report my suspicions to the proper authorities. I kept track of this man's activities until he disclosed his true colours in 1953 when he ran as the Labour Progressive's candidate in the Federal election. But according to our laws you can get into serious trouble if you call him a Communist.

The electors must insist that their members of Parliament find out :

(A) Who arranged for this man to enter the naval service ?

(B) Who was responsible for appointing him to a key position in the engineering branch ?

(c) Why was he not fully and properly investigated ?

(D) If his connection with the Communist Party was established by Naval Intelligence, as I know it was, then why was he retained in the Service ?

Case Three. A young French-Canadian received a Commission. His father is very wealthy and a great politician. I think investigation would prove that this family were the only guests permitted to retain their accommodation in the "Chateau" in Quebec during the Top-level conferences held during the war. The officer in question served under me in 1940-1941.

This man was a known "Red" during his university days. He was so radical that the firm to whom he was apprenticed to study law terminated the agreement. I heard him tell these things boastingly. He also boasted that after having his law studies terminated he was introduced into the International Smuggling Ring. He claimed he made good ·money diamond smuggling in the West Indies and countries located in the north of South America. I heard him say "The police finally got hot on my trail, so I returned to Canada and got my father to get me a commission in the Navy". I naturally watched this man's actions as carefully as possible because his duties required him to make up the top-secret cypher messages sent out every night to inform the proper naval authorities of the movement of our merchant ships. This man had knowledge of where every ship, loading in the St. Lawrence ports, was going. He knew when they were sailing, and the route they had been given to follow. Is it any wonder we lost ships in the St. Lawrence and as many as sixty in one Atlantic Convoy ?

I found this man to be a purveyor of foul and obscene pictures. He could obtain the worst of pornographic literature. He suppled it to ratings who served under him. I ordered him not to bring his filth into the office of the Naval Control Service. I was inclined at first to consider him as just a "crack pot" but I discovered he was meeting beautiful and expensively dressed young women in a certain hotel frequently.

Investigating this angle I found out they were different girls nearly every time. They came from the U.S.A. on trains and returning by train.

This man had all the ear-marks of a subversive but, when I made my suspicions known to the proper authorities and asked that he be removed from my staff and investigated by the R.C.M.P., I was the one who was removed. Because I had received the highest written commendations from N.S.H.Q. and the British Admiralty for the manner in which I had organized the Naval Control Service on the St. Lawrence and conducted my duties, and because my immediate superior officers had also written and thanked me for performing work *far in excess of what my duties required of me,* I naturally asked **WHY** I was being removed. No explanation was forthcoming. The subversive influence obviously extended higher than N.S.H.Q.

I followed this young man's naval career. He was promoted. He was sent over to Britain on some mission. When he returned he grew a beard. He was continually condemning the British. I have a well founded suspicion that beards, trimmed, in a certain way, were worn by "Comrades" to indicate their rank in the "Apparatus". The next time I ran into this young punk he was "Intelligence Officer" on the staff at N.S.H.Q. His particular duties were connected with the top-secret Bomb Disposal School. In this capacity he was able to obtain *all* information available regarding *every* type of bomb being used by *all* the warring nations because it was in this school that officers were trained how to dispose of unexploded bombs of every size and type.

I personally informed his commanding officer what I knew of this officer's record, both in and out of the Service. He shrugged and asked, "Do you know who his father is ?" I admitted I did. I feel certain this is the same man whose subversive activities were brought to the notice of the Royal Commissioners who investigated the Soviet Espionage Service. But he was only referred to as a naval officer on the N.S.H.Q. in the report of the Royal Commission. His identity was never disclosed. WHY ?*

Case Four. A man who had been dismissed by a big Ontario manufacturing firm for stealing the Company's money was afterwards worked into a Veterans organization as its President. I tried to prevent this. The man's supporters always used the argument, "Every one can make a mistake... Everyone deserves a chance to make good". Those who opposed this man were smeared in true Communist fashion as "Persecutors" or worse. After this man was elected President the morale of the organization began to deteriorate rapidly, but the popularity of the President increased among a certain group because he was always a "Good Fellow" a "Good Mixer". He was, despite his unsavoury record as far as honesty and morals were concerned, popular with certain politicians in City Hall. He could obtain unlimited "free" beer for picnic and stag parties from Ontario breweries. He was well in with certain police officials, and with a certain section of the Press. He could obtain obscene movies.

It happened that his itching fingers could not keep out of the organization funds. The evidence against him was clear as crystal, and complete. I was asked to take over his duties which I did. I mention this to prove I am fully familiar with the facts of this case, as I am with the others. I wanted to prosecute but certain influential people in the Press; the police force; and within the other veteran organizations, tried to persuade me not to lay charges. I finally insisted that the matter be decided at a general meeting of the members. It was typical of many other meetings dominated by subversives. The scrutineers had to be appointed by nominations from the floor, not by the presiding officer. The result of the vote was "Against prosecution". Immediately the scrutineers announced the result,

---

* Since writing this chapter an article appeared in the press in September 1955 which said the son of a prominent Quebec Liberal politician had been arrested by the R.C.M.P. for his connection with an international smuggling ring engaged in smuggling silks and tobacco into Canada. It would be interesting to know if this is the same man to whom I refer. How is he able to keep his name out of the papers ?

about six men jumped up to move and second that the ballot papers be **BURNED**.

This man was appointed in charge of a highly secret and important branch of the Naval Service. He was promoted. He became an honoured guest of men who were top level executives in the financial world. His popularity and the identity of certain members of his staff caused me to keep my ears and eyes open.

Among other things I found out was the fact that his immediate superior officers, although changed from time to time, were peacetime executives of breweries and distilleries. They were men who had been involved in the smuggling racket in the 1920s. They were millionaires when the war broke out. No pretense was made that they knew anything about ships (other than rum-runners) or about Naval service. They were made Captains apparently because of their executive ability and experience. It is more likely they were "Commissars" placed in position to see the policy of their masters was carried out.

The newly-rich were in the "society" in which the Naval Officer to whom I refer moved. One of these men took it for granted that Commander X. and I were personal friends, because he had heard us talk "old times". He invited me to be his guest for the week-end. I was back in civilization from Goose Bay at the time. I did not accept because I was expecting my wife to join me. His next remarks made me prick up my ears. He whispered confidentially : "You've been away from civilization for months... You come to our hide-away... we have everything. Women, song, wine, swimming pools, liquor... everything. A bunch of us bought the place for a song during the depression. Today it is worth a million. Two hundred and forty acres; bridle paths; good riding horses; miniature golf course; and **BROTHER**, you want to see the girls we have up there to act as hostesses for our guests. Pick any one you like... you can't go wrong".

When my "friend" had run out of adjectives telling what a fabulous place the hide-away was I knew it was another "Glass Club". I decided to make positively sure. I told him there was nothing I would like better than to accept his invitation but I couldn't possibly do so because I had arranged for "an old girl friend" to spend the week-end with me before I returned to duty.

My companion hit me a slap on the shoulder and said "Ahoy — You old sea dog... A woman in every port, eh ?... well, I don't blame you. But don't turn down my invitation... Bring your girl friend along... The more the merrier". And so it was arranged.

When my wife arrived I told her the story and she played her part well. The hide-away was another Glass Club similar to that I described operated during World War One in London, England. That it was the centre of espionage activities I couldn't doubt. Amongst the guests that week-end were two men whose missions were so Hush-hush that when I asked casually what their duties were they put their fingers to their lips significantly. They were in plain clothes. I was in uniform. I too, at that time, was Senior Naval Officer at Goose Bay, Labrador. This was another top-secret project at the time. Strange how three men engaged on top-secret projects were selected to be guests at a secret hide-away high up in the Laurentian mountains... and what a hide-away that was. The estate was self-contained because a certain acreage was farmed. It was equipped with its own gasoline tanks. Gas was rationed strictly at that time but everyone who drove a car to the hide-away was invited to fill up before they started back to the sea-port.

The hired help were all foreigners. They looked like Finns. They all lived on the estate. Liquor flowed like water from the time we arrived Friday night until late Sunday night. My host, four other men, my wife and I and six women comprised the party that week-end.

My wife complained of a bad headache and retired from the party about midnight. This gave me a free hand to do as I liked. It was really "some" party. It grew wilder as time went by. A dip in the pool before retiring was suggested. I demurred saying that I had no bathing suit with me. One of the girls screamed with laughter and everyone else joined in. This was considered the joke of the night. Bathing suits... who bothered with bathing suits ?... Ha... Ha... Ha... Big joke.

Apparently somebody had slipped up. One girl was extra because I had taken my own girl friend along. This led to an argument. When it came time to retire the two girls got into an argument that developed into a fight over who was going to sleep alone. They were both higher than kites at 3.30 a.m. They debated the merits of their claims and counter claims while wrapped in towels which they had thrown around them when they emerged from the outdoor swimming pool.

The argument over who should sleep alone started in the big living room after the swim. Everybody except the two girls and I had retired. The host was the only one who had retired to his room alone. The girls stayed behind to decide which would be his partner for the night. When he went to his room he made a remark to the effect that he wasn't going to play favourites. When the fight broke out all the guests rushed into the living room in various stages of undress. The fight was stopped and, because the living room looked like the stage of a comic opera, everybody began to laugh.

One of the male guests asked our host : "When and where can one obtain a "Corpse reviver" in the morning ?" This brought an abject apology from our host. He said he was sorry he had forgotten to tell us but, any time anyone wanted a drink, after the servants had retired, all they had to do was help themselves. He then showed us were the liquor supply was kept in pigeon-hole compartments under the winding stair-case. I estimated there were at least twenty four cases of various kinds of liquor stored, according to their brands, under those stairs. At that time liquor, like gas and food, was supposed to be strictly rationed.

I had drank a great deal less than the others thought I had consumed. Next morning I got up early and made everyone a John Collins and took the drinks into the various rooms. The two girls who had got into the fight were both in the same room with the host. They were apparently the best of friends again.

The guest house was furnished in a most luxurious manner. All the guest rooms were equipped with private bath. The service was perfect except that the servants didn't speak very good English or French. The food was excellent and in great variety.

Don't lets be naïve. Such hide-aways cost millions to equip and operate. Where does the money come from ? It required a great deal of influence, high up, to obtain unlimited quantities of gasoline and motor oil. Who was the man who could order such a breach of wartime regulations and get away with such criminal actions ? Who were the foreign-speaking servants ? Guests were requested not to speak to any of the staff other than those who waited on them in the house. How was the liquor obtained ? Our War-time host is now a Top-level politician in the province to which I have reference and an extremely wealthy man. He was a great friend of the father of the man referred to in "case three". All these hook-ups and connections can't be pure coincidence.

In 1944, I was able to find out how the gasoline was obtained and from whom. I also found out that a R.C.M.P. officer had also obtained the same information and reported it in the regular manner. The evidence implicated the men right at the top of the Government administration. Like the Stevens investigation proved in 1926, the R.C.M.P. could not prosecute unless instructed to do so by the minister of the department concerned.

These events occurred in August of 1943. Before flying to Goose Bay I told a naval officer attached to the Staff that I was convinced the set-up in the Laurentians was the same as that in London. I advised him to consult with naval intelligence and the R.C.M.P. As far as I know no action was taken against the higher-ups who made the operation of such a den of iniquity possible. It is obviously no use whatsoever reporting these matters to the "proper" authorities. Nothing ever happens to those you report and those who report them are usually taken for a ride. Only united action by the electorate can correct these subversive activities. A similar house was operated in Halifax all through the war. Officers only were invited. I spoke to Naval authorities and the R.C.M.P. but no action was taken in this case either.

During the course of my duties I met the son of the man who made it possible for those who ran the hide-away to obtain unlimited supplies of gasoline. He was in full charge of all gasoline stored at one of our larger air-ports. His father was a top-level executive on one of the Federal Governments Control Boards. How very convenient. Putting two and two together I got acquainted with people who knew his father intimately. I learned that *all* his friends could obtain gasoline in excess of their rations also. Further investigation revealed that this controller held "Wild Parties" in both his town and his country homes. In addition to women, wine, song, and gambling, this man also specialized in showing obscene movies. I know that the police were informed regarding this man's activities. I know that the police tried to do their duty and were not allowed. When the police pressed for action this man resigned so as not to embarrass those who had placed him in his top-level position in case those he worked for could not protect him for his crimes. But they did. He was never prosecuted to my knowledge.

I say again that the vast majority of police officers are honest men and willing to do their duty without fear or favour when they first start their careers, but when on the beat, and until they reach Inspectors' rank, they are continually being subjected to temptation and pressure from the conspirators' agents working at the "bottom". After they reach Inspector's rank they are subject to the influence of the same conspirators' agents working at the "top". They can do very little wihout public support. The wonder is that as many as do remain honest in spite of all temptation. They do their duty. Their authority only extends so far. If those higher up refuse to prosecute there is nothing they can do to make them. If they resign as I did, in order make the facts known to the highest authorities in the land, they will get nowhere as I have got nowhere to date.

I have discussed these matters with responsible police officers of many ranks in all parts of North America. Secretly they have wished me luck. Many active and retired police officers will recognise the cases I have mentioned briefly in this chapter. They know what I say is true. Public opinion in Montreal helped clean up a good deal of the mess there. It will take the united public opinion of the majority of the electorate to clean up the mess in other cities of Canada. It is up to you to act. Act at once. Tomorrow may be too late.*

We have again tied in the "Bottom" with the "Top". The Protocols devote several articles telling how they control the police. The conspirators have a healthy regard for many of the police. To avoid letting the police know any more than they can find out, their plan includes organizing their own police and spy rings to obtain all the information they require to further their secret plans and ambitions.

In order to prove still further what I say let us review the evidence given before the Royal Commission appointed to investigate Soviet Spy activities in 1946. The evidence showed that the mounted Police had done their duty and laid charges against the Communist leaders after they had surrendered in September 1942. The evidence proves that every one of the charges laid against them under the "Defence of Canada Regulations" were proven. But these arch-conspirators were released by order of Judge Roland Miller; Professor C. N. Cochrane, and A. S. Simpson. These gentlemen comprised the "Advisory Committee" appointed by our government to deal with people prosecuted under "The Defence of Canada Regulations". Here is the "top" working together with the "bottom" again. The people who are used as "instruments" by the conspirators often don't know they are being used in that manner.

Other evidence given before the Royal Commission proved that all the Communists released returned immediately to their subversive activities and worked as Spies for the Soviet embassy. The excuse given by those who ordered their release was that they considered them no longer a security risk after Russia had entered the war on

---

* The exposure of vice conditions in Toronto made in October 1953 prove the truth of this statement.

the side of the allies. Is it possible that men who have reached such high positions could be so innocent as to what is going on ? Is it possible they could be so ignorant regarding political intrigue ? Those who made such an excuse should know as well as I do that *Russia* doesn't enter into the International conspiracy... no country does... Two groups are involved in the International Conspiracy. The Communist dictators and the Capitalist dictators. They travel the same road. Only the top-level conspirators know when they will divide.

The advisory committee members also said that by releasing these arch-conspirators they thought they would contribute to the Canadian war effort. Any one with common sense will agree that if the Commie leaders had been imprisoned for the duration of the war, the Canadian war effort would not have suffered in the least possible way. The reverse is true. But the continued detention of the Communist leaders would have seriously handicapped the smooth progress of the international conspiracy. I don't for one moment even insinuate that the gentlemen concerned realized what they were doing... but they did it all the same.

I warned the proper authorities to expect riots in sea-ports and cities after V-E day. The warnings were ignored. A naval officer was made the scape-goat for the Halifax riots. WHY ? I warned the authorities they could expect mutinies and wholesale desertions immediately the government announced its change of policy regarding sending Zombies overseas as reinforcements. In December 1944 my predictions came true. But no effort had been made to prevent 100,000 desertions. The "mutiny" in Terrace, B.C. only failed to accomplish its purpose because officers of the units affected took notice of the warnings given them *privately*. The mutineers were overcome, arrested, and charged properly. But the Prime Minister of Canada ordered the charges reduced to minor charges of infractions of discipline. WHY ? His lame excuse given to the press was to the effect that to have imposed strict discipline and maximum penalties at that time would have resulted in anarchy throughout the Dominion. *Think this statement over.*

One could go on and on and write volumes. To clean up the mess is a major operation. It will require many honest and courageous men to do the task properly. For obvious reasons another Royal Commission will *not* effect the purpose. After investigators have obtained the evidence and proved an International Conspiracy does exist which endangers Canadian memberships in the British Commonwealth, that evidence should be heard, and judged, by parliament sitting as a committee of the whole. Parliament should judge. Parliament should set the penalties. Parliament should decide what action shall be taken to prevent the conspirators continuing with their diabolical plans.

CHAPTER X

Organized Labour and the international conspiracy

BEFORE studying HOW subversives infiltrate into the ranks of organized labour it should be understood how both the Communist and Capitalist conspirators have planned to use organized labour to further their ambitions to bring about a One World Government.

Dealing with the Communist plan first we have Lenin's own words "All revolutions must start from within the ranks of Labour". Ever since the First Congress of the Red International of Labour Unions the Communist policy has been to infiltrate their "Cells" into Labour organizations in order to obtain control of the individual unions so that the conspirators can ultimately control the national and international labour organizations.

Predicting the development of the General Political Strike on a National and International scale the Protocols say. Article III, Par. 11. *"This hatred (against Capitalistic oppression) will be still further magnified by the effects of an economic crisis, which will stop dealings on the exchanges and bring industry to a standstill. We shall create by all the subterranean methods open to us, and with the aid of GOLD, which is in our hands, a universal economic crisis whereby we shall throw upon the streets whole "mobs" of workers simultaneously in all the countries of Europe. These "mobs" will rush delightedly to shed the blood of those whom, in the simplicity of their ignorance, they have envied from their cradles, and whose property their will then be able to loot.*

Pa. 12 states. *"Ours they will not touch because the moment of the attack will be known to us and we shall take measures to protect our own".*

This policy was carried out on a national scale in every country subjugated todate. The "mob" do the dirty work and then the agentur of those who direct all angles of the international conspiracy take over. Plans to put this conspiracy into effect on an international scale are now being developed by amalgamations of unions and banks as well as industries.

The reason the Communist conspirators work to obtain control of the national and international labour organization is to place them in position to call national and international general political strikes. The general political strike is used to back up all revolutionary efforts made to overthrow a national government. It is planned to use the international general political strike in the final stage of the Communist world revolutionary movement to bring into subjection all the nations which at that date have not been previously subjugated.

The Capitalist conspirators plan to use organized labour for a similar purpose but, they plan to obtain control in a different manner. William Lyon Mackenzie King drew up the blue print by which the international capitalists would obtain control of organized labour back in the early 1900s. He became secretary of labour back around 1907. That his plan was accepted by the international capitalists is proved by the fact that he was invited by John D. Rockefeller to work for him.

Mackenzie King's plan to bring organized labour under control of international capitalism only failed in the United States during World War One because some labour leaders got wise to his plans. This is explained fully elsewhere. The Mackenzie King plan has been steadily at work in Canada since 1921 when he became Prime Minister. The plan is simple. Men the capitalists picked secretly were trained, and their education was paid for, under various scholarships provided by the foundations set up by various multi-millionaires. These agentur were found positions within labour organizations as "specialists" and "advisers". The task they were given was to unite all national labour organizations into ONE and then unite all international labour organizations into ONE also. The reader does not require me to tell exactly how far this plan has progressed to date. This year, 1955, we find the national labour organizations in both the United States and Canada being united in exactly the same way banks are merging in preparation for the possibility of a One World Government. This unity was made possible because the members were convinced by their non-communist leaders that it was necessary to unite to defeat the Communist conspiracy. That statement was perfectly true, but union men must be very, very careful that having stepped out of the Communist frying pan they haven't stepped into the Capitalist lit fire.

The men who plot and plan the capitalist international conspiracy are clever, shrewd, unscrupulous, and ruthless men. Their agentur can make people believe black is white. They fooled me for quite a while regarding their plans to obtain control of labour and I am sure they fooled quite a number of labour leaders who are real labour men also. It is in order that they may judge the facts for themselves that I publish this chapter.

In 1944 when I was serving on the staff at Naval Service Headquarters I was engaged in writing briefs which were intended to give my superiors the information I had gathered over the years. I was warned that the contents of my briefs were being made known to the leaders of the Communist Party in Canada before they reached the Chief of Naval staff. I was also warned to be careful not to accept what might appear to be highly important information and pass it on to my superiors until I had checked the source and the origin of any documents that were placed in my possession. I was told that such a plot had been hatched for the purpose of discrediting me in the eyes of my superiors.

Even after I had received this warning from a man I knew I could trust I nearly fell into the trap set for me. The plot was almost identical with that used to deceive Professor Nilus into innocently serving the purpose of the Illuminati. In order to remove any suspicions I might have had the information regarding an alleged plot by which the Communists were to obtain control or wreck existing labour unions was placed in my hands by a Naval Chaplain who told me it had been obtained by a man who worked as a spy within the Communist Party. The graph, and the accompanying report, was alleged to have been stolen from Communist headquarters in Toronto. It was claimed that the blueprint had been drawn up in Moscow and distributed to Communist leaders throughout the world in order that they could act unitedly to secure control of organized labour. Had I passed on this information I would have been ridiculed.

Study of the graph at first convinced me that it was the genuine article. I had photostat copies made at N.S.II.Q. but because of the warning I had been given I was determined to find out the source and the origin. The Padre said he was not privileged to tell me who had asked him to give me the information. All he would tell me was that it came from one of his superiors who knew that I was actively investigating the Communist conspiracy.

Shortly after the graph had been placed in my possession I was informed that letters were being received by the Naval Minister from wealthy and influential men condemning me on every conceivable count and threatening to make the matter an issue on the floor of Parliament if he did not remove me from his staff. The Minister had my record traced and checked right back to 1914. While this was going on the most vitrolic letter of all arrived and was addressed to the Minister and marked "Personal". The letter itself was marked "Strictly Confidential". It was signed by one of Canada's foremost news-broadcasters. I knew this man was anti-Royalty, anti-British, and anti-Christian. I had placed him in the same class as Brock Chisholm, but 1 knew they were not Communists. Here again as clear as could be was proof the Commies were stealing information from documents at the "bottom" and the agentur of the international capitalists gunning for me at the "top".

The more I studied the graph the more convinced I became that it was a genuine plan exactly as the contents of the mis-named protocols were a genuine plan. The word "protocol" meant "scheme" and that covered the contents of the protocols to a nicety. It was the additional words "of the Learned Elders of Zion" which placed the blame for the diabolical nature of the "scheme" on the shoulders of the Jewish people, that was wrong. In the case of the graph I found out that it had originated in the office of "Responsible Enterprise". The man who passed it to the religious dignitary was the same person who afterwards had documents planted in the office of parliament buildings Queens Park, which caused the C.C.F. leaders to accuse the Provincials government of conducting a Gestapo — charges they couldn't subtantiate. The repercussions swept the C.C.F. out of parliament almost to a man.[1]

---

[1] The man who signed the graph, and accompanying documents, is the same man who was hired by Mr. A. Brown to try to wreck the Poppy Fund Industrial Department 1932-1935, as in explained in the chapter on Communist activities in Canada.

I concluded the plan to obtain control of labour was genuine enough but it wasn't a Communist document, it was the Capitalistic plan and it followed the Mackenzie King theory as developed during the time he worked for the Rockefeller Foundation from 1914 to 1920.

This has been one of my latest investigations and the result has convinced me more than ever that the plans used by the Communist and Capitalist conspirators are almost identical. They all lead to a common goal... a One World Labour Organization... a One World Court of Justice... a One World government. Now we have just two groups in organized labour the same as we have in international affairs, Communist and anti-Communist. I cannot see any reason why the directors of the Illuminati, having directed both angles of the international conspiracy to this point would hesitate now to plot to throw one side against the other. The side which wins the struggle will be hopelessly weakened in every respect. The winning side will be forced to turn to the international financiers, who are the Illuminati, for help. At this point, if we allow the conspiracy to reach this far, the agentur of the Illuminati will take over. The despotism of Satan will be forced on the human race and it will continue until destroyed, as promised in the Scriptures, by Divine intervention.

The reader may wonder why Naval Headquarters staff would be interested in studying Communist infiltration into organized labour. I had discovered that the Communist conspirators considered it absolutely necessary to destroy Britain and her Empire before they could put into effect the final stages of their revolutionary effort and bring about an international dictatorship. The information I had obtained convinced me that the Communists would try to destroy Britain by forcing the population into abject submission by ruthless starvation, brought about by an International General Political Strike, (I.G.P.S.). This strike will not likely be called until the Soviet submarine fleet had been built up to one thousand vessels, about 1960.*

That my information was judged to be worthy of consideration was indicated when it was discovered that Stalin had written a book in 1927 entitled "Notes of Contemporary Themes". This book had been kept as a top-secret document. It was used to inform top-level conspirators in regard to the Long Range Plan for an International Dictatorship. An extract from this book was quoted by Manuilsky on March 11th, 1938 when he was reporting on behalf of the delegation of the Communist Party of the Soviet Union in the Executive Committee of the Communist International to the 18th Congress of the Communist Party of the Soviet Union in Moscow. Manuilsky said "British capitalism always was, is, and will be, the most vicious strangler of popular revolutions. Ever since the Great French Revolution at the end of the 18th century down to the Chinese revolution that is now in progress, the British bourgeoisie has always stood in the front ranks of the butchers of the liberation movement of mankind. But the British bourgeoisie does not like to fight with its own hands. It has always preferred to wage war through others". Manuilsky then

* Janes "Fighting Ships" places the strength of the Soviet submarine fleet in 1955 at approximately 500 vessels.

let slip the fact that Stalin was the author of those words by paying him a tribute. Manuilsky said 'Those words written by Comràde Stalin in 1927 are as true today i.e. 1938, as the day they were written'".

When a delegate attending from Canada asked "If the new war being prepared to take place between the capitalist countries, Britain and Germany, takes place as planned, which side should we Communists support?"

Manuilsky is stated to have replied :

"Britain is the rock upon which the waves of revolution have so far dashed themselves in vain. Britain and her people must be destroyed before we can reach our ultimate objectives."

When one considers these statements in connection with the statement repeatedly made by the late President Roosevelt that "The dissolution of the British Empire was necessary to the future welfare of the world" one is impressed once more with the certainty that international communism and international capitalism are travelling the same road to the point when a One World Government is to be formed.

That the international capitalist conspirators wouldn't object to seeing the people of Britain starved into submission is proved by the fact that they stood by and did nothing to guard the British nation against the threat of German U-boats before both World Wars One and Two, as told in the chapter dealing with subversion in the Mercantile Services. If British politicians can't be made to accept the Capitalist conception for a One World Government then it is obvious that the American conspirators would want to throw the British and Soviets at each others throats. It wouldn't look very nice if Uncle Sam attacked Mother England. We will prove that the late Mackenzie King favoured such a policy in both world wars. Terrible but true. Letters written to friends in the United States and signed by him prove this statement to be true.

An International General Political Strike would tie up shipping in every port in the world. If backed up by a blockade of the British Isles by Soviet submarines it would accomplish in four weeks what German U-boats just failed to accomplish in both World Wars in four years. It is the duty of the naval staff to inform the Government regarding such matters as they affect our external and internal security. The trouble in the past has been that the ministers who formed our governments did not take notice of the advice their naval and military advisers gave them. Only too often have top-level officers been rudely informed that it is the responsibility of the government to decide policy and the duty of time-serving officers to carry out the orders given to them. It is only once in a while that men like Nelson, Jellicoe, and Gen. Douglas MacArthur are born. They are never very popular with the politicians.

I informed the Chief of Naval Staff in 1943 that I suspected Stalin would use the World Labour Congress, scheduled to take place in London, England, June 8th to 20th, 1944, to further his new plan. Communists everywhere had been ordered to see that, if at all possible, only Communists be nominated to attend the London conference as delegates. In a further report I pointed out that Vincente Lombardo Toledano, head of the Trade Unions Confederation of Latin America, was touring the United States for the purpose of seeing that American Labour sent Communist delegates to London as he had already arranged to be done in all Latin American countries. The majority, if not all, the delegates from Canada were Communists.

The "plugging" tactics of the Communists were so successful that the A.F.L. of the U.S.A. refused to send any delegates.

It was about this time that I received information that Dewar Ferguson, then an official of the Canadian Seamen's Union, was sending a report to Moscow by Pat Sullivan, a Canadian delegate, to the World Labour Congress that the strength of the Communist Party in Canada was 28,000 members and 560,000 "Fellow Travellers". Any person who subscribes to the Communist theory that needed reforms can only be brought about by revolution is considered a "Fellow Traveller". Everyone who lives outsides the law, or is weak enough to have allowed him or herself to be framed, corrupted, or bribed, is used as a 5th Columnist.

In May, 1944, about a month before the London conference was due to take place, the Central Executive of the Communist Party in Canada met at 73 Adelaide Street, West, Toronto. The members completed plans by which they hoped to gain minority control of organized labour and connect every union in the Dominion with the Communist controlled, Moscow directed, World Confederation of Labour, scheduled to be organized in Paris, France, in October 1945. Control of Canadian Unions was to be obtained by the following methods :

(A) Take advantage of the indifference of the majority of members by having every Communist and "Fellow Traveller" turn out to important meetings, especially those called to elect officers. To nominate only Communists for office, and then vote them into power.

(B) See that only Communists or sympathizers be appointed as Shop Stewards.

(C) Use character assassination to discredit officials who were anti-Communistic.

(D) Record the names of all union members who are anti-communist for liquidation when the right moment comes.

(E) Wreck all unions which can't be controlled.

(F) If enough Communists and sympathizers were not present to put across the Party Line during a meeting then the Communists were to argue and prolong discussions until all except Communist members grew tired and left. When this happened the Communists were to make motions in accordance with the Party Line and rush them through because of the lateness of the hour.

The Directors of the World Revolutionary Movement are convinced that they must control the movement of shipping before they can organize an International Political Strike which is 100% effective. In order to control shipping, communists place at least three "Cells" aboard each ship flying the flag of countries not yet brought under Communist domination. The men are trained saboteurs, willing to obey their leaders, and ready to damage or sink the ships.

Communist directives insist that Seamen's Unions be affiliated with Long shoremen, Freight-handlers, Communications and Railway and other transportation workers unions. The objective is to make certain that no cargo will reach ships, once a general *strike is called, even if naval crews are placed aboard to sail them.* All the strikes which have taken place along the waterfronts of the world from 1945 to date are primarily called to ascertain progress, and to test organization efficiency, from the Communist point of view.

I mentioned Halifax as a possible danger point around VE-day because I heard Tim Buck had been visiting Halifax and discussing matters with an official of the Canadian Seamen's Union named, L. Avery. At that time he resided at 162 Argyle St. Halifax.

I also knew that Avery was in communication with Communist "Cells" placed aboard ships to spread Communist Propaganda, and wreck the British Seamen's Union because the leaders would have neither truck nor trade with Communism.

Revolutionary experts, who organized the World Confederation of Trade Unions in Paris, 1945, decided it was essential that Seamen's Unions, throughout the world, be affiliated into one big international Seamen's Union. This idea was advanced on the theory that all Seamen should receive the same pay, the same quality of food, and the same working conditions, regardless of what flag they served under. It is hard to argue against such sound reasoning. It is the fact that Moscow's plotters intend to use such an International Union of Seafarers to further their diabolical conspiracy that puts a different complexion on the matter.

The British Seamen never went on strike in World War One and Two. They are definitely anti-communistic as they were anti-Nazi A Communist named Francis W. Hutchings was detailed to further Moscow's plans amongst seamen. Hutchings wrote Avery as follows :

I quote : "Dear Louis; I apologize for not writing as soon as I arrived in the U.S. as promised, but affairs have been progressing so unsatisfactorily I had nothing much of interest to report.

The controlling body of the N.U.S. (British National Union of Seamen) refuse to have anything to do with our scheme of carrying a ship's delegates and committees... "We want to keep the N.U.S. clear of any filthy Red Element" I was told... So the only way for us to attain what we desire is to keep worrying at the foundations until their whole rotten structure collapses."

This radical boasts to his Canadian Comrade : "Already I have recruited over thirty efficient rank-and-filers who, in their ordinary capacities on board ship, are organizing and educating the others."

Comrade Hutchings continues : "Several weeks ago I endeavoured to hold a mass meeting in Liverpool, England... The Party put a hall at my disposal. After going aboard every ship in port, I obtained the promises of almost a thousand seamen to attend... but only 53 turned up. They only turned up because they were broke and had no place else to go. This attitude is unfortunately typically British. Only yesterday a chap refused to joint a ship's unit I was forming because, he said, "If the "Reds" got the power they would burn all the churches and rape all the nuns."

Hutchings then went on to tell of his efforts to sell the N.M.U. (U.S.A.) the C.S.U., (Canadian), the Australian, and New Zealand Seamens' Unions the idea of an International Seamen's Charter. (This is what the Communistically-controlled Inter-National Federation of Trade Union Executives want.)

I'll quote Comrade Hutchings again :

He writes, "Dear Comrade Louis : We have a long, arduous fight ahead. Our ultimate success depends on you, and others like you to arouse the men's interests and prove... *our only hope for international equality depends on our uniting of all seamen.*"

Comrade Hutchings signed himself :

Until then... so long, and thumbs (or fists) up.

Yours fraternally,

Francis W. Hutchings.

Then he adds a P.S. - "In your reply, would you kindly enclose your reports on, and your attitude towards, the International Seafarer's Charter and also the International Transport Federation."

In March 1947, Avery arranged for a communist named Murphy to address seamen on British ships visiting Canadian ports to tell them **WHY** they should get rid of their anti-communist leaders. Murphy hasn't a drop of Irish blood in his veins. He is a Moscow trained spell-binder whose real name is, I believe, Abie Chernikovsky, who has since become leader of the Mill, Mine and Smelter Union in Canada and Vice-president of the International Union.

Pat Sullivan resigned from the Canadian Seamen's Union the same year because it was absolutely dominated by Communists. His published announcement proved every word I had written in 1944 regarding Communist plans for controlling our merchant seamen, and through them, our ships and railways and the movement of food and supplies.

Pat Sullivan also confirmed what I had said regarding Dewar Ferguson making reports to Moscow's agents, who attended the London Labour Conference in June 1944, as advisers. It is now an historical fact that in Paris the next year, i.e., 1945, the World Federation of Trade Unions was formed and the officers elected were *all* Communists or Sympathizers with many years experience in international labour affairs. Thus Moscow has obtained virtual control over 75,000,000 organized workers in the remaining free countries of the world.

The Communist dictators do not want a Third World War on a global scale - why should they? They are doing very well as it is. They are making progress everywhere. They are working to perfect their plans for the day of Popular World Revolution and the advent of the International General Political Strike.

In my opinion the order for the International General Political Strike will not be given until after the end of the third Five Year Industrial Plan, i.e. 1960.

One of Moscow's economists attached to the Soviet Embassy in

Ottawa told the truth when drinking at the party given to celebrate the Twenty-fifth anniversary of the founding of the Red Army. When well in his cups, he said : ''You Canadians fear you may have to fight the Red Armies some day. That is not correct. We don't want to fight a global war. When we are ready we will flood the markets of the world with raw materials; agricultural products, and manu-'factured goods, at prices so low it will be impossible for capitalistic countries to compete. Do you think organized labour will accept another depression with unemployment, and economic chaos quietly ? I am telling you my friends that Capitalism is doomed. How can Capitalists hope to compete with the Soviets when we control the cost of production from the raw materials to the finished article. We use enemies of the State to develop our natural resources; we set a mini-mum quota for each man's working day; we absolutely control the rate of wages paid. Those who accept our demands and respect our orders serve the State. Those who exceed our demands receive rewards. This enables us to set new increased quotas for their kind of labour. Those who fail to deliver the goods are convicted as enemies of the State and are condemned to forced labour until they change their attitude, or die''.[3]

This Soviet economic expert was known as the ''Professor''. When the drink is in, the truth comes out. He informed those who were willing to listen that an economic depression, even worse than that of the 1930s, would be brought about after the war... it might be ten... it might be fifteen years after... but it would occur when the Soviets were ready to subjugate the rest of the Capitalist countries. He said, ''When this happens the workers will not sit back and do nothing like they did in the 1930s. They will revolt. They will destroy Capitalism and we will be ready to show them how to run their countries after the revolutions are over''.

I was informed that when Soviet Spies, within Naval head-quarters, reported to the Soviet Embassy that the Canadian officers attending the celebration had reported to their superiors what the ''Professor'' had said, the ''Professor'' was recalled to Moscow and suffered a fatal attack of lead poisoning shortly afterwards.

The Capitalist conspirators plan to let this struggle against the Capitalist oppressors proceed to the stage when the proletarian dicta-torship is about to be formed and then their agentur will take over as they did in Russia in 1917, appearing as the Saviours of the workers, they will free them from their oppressors only to lead them into the subjection of a totalitarian dictatorship such as happened in Russia in 1917.

The Protocols Article III, Par. 7 say : ''*We appear on the scene as alleged saviours of the workers from this oppression when we pro-pose to him to enter the ranks of our fighting forces — Socialists, Anar-chists, and Communists, to whom we always give support*''. Could any other words define the ultimate aim of this very complicated conspira-cy more clearly ?

---

[3] The policy of selling our surplus agricultural produce to Soviet countries plays right into the hands of those who plot to destroy us.

Why is it the rank and file of the labour movement can't see and understand the double conspiracy ? It must be apparent to all working men that they can't keep on forever increasing wages, shortening hours of labour, and slowing down production while, at the same time their employers increase their profits by taking the full rise on the greatly increased costs of each and every article. Under the present monetary system it is impossible for the English speaking people to exist without their export trade. How can we expect to sell manufactured goods which cost $1.50 an hour, and more, to produce, to people who are only paid $1.50 a day for their work ?

How can we expect to sell our surplus agricultural produce to the Soviet Countries and starving Hindus and Chinamen who only receive $1.00 a day wages when our governments set the price of wheat at over $2.00 a bushel ? We can't. And yet it is a fact that in Canada five out of every eight wage earners rely on our export trade for their weekly pay envelopes. Both the union leaders and their employers seem to be leading the workers into economic slavery when they persist in taking all and giving nothing.

After resigning from the Labour Progressive Party (Communist Party), Pat Sullivan stated in the Press ''When trust is repaid with treachery, it is time for decent people to beware. I would like to do what I can to arouse the people of Canada, and especially the honest decent men who compose the overwhelming majority of the labour movement in Canada, to the danger of the situation before it is too late. The Communist Party has many secret agents in *Canada and extends into the Government services*''.

The Communists claim Pat Sullivan went over to the Capitalist side of the conspiracy as many other labour leaders are accused of doing. The series of articles written by Pat Sullivan and published in the Toronto Evening Telegram did not disclose to the public what I know he knows, about both the Communist and Capitalist conspiracies. Sullivan wrote :

''The Canadian Seamen's Union is fully controlled by the Communist Party. The same apparatus is in existence in quite a large number of Unions throughout the country. *Throughout the country there are so many Communists one doesn't know who to trust''. The ''Secret'' list of Party Members is known only to the Central Committee of the Communist Party in Canada''*.

Sullivan also said : ''The policeman's strike in Montreal a few years ago was financed to the extent of $9,000 from Communist Party Funds. In 1937 the entire labour section of the Communist Party was thrown into action to raise funds for the strike against Lake Ship Owners. During that strike some of the C.S.U. executive received funds, receipts were given under various names, and the money was repaid to the Communist Party prior to an audit being made of the union's books. From then on, as the union opened additional offices the staff was chosen from Communists or men sympathetic to the Communist Cause''.

On March 18th, 1947, Sullivan warned the workers ''Communists in the C.S.U. executive plan to switch the organization from its affiliation with the Trades and Labour Congress of Canada into the control of the Longshoremen's C.I.O. Union, which is headed by Harry Bridges, U.S. West coast Communist Labour leader and storm centre of Maritime strife". Sullivan complained that thousands upon thousands of dollars belonging to the Union's funds had been used by Communists on the executive of the C.S.U. for personal or Party reasons. He charged that Secretary McManus made trips to the east Coast and the U.S.A. acting on instructions from people outside the Union.

Sullivan further charged that McManus also had discussions with representatives of Harry Bridge's Longshoremen's organizers in the U.S.A. and was laying the ground work for a raid to be made on the existing Brotherhood of Railway Steamship Clerks and the International Longshoremen's Association. Sullivan finally declared that he refused to continue to be a "Rubber Stamp" for the Labour Progressive Party".

Pat Sullivan confirmed in 1947 practically everything I had warned the Canadian Government, and Senator Patterson, was taking place in 1943-44.

Harry Bridges (since ordered deported by the United States Government for his subversive activities) is I believe the same man who was in China with me in 1911-12. The trips McManus took to the U.S.A. were to further Moscow's demands that all Seamen; Transportation workers; Freight handlers; and employees of communications systems, be affiliated under Communist leadership so that rapid progress could be made perfecting the preparations for an International Political Strike.

President A. R. Mosher, President of the Canadian Congress of Labour, in an article in the February issue 1947 of the Canadian Railway employees' monthly, wrote :

"It is not too much to say that the Communist Party is one agency of a secret foreign-controlled conspiracy designed to bring about a revolution, presumably along the Russian model, and place Canada under Communist control".

"Neither the Brotherhood, nor any other labour union, has a right to dictate to a member as to the political party to which he should belong, but the Communist Party is vastly more than a political party. It is essentially a secret organization the members of which have assumed an obligation to follow a party line controlled from Russia, who place their allegiance to Russia higher than their allegiance to Canada, and who do not hesitate to use their unions to promote the purposes of the party rather than the welfare of the Union membership". By making such a statement he shows that he only knows and fears one angle of the International Conspiracy.

I have stated that Communists, who were members of the American National Maritime Union, were sent to Canada, Britain, Australia, and New Zealand etc. to further the Communist plans to organize all seamen's unions into one World Federation of Seafarers under Communistic domination and control. I explain how active Communists obtained control of the key and executive positions in unions by taking advantage of the indifference of the general membership. To prove the above points I will quote Joseph Curran, President of the National Maritime Union. He published an article in the "Pilot", the official publication of the Union, March 28th, 1947 :

"Out of a total membership of between 70,000 and 80,000 seamen there are only about 500 Communists in the National Maritimes Union, U.S.A. We have 150 elected officials. *Of the 150 officials, 107 are members of the Communist Party in America. They are more interested in assuring their leaders that your union has become a stooge of the Communist Party than they are in keeping it an instrument belonging to the rank and file seamen who built it"*. Here we have the official confirmation that in a National Union, in which less than one percent of the total Membership are Communists, the Communists succeed in electing fellow Communists to 70% of the available "Key" positions, within the Union.

A Conference of delegates from Maritimes Unions met on Saturday, March 15th. 1947, in Washington. I can state, without fear of contradiction, that they discussed the ulterior motives of the Communist Party and then, with very few dissenters adopted a resolution to eject Communists from the Unions.

My prediction made in 1944 that only Communists would be elected to all "key" positions in the World Federation of Trade Unions, in 1945, also proved correct. Washington Press reports, October 10th, 1945, say : "A new world labour organization, claiming 75,000,000 members under mixed Communist, Socialist, and Left Wing Leadership is making its first public bow this week.

"The organization was established October 8th in Paris after a meeting of delegates representing 46 countries. The meeting began on September 25th. The United States was represented by an all C.I.O. delegation led by Sidney Hillman.

"The name is the World Federation of Trade Unions. Its creation drives another wedge between the Congress of Industrial Organizations and the American Federation of Labour here. The A.F.L. has refused to participate in any international labour organization in which the Soviet Union or the C.I.O. were represented."

Meantime the World Federation of Trade Unions got going with a Frenchman, Louis Saillant of mixed Communist and Socialist sympathies, in the driver's seat. He was 35 years old. He was a leader of the French underground resistance to the Germans after the 1940 Armistice. He has no political affiliations, but has supported Communist policy as often as Socialist views in the day-by-day development of French politics.

Last, but by no means least, is the way Communists within organized labour wangle matters so as to have 5th Columnists placed in "Key" positions in all levels of our national life and activities. They work to have a Communist placed where he can pull the switches which control electric power and light; they have others placed where they can stop public utilities and prevent the rendering of essential services; still others are placed where they can control all communications systems. Still others are worked in key positions in the Water-Works and other essential municipal services.

Having investigated Communism in the Canadian north in 1934-1937, I decided to see how it had developed, and in 1949, I returned to

Sudbury and took over the management of the Sudbury Memorial Hall for a group of local business men who had guaranteed the mortgage of $250,000. This gave me the opportunity to resume my investigations where I had previously left them off.

The manner in which the Communist Party obtained control of the Mine, Mill, and Smelter Unions will illustrate the policy they use to control labour organizations everywhere.

The Mine-Mill International is the continuation of the old Western Federation of Miners formed in Butte, Montana, in 1893. The original organization was led by men who were militant socialists. As the result of expensive strikes and internal disputes over leadership the W.F.M. broke up.

In 1934 Reid Robinson was elected President of the International. He was a man with plenty of drive and ability. He was supported by the "Right Wing" group. If he had any connection with the Communist Party at that time he concealed his association very well. But in 1940 Robinson seemed to go over to the "left". He became the captive of the Communist Party within the Union. Regardless of this fact the "Right" Wingers still held control of the Union's affairs.

In 1942 the Pittsburg Purge took place, It looked as if the "Reds" were going to be cleaned out. Seeing they could not control the M.M.S. by aggressive action the "Reds" adopted a "Let's stick together" policy. The slogan "All for one, and one for all" got a new airing. The friendly "unity" policy enabled them to dig themselves in deeper. It wasn't long before the "Left Wing" factions were being openly led by Robinson. The Communists within the M.M.S. did in 1942 exactly what those in the U.N.O. are doing today. We will see what happened.

The non-communist members were lulled into a sense of false security and, when at last they did awaken to their danger, it was too late. At the Convention held in Cleveland 1946, the "right" wing members tried to stop the Communist infiltration into the executive positions but they were unsuccessful. The election placed Communists, and Fellow Travellers, in the executive positions. The election itself was afterwards condemned as a fraud. Charges that the election machinery was "rigged" and "controlled" were made. The C.I.O. was asked to investigate. After doing so the C.I.O. offered to appoint an administrator to put the union on a sound and democratic basis. The "Reds" within the Mine-mill union started a smear campaign against the C.I.O. The situation deteriorated until in 1950 the C.I.O. expelled the Mine-Mill union together with a number of other Communist controlled unions.

The method of infiltration into politics was ably demonstrated in the Sudbury district. There had been an unnecessary and abortive strike organized in the Kirkland Lake Mining area in 1941. An unbiased investigator would have to admit that it looked as if the "Red" element within the Union and the international clique within the mine management were in league to bring about this strike. About the only thing the strike achieved was to turn a great many miners from the Liberal and Conservative parties and sell them solidly on the socialist C.C.F. ticket. Bob and Kay Carlin, and several other

Mine-Mill organizers, moved into Sudbury which by this time had a population of approximately 40,000. It is estimated that there are more than twenty ethnic groups living in Sudbury and district. Carlin disclaimed being a Communist. He was loyal to Robinson as far as union business was concerned. Carlin considered conditions were ripe in Sudbury for him to get into politics. Because of the war the men were frozen on the job. Nickel was much in demand for war production purposes. Carlin decided to run on the socialist C.C.F. programme. He received the solid support of the union men.

Then an incident happened which is absolutely unexplainable unless one is willing to accept the theory I have mentioned so often, that while Communists undermine at the "bottom" the agentur of the Capitalist conspirators work at the "top" and direct matters so they serve the purpose of their masters.

A gang of goons attacked the union offices and wrecked the place. Then the International Nickel Company (I.N.C.O.) formed a company union, the U.C.N.W. exactly the same way as the Rockefellers had done under Mackenie King's direction in Colorado in 1914. The two incidents were so alike they must have had a common origin. The only difference was that in some miraculous way there was no loss of life in Sudbury. These two incidents unified the workers as nothing else could have done. The workers obtained the sympathy and the support of the Steel Workers under C. H. Millard; the C.C.L. under Conroy and Mosher. The C.C.F. leaders, Jolliffe, and Leavens made political hay in that particular kind of sunshine.

Local 598 of the Mine-Mill and Smelter was granted its charter in 1943. Carlin ran for the provincial parliament and was elected in a landslide. Then, after the election, rightly or wrongly, the C.C.F. party decided Carlin was a Communist. The C.C.F. leaders claimed he had been elected while flying false colours. They kicked him out of the party while he was still a member of the provincial parliament.

The first President of local 598 was Mel Withers. He was a good solid union man and certainly not a Communist. His only fault during his two terms of office was that he didn't seem able to fully appreciate the extent of Communist intrigue, and their double-talk, and double-cross methods. Jimmy Kidd was elected President of 598 in 1945. He also was a solid union man. Kidd knew every dodge the Communists used. He was soon in head-on collision with Carlin. Earl Browder, the leader of the Communist party in the U.S.A., sent a personal message that the local Communists had to "get" Kidd. His fate was to be decided by character assassination. Not a knife or a bullet. When those who are ordered to apply modernized L'Infamie get after a person he is made to suffer more than any knife or bullet could make him suffer.

In order to "get" Kidd, the Communists employed one man full time, and four men part time. *All* party members were ordered to lend a hand. A "Whispering campaign" was started in the beer parlours; it was extended to the street corners, into the pool-rooms; into the service clubs; into the various church organizations. Having been subjected to similar treatment 1949-51 by the same people I know exactly what Kidd went through.

It took the "Reds" eighteen months to put the skids under Kidd but when they did Nels Thibault took over. The Communists have been in control ever since. The thing that interested me most was the fact that L'Infamie worked in Northern Ontario in 1944-46 exactly as it did in France in 1778-1789. Non-Communists refer to those in control of their union as "The Present Executive" because the Commies object to being called Communists. I asked many miners "Is it not true that the members of local 598 made their greatest gains, both as regard to wages and working conditions, during the years Jimmy Kidd was President ?" The majority admitted that was true.

When I asked them "WHY did you desert Kidd in 1946, and let known Communists get control ?", most of those I talked to admitted they had believed the slanders told against him. When I asked them "Why don't you vote the Commies out of office Now ?" I was informed "There hasn't been an honest election since 1946... Those who are anti-communistic can't even appoint scrutineers. The ballot boxes can be stuffed to the lids and we can't do a thing".

Rank and file candidates are lucky if their names are even mentioned in the local 598 News before election day. They get no help from the union's very efficient propaganda system which can put a leaflet in the hands of every workman in the city and district in 24 hours. This makes it very hard to defeat the "Present Executive".

The main Union hall is sometimes known as the "Little Kremlin". It is a modern yellow brick structure which cost about $400,000. Investigation showed the deed was registered in the name of the International Union in Denver. This was obviously a protective measure in case the local members ever decided to leave Mine Mill.

Activities in the union hall include lectures, concerts, movies, dances, a school and a summer camp for members' children. Each summer the union sponsors a week-long midway. The girlie show once saw the inside of the local bastille when city police objected on moral grounds.

The touring Soviet artists were featured at the Union Hall. The Communist propaganda movie "Salt of the Earth", made in Mexico by Communists fired from Hollywood, was sponsored by the Union. Their propaganda machine went all out to promote this project. The "Present Executive" has made several attempts to get control of the city playgrounds, but alert officials prevented it.

Perhaps the most disturbing feature is the Communist youth activity. This consists of a school and summer camp. This project is under the direction of Ruth and Weir Reid, who conduct classes in art and public speaking. Weir Reid's spacious office is the size of a small hall. The art consists mostly of charcoals of thin Mexican mothers suckling thinner children, and well muscled labourers straining at impossible tasks. This claptrap is known as "Labour Art". To attract children of impressionable age a Communist physical training instructor and expert dancer gives them lessons free. The library in Mr. Reid's office contains no copies of "das Kapital" but plenty of Jack London, and such like books which are a palatable dose for teen-agers, and admittedly good transition material. The Reids also run the big Mine Mill summer camp, at Richard Lake.

Children of Union Members may spend one week at $1.00 per day per child.

One Protestant Minister spent the better part of two years training youth leaders for his church camp. He received a bitter disappointment when the Reids, who had no youth leaders, hired all the minister's leaders at more money than his church could afford to pay.

The Union Hall has always been open to any pro red who held a union card, and to some who did not. Union business has even been suspended to allow out-of-town Communist spell-binders to address the comrades in Local 598. They have to attend whether they want to listen or not.

Rev. (?) Dr. Endicott, winner of the Stalin Peace Prize, used the Union Hall on a Sunday afternoon in 1950. Certain men I suspected were agentur of the Capitalists international group tried to organize a big violent anti-communist demonstration. They tried to get the members of the Legion to back up the idea. But those of us who knew this would serve the Communists Cause prevented it happening. We advised giving Endicott the silent treatment. The only people who attended the meeting were those who already knew what he was going to say.

Known Communists like Tim Buck, Leslie Morris, Joe Salsberg, who are not directly connected with organized labour, use the smaller Communists halls when in town. Their presence at the "Little Kremlin" might give the place a bad name, and embarras the "Present Executive". Besides, to entertain them officially in the Union Hall would give the Rank and Filers a strong talking point.

None of the "Brothers" on the "Present Executive" has ever been known to say anything of a disrespectful nature about any of the Communists bosses, either at home or abroad. They rant and rave about the wicked industrialists, but they curiously enough never say anything bad about the enormously wealthy International Bankers. It is possible they know who is financing them.

The Present Executive have tried to get their men on the City Council and Board of Control. Sudbury has three Aldermen to each ward and every voter is entitled to vote for three. The union ran *one* man in each ward and *one* for Board of Control. They instructed their Comrades to vote for the union candidate *only*. This had the effect of trebling the votes for the union slate. They were very disappointed when they only elected two men, one Alderman and one Controller. With these "Reds" in the City government there was a steady stream of "pinks" bothering the City Council. They have one "Cell" in the City Hall who is in position to inform the Party of everything that is going on.

In 1954 the "Present Executive" tried to get complete control of the city government. Their candidates however were too well known. The union spent money like water but not one of their men was elected. One non-Communist candidate defeated them when he said on T.V., the eve of the election — "Fellow Sudburians ! Let's make this a **WHITE** Christmas, not a **RED** one".

The Provincial Governments would do well to amend civic election regulations. May we suggest that any ballot marked for *fewer* than the *required number* of candidates should be counted as *spoiled*. This would counteract subversives tactics. In recent years it has been subversive policy to support so-called Independent candidates, rather than open Communist candidates.

In Sudbury City constituency Hall Proctor, L.P.P. (Communist) candidate in the 1955 Ontario election dropped out in favour of "Independent" Nels Thibault, Canadian President of Mine Mill. The Sudbury Daily Star in a front page editorial invited Thibault to denounce the Communists, and refuse their support, but he failed to do so. Thibault and Bob Carlin ran for election against two "Brothers" in the Union, who ran as C.C.F. (Socialists). The latter took a terrific barrage of abuse from the union propaganda machine.

The Independent candidates were beaten by Conservatives, but they polled 8,000 votes. By running as Independents they assured the defeat of the two Socialists. Here again is seen the combination of Communist and Capitalists uniting to defeat a common enemy — two Socialists.

When I was plagued with Communist infiltration into the local branch of the Legion, and into the Civil Defence organization, I asked the R.C.M.P. for assistance. I asked them if they would tell me which members and applicants were Communists and I was informed that to do so would be against orders. Discussing this angle of the international conspiracy with a man who had been actively anti-communist for years, he said : "There are a great number of anti-communists in this community who are beginning to wonder just why it is that we cannot get any worthwhile support from the Government authorities, big business, or the executives who operate the mines, the mills, and the smelters of Canada. It is getting harder and harder every day to convince the members of the union, who are non-communists, that the Communist talk of anti-capitalism is as phoney as a three dollar bill. More and more members are becoming convinced that the Communist Party is the tool, and striking force, used by those who favour international capitalism".

With that expression of opinion I must agree. What union members must guard against is the danger that, having cleaned the Communist element out of most of the unions, they don't relax to the extent that they allow the "specialists" and 'advisers" (bred, trained and educated from birth to act as agentur for the Illuminati) to lead them from the old oppression into a new subjection through the rather enchanting meadows of a welfare state. The sign — This way to :

A ONE WORLD GOVERNMENT AND
PERMANENT PEACE AND PROSPERITY

is painted in fine colours. It can be seen clearly in the sky beyond the horizon. But we must remember there is a precipice of tremendous depth dangerously hidden by the luxuriant overgrowth of bribes, disguised as grants for social security, between us and the promised land. The only safe way to avoid a Third World War, a revolution on an international scale or a Capitalistic Dictatorship, is to **TURN**

BACK NOW. We must turn back and pick up the path, on which Christ started us out, on at the point where we left it.

To prove the dangers I name do exist I quote the report of the secret committee by Pres. Roosevelt March 4th. 1939. ''I am making no concessions to business, or for relief. I have a military machine sufficient to stop any organized revolt. I am putting *MY PEOPLE ahead* of all instruments. I have had a full understanding with Chamberlain, and we will destroy this unemployed condition with a WAR, and a WAR only. To Hell with the American people, as far as a Democracy is concerned. It does not exist. It never did, and we will never let it happen that way. I am going to crush business, infest America with all the aliens possible, and in the last analysis, declare Martial Law, and confiscate everything I need for a true and forceful Dictatorship. My New Deal is a failure, and I know it, but no one else will tell me that I must discontinue my present activities, and program.''

From the Secret Audience with the Military Appropriations Committee.

The Ways and Means Committee.

The Special War Finance Committee.

This copy was presented to me by mail through Senator Lundeen.

CHAPTER XI

Subversive elements in Navy and Merchantile Marine

THE facts reviewed in this chapter, concerning the history of naval warfare and its effects upon the Mercantile Marine from 1340 to 1935, were brought to the attention of both the British and Canadian naval authorities from 1930 right up until the outbreak of war. Evidence was submitted to prove that new designs and inventions made the modern submarines, then being constructed in Italy and Japan for Germany under the direction of German engineers, invulnerable to the ASDIC gear on which the ''Big Ship'' naval officers were placing so much reliance. The brief, the warnings, the evidence, and the urgent requests that both navies build anti-submarine ocean convoy vessels, were accompanied with plans for such a vessel drawn by ''Bingo'' Benson of Toronto. He was a well known naval architect. He obtained technical advice from internationally known engineers and ship builders in Britain, Canada, and the United States.

As far as all these men were concerned it was a labour of love. I had convinced them, as I had failed to convince the naval officials and responsible government authorities, that if we didn't have a fleet of at least fifty anti-submarine ocean escort vessels ready when war broke out, the German U-boats would take tremendously heavy toll of our merchant ships and could, quite possibly, starve Britain into submission in a few months.

The committee working on this project made a large scale model and, after first testing it in a tank made available by Mr. Harry Greening, of Hamilton, the model was tested in Hamilton Bay. Naval representatives were present. The craft, designed by "Bingo" Benson, was the smallest of its type that would have 2,000 miles cruising range. It had engines which could patrol at 8 to 12 knots and speed up to 35 knots in emergency. Mr. Benson stated quite clearly that larger prototypes of the original could easily be made to provide a larger cruising range, and carry heavier armament, by simply changing the hull design slightly. Both navies turned thumbs down on the project.

Instead of the craft we designed, — free and gratis – the Canadian Navy was supplied with "Fairmiles", an absolutely useless type of patrol vessel that failed to accomplish anything useful during the entire war. The "Fairmiles" cost the tax-payers millions. Commander "Andy" McLean, has published enough about "Fairmiles and Foul". He retired from the Canadian Navy in disgust 1942 after he had resigned from command of the Fairmile flotillas. I had them under me in 1942, after his resignation. They were just no good.

The man who was mainly responsible for obtaining contracts for the construction of Fairmiles from the Canadian Government was an Englishman who had previously faced criminal charges for perpetrating frauds against the British Government in regard to patrol craft in World War One. This man was the representative for internationalist financiers who made fortunes from Government contracts. He always had unlimited sums of money available for entertaining and other purposes. Apart from all other considerations the fact remains that the responsible Canadian and British officials turned down flat the anti-submarine craft designed by Mr. Benson, which international experts claimed would be efficient, and accepted a craft which proved to be absolutely inefficient. The plans of the craft designed to my specifications by Mr. Benson were offered to the government without any strings attached. The Fairmile deal cost the tax-payers plenty.

An even worse illustration of how the people at the top sabotaged the war effort, and made several million while doing so, was the purchase of old, dilapidated, and unseaworthy yachts which were also used as anti-submarine patrol vessels. These yachts were purchased mostly from Americans who had laid them up when the depression hit in 1930. Most of them had been allowed to deteriorate until they were only fit for wrecking. But when the war broke out the owners were paid ridiculous sums of money. I examined six of the vessels purchased while they were being reconditioned in Quebec in 1940. I condemned four of the six as beyond repair. I staked my reputation as a Master Mariner that results would prove that no amount of money could make four of the ships seaworthy. I explained to the proper authorities why none of the ships could ever be made into efficient anti-submarine patrol vessels. I warned the responsible authorities that if four of the six yachts were sent to sea they would in all probability founder. Three ships I so emphatically condemned did founder. Two of them disapeared so suddenly beneath the waves of the lower St. Lawrence that they were lost with all hands. The third vessel I condemned foundered off Halifax with heavy loss of life. A few survivors were saved because other naval craft happened to be in the close proximity. Among those lost with H.M.C.S. OTTER was the younger brother of Mr. George Drew. Not only had I condemned this yacht as being beyond repair while in Quebec but I had warned the officer who was appointed to command her that he was endangering the lives of his crew if he took the vessel beyond the gate-vessels. The forth vessel I had condemned survived the war. I understand she was tied up to a wharf and used as a venereal disease hospital.

When one of the three vessels which foundered was sent to me for anti-submarine patrol duties in 1942 I refused to send her to sea. She was taken away from me and sent elsewhere. She foundered shortly afterwards. I have the documentary evidence to prove these serious charges. My efforts to have these facts brought before Parliament in a proper manner were frustrated. Neither the Government or the opposition would act upon the evidence I submitted.

Here we have another flagrant illustration of how public funds were recklessly squandered by the top-level government officials and given to Ex-millionaires in the United States, most of whom had made their fortunes out of government contracts in World War One. To give some idea of the type of owner from whom these death-traps were purchased it is sufficient to say that one of the vessels was especially fitted out as an ultra-luxurious floating brothel. Another had been specially designed as a rum-runner. Another was so equipped that the partition between the owner's cabin and the one next to it pivoted around and made the two into one.

The responsible officials had been fully informed that experience gained in World War One had proved that yachts, such as these, were not dangerous to the enemy in the slightest degree. Any modern submarine could send them to the bottom with only a small cost in ammunition. The yachts were so utterly harmless to the enemy that some submarine commanders wouldn't even waste a single round of ammunition on them. They kept their ammunition for merchant ships which were carrying valuable and much needed cargos.

While the Canadian tax-payers were being robbed of millions, and Canadian seamen were being sent to their deaths for no good cause, "Reds" and "Pinks", safely employed in the government's information bureaux, informed the public that the Canadian Navy had been 'ncreased by more than one hundred ships in the space of less than one year. To prevent this being an outright lie orders were issued that every harbour craft was to be given an official name or number and entered in the navy list.

It is necessary to review briefly the history of the Merchantile Marine in order to learn how the international conspirators have used the merchant ships and seamen to further their cause. International financiers have proved themselves utterly indifferent to the welfare of seamen during the past 600 years. There have been some improvements recently but they have been grudgingly given.

Six times since 1340 the British have fought wars at sea. We won't discuss the merits of the wars. The fact remains that British seamen had to fight the Dutch, the French, the Spaniards. Sometimes they had to fight combinations of two or more of them. They did remarkably well. But what I'm getting at is this. The British Navy was originally intended "TO PROVIDE PROTECTION FOR THE MERCHANT SHIPS SO THEY COULD PROCEED SAFELY UPON THEIR LAWFUL OCCASIONS."

As time went on the navy was used more and more to convoy troop-ships; to cover the landing of armies and engage in foreign wars. Six times between 1340 and 1914 Britain engaged in wars at sea as well as on land. When these wars broke out England didn't have enough naval ships to provide her merchant ships with the protection needed. For the first two or three years of each, and every war Britain lost up to 45 per cent of her merchant ships. Most of the seamen who sailed those ships went to the bottom, or were captured, simply because the Navy wasn't able to perform the duties for which it was intended.

It wasn't the fault of the naval men. It was the merchants, the politicians, and the government, who cut the navy right down to the bone immediately after each war was won and over. If the Capitalists hadn't been so greedy, the merchant seamen wouldn't have been left at the mercy of the enemy for the first three years of every war. But Capitalists don't have to stand defenceless to be shot at. They don't have to drift about for weeks and months in open boats. They don't have to suffer years of imprisonment..... Oh no!..... They make plenty of money. They can afford to cheer.

In 1914 Winston Churchill was First Lord of the Admiralty. He'd been First Lord ever since 1911. Mr. Churchill is one of our big national heroes. He takes credit for having the British Navy mobilized, and ready for action, when war broke out in August 1914. The British Navy wasn't ready in August 1914. Like had happened before, the British Merchant ships were without proper protection from August 4th, 1914 to July 30th, 1917. During those three years we lost 60% of our merchant ships and 42,000 officers and men. We had to take that beating just because Churchill didn't keep the navy up to strength.

Admiral Sir John Jellicoe had tried to tell Churchill and his friends in Whitehall that our naval policy was wrong. After Jutland he wrote an official report stating that unless the naval policy was changed it would be only a matter of time before Britain would be starved into the position of having to seek peace under terms which would be far from satisfactory to our allies.

When Jellicoe didn't get a satisfactory reply he left the Grand Fleet in Scapa Flow in command of Admiral Madden. He proceeded to Rothsyth and held a conference with Admiral Beatty, who was then in command of the Battle Cruiser Squadrons. Together they wrote another brief urging the absolute necessity of reallocating destroyers away from the Grand Fleet to protect merchant ship convoys. They stated bluntly that if such action was not taken we would lose the war. Both Admirals signed the brief. Jellicoe took the document to Whitehall.

Churchill never had any use for Jellicoe. Churchill's reports made the public believe that Jellicoe had been at fault at Jutland. Then, immediately after Jutland, Lord Kitchener was lost with H.M.S. Hampshire. Churchill again tried to make Jellicoe the goat. The public failed to realize the fact that these two adverse reports caused the bottom to fall out of the stock-markets in all allied countries. The international financiers sold stocks and shares short on all the exchanges. Then, just before the corrected reports were issued, they bought everything they had sold back again at half the price. The international bankers made fortunes, just like the Rothschilds did after Waterloo...

When Jellicoe met the Cabinet, in October 1916, Churchill asked him by whose permission he had left the Grand Fleet?

Jellicoe told him he left on his own responsibility.

Churchill is then alleged to have remarked, "If you consider the matter so very urgent perhaps you would be willing to relinquish the command of the Grand Fleet and stay at the Admiralty and solve the problems?"

To the surprise of everyone present, Admiral Jellicoe said he would. Those were the circumstances which caused Admiral Jellicoe to leave the Grand Fleet in November 1916 and go to the Admiralty.

After Jellicoe took over at the Admiralty he had a bed moved into his office. He had his meals carried in when he was hungry. He worked from eighteen to twenty hours a day. He called in all the brains available to study every suggestion for anti-submarine devices. The Q-boats; depth charges; mined nets; and listening devices were introduced in ever increasing quantities. A system of ocean convoys was worked out and put into effect as soon as escort vessels were available.

Churchill was made Minister of Munitions. In this capacity he had to be in very close touch with Jellicoe. On Christmas Eve, 1916, Jellicoe sent Churchill a personal note by Admiralty messenger. He told Churchill that because he hadn't been able to spend any time with his family during the past six weeks he was going to go home for a few hours to arrange for his children's Christmas. He said he would be back at the Admiralty by midnight. The messenger brought back Churchill's reply. It was scribbled on the back of the original note. It read, "Go home, you damn fool and stay home"... That is how Jellicoe left the British Admiralty December 24th, 1916... Dozens of people got to know him during the next two weeks because, as soon as he got home, he immediately joined up as a special constable and did his regular beat as air raid warden. Churchill's insulting behaviour could have caused a national crisis.

Admiral Jellicoe was asked to go back to the Admiralty. Putting his personal pride in his pocket he did as requested.

After that, Jellicoe made Admiral Duff his right hand man. They organized the *Anti-Submarine Detection Investigation Committee* to study every possible way and means to counter-attack enemy submarines. That is how the "Asdic" gear we used in this last war first got its name. The word ASDIC is made up of the first letters of the words which named that special committee.

In February 1917, the Germans declared unrestricted U-boat warfare. Jellicoe and Duff, and their experts, proved equal to the task. By the end of July 1917 they had broken the back of Germany's U-boat campaign. They made it so dangerous for a U-boat to attack a ship in convoy that the morale of the U-boats crews broke. We won the war. It only took Jellicoe and his staff eight months to correct the mistake that originated during the six years of Churchill's administration as First Lord of the Admiralty. From August 4th, 1914, to July 30th, 1917, we lost over 60% of our merchant ships, their cargoes, and 42,000 officers and men. From August, 1917 to November, 1918, our losses at sea were negligible. Once the war was won the navy was cut again. The same sad story repeated itself in World War II.

When the war broke out in September 1939 Britain didn't have one solitary anti-submarine ocean convoy escort vessel in commission, or building. Between September 3rd, 1939 and April 3rd, 1943, a little over three years, the same thing happened to our merchant ships, and seamen, as happened during the first three years of World War One. In answer to a question Prime Minister Attlee informed the British House of Commons in November, 1945, "Our Merchant Seamen suffered a total of 45,411 casualties during World War Two; 30,189 are known to be dead; 5,264 are missing; believed to be dead; 4,402 were wounded; and 5,556 were made prisoners of war and interned."

Sir Philip Halding threw further light on the subject when he addressed the British Chamber of Commerce. He said, "Despite the experience gained in World War One, 1914 to 1918, few responsible officials foresaw that damage from U-boats would be so severe or so wide-spread. Nearly 75% of the 750 deep sea tramp-steamers, operating when war broke out, were sunk. Up to the spring of 1943, when conditions improved, Britain lost 545 ships. We lost only 26 more from then to the end of the war".

Between September 3rd, 1939 and April 1943, we lost the 545 ships and we suffered 33,500 casualties of which 29,000 are known to have died. From April 1943, after our merchant ships were given proper protection with air-craft and escort vessels, to the end of the war we suffered only 11,911 casualties and of this number only 889 were killed. These figures are a matter of great importance. They show that while our merchant ships were unprotected, due to the stupidity, or criminal negligence, of those who were responsible, 77% of the men aboard ships sunk by enemy action during the first three years of the war lost their lives because there were no escort vessels to pick them up out of the water, but after April 1943, only 13% lost their lives.

Admiral Jellicoe told me about what had happened, during the battle of Jutland, when he visited Toronto in 1934. He said : "If I had been given information, which was available to those at the Admiralty at the time; had I been told that the enemy were passing to my rear during the night, the battle of Jutland would have ended very differently". Admiral Jellicoe also told me of the differences he had with Government officials over failure to use destroyers attached to the Grand Fleet as escorts to Merchant vessels. Convoys are only safe if they are properly escorted and defended against both aerial and under-water attack.

Admiral Jellicoe was too much of a gentleman to inform me of the Christmas Eve episode at the Admiralty in 1916, but a Captain of the Royal Navy, who served on Admiral Jellicoe's staff in 1917, confirmed that the episode took place. These conditions have proved costly in ships, cargoes, and man-power in the past. The only way to correct the situation is to arouse public opinion and prevent maladministration in the future.

Communist leaders in seamen's organizations know everything that has happened detrimental to the welfare of naval and merchant seamen. They use this knowledge to try to subvert the seamen. The question may well be asked, ''Just how high in Government administration have the agents of those who plot and plan popular world revolution been placed?'' Who advised or forced top-level officials to blunder so badly?

Communist leaders try to place three communist ''cells'' aboard every merchant ship belonging to countries not yet Sovietized. Communists hold a large percentage of the key executive positions in both Canadian and American Seamen's Unions. On a world wide basis the Communist agents would be able at any time to put into effect an international general political strike which would cripple the ocean transportation of the world. If this strike is ever called, all transportation workers, freight-handlers, and communications employees etc. will be forced to take part.

The situation is very serious because, while public opinion is being centred upon the possibilities of atomic warfare, the Soviet leaders are concentrating on perfecting the organization in all countries, to execute an international general political strike.

Local strikes are first used to introduce limited revolts. General national strikes are used to introduce nation wide revolution. Communist leaders of the world revolutionary movement are now organizing the World Federation of Labour, formed in Paris, France, 1945, so they can use the 75,000,000 workers to back up an international general political strike to introduce World Revolution.

In such a strike the merchant seamen would play an all important part. If an international general political strike is called it is the equivalent of an open declaration of war, because the purpose is to force the governments of all nations to hand over the administration of their countries to the leaders of the Communist parties. These minority groups plot and plan so they will be able to stop the wheels of industry completely, and halt all methods of transportation, and silence all communication systems. There can be no doubt that when the leaders of the world revolutionary movement decide to take this drastic step the Soviets will back the effort up with every kind of armed intervention. These facts explain the reason the Soviets are building *one thousand submarines* to be ready by 1960. In the event of an international general political strike, or war, the submarines could be used to clean up any shipping that gets to sea from strike bound ports.

The study of global warfare, and global maps, will show how the Soviet nations can supply themselves without aid of ocean-going transports, whereas other nations are dependent on ocean transportation to keep their war potential up to the mark.

The 57,000,000 people in Great Britain could not survive more than one month if ships were not allowed to enter British ports with food. People hear much about the hydrogen bomb and its capabilities of destroying a *whole city* with possibly a million human lives, but an international general political strike, backed by Soviet submarines, could starve the population of the British Isles into submission or death in a few weeks. This devilish conspiracy has been tried twice since 1914. If we permit the revised plan to be put into effect Britain and her people are doomed.

We are making the same foolish or criminal mistakes regarding naval policy today as we did before World Wars One and Two. Those responsible are not taking notice of the lessons taught by history. The Soviet powers are concentrating on hundreds of submarines with which to enforce a tight blockade of Britain. We seem to be concentrating on air-craft carriers rather than on building dozens of smaller anti-submarine ocean escort vessels. When aircraft have the range they possess today they don't need sinkable aircraft carriers. They need sea-plane bases. Landing fields, like air-craft carriers, can also be destroyed by bombs but the sea will always find its own level.

Search for an explanation for such stupid, if not criminal maladministration, and the only place one can find the answer is in the Protocols. Article 10, Pars. 18-19 and 20 say : "The recognition of our despot may also come before the destruction of the constitution; the moment for this recognition will come when the people, utterly wearied by the irregularities and incompetence of their rulers... a matter which we will arrange for... will clamour "Away with them and give us ONE KING over all the earth who will unite us and annihilate the causes of discords... frontiers, nationalities, religions and State debts... who will give us peace and quiet which we cannot find under our rulers and representatives".

"But you yourselves know perfectly well that to produce the possibility of the expression of such wishes by all the nations it is indispensible to trouble in all countries the peoples' relations with their governments, so as to utterly exhaust humanity with dissension, hatred, struggle, envy, and even by the use of torture, by starvation, by the inoculation of diseases, by want, so that the Goyim sees no other issue than to take refuge in our complete sovereignty in money and in all else. BUT IF WE GIVE THE NATIONS A BREATHING SPACE THE MOMENT WE LONG FOR IS HARDLY LIKELY EVER TO ARRIVE".

The point we must never forget is this. The ONE KING the Illuminati intend to crown to rule the universe is a man who will exercise the Despotism of Satan. Only pressure of public opinion will make those who believe in a One World Government halt before they lead us intentionally or otherwise into the Despotism of Satan.

CHAPTER XII

Communist activities in Canada

Moscow trained Communist emissaries came to Canada in June 1920 and, being well financed, their subversive activities grew rapidly. Inspector John Leopold of the R.C.M.P. came from undercover in 1930 and, at the trial of the Communist leaders, which included Tim Buck, he gave evidence he had gathered while working with them for ten years. Buck and others were sent to prison for plotting the overthrow of the Canadian Government by force. While in Kingston, Tim Buck preached his revolutionary ideology to fellow inmates, and he recruited many as "Fellow Travellers". When he succeeded in organizing the Kingston penitentiary riots in 1931 he won the admiration of his Moscow masters and qualified himself for the leadership of the Communist party in Canada.

Notwithstanding the evidence given at the trial of these revolutionary leaders; and the fact that they were found guilty of treason and subversive activities calculated to bring about the overthrow of constitutional government by force of arms; and the further fact that Tim Buck openly declared that in the event of war between Canada and Russia, he would fight for Russia, he was soon released from prison.

Communists throughout Canada never rested until they had convinced a great many people that Tim Buck was a sincere "reformer" who was being persecuted. They capitalized on the fact that a prison guard was alleged to have fired a shot-gun at Buck while he was in his cell during the riot. This alleged outrage won for Tim Buck the sympathy of thousands of soft-hearted citizens. They joined the Communists and clamoured for his release. These simple minded citizens never stopped to reason that Tim Buck had, in all probability, arranged the shooting incident himself, in accordance with Communist practice, to make it appear to the public that he was a martyr. They never stopped to think that it was absolutely impossible for a guard to have fired at Buck in his cell and missed unless he had wanted to miss.

Prison guards, and other prison officials, are underpaid when compared with other wage earners. It is a well known fact that prisoners, who can obtain money from outside, can purchase almost anything they desire from guards including tobacco, dope, and even temporary leave of absence. There have been several cases in the United States where convicts were proved to have obtained temporary freedom. In Nova Scotia one man went in and out of a local jail just as he pleased.

Communists have always placed great importance on having "Cells" in all penal institutions so they can work on the prisoners, who have proved themselves to be anti-social and, therefore, are good prospective revolutionary material. In all revolutions staged to date prisoners have been released, armed, and used as fighting men and to stir up the blood-lust necessary to bring about the preconceived reign of terror.

In 1953 I was able to prove that one of the senior officials in Kingston Penitentiary at the time of the riots was a Communist. He ran as Labour-Progressive candidate in the 1953 Federal election. During the last war this same man held important executive positions in the Royal Canadian Navy. At one time he was engineer-commander in charge of training engine-room personnel at Halifax dockyard. If the "Powers that be" could have placed him in a better position to suit their subversive requirements it would be difficult to think just where it would be.

No sooner was Tim Buck out of jail than he and his followers proceeded once again to carry out subversion in Canada. It is criminal folly to underestimate the ability of the Communist leaders, the organization, the discipline maintained by the party, or the number of its Fellow Travellers. To emphasize this point, let us remember the fact that after being released from Kingston Penitentiary, Tim Buck received almost enough votes to elect him Mayor of Toronto. His lieutenant, Stewart Smith, was elected to the Board of Control, several years in succession.

The subversive leaders have set up "training schools" in Canada exactly as they did in Spain. They have organized the distribution and sale of crime comics, pornographic literature, moving pictures, photographs and phonograph records. They work to corrupt the morals, and destroy the loyalty, of both young and old. In 1929-30, they organized the March to Ottawa, the Queen's Park riots, and they have led a continual fight to weaken the public confidence in constitutional authority ever since. They have aroused public resentment against the forces of Law and Order whenever a political error, or an individual indiscretion, gave them the opportunity. In all these activities they were trained in Moscow and directed by the secret power which directs the world revolutionary movement at home.

To prove these statements, I quote from the theses and statutes of the Communists International. "The task of the proletariat is to blow up the whole system and machinery of the bourgeoisie, to destroy them and all parliamentary institutions with them. This must be done irrespective of whether they be republican, or constitutional monarchial".

The following extract from the theses should convince those who are responsible for the maintenance of law and order, and the internal and external security of democratic countries, of the necessity of probing to the bottom all illegal practices. The leaders of the popular world revolutionary party say, and I quote :

"The Communist Party Leaders must learn to unite systematically legal with illegal work, but all legal work must be performed under the direct control of the illegal party."

Could anything be plainer ? The Labour-Progressive Party in Canada has been given legal status, but its members must carry on their work under the direct control of the illegal Communist Party, and this is controlled by the agentur of the Illuminati, who operate at the top levels. The same system controls all Communistically inspired movements in any country in the world.

Communists Front-men are delegated to engage in the political field. Leslie Morris, editor of the "Tribune", (the official organ of the Communist Party in Canada since 1923) is now one of Canada's most active top-level Communists. He was born in England in 1904. When he was only twenty he was made national secretary of the Young Communist League in Canada. In 1927-29 he studied at the Lenin University in Moscow. All his expenses were paid by the party. He studied the Communistic technique of propaganada as well as the theory of revolutionary warfare and the art of street fighting. Closely associated with Leslie Morris were Stewart Smith and Fred Rose. Leslie Morris was in 1954, a very important member of the central executive council of the Communist party in Canada. He directs publicity and public relations work. He was, also organizing secretary of the Labour-Progressive party in Canada.

In 1929, he preached sedition, and Atheistic doctrines to the youth of Ontario. He was by his own statements anti-everything except Communist. He was an openly avowed disciple of Marx, Engels, Lenin, and Stalin. He was a fiery orator. He advocated revolutionary action on every possible occasion. From 1939 onwards, he did everything possible to obstruct and defeat the British war effort, even after the Soviets were attacked by Germany. These statements were proved when Morris was convicted of the charges laid against him by the R.C.M.P. in September 1942.

Together with Fred Rose, who figured prominently in the Canadian Soviet espionage case, and Stewart Smith, who was, until 1947, for several years, controller for the City of Toronto, Morris was closely connected with the organization and carrying out of the Queen's Park riots in Toronto during 1929-30.

The leaders of the revolutionary movement in Canada encouraged young Communists to create disturbances which would cause the police to use force to suppress their activities because it is the party's policy to bring the public into conflict with the Police.

Lilly Himmilfarb and Becky Buhay were two of the women leaders of the Young Communist league, who nearly created a serious riot one afternoon in December 1929 when the Toronto Police broke up the most serious demonstration ever staged in Queen's Park.

The Toronto Mounted Police handled the situation in a determined and masterful manner without resorting to any unnecessary force. The leaders of the Young Communist League tried to incite unemployed veterans to antagonize the police into using force. The Police behaved magnificently. They herded the masses of people out of the park. They split them up into three sections and herded each section into, and along, different thoroughfares.

One section of the mob was herded down University Avenue to Queen street. When the crowd reached Queen street, the police split it into two and guided one section east while the other half was forced to move West. The Young Communists plotted to heave bricks through store windows in the hope that such action would create a riot. They decided to take this action when they reached the spot where Queen Street widens, so that the members could escape down a back alley to a restaurant on Spadina Avenue which they had made their headquarters. It is the policy of the Communists, both young and old, to instigate the necessary action, create a riot or disturbance, and then escape and leave innocent onlookers to come into physical contact with the police.

As a newspaper reporter covering the "riots" I obtained evidence which proved that top-level newspaper executives worked in conjunction with University professors and organized the plans for the disturbances which were put into effect by the Communists. Because it was impossible to get the TRUTH published in the paper I turned the evidence over to the police and General Draper used this knowledge to instruct his subordinates so they did not fall into the traps prepared for them. This is one more illustration of how the "top" directs while the "bottom" carries out the subversives plans.

On December 29th, 1929, Stewart Smith told members of the Young Communist League that he had been authorized by the Comintern to inform them that if they worked diligently, obeyed orders given them by their leaders, and remained loyal to party discipline "they would live to see the day, in the not too distant future, when the gutters of Yonge Street would run red with capitalistic blood". This speech was published in one edition of the Toronto Star. His record since 1929 would tend to prove this information to have been correct because he has made municipal politics his life's work since his return from Russia. He was elected to the Toronto Board of Control during 1945 and 1946. Incidentally, while he was a member of the Board of Control he proved he was well versed in municipal affairs. He has recently concealed his violent, bloodthirsty, ruthless revolutionary tendencies from the public. Since his utterances were published in 1929, most people think that Smith, at his worst, is only a radical reformer. They forget a leopard does not change its spots.

In the 1930's, the young enthusiasts of the Communist Party were told that the members of the Comintern were satisfied that British-Imperialism and German Militarism could be brought into conflict within ten years. (Mark the accuracy of all statements). They were instructed that when this happened it was the duty of all Canadian Communists to join the armed forces for military training but for service in Canada only. As far back as 1929 Stewart Smith stated quite confidently that the Canadian Government would never agree to compulsory military training for service outside of Canada. How did he know this important fact? He was well informed in regard to the policy the Canadian Government carried out from 1939 to December 1944. The government only changed its policy regarding its Armed Forces *after* Stalin broke with the Western Capitalist Internationalists.

Communists were told that once they were in the armed forces, it was their duty to work willingly, diligently, and enthusiastically, in order to win promotion and work themselves into positions of responsibility, and trust, where they would be best able to take over the armed forces, when the word to revolt was given. Communists were informed that the policy of the Comintern was to wait until both enemies of Communism were exhausted, and weakened in man-power and wealth, then, when the people of the conflicting nations were tired and weary of war and demanding peace, the Communists would arise in every country and overthrow the government and form Soviet states. The slogan was to be "A revolution to end wars".

After the Queen's Park Riots failed in their purpose, Messrs. Morris and Rose moved back to Montreal.

In Montreal, Morris kept busy as an anti-social, anti-British agitator. He worked hard to stir up religious and racial differences between different classes, colours, and creeds.

The purpose of such activities is this. The text books on revolutionary warfare point out that the strength of the revolutionary party increases pro rata to the disunity and confusion created amongst those who are not members of the Communist Party, or Fellow Travellers. Mr. Morris over-reached himself when he preached open sedition. He was arrested and found guilty. On January 20th, 1933, he was sentenced to one year in jail for seditious utterances. For his outstanding service to the Communist Party he won immediate recognition and reward from his masters in Moscow.

Upon his release from prison he was ordered to Moscow for further training. He spent most, if not all, of 1935 in Russia. He returned to Canada and was appointed a leading member of the central executive committee of the Communist Party of Canada, which position he holds today.

While Communist leaders throughout the world preach and pretend to advocate socialism, and will use it as occasion demands, they hate socialism as it is advocated by the C.C.F. in Canada, by the Labour Party in Britain, and in other parts of the Empire, as I proved in "*Pawns in the Game*" they hated it in Russia and Spain.

After studying Communistic and Fascist activities in Toronto, Hamilton and Oshawa from 1925 to 1930, I next made another trip to Europe. Upon my return to Canada I lectured under the auspices of the Canadian Club and Navy League in all the larger centres of population throughout the entire Dominion. In 1931-32 I studied the subversive activities going on in industry, amongst our children, in our educational institutions, etc. I saw only too clearly how the members of both subversive groups in Canada were rapidly spreading their heathen philosophy throughout the length and breadth of the country. The disturbing fact was that many decent citizens didn't wish to hear the truth because it upset their peace of mind.

After completing my Canadian tour I decided to investigate the conditions much more thoroughly in the Canadian north, particularly in the Northernmost parts of Ontario and Quebec. Information I had obtained indicated the Communist organizers in Canada were establishing revolutionary strong holds in areas they considered of greatest strategical importance in their plan for the Sovietization of this Dominion and subjugation of the U.S.A.

Some of the areas given special attention were the West Coast from Vancouver to the Yukon and Alaska; a large area centred right in Prime Minister Mackenzie King's own parliamentary constituency — Prince Albert, Saskatchewan; the twin cities of Port Arthur and Fort William at the head of the Great Lakes; Sault Ste. Marie, Sudbury Nickel Belt, and the big gold mining camps, the paper mills, and the lumber and pulp industries in Northern Ontario and Quebec.

In order to obtain information first hand I spent many months in the mining camps in Timmins, Noranda, Val d'Or, etc., and the camps of the Great Lakes Paper Company. I was able to find employment for my own son in the mines. He worked as a common labourer side by side with honest loyal Canadians and with those who were plotting revolution in Canada. The biggest piece of first-hand evidence I collected was regarding the power of their propoganda. I felt sure that my own son would be immune to Communist propaganda, but I was proved to be in error. A young man in his teens exposed to constant propaganda will inevitably break under their cleverly, continuously, applied pressure. My son for a time turned anti-Christian, anti-social, and just about anti-everything. Fortunately I finally changed his ideas by proving their propaganda was as untruthful as it was deceptive.

I intended at first to give the results of my own investigations conducted in the northern parts of the provinces in this book, but it so happened I spent a few days in March 1946 listening to the debate to the Speech from the Throne, in the House of Parliament, for the Province of Ontario, in Toronto. I was amazed to hear Mr. J. A. Habel, member for Cochrane North, cover in detail much of the same ground. I therefore quote Mr. Habel, who is now an M.P. in order to convince the reader that no matter from what angle an unbiased investigator studies the conspiracy, in all countries of the world, in all classes of society, and at all levels of Government they invariably reach the same conclusion, i.e. *that the ultimate and crowning motive is to bring about bloody revolution during which members of the Party can carry out deliberate, premeditated mass murder to liquidate all those they consider reactionaries and opposed to their own heathen philosophy.*

Mr. J. A. Habel was the member for Cochrane North. He is an extraordinary man in many ways. Mr. Habel represents a constituency in Northern Ontario which extends west from the Quebec boundary 255 miles and extends from the Sudbury riding north for more than 600 miles. It includes the most northerly polling booths in Ontario.

Mr. Habel addressed the House in 1946. He said : "I have the highest respect for labour leaders who are honestly working to improve conditions. The rights of all must be protected, otherwise there would be slavery". He pointed out "The trouble today is the fact that there are still too many selfish employers, and too many labour agitators, deliberately confusing the minds of the citizens of this Dominion until the majority are wondering in which direction they should go". Mr. Habel evidently sensed the double nature of the conspiracy also.

Mr. Habel then turned towards the back bench in the House where Communist members Messrs. Salsberg and McLeod, sat. He said : "There are certain people in this country who classify themselves as Canadians. To my mind they are not Canadians at all. In order to qualify that remark Mr. Speaker I must go back to 1934... There were a considerable number of strikes up North in the bush that year... the very same men who today are claiming to be the champions of Labour and Freedom, (like the member for St. Andrew said yesterday), those very same men came into our bush camps up North in 1934 and *drove* the lumbermen out of the camps. They used such force that one contractor was confined to hospital in Cochrane for ten days afterwards''.

Mr. Habel explained how the Communist Party Organizers had collected together ''Fellow Travellers'' from Port Arthur, Fort William, Sault Ste. Marie, and Sudbury and brought them into Cochrane. He told how armed bands went into the bush, entered the lumber camps, and made the lumberjacks prisoners because they refused to strike. He told how the Communists forced the lumberjacks to march to a Communist hall at a small place named Driftwood, some eighteen miles from the camp. They were kept locked up for two days and then transferred another eighteen miles to Cochrane where they were imprisoned in a house for a further eight days and fed nothing but bread and water. The member for Cochrane North then explained how Communist bands had entered another lumber camp twenty-six miles north of Cochrane and forced the men, who didn't want to strike, to march through deep snow, in zero weather, twenty-six miles into Cochrane. The men arrived at Cochrane at one o'clock in the morning and were crowded in with the others.

Mr. Habel then remarked, ''The same men who forcibly imprisoned honest working men, because they felt they had no quarrel with their employers, are the same individuals who are making such a holler regarding the Federal Government's action in arresting people and holding them for interrogation on authority of a secret Order in Council, after the Government of Canada had satisfied itself they were plotting against the security of this Dominion''. He was referring to the Ottawa investigations into Soviet Spy activities in Canada.

Mr. Habel told how he and other citizens formed a local Constabulary and liberated the imprisoned men. They arrested five of the Communist leaders. The Communist leaders were found guilty and sentenced to jail for six months. Could any thing be more ridiculous ?... Mr. Habel said : ''The leaders of the Communist Party of Canada *are following exactly the same destructive policy today as they were in 1934, despite the fact that they are trying to convince the public that they are acting in a constructive manner in the interests of the working class population''*.

Mr. Habel then told how two men had come to his home in Porquis and threatened that ''If he didn't lay off his activities against the Communists he would be buried under six feet of clay''.

Mr. Habel continued : ''In 1935, the members of the Central Executive Committee of the party further consolidated their position in the Northern section of Ontario by ordering Finlanders and other foreigners, who had been chased out of their own countries by anti-Communists, to infiltrate into the great gold producing mines. They were followed by Jewish Communists from the Ukraine, and ''Polish

Reds". High-grading, the White Slave Traffic, organized gambling, and labour unrest, swept through the whole of the largest mining camps in Canada, like a forest fire on a windy day".

Decent citizens called a meeting to discuss the conditions and formulate a plan of action to deal with the situation. About 3,000 gathered in a hall in Timmins. According to Mr. Habel's statement the Communist leaders spread their followers all through the hall and every time a decent citizen got up on his feet to speak, they booed, and heckled him, until a riot broke out. They hoped the police would break up the meeting. Mr. Habel pointed out that if the police, at the request of decent citizens, acted against the Communists to prevent the spread of their heathen philosophy, and to prevent them perfecting their plans to usurp the rights of the people by the use of armed force, they, the Communists, cry to high heaven they are being refused the rights of democratic citizens. But when the democratic citizens try to expose their subversive activities they immediately take action to cause the police to break up the citizens meeting by creating pre-arranged riots.

The witty and courageous French-Canadian told how he stopped the riot ,and proved to the Communists, that the vast majority of citizens in the Canadian North were true to their faith and loyal to their King, by ordering the pianist to play the National Anthem. "Everyone stood to attention... even the Communists", Mr. Habel explained. "If they hadn't it would have been just too bad for them".

Mr. Habel continued, "In 1937 I was in Toronto. I had been to worship in my own church one particular night. As I left the church after the service I walked past Massey Hall where large crowds were gathered. They were Communists, and their Fellow Travellers, waiting to enter Massey Hall for the purpose of celebrating the twentieth anniversary of the Red Russian Revolution". Mr. Habel continued, "The speakers that night included Tim Buck, Stewart Smith, and the honourable member for St. Andrew, Mr. Salsberg. I entered the hall and took a seat in the top balcony. I heard the honourable member for St. Andrew say : *"To-night in Moscow, in that big red square, millions of people are celebrating the twentieth anniversary of the Russian... the Soviet Revolution. The people are listening to Stalin's speech. At each corner of that big square, powerful searchlights are sending their glares to heaven, defying God to come down with his angels and prevent the Soviets doing what they are doing..."*

At this point Mr. Salsberg could sit still no longer. He jumped to his feet and appealed to the Speaker. He said : "Mr. Speaker. I rise to a point of order. I declare without hesitation the honourable member is putting words into my mouth which I never uttered..." He added after a moment's hesitation. "As far as my memory serves me..." This caused a big laugh. "He certainly can't remember what I said in 1937. I must ask the honourable member to quote or I should be entitled to say he is not reporting the truth", Mr. Salsberg continued.

Mr. Habel replied with a smile, "I was expecting that, Mr. Speaker... I know how they wriggle once they are on a hook".

Mr. Habel dug into his pockets and produced numerous letters, pamphlets and other documents. "I didn't wish to bother the members with reading extracts from documents but now I'll quote a few". He then waved one paper, "Here is a confidential report of a pre-convention meeting held by the provincial secretaries of the Ukrainian Labour Farmer Temple Association at 300 Bathurst Street, Toronto, on Saturday and Sunday, August 18th and 19th, 1934. They are all Communists and their organization is to advance the Party Line. The General Chairman of that meeting was J. Pacino. He was assisted by the Secretary, N. Yofan of Hamilton ,and J. Dolyinsky of Port Arthur. The Presidium" of the association are first "Stalin, Joseph, address Moscow, U.S.S.R. Next Thaelman, Ernest, address Germany (in prison). Next Buck, Tim — address Kingston Penitentiary, and last, Ewen, Tom, address also Kingston Penitentiary". Mr. Habel then quoted recommendation No. 10.

"Recommended by Shabrura that Eulik make strenuous efforts and organize all lumber workers in the Thunder Bay District, and to urge Makella, Jack Gilbanks, and other leaders in the Lumber Workingmen's International Union to speed up propaganda and organization work in the lumber camps and to urge each one *to do his best to break up the Canadian Bushmen's Union.*

No. 12. Shabrura recommended that in the event of a strike, if strike breakers are employed, the food in the camps concerned must be damaged by pouring coal oil and gasoline on it. If, after a period of two or three weeks, the strike is not settled, and strike breakers are still employed, *the food must be poisoned and the strike-breakers subjected to man-handling".* Mr. Speaker, I am quoting from authentic documents.

Mr. Habel continued. "Two men named Lawryss, and Czyz, recommended that instructions be sent Peter Harpuk, of Kapuskasing, to get all members of the L.W.I.U. together and make final preparations for a strike in the lumber industry to take place not later than November". It had been reported at that meeting that the local unions in Kapuskasing and Sudbury could not arrange a strike, but a white collar organizer of the Communist Party in Canada, sitting in Toronto, *ordered a strike to take place in the Canadian bush that November.*

It was next recommended, "To popularize the next strike in each city, and in order to obtain accommodation for the strikers, a mobilization of the women and children should take place so they will be given an active part in the strike collecting food and funds, and participating in picket duty."

Having recommended... ordered... that women and children should be involved in the strikes, resolution number 19 reads, "Recommended by Hucalak that the Miners' Local of Kirkland Lake and Sudbury, send the Lumber Workers International Union *a few cases of dynamite with which to blow up the camps and other buildings in case of a prolonged strike."*

There was an audible series of "Ho.o.o.o.o" as the member for Bellwoods, Toronto, jumped to his feet. He shouted. "Mr. Speaker. I rise to a point of order. I believe under the rules of the House when an honourable member is quoting something to the House he is obliged to give the source of his information". Mr. Speaker then ruled, "In case of documents the Honourable member can be asked to table the documents, but if it is a confidential report or letter... no".

Mr. Habel continued. "Clause No. 22 reads : 'Andreyczuk recommended that some damage should be done at the Great Lakes Paper Company property *because this Company has fired so many members of the U.L.F.T.A. and W.U.L.*' "

Mr. Habel continued. "Here is a statement written by a fellow named Zadaczny, quotation No. 28. 'The foreigners do not care a great deal if they lose their jobs or not. They are spreading our propaganda in the places where they are employed in the true revolutionary spirit. I hope sincerely we will meet again next year in Hamilton... and if not that, we will be shoulder to shoulder at the barricades on the streets fighting against capitalism' ".

"To prove one other point I will quote clause No. 30 — "The convention was closed with an especially fiery speech by Antoni Kiernicki. He concluded his speech with these words : *"Our organization is not only fighting in the interests of the workers, but is a member of the International, and we receive our orders from Moscow. We must be ready at all times and prepare the workers for the defence of Soviet Russia. We must never forget that the aims of this organization are to crush capitalism and to establish a Soviet Canada".*

"Messrs. Salsberg and McLeod were associated with these revolutionaries", Mr. Habel said "from 1939 to 1942 both honourable gentlemen were running around this country trying to keep ahead of the R.C.M.P. but they still kept spreading propaganda calculated to obstruct the war effort of the Allied Nations".

Mr. Habel concluded with these words. "Mr. Speaker, the people of this Dominion must decide now, if they are going to sit back while men of the type I have exposed spread their false philosophy. How can these men justify calling themselves Canadians when they have sworn allegiance to the Head of Soviet Russia ? How can they claim to be champions of the Canadian workers when they know that in the Soviets the workers have no right to strike, no right to engage in collective bargaining, no right to do any of the things we hold most precious and dear... In 1775, our forefathers left us with a pledge, which was made again in 1812. I say there is no room in this Dominion for Soviet-Canadians who call themselves Canadians. We are part of the great British Commonwealth of Nations... I maintain we are more Canadian to-day than ever. Our nation has reached maturity. We stand for one flag, and that flag means we will not tolerate this intrusion of any foreign power".

Having spoken an hour longer than he intended, Mr. Habel apologized to the speaker and the Prime Minister and sat down, evidently well satisfied that he had used the time to good purpose.

The lesson to learn is this : Because the "Secret Power" hidden behind the scenes of government control the policy, the government does nothing to destroy the Communist 5th column. There can be no other reason than the fact that those who direct the international aspect of the Capitalist Conspiracy may wish to use the Communist 5th column one day to further their own secret plans and ambitions.

Communists preach Socialism to attract socialist minded people to their party meetings few socialists know that the Communists in Canada, as in other countries also, received a directive that they were to wreck the C.C.F. Party. Mr. Leslie Morris was chosen as the "Voice" and the "Pen" which should do the slaying. He published a pamphlet called "The C.C.F's Betrayal". He denounced the C.C.F. for trying to achieve socialism by the use of *ballots* instead of *bullets*. He berated the C.C.F. Leaders because they advocated parliamentary methods for reforms rather than revolutionary action. He wrote : "They... the C.C.F. Leaders... abhor struggle like the devil hates holy water. The foundation of class collaboration, of the gradual winning of a parliamentary majority which will painlessly usher in socialism lies at the bottom of all the treachery of the C.C.F. leadership between 1929 and 1939".

Another extraordinary illustration of how international capitalists work at the "top" while international Communists work at the "bottom" to defeat a common enemy was provided in 1945 when Responsible Enterprise, directed by Mr. Gladstone Murray organized a plot intended to kill any chances the C.C.F. had of forming a Government in Ontario. The newspapers covered the story in detail. It is sufficient to say here that papers were found in an office occupied by the Provincial Police in the Parliament Buildings, Queens Park which led the C.C.F. leaders to believe that the provincial government were using the Provincial Police as a Gestapo to spy on C.C.F. members and make out they were Communists. The C.C.F. leaders took the bait placed for them and swallowed it hook-line and sinker. They made a lot of wild and irresponsible charges which is what the plotters expected them to do. When they couldn't prove their charges public reaction was such that they lost all hope of winning a party majority in the provincial government.

I have known the man who placed the bait since 1930. He used the code D-208 when signing reports and investigations he made for Mr. Murray. He tried to wreck the salvage business I organized to help needy Veterans in 1931. Who controls the Industrial Department of Poppy Fund today ? It is certainly not the Communists. The control is in the hands of an international combine. The officials responsible for enforcing the anti-combines act have been informed but have failed to act. The men who control the international ramifications of the Salvage business are multi-millionaires. Few people realize that the salvage business is big business and when strictly controlled the profits are very great.

Because I refused to sell out the Poppy Fund Industrial Department, to the Canadian representatives of the International Cartel which controls salvage collections all over the world, every effort was made to put us out of business. This quite unexpectedly provided me with an excellent opportunity to study another angle of the international conspiracy.

In order to pick up the threads of this very complicated business it is necessary to relate, very briefly, my connections with the Poppy Fund of Toronto. Poppy Day was introduced into Canada by the late George Moore to raise funds to help *deserving* ex-service men and their dependents who found themselves in need through no fault of their own.

The collections were usually held on the Saturday nearest to the anniversary of the Armistice signed November 11th, 1918. The sale of Poppies grew until the organizers realized as much as $47,000 in Toronto alone. Those who directed the international conspiracy decided they had to obtain control of the Poppy Fund as they obtain control of everything else which affects the lives of those who suffer poverty or affluence.

The first steps taken to obtain control was to use subversives attached to the Communist Party to bring the Poppy Day Committee into disrepute. The second step was to appoint agentur of the Capitalists to control Poppy Day Fund's activities. In 1926 one of the executive was persuaded to have a load of coal delivered to his own home. Those who tempted him argued that he was entitled to it in return for the tremendous amount of voluntary work he had put into the annual project. He knew that others connected with the fund were taking expense money. As soon as this "Pawn" fell for the suggestion, so cunningly offered, he was exposed in the Press by the very men who had tempted him.

The agentur of the Capitalists immediately used this incident as justification to demand that the City Fathers of Toronto name a committee of outstanding citizens to act as directors of the Poppy Fund. The man who had been used as a "Pawn in the game" came to me for advice. He told me a great deal regarding what had been going on behind the scenes This man had lost his job because of the publicity and as he had a wife and family I offered to see that those who had led him into disgrace were removed from the Poppy Day Committee also.

I did not know as much about the ramifications of the conspiracy then as I do now. I went to one of those who were putting pressure on the City Fathers to reorganize Poppy Day and told him all I had found out and asked him to use his influence to give the man another chance. I don't know what happened after that interview. I told the man concerned that I was satisfied the matter would by straightened out and that he would get another job. He was happy when I left him. That is why I cannot help but suspect foul play because, the next morning, his body was found smashed and broken in the Don Valley Ravine. It was taken for granted he had committed suicide.

I kept in constant touch with the Poppy Day Committee. Its activities were taken over by a group of men selected by the City Fathers and others appointed by the executives of various Veteran organizations. In 1926 I became active within the administration when I was asked by Colonel Le Grand Reed to try to straighten out H. J. who had been appointed to organize the Poppy Day Campaign for the new executive. Mr. H. J. had not been sober for nearly two weeks. I was innocent of the facts regarding this man's character at the time so I took him into my own home and tried to sober him up.

Mr. H. J. repaid my kindness by bribing my own young children to smuggle patent medicines containing alcohol into him after I had spent three days trying to sober him up. He had pleaded that if I cut him off completely he would go insane. I guess my method of trying to help him was not based on scientific knowledge, but I do know that the most effective way to bring druken seamen out of their stupor the day after leaving port is to give them an occasional shot of rum mixed with a laxative flavored with lime-juice.

My surprise can be imagined when I returned home from work that evening to find my wife and children terrified. My guest was in the D.Ts. I called Christie St. Hospital and the doctor (who treated him for his war disabilities) came to see him and placed him under treatment. The doctor said that if I would still look after him it would be the best kind of treatment. He confided to me that Mr. H. J. had started this last drinking about after his wife had decided to leave him but he didn't tell me why.

What a boob I turned out to be. While in the stages of remorse my "guest" insisted on telling me of his domestic unhappiness. I listened because it is said "Confession is good for the soul". My horror can be understood when he voluntarily confessed he was a sexual pervert and had sunk so deep that he had used his own children to satisfy his unnatural cravings. I immediately got in touch with his doctor and insisted that the man be removed from my home. The thing that puzzeled me most was the fact that this type of human monstrosity had been made organizer for the Poppy Fund Campaign when hundreds of decent and capable men were available.

A careful check of the members of the new Poppy Fund executive showed that the vast majority of the members were men whose characters were above reproach. Two members did not, however, measure up to the standards of decent citizenship, although they were prominent in society and industry. Investigation showed that Mr. H. J. had been recommended for the position of campaign organizer by these two men.

I warned Colonel Le Grand Reed and the Rev. Canon Hedley about the peculiar character of their organizer because I feared their good name might have suffered seriously if this one man's actions brought the whole executive into disrepute as had happened to the previous executive.

It was shortly after this episode that Colonel Le Grand Reed, backed by Canon Hedley and several others, asked me to become secretary of the newly formed Christie Street Hospital Branch of the Canadian Legion.

To show how extensive the control of the directors of the subversive conspiracy really is investigation proved that on the staff of the reorganized Poppy Fund were three men and one woman who were definitely subversives. Two were secretly working with the Communists and two had for a long time been working for the Capitalist conspirators. All complaints and charges brought by certain members of the Poppy Fund Executive against these subversives were glossed over by other members who claimed they could not be substantiated. By this time (1929) I was becoming convinced that these extraordinary things just didn't happen by accident. I determined to dig right down to the bottom and discover the "Causes" which produced such revolting and extraordinary "Effects".

I took only three persons into my confidence : Colonel Le Grand Reed, General John Langton, and General D. C. Draper. We didn't trouble Canon Hedley with any details because they would have offended his deeply religious and sensitive nature.

As early as 1928 I predicted there would be a World Wide depression. I urged my three friends to persuade all those interested in Veteran welfare work to prepare to take care of those who would be the first to fall victims to this phase of the international conspiracy. I am sorry to say those in a position to have averted the disastrous times that followed in 1930 refused to listen to these warnings.

I explained to the above named gentlemen how I expected the leaders of the Communist Party in Canada would use the depression to spread discontent amongst ex-service men and suggested that a huge salvage campaign be organized to help Veterans who would be thrown out of work and disposessed. My friends on the Board of Directors tried to persuade the other members to appoint me as General Manager of the Poppy Fund of Toronto with full powers to :

(A) Organize a house to house collection of furniture and other household goods and clothing which could be repaired and used for the relief of Veterans and their families found in need.

(B) To organize a salvage department in connection with the above collection and distribution service to provide employment and help defray the cost.

(c) To train Veterans so they could stand a better chance of obtaining steady employment on the competitive labour market.

My friends made absolutely no head-way until **AFTER** the depression struck.

I organized the industrial department November 1930 and was appointed Manager of the Poppy Fund in the Spring of 1931. Records will show that the tag day collections of Poppy Fund had dropped from nearly $50,000 a year in the early 1920s to less than $10,000 in 1930.

During the depression under my management the affairs of Poppy Fund prospered until the organization owned its own plant on Atlantic Ave. The employment and industrial records reached an all-time high in 1938-1939. I can prove (by records given out by the directors since 1940) that the volume of employment and business has decreased steadily ever since. This steady decrease had taken place during the "boom" years of 1941 to 1955.

I mention these facts so the reader will be able to believe the following statement : After I took over Poppy Fund I was attacked at the "bottom" by the Communists who wished to exploit the sufferings of needy Veterans to the limit of their capacity, and by the Capitalist conspirators at the "Top" because I entered the commercial field for salvage and thus interferred with the absolute control held by an international cartel. If my investigations conducted between 1927 and 1929 hadn't proved that the tremendous profits to be made out of salvage would carry the cost of collecting and repairing the furniture and other household goods and clothing, which we supplied to needy Veterans free of charge, there would have been no merit to my suggestions. But once my project was launched Poppy Fund was subjected to every kind of opposition from the "bottom" and at the "top". There were agents of the conspirators on the Board of Directors.

The first move of the conspirators was to divide my authority. Colonel Lidstone was appointed Manager of the Relief Department in the middle of 1931. There was no need for this additional expense. He was also appointed secretary to the board so those who did not want me to attend meetings could say my presence wasn't required.

Subversives sabotaged the work we were doing. They stole thousands of dollars worth of goods and always found a ready market amongst the lowly salvage dealers who are controlled by "The Big Three" dealers. We had three mysterious fires. Each one was calculated to put us out of business but, thanks to my friend Colonel Le Grand Reed, we were always able to obtain sufficient insurance to cover the value of our stock on hand, even when it had accumulated to almost a thousand tons, when "The Big Three" dealers closed us out of the Canadian markets. Every dirty trick was tried to put Poppy Fund Industrial Department out of business, but an answer was found for everyone of them. This dirty trick method of doing business is referred to in the salvage business as "Chiselling". It consists of sabotaging the opposition's business. Any means possible are used, from putting sugar in the gas tanks of trucks, to tricking competitors into costly contracts which the conspirators make sure they cannot fill; Breaches of contract can lead to costly litigation. Fighting the Communist "Cells" attacking at the "bottom" and the agentur of the International Capitalists attacking at the "Top" gave me nine of the most interesting years of my life.

A Mr. A. Brown controlled the Canadian section of the international salvage monopoly. He had come to Canada from England as a Barnard's Home Boy. His exploitation by a miserly farmer had hardened his character. He reached his objective no matter how many people he crushed under foot. Because of the brutal treatment he had received when a boy he sought the aid of the Salvation Army and was given employment in their Salvage Department. He decided to leave the Salvation Army and play along with those who controlled the Salvage business in Canada. Because of his ability and hard-boiled business methods he was soon appointed general manager of the Canadian Combine.

When I first organized the Salvage Department for Poppy Fund, Mr. Brown made me an offer of permanent employment at a generous salary if I would throw in my lot with the "Big Three" dealers. When I refused, his task was to put the industrial department of Poppy Fund out of operation. Mine was to see he didn't succeed.

Thanks to the generous support of the public the Poppy Fund

came out of the doldrums into which it had sunk between 1926 and 1930. In 1931 we helped rehabilitate over 3,000 veterans families. In order to meet the expense of collecting furniture and clothing from house to house we had to build up the commercial end of the salvage business. This wasn't hard to do, because the "Big Three" had never paid their customers more than about one third what their salvage was worth. We took over 500 tons of commercial business away from the "Big Three" dealers within two months. We paid those we dealt with a fair price. I broke up Mr. Brown's attempts to close the markets to Poppy Fund because I learned of a war going on at the international level to decide whether the representatives of the Axis Powers, or the international capitalists were going to obtain control of the salvage business which becomes a matter of the greatest importance when the world is being prepared for war. I played one group against the other and Poppy Fund continued to prosper.

By 1934 most of my friends had either died or been replaced on the Board of Directors. The new board ordered me to return to the Big Three dealers accounts amounting to over 250 tons a month. I fought this ORDER bitterly at first, but then decided I would obey in order to obtain conclusive evidence that a combine did exist. The directors next entered into an agreement with the Big Three dealers under which Poppy Fund was to pay the "Big Three" commission on all tonnage sold to the mills. I protested this agreement, pointing out that we did not need anyone to dispose of our stocks. I refused to pay the commissions demanded.

Brown tried every trick he knew. He always used others to do his dirty work while he remained in the clear. At every opportunity I appealed to his better self. After a time I knew he was beginning to weaken. In 1936 we reached a private agreement under which he promised to "lay off Poppy Fund". We didn't dare let his or my directors know that he had weakened in his determination to put the Poppy Fund Industrial Department out of business.

There must have been a leak somewhere, because a big reorganization of the Big Three Salvage companies took place in 1937. Mr. Brown's authority was limited. Early in 1938 he took suddenly ill. He died shortly afterwards.

Just before Mr. Brown died he sent for me. He was at that time confined to his bed. He said he wanted to make a clean breast about everything that had happened. He admitted having financed three ex-officers to work in opposition to Poppy Fund with the intention of dividing public support and causing business failure. He admitted having worked subversives into the staff of the industrial department for the purpose of sabotaging our efforts from within. He admitted responsibility for practically everything that had happened except the three fires which had demolished our plants. He gave the names of the ex-officers he had employed to try to wreck Poppy Fund's business. All of them had previously been used as subversives in the Veteran movement. One of the men he named worked for Mr. Gladstone Murray and his so-called Responsible Enterprise organization. When working for Murray he used the code-name D-208. This is the same man who tried to give me the bum steer regarding the Communist conspiracy against organized labour in 1944. He is the same man who placed the documents used to bait the capitalist angle of the conspiracy against the C.C.F. in 1945. In return for services rendered he was nominated and financed to run for the Provincial Parliament in a by-election in 1947. He did not represent the L.P.P. or the C.C.F. parties. When I returned from active service the Directors refused to reinstate me as manager of the Poppy Fund industrial department. I appealed to the government under the veteran legislation and the government of Canada upheld the decision of the Directors of Poppy Fund. During the war they had sold out the interests of the Veterans to the internationalistic combine.

Here were two different cases in which capitalist internationalists worked at the "top" while communist internationalists worked at the "bottom" to achieve the same common purpose. The important thing to notice is the fact that in this case, as in others, the man who acted as the "link" was well paid for his services. He was financed so that he could run as a candidate in the provincial elections. Because I had dared to challenge the power of the men at the 'Top" they made sure I didn't return as manager of the Poppy Fund Industrial Department after I returned from World War Two.

The Secret Powers behind World Revolution do the plotting and the planning; they provide the trained agentur and experienced revolutionary leaders; they pile up tinder suitable for starting revolutionary fires; they give government administration bad advice; they strike the spark that makes the blaze; they use the working people, who for diplomatic reasons they term the Proletariat, to fight behind the barricades. Behind the scenes the Proletariat are referred to as "Cattle", the mob and, the Goyim. But finally it is the agentur of the Illuminati who take over political and economic control.

A well known Communist during a discussion I had with him, told me : "Once Popular World Revolution is an accomplished fact, there will be no need for members of the Communists Party to be dishonest, corrupt, or disloyal. They will have everything they need. They will have all the heart of man can desire. It will be theirs without the asking. We leaders of the Communist Party in Canada today, will be the Commissars of the Canadian Soviet Republic tomorrow. We will look after ourselves well, and our friends", and, he added with a grim smile, "We will also look well after our enemies".

There in a nutshell you have the reason which gives all members of the Communist Party the WILL, and the DETERMINATION, and the ENERGY, to work night and day to bring about popular revolution. They will suffer persecution, imprisonment and abuse, but they will not slow up for a single instant. They keep their eyes fixed on their ultimate goal... popular world revolution. They are playing for gigantic stakes. With them it is a case of "Winner Takes All". They don't realize they are being used as pawns in the game of international intrigue.

Toronto citizens elected several Communists to municipal offices year after year. Stewart Smith was a controller for several years, others were Aldermen and members of the Board of Education. It is no exaggerated statement to say the Communists required approximately 50,000 followers to elect so many members of the Communist Party to positions in Toronto's civic affairs. Similar conditions are prevalent in other Canadian cities.

If there are fifty thousand Communists, and Fellow Travellers in Greater Toronto, which has a population of approximately 1,000,000 people, then it is not unreasonable to suppose that in large centres of population, which are less British, the percentage could be much higher.

In 1946 those directing the world revolutionary movement ordered the leaders of Communism in all the remaining "Free Nations" to purge their parties ruthlessly of suspected reactionaries, diversionists, traitors, and possible spies. This general house-cleaning program was extended to include "Fellow Travellers". As the result, the numerical strength of the card bearing members was reduced to approximately 18,000 and the Fellow Travellers to 180,000.

I mention the above facts in order to prove that the Communist Party in Canada, and their Fellow Travellers, are strong enough numerically to carry on the organization and administrative work necessary for a successful revolutionary effort at any time the signal is given.

History reveals that when Lenin started his Bolshevik Party in 1903 he had only 17 followers. In 1917 he had 43,000. Pro rata to population, Communists and their fellow travellers are far stronger in Canada and the U.S.A. than they were in Russia when Lenin overthrew the Kerensky Republican Government in 1917.

It was necessary that Lenin and Trotsky had the financial backing, and the political support, of the international minded Capitalists in order for them to accomplish what they did. It is obvious that international-minded Capitalists still support Communists secretly here also. No other reasoning makes sense.

This is a matter of the utmost public importance. Members of Parliament should enquire **WHY** the Minister of Justice tried to convince them on July 8th 1955 that the Communist Party and their Fellow Travellers now only number approximately 63,000. By trying to make the public believe such utter nonsense he insults their intelligence.

Apparently the members of the Canadian Cabinet forget, or ignore, the fact that the will of the electorate is still supreme. They forget, or ignore, the fact that it is the duty of every member of the government, and every member of parliament, to keep the electorate **FULLY** and **PROPERLY** and **TRUTHFULLY** informed on *all* matters of the Governments business in order that the electorate may study *all* problems in an *intelligent manner* and then inform the government, through their elected representatives, what they wish them to do. Under both the British and the American constitutions the will of the people is absolutely supreme.

From the evidence under review it would appear that the cart is definitely before the horse. The electors would be justified in asking if the government and Parliament are in conspiracy to keep the electors in ignorance on all matters of political and economic importance so that they will remain unable to express their will? If the electors permit this shocking state of affairs to continue it is only a matter of time... a very short time... before we lose the opportunity to take an intelligent interest in the affairs of our country. Despotism as described in the "Long Range" plans will be all supreme. All human beings will become slaves to Satanic despotism, body... soul... and mind.

In order to prove how dangerous is the road internationalists are treading, regardless of whether they be Communists or Capitalists, I quote from a letter written by the late Mr. P. N.. Miliukoff in 1917 when he was leader of the Constitutional-Democrat party in Russia. It was written in answer to one he had received from Prince Paul Dolgeroukoff who at that time was Chairman of the Central Committee of the party.

The letter proves that the conspirators used the Menshevist-communists to overthrow the power of the Czar in order that they could seize power. They backed Kerensky to form his Provisional Government. Miliukoff became its Foreign Secretary. The letter admits that their plans were defeated because they failed to recognize the power of the leaders of the extreme "right" (the agentur of the Illuminati). It was the agentur of the Illuminati... the international capitalists... who financed Lenin and Trosky, and obtained for them the political backing of members of the Allied Governments. This enabled them to overthrow Kerensky's Provisional government and turn the Russian administration into a totalitarian dictatorship which was operated under the direction of the Illuminati until Stalin kicked over the traces. When Stalin decided he would break with the Illuminati and establish his own form of Imperialistic World Government the world remained on the verge of World War Three until he died or was disposed of. We will let the letter speak for itself.

"In reply to your questions as how I look upon the coup d'état which we have brought about and what I expect of the future and how I evaluate the rôle and influence of the existing parties and organizations, I write you this letter, I confess, with heavy feelings. That which happened we had, naturally, not wanted. You know that our aim was limited to the achievement of a republic or a constitutional monarchy with an Emperor having nominal powers, with the dominating influence in the hands of the intelligentsia of the country, and equal rights for the Jews. We did not want complete ruin, although we knew that the coup d'état would at any rate have a bad effect on the course of the war. We assumed that power would be concentrated and would remain in the hands of the first Cabinet, that we would soon stop the temporary disorganization of the army and, if not by our own hands, then with the help of the Allies, we would attain victory over Germany, having paid for the overthrow of the Czar only with the temporary postponement of this victory. One must admit that some even in our party had pointed out the possibility of that which later happened, and we ourselves watched the organization of the working classes and propaganda in the army not without some worry. There is no escaping it, we were wrong in 1905 in one direction, now we are wrong again in the other. Then we made a wrong estimate of the strength of the men

of the extreme Right, now we did not foresee the dexterity and cons-
ciencelessness of the Socialists. The results you can see for yourself.

It is quite obvious that the leaders of the Council of Workers'
Deputies are leading us quite consciously towards financial defeat and
economic collapse. The shocking formulation of the question of peace
without annexations and compensations, apart from its complete sense-
lessness, has already now fundamentally spoiled our relations with the
Allies and undermined our credit. Of course this was no surprise for
the inventors. I shall not explain to you why all this was necessary. In
short I shall say that there was played, in part, a role by conscious
treason, in part by the wish to fish in troubled waters, in part by a
craving for popularity.

Of course we must confess that the moral responsibility for that
which happened lies on us — i.e. the Bloc of the State Duma. You
know that the firm decision to take advantage of the war in order to
bring about a coup d'état had been taken by us soon after the beginning of the war. You also know that our army was to have gone over to
the offensive, the results of which would at once have stopped, at the
root, any hints at dissatisfaction; and would have called forth in the
country an explosion of patriotism and jubilation. You will now understand why I hesitated at the last moment to give my assent in the
carrying out of the overthrow; you will also understand what must be
my inner feelings at the present time.

History will curse the leaders of the so-called proletarians, but
it will also curse us, who called forth the storm. You may ask what
one must do now — I do not know, i.e. inwardly we both know that the
salvation of Russia lies in a return to the Monarchy, we know that all
the events of the past two months clearly prove that the people were
incapable of receiving freedom, that the mass of the population, which
does not participate in meetings and congresses, is in a monarchist
mood, that very many indeed who vote for a republic, do so out of
fear. All this is clear, but we cannot admit it, an admission is the
collapse of all our work, of the whole of our life, the collapse of our
entire ideology (Weltaischauung — G.K.), of which we are the representatives. We cannot admit, we cannot counteract, we cannot join up
with those of the Right and obey them, having struggled against them
for so long and with such success — that we cannot do. That is all I
can tell you."

I only wish to make one comment. The writer admits that the
masses of the Russian people were in favour of the limited monarchy
and that those who used the Menshevists wanted to secure power for
the intelligentsia, i.e. for Miliukoff and his clique. In view of this fact
we must consider his statement that "the Russian people were not ripe
for liberty", mere demagogy. The conspirators were not interested in
giving the people liberty. They already had liberty. They were only
concerned in securing political and economic power for their own
group. The agentur of the Illuminati permitted them to proceed to
the point where they had overthrown the power of the Czar and then
weakened the Menshevists so they could form their own government.
They in turn were then subjugated by the agentur of the Illuminati
who at that time happened to be Lenin and Trotsky. Trotsky was fore-

ed to exile himself when Stalin decided he would no longer obey the Illuminati. While in exile he wrote that if the Russian White Armies had fought the Civil War under the banner of a people's Czar they would have won in two weeks. In other words if the people had the sense to return to the rule of a limited Monarchy such as we enjoy they should have been free today.

In order to prove that these things did not just happen Paragraph 14 of Article IV of the Protocols is quoted. "When the populace has seen that all sorts of concessions and indulgences are yielded it in the name of freedom it has imagined itself to be sovereign lord and has stormed its way to power, but naturally, like every other blind man it has come upon stumbling blocks, it has rushed to find a guide, IT HAS NEVER HAD THE SENSE TO RETURN TO THE FORMER STATE and it has laid down its plenipotentiary powers at OUR feet."

High Officials in both Provincial and Federal Governments to whom I have made known the facts published in this, and my previous books, almost invariably pass the same comment. "But all that you are telling us took place years ago. We know all about them. What is the use of raking over dead coals... What is the use of digging up a rotting corpse?"

If I didn't know those people had plenty of brains, and were intelligent and clever, I would have been deceived into believing they were ignorant, or gullible, or both. But they are not fools. And, if they are not fools, they must of necessity be knaves.

In Article II, Par. 2 of the Protocols the speaker is recorded as telling his listeners. "*As is well known to you, these "specialists" of ours have been drawing, to fit them for rule, the information they need from our political plans from the lessons of history, etc., etc.*" The speaker then says : "*The Goyim are not guided by practical use of unprejudiced historical observations made of the events of every moment as it passes*". If the directors of the conspiracy, who planned to destroy us, place so much importance on the study of the lessons of history, how then can we justify considering past events of no importance ? A careful study of unprejudiced history, both ancient and modern, is the only way we can fully appreciate our immediate danger and gain sufficient knowledge to take action which will offset the future plans of the enemy.

The conditions PROVED to exist in 1925-1927 still exist to-day. The treasury is still being defrauded; Corruption and graft are still rife among high officials as I will prove; Many of the agentur of the international conspirators who did the "dirty" work in 1925-1927 are now millionaires, they have turned respectable, since they qualified for membership in the new aristocracy founded on the amount of wealth a person has. They exercise tremendous influence on the members of governments and the leaders of all political parties.

Through their agenturs they contribute to the campaign funds of all political Parties. They back all "political" horses entered in the provincial and federal election "right across the board". They operate on the principle that it costs them a lot of money to make sure they have backed the winning political horse but that is of little consequence providing they can control the political stable to which horse and jockey belong. Once they control the stable they can then tell *all* jockeys, they put up on mounts, how they must ride the races in which they are entered.

I also claim history teaches that it has often been necessary to exhume corpses, some of which had been a long time dead, to prove that those bodies had been murdered and had not died from natural causes as the original death certificates indicated. I state that the empires, and the nations, which have been destroyed to date did not die natural deaths. They were murdered by the agenturs of the international conspirators. The agenturs used the unlimited amounts of money supplied by the international bankers to inject the veins of the body politic with the deadly virus of corruption and graft. When the poisoned body was sick and weak then the international conspirators turned loose their Communist 5th columns like packs of wolves to destroy them. History does not record a single successful revolutionary effort which was not planned, financed, and directed by the agents of the international conspirators.

The agenturs of the conspirators cunningly make known the failings and short-comings of their victims in such a manner that they lure thousands of citizens into the Communist or Capitalist groups of the international revolutionary movement either as party members or "Fellow Travellers". What these dissatisfied and disgruntled individuals don't realize is the fact that even if their activities proceed to the revolutionary stage the men who direct the international conspiracy have no intention of allowing the leaders of the Communist Party to rule. This fact is clearly stated in Article I, Par. 7 of the Protocols which reads. *"In our day the power which has replaced that of the rulers, who were liberal, is the power of GOLD. Time was when Faith ruled. The idea of "freedom" is impossible of realisation because no one knows how to use it with moderation. It is enough to hand over a people to self-government for a certain length of time for that people to be turned into a disorganized mob. From that moment on we get internecine strife which soon develops into battles between the classes, in the midst of which states burn down and their importance is reduced to that of a heap of ashes".*

Paragraphs 20 and 21 of the same article say. *"A people left to itself, i.e. to upstarts from its midst, brings itself to ruin by party dissensions excited by the pursuit of power, and honours, and the disorders arising therein. Is it possible for the masses of the people calmly and without petty jealousies to form judgments, to deal with the affairs of the country, which cannot be mixed up with personal interests ? Can they defend themselves from an external foe ? It is unthinkable, for a plan broken up into as many parts as there are heads in the mob, loses all homogeneity, and thereby becomes unintelligible and impossible of execution".*

Paragraph 21 continues : *"It is only with a despotic ruler that plans can be elaborated extensively and clearly in such a way as to distribute the whole properly among the several parts of the machi-*

nery of State; from this the conclusion is inevitable that a satisfactory form of government for any country is one that concentrates in the hands of ONE responsible person. WITHOUT AN ABSOLUTE DESPOTISM THERE CAN BE NO EXISTENCE FOR CIVI-LIZATION WHICH IS CARRIED ON NOT BY THE MAS-SES BUT BY THEIR GUIDE WHOSOEVER THAT PERSON MAY BE. The mob is savage, and displays its savagery at every op-portunity. The moment the mob seizes freedom in its hands it quickly turns to anarchy, which in itself is the highest degree of savagery".

Could the objectives of the international conspirators be more clearly stated ? The international conspirators deliberately undermine the economy of the countries they wish subjugated. They corrupt its government and bribe its officials in order to disgust the people and make them revolt. Then they employ the Communist Mob to over-throw the government. They give them sufficient time to introduce "Terrorism" and to bring themselves to ruin, as stated in Paragraph 20, Article I, and then the agentur of the International conspirators take over. They first deceive the masses by saying they are forming a Proletarian Dictatorship to restore law and order, but no sooner is this done than they turn the Proletarian Dictatorship into a totalitarian dictatorship. The totalitarian dictatorship is then turned into the absolute despotism of ONE man.

This plan has been put into effect in every country subjugated to date. The fact that both Eisenhower in the U.S.A., and C. D. Howe in Canada, obtained the powers to declare a state of emergency and assume despotic powers in July 1955 proves that those who direct the international conspiracy intend, in the event of war or revolution, to use them here as they used Lenin in Russia in 1917.

CHAPTER XIII

Spy Rings

S CHMIL KOGAN arrived in Canada in 1924 from Russia. He was only 18 years of age but he was a graduate of the Lenin Institute of Moscow. This is the man who afterwards changed his name to Cohen and then again to Sam Carr. (No relationship, by the way).

His first task was to travel with the harvesters going from eastern to western Canada. His job was to demonstrate "mob" psychology to fellow Communists. I actually watched this young revolutionary at work. I was able to prevent a serious riot in West Toronto station in 1925 because I was able to explain to other police officers exactly what he was trying to do. His effort to create a riot in West Toronto amongst the people on the "harvest specials" fell flat because the police refused to rise to the bait he kept throwing out to them. But a Communist never gives up and the young revolutionary succeeded in creating a full scale riot when the train reached Chapleau in Northern Ontario. The "mob" wrecked the station restaurant, and several women were brutally assaulted. One was raped. The subversives who actually caused the riot stepped into the background and left others to take the blame.

When Cohen changed his name to Sam Carr he was made head of the Canadian spy rings. After his army of spies obtained the necessary information Sam Carr put the finger on the key men. He "persuaded" them to act as "fronts" to all the different Communist organizations. Prominent men and women who had departed from the path of virtue, and others who had foolishly permitted themselves to become involved in shady politics or crooked business deals were "persuaded" to "donate" substantial sums of money, and sponsor Communist "charities" and "welfare organizations".

Communist organizations, such as the League for Peace and Democracy; the Soviet Friendship League; The Civil Rights Committee etc.; would not have any great value if the Communists couldn't get outstanding citizens, of great influence and considerable social standing, to sponsor such organizations and take an active part by "chairing" meetings etc.

Time and time again one hears the remark, "I wonder why so-and-so is mixed up with those Commies. He knows they are as phony as a three dollar bill and yet he is out night after night trying to convince the rest of us that we should all be one big happy family ?"

Investigation proved the majority of the "front men" had been caught in the meshes of either the Communist or capitalist organized spy rings. Because many of the victims are still alive we can't give their names but the story of the predicaments in which some of them found themselves is told so others may avoid a similar fate.

Case one : Involves a father and his son. The men in question belonged to one of the best known families in Canada. The father was one of Canada's top-level executives in commerce and finance. Both were members of interlocking directorates of big business. Why did both father and son lend themselves to Communist organizations and further the plans of the international conspirators in Canada ?

There were very good reasons. Sam Carr's spy rings had obtained information regarding their private lives and business transactions they just couldn't afford to have made public. To put it crudely they were the victims of blackmail. Another reason was that they were, willingly or unwillingly, also hooked up with the international capitalists conspiracy. They had to obey the orders they received from the top-level agentur of the Illuminati. I never suspected this second reason until after I had investigated the Communist angle. This is what I discovered.

While at the University the son was rather "wild". He was no different from thousands of other students in their early twenties. The Communists had members going to the University also. The "Reds" made friends with influential fellow-students. Very often, the friendships carried over into their post-graduate days.

Nothing of a serious nature happened until after the victim's marriage to a well known society debutante. Then he allowed himself to be infatuated with a "red head". Her hair was as 'red" as her convictions. These she kept carefully hidden. This girl was very well educated and exceedingly clever. She was exceptionally good-looking. The man set her up in an apartment. Everything was lovely until he wanted to terminate the "love" affair. Then, to his consternation, he found that the "red head" had obtained recordings of their conversations and photographs of their bedroom behaviour. From that day on he did as he was told — or else.

This particular man wriggled a great deal trying to get off the hook but it was no use. He was persuaded to write cheques for very considerable amounts as "voluntary" contributions to Communist sponsored organizations. He was so completely dominated by those who headed the spy rings that he nearly went insane. They forced him to lead other influential men and women into the nets they set so cleverly. This young man finally decided to tell his father everything and seek his advice.

One can realize the young man's shock when he learned his father was one of the top-level agentur of the capitalist conspirators. He admitted he had been involved in the conspiracy to bring about a one world super government since 1914. He tried to justify his actions by saying he was convinced only a one world super government could ensure peace and prosperity.

I found out that until the son was involved by the "red head" in 1928 the relations between father and son were decidedly strained if not outright unfriendly. After the son had been compromised by the Communists the relationship between father and son became decidedly cordial.

Investigation disclosed the following facts.

1. The father had been a close friend of Mackenzie King from his University days onwards.

2. He had been introduced to the Rockefeller family by Mackenzie King when the latter was employed by them to improve public relations between the Rockefellers and the American public. The public hated the name Rockefeller after the Rockefellers' armed thugs had shot and killed about thirty men, women and children during the strike at the Colorado Fuel and Iron Co. in 1914.

3. Mackenzie King, Ivy Lee, and the Rev. Frederick T. Gates, were the three geniuses who conceived the plan to re-gild the Rockefeller lily. They launched a multi-million dollar propaganda campaign which made the vast majority of American citizens believe that the Rockefeller family were a group of patriotic philanthrophists and not a family of ruthless internationalist gangsters who didn't stop at anything they thought necessary to further their plans to bring about a one-world super government.

4. After he became acquainted with the Rockefeller monopolists he was shown how to make a huge fortune quickly. When World War 1 broke out he was introduced to Canadian Government officials. In no time at all he was enjoying government contracts. He was alleged by the Press to have done so much for Canada's war effort between 1915 and 1918 that he was honoured by the British Crown for his great services to the Empire... In actual

fact he had been furthering the plan of the Rothschilds, the Warburgs, The Kuhn-Loebs, the Morgans, and the Rockefellers, to
destroy the British Empire, as will be proved in another chapter
dealing with international politics.

5. Before the international capitalist conspirators could place unlimited confidence, and trust, in this Canadian they had to place
themselves in position to be able to destroy him, his family, and
his newly acquired fortune if he so much as hesitated to obey the
commands of the supreme directorate who comprised the Illuminati. They obtained this hold by involving him, and his associates,
in shady deals with the government. They supplied food and materials for use of the armed forces which were greatly inferior in
quality to what the contracts called for.

6. One deal involved hundreds of tons of second and third grade
meat which was shipped overseas to feed Canadian troops in
Europe. This meat passed through a warehouse before being
loaded aboard ship. While in cold-storage the meat was stamped
with "A" grade markings. Men who handled the beef told me
that some of it was so rotten that it could not have been handled
if it had not been hard frozen. Checking these statements showed
that army cooks in Europe had refused to cook some of the meat.
Further investigation showed : the Port of London health authorities had condemned a whole cargo as unfit for human consumption.

7. Other subversive activities, which involved high-level capitalists,
included supplying army boots made of poor quality leather;
rifles that jammed after firing a few rounds, and collar-type life
preservers which broke the wearers neck when he jumped into
the water.

8. During the period 1930-38 the elder of these two conspirators was
mentioned in the "scandal sheets", and the Communist press. He
was accused of shady dealings in regard to stocks and bonds and
his employees. His activities in Canada were patterned on the
Rockefeller activities in the U.S.A. and the Rothschild's activities
in Europe; so much so that when the Rockefeller's name began
to stink again in the United States, because of the unethical and
treasonable conduct of members of the family in Asia, Africa,
Europe, and South America, they removed their names from the
directorates of all the companies involved and so did he. This
policy of pretending to retire from active participation in the
affairs of these international combines and cartels while secretly
deciding policy and financing and directing operations from
behind the scenes, is in keeping with the joint stock company policy
of the Illuminati.

9. Just a few years before World War Two broke out two Communists who were experts in the manufacture of synthetic fabrics
left their home in central Europe because Hitler was making conditions too hot for them. They were welcomed to Canada by the
man whose activities I was investigating. It is obvious that these
two "Reds" arrived with credentials from men who were high
level Agentur of the Illuminati because, without delay, they were

provided with a factory and the equipment necessary to manufacture synthetic wool. All this was done with the greatest of secrecy. I was manager of the Poppy Fund industrial department at that time and it was my duty to find the most favourable market for the waste products produced by the salvage division. The people I refer to offered me a better price for our "shoddy" than I could obtain elsewhere. This fact caused me to wonder. I finally obtained evidence that these foreigners, backed by some of Canada's leading industrialists, were using 60% wool, of which most was shoddy, and 40% wood-fibre to make a product which they sold to the public as "4 ply pure Scotch fingering wool". The synthetic product was such a good imitation that only an expert wool buyer could detect the fraud. The majority of the people employed in the plant were foreigners and a check showed most of they were interested in communist activities of all kinds.

Soon after the war broke out a shortage of wool developed because the Wool Control Board "froze" the supplies on hand. It was needed to manufacture blankets and uniforms for the armed forces. Notwithstanding the war-time restrictions, the retail sales organizations, with which the man I refer to was connected, continued to advertise and sell what was claimed to be 4 ply pure Scotch fingering wool. It was expensive. It was advertised as being in very short supply. I made enquiries and found I could buy the same wool wholesale *by the ton*.

The Red Cross bought several tons of it. Acting as purchasing agent for various women's auxiliaries, I purchased large quantities also. I couldn't understand how the firm could obtain in such quantities "pure Scotch four ply fingering wool", when the government restrictions were so rigid. I decided to investigate. I took a sample of the "pure" wool to an experienced wool buyer who had learned his trade in England. He examined the sample and immediately said "That is not pure wool but it's about the nearest thing to the genuine article I've ever fingered".

I next sent a sample to the University of Toronto and had it analyzed. The report came back that it was 40% wood fibre. I next had my wife knit socks for my two sons who were in the Army, and I had women whose men-folk belonged to various Toronto Units knit socks from this same wool. I had photographs taken of the "Special Wool Counter" which handled the retail sale of this wool in the store. I bought quantities of the product being sold retail as genuine four ply Scotch fingering wool" and had it compared with what we had bought wholesale to make sure they were the same quality goods. Having obtained all the evidence obtainable I waited until the first socks had been tried out on soldiers feet during a route march. The perspiration caused the synthetic wool to turn hard as a board and the men who wore the socks had to receive medical treatment for sore feet. The wearing qualities were also proved to be unsatisfactory. I took all this evidence to General D. C. Draper, who was then Chief of Police but all he said was : "I'm going to be through here shortly... I'm not getting mixed up in that mess... You'd better tell the head of the store detectives what you know".

I made the store in question take back the synthetic wool and deliver pure wool to the Poppy Fund, as my contract called for. Where they got the pure wool I don't know. I placed the evidence I had obtained in the hands of the Red Cross officials but they didn't even pay me the courtesy of telling me what action they had taken.

I fully appreciate the fact that those involved in this gigantic swindle were great supporters of the Red Cross and other charities. Why shouldn't they be? They were only giving them money they had stolen from the public and, if they hadn't given their surplus profits to charity and obtained the value of their donations in free publicity, they would have had to pay higher income and excess profit tax.

I reported the matter to the Federal Wool Board but again the matter was ignored. I found it utterly impossible to get the police or other government authorities to act against the Canadian industrialists who were involved in such a tremendous swindle. The directors of Poppy Fund Incorporated were informed but they refused to do anything. The business men involved were friends of theirs. This case illustrates how the Illuminati working at the top, and the Communist "cells" working at the bottom, co-ordinate their efforts in a way that enables them to black-mail men and women high up in society and in the top levels of our government administrations, into doing their will. If I did not still have the evidence to prove the truth of what I write I would never have dared mention this particular case.

Then a strange thing happened. I had volunteered to go back in the navy but had been rejected. But when I was trying to get action on the synthetic wool racket I suddenly received orders from Ottawa to report forthwith to the senior naval officer at Quebec, for duties connected with the naval control service for the St. Lawrence.

The point I am making is this. Sam Carr's spy ring knew all about this rotten business; so did the agentur of the International Capitalist conspirators. They in turn passed it along to the Comintern in the case of the Communist, and the Illuminati in the case of the capitalist conspirators. The directors of the World revolutionary movement are then able to use such information to further their plans. In this single case we have the top-levels of industry, top-executives in commerce, the international Red Cross, the local and Federal police all involved in a dastardly swindle. The subversives can arouse the "mob" if and when they so desire by proving that there is definitely one law for the rich and another law for the poor.

An important fact to remember is this. Large national industries and business houses which have been involved in crooked deals have *all* been forced into International mergers. Labour leaders who negotiate with management have been known to use information such as I disclose to "force" management to agree to terms. Now let us see how these conditions fit into the "long range" plans of the international conspirators. The man who was explaining the plan to top-level agentur in 1900 made it extremely clear that it was essential that chain-stores should take the place of independent store-keepers; that national business and industries should be merged; just as the financial and banking business had been merged, because when the time came to make their wrong doing known to the "mob" — See Article III, Par. 11... "We shall create by all the secret methods open to us and with the aid of gold, which is in our hands, a universal economic crisis whereby we shall throw upon the streets whole mobs of workers simultaneously in all the countries of Europe. These mobs will rush delightedly to shed the blood of those whose properties they will be able to loot. Ours they will not touch because the moment of attack will be known to us and we shall take measures to protect our own".

That the introduction of illegal practice into business and industry has been deliberate and for a specific purpose is clearly stated in Article IV, Par. 7 of the "Long Range Plan". It says :"To complete the ruin of the industry of the goyim we shall bring to the assistance of speculation the luxury which we have developed among the goyim, that greedy demand for luxury which is swallowing up everything. We shall raise the rate of wages which, however, will not bring any advantage to the workers for, at the same time, we shall produce a rise in prices of the first necessities of life... we shall further undermine artfully and deeply sources of production, by accustoming the workers to anarchy and to drunkenness and side by side therewith taking all measures to extirpate from the face of the earth all the educated forces of the goyim".

Par. 8 reads : "In order that the true meaning of these things may not strike the goyim before the proper time we shall mask it under an alleged ardent desire to serve the working classes and the great principles of political economy about which our economic theorists are carrying on an energetic propaganda".

The member of the Illuminati who was explaining the working of the "Long Range" plan told his audience that the purpose of merging small businesses and industries into larger corporations was to ensure better control. He said "Economic crises have been produced by us for the goyim by no other means than the withdrawal of money from circulation. Huge capitals have stagnated, withdrawing money from the states, which were constantly obliged to apply to those same stagnant capitals for loans. These loans burdened the finances of the state with the payment of interest and made them the bond-slaves of these capitals... The concentration of industry in the hands of the capitalists, out of the hands of small masters, has drained away all the juices of the peoples and with them also of the State".

When I was a reporter on the Toronto Star 1928-30, I was asked to investigate the mysterious death of a very prominent business man. He was highly regarded as a Churchman. He was considered as absolutely above suspicion as far as his personal habits, business dealings, and social behaviour were concerned. He belonged to the upper "400" and was related to the men who were responsible for the maintenance of law and order in the province at that time.

He had been found drowned under circumstances that made it appear he had committed suicide. I hadn't been on the case two hours before I had dug up evidence which convinced me he was hooked up with the illegal traffic and trade racketeers. I was soon convinced that he had been bumped off because he had either tried to double-cross his underworld associates or else he had tried to break away from blackmailers. The further we dug the more dirt was uncovered. The man was dead and his friends had enough influence to have the matter hushed up to avoid a national scandal. Two facts convinced me the man did not commit suicide. He was known to have been wearing a hat when he left his house late at night in response to a mysterious telephone call. The hat was not found anywhere near the body. I mentioned this fact in the story I wrote in the Toronto Daily Star. The day following, a boy found the missing hat near the pond. It must have been *placed* there afterwards by those who put the body in the water.

The other peculiar feature about that "drowning" was the fact that the man's shoes were not full of mud. How did he walk out into water deep enough to drown himself, over a muddy bottom, without getting mud over the tops of his shoes ? The third thing I noticed was the fact that there was neither mud nor dirt under his fingernails. Usually mud or dirt is found under the finger nails of a man who drowns in comparatively shallow water. A drowning man automatically clutches as he struggles but the nails on the fingers of this *dead* man looked as if they had been recently manicured. Investigation disclosed that underworld associates drove a car he owned back and forth between a garage on Queen Street west, Toronto, and Buffalo.

Another angle was that a man named M... who had done time in Kingston... acted as go-between for the business man and his underworld associates.

Case Four. Another mysterious death was that of a well known politician. He died as the result of a motor accident. At least that was the finding of the coroner's jury. The man in question was driving very fast to his home in the country about 3 A.M., when he went off the road and hit a telephone pole. The theory was that he had probably fallen asleep. Private investigation showed that this man had been worried for months before his death.

He had refused to take his most intimate friends into his confidence. I wondered if it was sheer coincidence that the "red head" who played such a prominent part in Case One, happened to be a stenographer in the politician's business office for six months before he died ?

I decided to investigate the matter from the angle of the "Red Head". She was involved. Not only had she infiltrated spies into his office, but she had also used her domination over him to infiltrate others into City Hall. They had been worked in as secretaries and stenographers of important Civic officials. Particular emphasis had been paid to the assessment department. One city father became so outraged because top secret information seemed to leak out from City Hall at the most inconvenient times that he demanded a police investigation. The police officer detailed to the job took a look around City Hall and then informed the irate official that his secretary was a member of Sam Carr's spy ring. The head of the Anti-subversive Squad added : "The other offices appeared to have their quota of subversives on the staff also"

Further investigations showed that the deceased politician had worked in his office late the night of his death. He had put all his affairs in order. He had cleaned out his desk and burned a lot of papers. Knowing the terrific pressure that is put on men who are in possession of highly confidential and secret information, I could appreciate that, after the mess he had got himself into, death was the only way to escape from the clutches of his inexorable blackmailers.

To protect his family against financial troubles he had taken sleeping pills just before he took his car from a down-town garage. They took effect soon after he got beyond the city limits. According to a milkman, he was going at least 70 miles an hour when the car first started to zig-zag and then swerved off the road and hit the telephone pole.

One man who was convicted as a spy since 1946 was very different from other people who have become associated with subversive activities.

The man in question is wealthy in his own right. He is an exceedingly clever scientist. He was very philanthropic. He detested class distinction, racial hatreds, and colour discriminations. He was a One Worlder.

He married a very beautiful Jewess several years younger than himself. By marrying her he showed his friends he was sincere in his wish to do away with racial hatreds, religious bigotry, and colour distinctions. When the war broke out he was asked to engage in research work necessary to the allied war effort. He agreed, although he would much rather have worked on research that could have been of benefit to peaceful living.

He worked long hours and did very little gadding about. Life was rather dull for his wife and she went out quite a lot and took an interest in social welfare work.

When his wife suggested it would do them both good if they entertained a little more, he agreed. When she arranged a dinner to which his scientific friends were invited, he was delighted.

The man we are discussing discovered a formula for a new and most powerful explosive. His government passed the new formula over to other allied governments but not to Russia. The man who discovered the new explosive was openly outspoken in denouncing his government's policy. Other scientists agreed with him. They claimed that *all* knowledge should be made available to the scientists of the allied governments because the solution to problems was often delayed for years, because the interchange of information was seriously restricted.

Among the guests who were made welcome at the home of the professor was a top-level authority on atomic energy. Pretending that she was suffering from boredom the older scientists's wife started a flirtation with the handsome young scientist. Intimacy developed. Knowledge of his infatuation for a colleague's wife was used to "persuade" him to pass certain valuable knowledge on to the Soviet spy ring.

When Gouzenko deserted from the Soviet Embassy and in 1946 proved a Soviet Spy Ring was operating in Canada and the U.S.A. both the older scientist and the young professor were arrested, tried, and found guilt of communicating "Top Secret" information to the Soviet's spies. Strange to relate the woman in the case went Scott-free. Investigation into this angle of the conspiracy proved that subsequent to the events related here the Canadian Scientist and an American millionaire, who has also been convicted of subversive activities, in the U.S.A., agreed to "swap" wives... and did. These people were not Communists as charged, they are agentur of the Illuminati. They contribute to Communist Front organizations, and pose as Communist Fellow Travellers, in order to confuse investigators and conceal the identity of the men who constitute the Secret Power, which directs ALL aspects of the International Conspiracy.

I proved to General Draper, Chief of the Toronto Police Force, as far back as 1939, that Communist 5th Columnists had located party members in stores, or apartments, or buildings, which gave them virtual control over every police station, fire hall, and all important cross streets leading to and from military barracks and naval and air force establishments. I proved to General Draper *that while in his office he was in a position to be covered by a Communist who ran a bootlegging joint.* General Draper was one of the few men who seemed to realize the danger from the Communist 5th Column and because he did so he was subjected to continuous criticism and attack by Communists on newspapers staffs.

Because of perfect organization, Communists, while in a decided minority, are so placed that they could absolutely paralyze the life of any city, town, and village, in Canada or the U.S.A. within a few minutes of the order to revolt being given by Moscow. To prove that this statement is no exaggeration, the Communist plan was tried out during the war by a small military force. This small force representing the Communist 5th Column descended from Camp Borden upon Toronto during the hours of darkness. When the city woke up "5th Columnists" were in control of the City Hall, all police stations, Parliament Buildings, the railway stations, the barracks, waterworks, transportation systems, bread and milk distribution centres, etc., etc. The element of surprise is, of course, all-important.

So complete are the preparations for popular revolution that the Communist spy rings have supplied the planners of wholesale murder with information regarding the personal and family habits of all important citizens. Those who will direct the revolution know exactly when the mayor and controllers leave their homes, and the route they travel to the City Hall. They know the exact time every policeman and fireman changes shifts. They know the exact location of every electric master-switch in the city. They have their list already compiled of those who are to be liquidated exactly as they had them in

Spain. In several countries already subjugated spies disguised as knife-grinders were used to gather information for the master plotters. They have recently increased in numbers in all Canadian Cities.

The revolutionary leaders have been supplied with a secret but simple code. Moscow can contact them and they can contact each other by innocent sounding messages over the air, by drawings and words in comic strips, and through the "personal" columns in the newspapers. Communists and fellow travellers have for years practised evacuating cities and towns marked for bombing by Moscow. This has been done under pretense of going on picnics and rallies and to camps and country resorts on Saturdays and Sundays. The revolutionary leaders have organized an efficient transportation system by which they can move their 5th Column quickly any place they wish. They have their own cycle and motor-cycle corps organized. In fact they haven't overlooked a single detail in preparation for the day of popular revolution.

CHAPTER XIV

The conspiracy in the social sciences

ANY group that has plotted a conspiracy against other human beings always considered how they can use poisons to help accomplish their purpose. Poisons have been used as far back as can be traced to contaminate the water supply of a city or village. When Arabs were pursued across the desert by enemies they invariably poisoned wells after they had obtained their own supply of water in order to force their pursuers to turn back. The Illuminati have used poisons, to aid in their diabolical plans, down through the centuries.

Fluorine was discovered by Scheele in 1771. Because of its intense affinities for so many other elements it was regarded as "the villain" of the chemical world and the most dangerous poison known to man. Because of its many puzzling features it was not produced in gaseous elemental purity until 1886 when Moissan accomplished this task. The leaders of the W.R.M. again ordered further research to see if "the devil's poison" could not be used to subjugate the people of a whole community more quickly than fighting them into submission. They were looking for a poison with qualities which would permit the effects to be regulated in a scientific manner.

Experimentation developed to the point where human beings were required to be used as guinea-pigs, because animals can't talk. Those conducting the experiments had to find out how varying doses of the poison affected human beings.

The experiments on human beings revealed that sodium fluoride is entirely different in its characteristics from organic calcium-fluoride which is provided by nature to take care of the requirements of the human body. No HONEST medical man or scientist will deny the truth that nature provides an adequate quantity of calcium-fluoride in water, vegetables, meat, and fish to meet the normal requirements of the human body regardless of where people live. That is one of the marvels of nature. In the frozen north the fluorine is provided in the sea-food the people eat. In many inland places it is found in suitable quantities in the waters of rivers and streams. In other places vegetables supply the body's requirements. All over the world people who ate a NATURAL diet had perfect teeth. Cavities due to caries, and deterioration of the bone structure of the jaws, did not occur until after the inhabitants of various areas began to eat foods which had been denatured in the process of manufacturing in order to give *them* a more pleasing taste or appearance. Denatured flour, refined sugar, soft drinks, over-cooked foods, and candies affect the dental health of ALL those who eat that kind of food.

If the people are really concerned about the health of their childrens' teeth, they must correct their eating habits. Medical "baby specialists" like Doctor Allan Brown argue that because people will *not* correct their eating habits, we must strengthen the dental enamel by adding fluorine to the drinking water of the whole nation. No suggestion could be more illogical. Sodium fluoride is such a deadly poison that the addition of even the most minute quantities to the amount provided by nature in a normal diet can produce immediate ill effects to the bowels, nerves, and other organs of the body. But more important still is the fact that the cumulative effects of fluorine poisoning do not, as a rule, show up for a considerable time — as long as seven to ten years — depending on the quantity of poison absorbed into the system. As the ill effects progress the victim suffers mental physical and nervous disorders which can actually cause paralysis. Serious changes in the bone structure are also found in the bodies of people who have ingested too much fluorine. Fluoridation of the drinking water could not be regulated with sufficient accuracy to eliminate serious danger. The person who drinks ten glasses a day of beverages made with fluorinated water absorbs ten times as much of the poison as the person who only drinks one glass. Tea has a very high fluorine content compared with most foods and beverages. What is going to happen to the heavy tea drinkers who brew the tea with fluorinated water ? The first visible signs that show a person is suffering from chronic fluorine poisoning are mottled teeth and finger and toe nails.

The "specialists" and "advisers" who have been promoting the idea of fluoridation have been telling a number of lies. The medical men who have advocated fluoridation must have had an ulterior motive because their education must have made the true facts regarding fluorine known to them.

Lie Number One. Those who advocate the introduction of fluoride into our drinking water claim it will give our children better teeth. Fluoride only *helps* to prevent caries. This limited benefit is obtained at the danger of losing the whole set of teeth while people are in their thirties. Dentists know that in all areas where fluoride is found in the drinking water most of the people develop gingivitis and pyorrhoea to a degree that makes extraction the only remedy.

Lie Number Two. Those who advocate fluoridation claim that little is known about the cumulative effects. They say that what little is known indicates the long range effects would not be seriously harmful to the human body. Medical men know that extensive research work has been done to ascertain the cumulative effects of fluorides. In British medical journals alone thirty four articles have been printed on the subject. More than double that number have appeared in medical journals in Canada and the United States. Because science proved the harmful cumulative effects, the British Government passed legislation which absolutely prohibited the use of fluoride as a preservative in any kind of food or beverage prepared for human consumption. Similar legislation was passed under the Pure Foods and Drug Acts in Canada and the U.S.A.

Research workers in the U.S.A. found that the accumulation of fluoride in the bones of animals over two years of age was so great that it constituted a danger to the health of people who ate foods containing bone meal. A law prohibited manufacturers from using the bones of older animals.

In Canada the findings of research workers in regard to the harmful cumulative effects of fluorides on the human body caused the government to introduce a clause into the "Pure Foods and Drugs Act" which made it unlawful for any food or beverage prepared for human consumption to contain more than .2 parts per million with the exception of certain canned fish which naturally contains a higher percentage than .2 Parts per million.

Notwithstanding the above facts Drs. Allan Brown, Drake, Tisdall, Jackson and others made up a formula for Pablum, "The perfect baby food", which included so much animal bone meal that the babies of America, who were fed "Pablum", actually took into their little bodies anywhere from 6 to 22 P.P.M. of fluoride. Research conducted by Professors Mary P. Ham and M. Doreen Smith in the Food Chemistry Department of the University of Toronto prior to 1953 proved that Pablum contained an average of from 11 to 12 P.P.M. of fluorine. This policy of serving rat poison to the infants of America continued from the day Pablum first went onto the market nearly twenty years ago until early in 1954. Medical men with whom I have discussed this matter inform me that ingestion of such quantities of fluorine cannot help but have a harmful cumulative effect.

An investigation was conducted into this matter and it was found that a number of children who had been raised on a Pablum diet had, between their fifth and seventh years, developed symptoms of chronic fluorosis. They didn't seem to know exactly what was wrong with them. One day they had bowel complaints, spasms of pain, diarrhoea, cramps, etc., etc. Another time it would be bladder trouble and chronic constipation. Mostly the pain seemed to centre around the diaphragm. The symptoms were usually obscure. Doctors usually made a diagnosis of Colitis or Coeliac. Repeated hospitalization of some children failed to obtain a more definite diagnosis. Coeliac is only a general term for ailments affecting the area of the diaphragm. When I asked several doctors if the obscure symptoms were not in keeping with chronic fluorosis, the doctors were strangely silent.

One little girl, seven years old, complained of pain in her groin. The doctors at first couldn't find any reason for the pain. The pain continued for a whole year. Finally X-rays disclosed a *decided* bone change in the hip joint. The doctors say it isn't T.B. of the bone. They say it isn't arthritis. They won't say what it is. One doctor suggested that the child be taken to a specialist and that he be asked to consider the possibility of fluorosis. If little is known about the cumulative effects how is it there is a disease known as fluorosis ?[1]

Professors Ham and Smith of the Department of Food Chemistry, University of Toronto, wrote two scientific papers on this subject : "Fluorine Balance Studies on Four Infants," and "Fluorine Balance Studies on Three Women." Both papers were published in the "Journal of Nutrition", Vol. 53, No. 2, June 1954. Investigations went to show that these two professors had been pointing out for years to those making Pablum the harmful effect 12 P.P.M. of fluorine could have on those who ate the baby food.

Investigation also proved that one doctor who was associated with those making and selling Pablum took a very serious view of the facts discovered by Professors Ham and Smith. He told the person I interviewed on this matter that he was going to insist that the formula be changed. He is alleged to have got into such a heated argument over this matter that he took a heart attack and died. THE STRANGE THING IS THAT THE FORMULA WAS NOT CHANGED UNTIL 1953 OR EARLY 1954. WHY?

I spoke to Dr. Drake, who claimed he had had most to say in preparing the original formula for Pablum, about this matter but I could get no satisfaction. He claimed the only reason the formula was changed was because the idea for the fluoridation of the water supply systems in the U.S.A. and Canada was catching on. He stated they didn't want to overdo the thing. I then wrote to Dr. Drake, who is on the Staff of the Hospital for Sick Children, and asked him a number of questions regarding Pablum. I regret to say that his replies were very unsatisfactory. In some cases they were untruthful. The most glaring untruth was his statement that the old formula didn't contain anywhere near an average of 12 P.P.M. He also stated the present formula from which Pablum is made by Mead, Johnson & Co. of Canada Ltd., only contains .2 P.P.M. the legal amount. A letter dated May 9th, 1954, written and signed by Mr. David Menzies, President of Mead, Johnson & Co. stated : "It is true... we used to incorporate powdered beef bone ash in our Pablum cereals. The chief reason was to provide adequate amounts of calcium and phosphorous to the diet. However the beef bone powder also caused the fluorine content to be raised to a point higher than normally required. We therefore changed to Tri-basic Calcium Phosphate which still supplies the same amount of calcium and phosphorous without unduly increasing the fluorine content. For dietary purposes therefore the product under the present formula is better than the product under the old." How very, very interesting. The

---

[1] The condition has now been diagnosed as Legg-Perthes Disease. Several medical men say the degeneration of the bone structure of the hip-joints could result from deficiency of vitamin 'C' and Calcium in the diet. Experts say that one of the effects of fluorine when ingested is to destroy vitamin 'C' and Calcium.

only trouble with such a statement is that Mead-Johnson & Co. advertised Pablum, as made under the old formula, as "THE PERFECT BABY FOOD". How can the new formula be better than PERFECT?

Mr. Menzies replied to another letter. It is dated May 18th, 1954. He wrote : "In reply to your latest inquiry, the fluorine content of Pablum used to be between 7.5 to 9.8 parts per million. The present Pablum has a fluorine content of between 1.5 to 2.2 parts per million". There is a lot of difference between the .2 P.P.M. Dr. Drake said it contained, and the 2.2 P.P.M. Mr. Menzies admits is still in the Pablum. It must be remembered we are discussing "The Devil's Poison", the most deadly and dangerous poison known to man. Professors Ham and Smith staked their professional reputations on the truth of their statement that the "old" formula contained from 6 to 22 P.P.M. of fluorine and that the average was 11 to 12 P.P.M. If Mr. Menzies statement regarding the contents of fluorine in the present Pablum is as far out as it was regarding the old, then there is still well over the legal limit of rat poison being shovelled down the throats of the babies of America under the false statement that Pablum is *the perfect food.*

My investigations went to show that the officials in Ottawa responsible for administering the "Pure Food and Drug Act", and enforcing its regulations, were fully informed in regard to the flagrant manner in which the manufacturers of Pablum disregarded the law, yet they took no action. WHY? Are the men who made fortunes out of this baby food above the law?

Lie number 3. Those who advocate fluoridation claim that it is possible to regulate the quantity of this deadly poison so that not more than 1 P.P.M. will be placed in our drinking water. Those who make such a statement know it is a deliberate lie. If the quantity of fluoride introduced into a supposedly scientifically prepared baby food varied from 6 to 22 P.P.M. under the old formula and varies as much as from 1.5 to 2.2 P.P.M. under the new, why should it be possible that those charged with introducing it into our drinking water would be more accurate? Those making the "perfect" baby food were supposed to be "experts" and medical "specialists"; those who look after our water works are just ordinary working men.

Lie number 4. Those who advocate fluoridation state that the majority of medical men and dentists in Canada and the United States endorse the idea. It was the fact that those who promote the idea claimed the A.M.A. and C.M.A. supported the idea that caused me to investigate this statement also. Lenin had on several occasions stressed the importance of revolutionary leaders having their "cells" obtain control of the Departments of Public Health and Mental Hygiene in the countries they planned to subjugate. I determined to find out WHY?

To deal with the first part of lie No. 4. A poll of medical men in Toronto showed that the vast majority were NOT in favour of fluoridation. The vast majority did not want to commit themselves. Inquiry amongst this group showed they were scared to death of what the C.M.A. might do to them if they dared to openly oppose those who were sponsoring this form of mass medication. Most of the doctors I spoke to demanded a promise that the talk be considered confidential.

Just a few were more concerned with the public welfare than their own interest and said I could use their names and give their reasons for opposing fluoridation. It would appear that these courageous medical men had tried to have the "free" press publish what they knew about fluorides but without success.

Before quoting the medical authorities who oppose fluoridation we will examine part two of lie No. 4. Those who promote the project stated that the A.M.A. and the C.M.A. both endorsed the idea. What do the A.M.A. and the C.M.A. consist of? Let's examine the history of the A.M.A. The authority we quote on this subject is Dr. E. M. Josephson, M.D. author of two famous books "Your life is their toy", sub-title "Merchants in Medecine" and, "Rockefeller Internationalist", Dr. Josephson was born in Baltimore, Maryland, 1895. He studied at John Hopkins and Columbia Universities. He obtained his B.Sc. and M.D. degrees in 1916-1917. He became Assistant Medical Director of the American Red Cross in Europe in 1921. He then engaged in studies in research in France and Germany returning to America to start practice. He specialized in diseases of the eyes, ears, nose and throat. His numerous researches and discoveries earned for him a reputation of international prominence. Backed by this reputation he became a fearless fighter for medical, social service, and public health reforms.

In addition to medecine Dr. Josephson made a study of sociology and economics to enable him to reason out WHY it was that the A.M.A. were trying to obtain absolute control of all doctors, medical institutions, etc. Dr. Josephson tells how "Doc" George H. Simmons, a monumental figure in the field of medical quackery and racketeering, emerged upon the scene in 1899 and gradually took over the rule and control of the A.M.A. (American Medical Association).

Simmons arrived in America from England in 1884. There can be no doubt that he was an agent of the directors of the international conspiracy. He first launched into Journalism in order to obtain publicity and a following. Then he took up politics in order ot make the necessary contacts among legislators. Having paved the way he set out to obtain absolute control of the medical profession, the hospitals, and institutions of learning, for his masters. Without any authentic medical education, or training, "Doctor" Simmons launched into business as an advertising quack and declared himself a "universal specialist in deseases of men, women, and children". He started "The Lincoln Medical Institute" and boldly announced that he had "Accommodation for a limited number of ladies in my residence". This was a stock phrase used by professional abortionists.

"Doctor" Simmons preyed so cleverly upon the sins, weaknesses, and sufferings of humanity that he became wealthy. He was able to obtain the backing of shady politicians. By reason of the influence of these international conspirators he obtained an appointment as Secretary of the Nebraska State Medical Society, and of the Western Surgical and Gynecological Society. Then, hooking up his journalistic experience with his medical achievements, he became editor of the "Western Medical Review" and started out to control the practice and thinking of the whole medical profession. His purpose was to make it conform with the policy of those who planned a One World Government.

To legalize the next steps in his programme he obtained a medical degree. "Doctor" Simmons was actually practicing as a quack in Lincoln, Nebraska, when registered as a student at the Rush Medical College, Chicago, which granted him his "degree". In 1899, "Doctor" Simmons seized control of the A.M.A. In order to control the A.M.A., he had himself appointed "organizer" to build up and select membership; Secretary to control its business; and editor of its journal to enable him to control the thinking of the members.

In 1901, at the St. Louis Convention "Doc" Simmons was elected "General Manager" of the Association. The directors of the international conspiracy then surrounded "Doc" Simmons with a notorious gang of racketeers whom they appointed his 'Specialists" and "Advisers". Just to make sure "Doc" did not grow too big for his britches the conspirators had the Secretary of the Kentucky State Board of Health appointed as one of his trusted lientenants. This "gentleman" was once arrested for a shortage of over $62,000.00 in his accounts. He didn't even trouble to deny the charges. He walked into court and waved a "Governors Pardon" under the nose of the Judge. Amongst other One Worlders placed to keep Doc Simmons in line was Dr. Morris Fishbein, who succeeded him in control of the A.M.A. when Simmons died in 1937.

Fishbein was ordered to cloak the A.M.A. with an air of respectability in exactly the same way the racketeers blossomed into society as philanthrophists after committing every crime listed on the calendar to obtain their wealth in the first place. Dr. Josephson says on page 14. "Fishbein proved himself a worthy successor... he carried the association to new heights of quackery and of powers and dominion over the medical profession, medical education, the Press, and the drug, and allied interests."

To prove how the public is deliberately deceived by the daily Press, in which the vast majority have been taught to believe implicitly. I quote from the influential New York Times. On September 2nd, 1937, the editors published an obituary to "Doctor" Simmons, headed "NOTED FOR WAR ON QUACKS"... well knowing that Simmons was the biggest and most ruthless quack of them all.

Dr. E. M. Josephson devotes 255 pages to proving how your life and mine have been made the toy of the merchants in medicine since Dr. Morris Fishbein took over direction of the A.M.A. in 1937. In the U.S.A. Fishbein is referred to as "The Hitler" of medicine. His lieutenant Olin West is called "The Goering" of medicine. The power exercised by the A.M.A. is so great that honest and respectable Physicians and Surgeons are forced to become members and once they do they are silenced by various means.

Just before the U.S.A. entered the First World War the A.M.A. obtained control of the medical aspects of military conscription so the international conspirators, who had pushed America into the war, could carry on their policy in this all important branch of the armed forces.

In 1917 the A.M.A. had the distinguished Professor G. Frank

Lydsten, of the College of Physicians and Surgeons, barred from military service because he exposed the corruption within the A.M.A. It was afterwards acknowledged that the records used to accomplish this purpose were false. If the A.M.A. can penalize a prominent physician and surgeon for speaking the truth it is only logical that the "ordinary" practitioner keeps his mouth tightly shut.

In June 1940 Dr. Nathan B. Van Etten was elected President of the A.M.A. He stated in an affidavit taken by the Notary Public, Bronx County, (Clerk's No. 197, Registers No. 235-M-41) on the 29th day of June 1940 that his sole office was that of president but that he had no executive or administrative duties. He swore the A.M.A. was completely controlled by Olin West and Fishbein and their own ring.

In Canada I had the opportunity to discuss the C.M.A. with many prominent medical men. From these conversations I reached the conclusion that a "Gang" controlled the Canadian organization in exactly the same way a "Gang" had been proved to control the A.M.A. Most of those who took me into their confidence asked me not to mention their names. Sir Frederick Grant Banting is now dead. Just before he took off on the ill-fated flight to England he told me a great deal about his opinion of the C.M.A., the A.M.A. and the Canadian Institute of Mental Hygiene. Dr. Banting and Dr. Best were both offered enormous fortunes to sell themselves lock-stock-and barrel to the agentur of the international conspirators. It is to their eternal credit and glory that they refused. Doctor Banting told me matters concerning his private life which showed how ruthless and unscrupulous the agents of the conspirators can be. What I learned involved a man I had long suspected used his literary abilities in so-called health magazines to cover his real activities as an agent for the Capitalists conspirators. This information was of such a startling nature that when I heard Dr. Banting had been killed I suggested to Naval Intelligence that the death of Canada's most famous research worker should be investigated further to make sure sabotage wasn't the cause of the plane crash. Dr. Banting was going on a very important and top-secret mission at the time. In 1945 I faced the intellectual with the statements Dr. Banting had told me about his despicable conduct and he admitted their truth. This man was intimately connected with the Health League of Canada and with those trying to force the Freudian theories in regard to psychiatry upon the medical profession and the public.

Now we will look at the B.M.A. Dr. Clarence Routley a CANADIAN was elected President of the British Medical Association in 1955. WHY? Dr. Routley is also president of the C.M.A. He has not been actively engaged in medical practice since the end of World War One. He has however, knowingly, or unknowingly, been furthering the medical phase of the international conspiracy since 1921. He was the creator of the World Health Organization with the U.N.O. He is a close associate of Dr. Brock Chisholm who advocates solving all racial problems by mixing Whites, Blacks, Reds, and Yellow races into one big slithering squirming mass of degenerated humanity. The director-general of the World Health Organization recently advocated miscegenation on a global scale also.[2] An English member of the World Health Organization recently advocated in the public press that in order to help these medical geniuses improve the health problems of the human race the U.N.O. should be asked to provide sufficient money to supply a "Safe, simple, and fool-proof means of contraception to all human beings capable of performing sexual relations". What nice, clean, healthy minded people are plotting our fate as human guinea-pigs. They must actually believe Satan's plan for creation is better than God's plan.

Investigations conducted to find out WHY the directors of the Red Cross, and those of the Poppy Fund, refused to prosecute those who, in 1939-1940, sold them synthetic wool at the price of pure wool brought to light the fact that those who direct all aspects of the International Conspiracy have worked their agentur into positions from which they can control the policies of professional social welfare agencies and organized charities. The vast majority of the "Workers" are honest, sincere, and charitably disposed Christian people, but they would do well to examine closely those who control the Budget Committees and enjoy the well paid executive positions. To illustrate what I mean. Basil O'Conner served without pay as head of the American Red Cross until General G. Marshall took over in 1949, The General, who helped put hundreds of millions of people under Communist control, drew $18,761 a year retirement pay but those who worked him into the position to control the American Red Cross "forced" him to accept $22,500 a year as salary and $6,000 additional as expense money. General Marshall is not a Communist but he was groomed, and educated, and trained, from early childhood to be a good and faithful servant of the Capitalist Internationalists. Because he was obedient to their commands he was made a Political Five Star General, a rank he could never have hoped to obtain had he been subject to the recognized rules for promotion.

Nearer home those who control the Community Welfare chests subsidize those who put into effect the international conspiracy, as detailed in the Protocols, and sell the public Satanism under the guise of "Modern Thinking", as advocated by National Health Leagues, and Mental Health Associations. Thus we see how the cunning directors of the international conspiracy arrange matters so the charitable and generous hearted public pay to put into effect their secret plans, and further their diabolical ambitions.

The beautifully printed annual report for the "Red Feather Campaign" Toronto, 1954, disclosed the fact that the budget committee of the Community Chest voted $82,000. to the Health League of Canada and $23,000. to the Mental Health Association of Canada in 1953-1954. Dr. Gordon Bates is head of the H.L.C. He like Dr. Routley has not actively practiced medicine for many years, yet he spent most

---

[2] A Reuter Press dispatch from Tokio dated Oct. 28th. 1955 stated that Doctor Elmer Pendell of Baldwin-Wallace College, Berea, Ohio, claimed that "The reckless reproduction of our relatively brainless citizenry has caused a decline in human standards." He advocated that "the government should establish a "legal" family limit and sterilize mothers who exceed that limit". That is exactly the kind of legislation that will be enforced if we permit the establishment of any kind of a One World Government.

of 1953-1954 promoting fluoridation throughout Canada. He bought valuable advertising space. His travelling expenses must have been great. It must be presumed that money donated for Charity to the Community Chests of Canada, is being used to promote this devilish project.

The Medical, Dental, Health, and Mental Hygiene Organizations are tightly controlled by those who direct the international conspiracy. Only a certain percentage of the medical men, and dentists, belong to the associations.

The A.M.A. and C.M.A. do not, as most people are led to believe, express the honest opinion of the best brains in the Medical and Dental professions.

Research into fluorine in food has been going on for years in the University of Toronto. One professor was provided with four bodies. His instructions were to ascertain the amount of fluorine in the bones of those cadavers. Two bodies were those of young people in their late teens or early twenties. The other two were the bodies of elderly people who had lived beyond three score years and ten. The professor reported that he found no appreciable difference in the amounts of fluorine found in the bodies of the four dead people. This particualr professor supports fluoridation. His report was calculated to remove the fears some medical men had regarding the harmful cumulative effects fluorine could have on the system, organs, and bony structures of the human body. His report was allowed to go out as official.

What those who issued this false report did not know was the fact that the feet of these same bodies were secured and tested by another fully qualified research worker who proved that the amount of fluoine in the bones of the old people was many, many, times as great as the quantity found in the bones of the young people. This professor's findings proved that fluorine does accumulate in the bones of human beings as it does in those of cattle. We may well ask how it is possible to perpetrate such a fraud in the research department of a University like Toronto's ?[a]

Having obtained this information, I asked a friend to write to Dr. Sydney Smith head of the University and ask him if any research work had been done into fluorine poison in the University of Toronto which, if made known publicly, would enable the voters to arrive at a sound understanding before they were asked to vote. The President's reply was in the negative. What reason would a man in his position have for adding another untruth to the many? Surely he must know what is going on in the University.

It was shortly after I sent the information I had obtained regarding fluorine to responsible authorities in our municipalities that those promoting fluoridation switched their policy. They claimed the matter should be settled by the medical and dental 'specialists" and "advisers" and not by a vote of the people. What cunning ! What guile !

[a] Information received since this was written proves that the Professor referred to also gave inaccurate reports when asked to do research work into the amount of fluoride Pablum contained and the percentage of fluoride retained in the body after ingestion. He has been closely associated with those who introduced Pablum and marketed it as 'The Perfect baby food'.

Important evidence regarding the harmful cumulative effects fluorine has on the systems, organs, and bones of human beings was obtained when Dr. Leo Spira did extensive research work to find out why so many men and women he examined after they joined the army were suffering from chronic fluorosis.

Investigation proved that fluorine had been introduced into the British working man's beer and ale during the early part of the century when the agents of the International Chemical Combine sold it as "The perfect" preservative for foods and beverages manufactured for human consumption.

The only logical reason fluorine would be introduced into an alcoholic beverage would be to study its effect on those who drank it. Beer and ale don't need added preservatives. The Public House in England is the working Man's club. Each Public House had its own clientele. It was a simple matter for those conducting the experiment to observe the immediate and cumulative effect this poison had on those who drank it. Among the patrons who frequented their favorite Public House regularly were men and women who were abstemious; those who drank moderately; and those old topers who filled themselves up to the gills every night. All of them absorbed different amounts into their systems. None of them ever suspected they were being used as human guinea-pigs. The after effects they suffered from fluoride poisoning was usually attributed to over indulgence.[4]

The symptoms of fluoride poisoning are obscure. They are similar to those which accompany many other ailments. A mild overdose of fluoride produces intestinal cramps, slight nausea, dry tongue and debility, with an abnormal amount of perspiration; A slighty increased dose produces an ailment which could easily be mistaken for "Summer complaint"; spasms of abdominal pain, violent disturbance to the nerves of the diaphram, vomiting and diarrhoea. A slighty stronger dose could easily be mistaken for ptomaine poisoning. A little more would produce complete prostration and loss of control of stomach, bowels, and bladder which could render the victims incapable of doing anything to help themselves for a period of one day to a week. A slightly stronger dose could be fatal. Fluorine is truly "The devil's poison".

The medical men who set themselves up as "specialists" and "advisers" on matters of public health know what I say is true. The editors of the daily newspaper have been fully informed regarding all these facts, Municipal, Provincial, and Federal authorities have been informed. The conspirators have such control of the press that it has proved impossible to warn the public regarding their danger.

Because scientists learned so much about fluorine poison the men who plot and plan the international conspiracy realized only one problem remained which prevented them using it for revolutionary purposes. The problem was how to have sufficient quantities of fluoride always stock-piled ready, and available, at the sources of the drinking water supply systems without creating suspicion ? The answer was

[4] When fluoride was proved to be in the ale in harmful quantities those responsible explained that it must have been introduced in the preparation used for cleaning out the boilers and fermentation vats. Beer drinkers should make sure the same slow poisoning isn't going on in Canada and the U.S.A.

to force fluoridation upon the citizens by stating that such mass medication would improve the teeth of their children.

Dr. Leo Spira M.D., Ph.D., M.R.C.S., London, England, Vienna, and New York, is considered the most outstanding authority on fluorine in the world. He reported the cumulative effects of fluorine on the human body to the United States Senate only recently and yet the devilish plot to put fluorine in the drinking water has been backed by officials in Washington since an ex-employee of the Aluminum Co. of America was made Secretary of the Public Health Administration.

Dr. Spira states that as the result of using aluminum cooking ustensils, plus the fluorine ingested with a normal diet, thousands of people are now suffering from chronic fluorosis which the medical men they consult diagnose as other ailments. While mottled teeth is a sure visible indication of chronic fluorine poisoning a person with mottled teeth should be asked the following questions.

1. Do you suffer from constipation to the extent that you have to frequently use aperients ?
2. Do you suffer from "pins and needles" in your fingers or toes ? Do they go numb ?
3. Do you suffer from boils ?
4. Do you have heat-spots, heat-bumps, or rashes ?
5. Do you ever notice loose, shrivelled skin between your toes ? Does it peel ?
6. Are your finger nails brittle ? Do they break easily ?

If you have mottled teeth or nails and can answer "Yes" to one or more of the above questions that is a further indication that you are suffering from the cumulative results of fluorine poisoning.

The symptoms encountered in more severe cases of chronic fluorine poisoning, which can result from ingesting just a little of the poison regularly, are as follows :

Constipation alternating with Diarrhoea.
Frequent attacks of common colds; running nose; sneezing; sore throats;
Severe gas formation.
Hoarseness; Huskiness of voice.
Neuritis and neuralgiae.
Bronchitis; catarrh of upper air passages.
Tender calves.
Irritation of the skin.
"Pins and Needles"; Deadness and numbness in the limbs, particularly hands and fingers.
Conjunctivitis, lachrymation.
Bleeding of the gums.
Excessive salivation, dribbling at the corner of the mouth.

Disturbances of hearing.
Excessive perspiration.
Skin eruptions; eczema.
Hardening of the skin on palms and soles.
Warts.
Loss of hair.
Changes in finger and toe nails.
White specks or lines on finger or toes nails.
Brown patches on skin.
General debility. Weakness, tiredness.
Varicose veins.
Swelling of the legs.
Mental disturbances.
Chronic gastric and duodenal disturbances.
Brights disease.

It is estimated that if people continue to use aluminum cookings utensils, and even as little as 1 P.P.M. of fluoride is added to the drinking water the doctors and dentists will begin to reap a real financial harvest because the cumulative effects of the poison will cause people to become steadily poorer in health as they advance in age. Diet high in calcium and vitamins "B" and "C" can help but will not cure those suffering from chronic fluorosis.

Parents of children raised on any of the so called "Perfect Baby Foods", which contained animal bone meal, should pay particular attention to their complaints.

The doctors said the child, referred to on page 163, would have to wear a special brace and splints for at least three years. Before subjecting her to this refined form of torture the parents placed the child on a diet high in calcium and vitamin "B". Subsequent X-ray showed great improvement. The special brace and splints were unnecessary.*

Every parent, whose child has been diagnosed as suffering from Colitis or Coeliac, should check throughly to make sure their son or daughter is not suffering from chronic fluorine poisoning.

The study of fluorine gives us another perfect example of how the men of the "Hidden Government". The Illuminati, who direct the international conspiracy, use the capitalists subversives at the "Top", and the Communist subversives at the "Bottom", to further their plans to bring about a One World Government. The international combines make huge fortunes out of the sale of aluminum utensils. They will make more millions if the public allow fluoridation to be put into effect because sodium fluoride is a by-product from the manufacture of aluminum.

If fluoridation is permitted this deadly poison will be stock-piled in sufficient quantities, at the very source of our water supplies, to permit subversives to use it in the event of a revolution. I can state, without fear of contradiction, that in England, during World War Two, water supplying army camps was found to contain as much as 1.4 P.P.M. of fluorine. Top level officials in the government absolutely refused to permit the medical officers, attached to the units, affected, to trace the source of the poison. Orders were given that the medical officers who discovered the presence of fluorine in the water were not to be permitted to enter the pumping stations at the source of the water supply. The fluorine introduced into the camps drinking water was in addition to the chloride used for killing bacteria. If Doctor Spira had not diagnosed cases of fluorine poisoning the fact that it was being introduced through the water supply system would never have been known or suspected. And still advocates of fluoridation claim that fluorine could play no part in a subversive conspiracy. I say they lie, and they know they lie. They lie for a purpose.

Fluoridation is one of the most dastardly plots ever attempted against the human race. I will quote a few authorities to prove that statement. Charles A. Brusch B.S., M.D. of Brusch Medical Centre, Cambridge, Mass. has circulated a scientific paper entitled "The action of fluorides on the body". For my purpose it is sufficient to quote the summary. He says "Artificial fluoridation affects every

---

* The calcium diet worked wonders. X-ray showed great improvement. The painful brace and splints have been discarded.

cell and system of the body... This forced experiment, with a protoplasmic poison which all must ingest, is mass medication is without parallel in the history of medicine... can cause symptoms of disease such as allergy, internal, and gastric upsets, such as colitis, blood conditions, gland and nervous trouble, diabetes, arthritis, muscular weaknesses, hardening of the arteries, kidney trouble and a long list of other serious diseases''.

Dr. E. H. Bronner of Los Angeles, California supports what I said about Lenin emphasising the importance of getting ''cells' into the Public Health Departments of our cities and towns. In a warning he sent out he asked. "Are our civil defence directors awake to the perils of water poisoning by fluoridation''.

As the Director of Civil Defence for the Sudbury district in Northern Ontario 1950-1951, I repeatedly warned authorities in local, provincial, and federal governments of the danger of fluoridation. I became the target for a ''smear campaign''. Fluoridation was put into effect in Sudbury. Many other centres of population in Canada, and over 125 in the U.S.A., have adopted fluoridation. Other centres are being brainwashed into following their example. In addition to being the most deadly poison fluorine is the cheapest, and the most effective poison known to chemists. It is colorless, odorless, tasteless. There is no known antidote. Once the machinery is installed in the pumping stations, and the necessary quantities of the poison are on hand, one turn of a valve, by one man, can render every person drinking the water helpless. With this ''Devil's poison'' it is possible to regulate the degree of disability and the length of time the immediate effects will continue. It is a very simple matter for the enemy 5th column to draw off enough water for their own use before the diabolical plot is put into effect. Experiments in fluoride poisons were conducted in the Soviets between 1919 and 1939. My informant told me ''Public officials and members of the Communist Party drank only pure water obtained from wells and springs''. WHY?

Dr. George L. Walbott, M.D., F.A.C.P., F.A.C.A., F.A.A.A. 2930 W. Grand Blvd. Detroit, 2, Michigan conducted extensive research into the effects of fluoride poison. He also published a paper on the subject in January 10, 1955. This paper is fully documented. He quotes 55 authorities in all. He unreservedly denounced the policy of fluoridation.

Congressman A. L. Miller, M.D. former state health Director for Nebraska, stated he had at first been misguided by the Public Health Service but later obtained overwhelming scientific evidence that definitely changed his mind on the matter of fluoridation.

Mrs. Lydia Arsens, M.L.A. stated before the Legislature in B.C. February 22, 1955, ''Among hundreds of professional men who strongly oppose fluoridation are such outstanding authorities as :

Dr. Geo. A. Swendeman, D.D.S. Grand Forks, N.D.
Dr. Chas. T. Betts, D.D.S.   Toledo, Ohio.
Dr. Royal Lee, D.D.S.   Lee Foundation of Nutritional Research, Milwaukee, Wis.
Dr. McCay   Cornell University (Prof. of Nutrition)

Dr. H. V. Smith   University of Arizona.
Dr. Paul Manning, D.D.S.   Springfield, Mass.
Dr. L. Spira, M.D., Ph.D., M.R.C.S. Author "The Drama of Fluorine".
Dr. F. F. Heyroth, M.D.   Cincinnati, Ohio.
Dr. Hans Neumann, M.D.   Columbia University
Dr. Geo. O. Boucher, M.D.   Long Branch, California.

The above named men are specialists in their field of medicine and research. They are not a bunch of Quacks, or men who call themselves doctors, although they haven't treated even a sick dog in years.

Charles Eliot Perkins biochemist and physioligist is internationally known for his original discoveries in the field of Cancer Research. He says, ''Chronic fluorine poisoning by ingestion in food or water can become a potent factor in accelerating the cancer progress. Kidney, heart, nerve, and brain tissues are violently attacked. Mental degeneration is rapid''. What more evidence is necessary to prove that the only reason the TRUTH regarding this matter has not already been made known to the public is because the conspirators control most outlets of public information.

Those directing the international conspiracy also work to prevent human beings from obtaining benefit from the discoveries made by men the internationl conspirators are unable to control. One of the most glaring cases of this kind is the persistent way the A.M.A. has persecuted Dr. Harry M. Hoxsey of Dallas, Texas. This man is a millionaire. He is no quack. He simply wants the public to benefit from his method of treating cancer patients. He has cured many people whose cases were pronounced hopeless by doctors who were experts in the of so called orthodox methods approved by the A.M.A. Dr. Hoxsey treats the blood of cancer patients. In April, 1954 ten doctors spent five days, April 8th to 12th, at the Hoxsey clinic in Dallas. They inspected the facilities and examined 21 people, who had been cured by Dr. Hoxsey after being pronounced incurable by other medical specialists. After five days ten doctors signed a statement saying, ''We, as a committe, feel that the Hoxsey treatment is superior to such conventional methods of treatment as X-ray, radium, and surgery. We are willing to use it in our office, in our practice, on our own patients, when at our discretion it is deemed necessary''. The ten doctors from many states all signed. And yet those who control the A.M.A. threaten to take away the degrees of any nurse who serves in Dr. Hoxsey's clinics.

Dr. Wm. F. Koch is also curing cancer patients who had been pronounced incurable by their own medical advisers. Why is Dr. Fishbein of the A.M.A. still doing everything in his power to block the efforts of these men to relieve human suffering? If those who control the funds allocated to Cancer research where honestly interested in getting at the roots of the cause of cancer, why have they persistently refused to spend one red cent to prove or disprove the treatment methods used by Drs Hoxsey and Koch? Dr. Hoxsey states cancer starts in the blood stream and he treats the source of the infection. He does not believe in the knife. He is curing cases which remained malignant after the victims had been subjected to all kinds of major surgery without good results.

There is not space to deal with the Polio question. I have studied this terrible scourge since the terrible epidemic in 1934. It is with a heavy heart that I must admit many doctors buried their many mistakes. Everyone has heard of the terrific fight the Australian Nurse Miss Kenny, put up to stop medical mal-practice that was doing polio victims more harm than good. The Medical Association control everything its members wish to put in the Press and that is bad. I know that war surplus ether was bought up by an allegedly reputable drug company. The cans containing the ether were from seven to twelve years old. The ether had deteriorated and it killed a considerable number of people undergoing only minor operations. I obtained the facts of this story, and, although I was employed as a reporter at the time, the C.M.A. were able to have it hushed up. WHY?

Please don't think I only see the dark side of the medical situation. I know plenty of doctors who have treated, and cured, dozens of cases who had been mistreated in the military hospitals. Three of the most outstanding pathologists in Canada stated that cases of mistreatment and false diagnoses were a disgrace to the medical profession in view of the knowledge and facilities that were now available to the profession.

This statement was submitted to Prime Minister King and his Minister of Health, Dr. King. It accomplished nothing worth while. Only the united weight of public opinion, properly directed and applied, will defeat the diabolical plans of the international conspirators who use Communism at the "bottom" and selfish capitalism at the "top" to further their secret plans and ambitions in regard to mass-medication. One does not need much imagination to realize what a financial harvest doctors and dentists will reap as the result of chronic fluorine poisoning if it is put in our water.

MOSCOW'S ATTITUDE TOWARDS RELIGION AND "RED" PROPAGANDA

Regardless of what propaganda experts may say, the evidence in this chapter will prove it is the intention of the Illuminati to ultimately erase the memory of religions which teach belief in a Supreme Being and a Life in a Hereafter from the minds of human beings.

Louis Budenz wrote a book exposing Communists and their methods of infiltration. Budenz says "For instance in New York City, Michael J. Quill functions as a leader of the Transportation Workers Union, the membership of which is overwhelmingly Catholic. Quill knows I have met him in Communist National Committee meetings. He knows we sat next to each other and voted for a Control Commission for the Communist Party. He knows we discussed together, on a trip from Philadelphia, his Catholic affiliations and his devotion to the Communist Party. He knows the Communists joke about how "Quill' leads the Irish around by the nose.

"Quill has never deviated from the Communist Party line and policy. Communists use two methods to carry their deception against the Church and Catholic Unions. The first method is to infiltrate

Communists into the ranks of Catholic Congregations, and Catholic organizations, where they can mislead honest men and women into doing the work of the conspirators. They get a few Catholics muddled and disgruntled and then they work upon them to become under-cover Communists. Nominally they remain "in the Church", but actually they use that advantage ground to spread Communist propaganda.

"The second method is to make false statements. The "Red" leaders say they will respect the Catholic right to worship according to their own beliefs. This is one of their most diabolical hoaxes by which they lead Catholics towards the Slave State. The current campaign against the Roman Catholic Church announced in THE NEW TIMES, and picked up by Communists everywhere, has only one goal, the destruction of Catholic worship. That, I found out definitely in the discussions on the Catholic question within the Communist executive".

What is true of infiltration into the Catholic Church is true of other denominations also. Whether the congregations know it or not the influence which formed the National Council of the Churches of Christ, is subversive also.*

Many people turn to Communism because they have become convinced that Christianity is a word rather than a live and practicing religion. The principal line of attack is based on the argument that those who profess the Christian religion failed to put the principles of Christian charity into practice in their daily lives.

The other attack is based on the Marxian argument that religion is the opiate of the people used by selfish Churchmen, Capitalists, and Imperialists to keep the public under control by trying to make them believe that everything that happens is God's will, while in actual fact wars and revolutions are a curse self-inflicted upon the human race because we allow the Powers of Evil and Darkness to usurp our God-given "Rights" and "Prerogatives". We get involved in wars because we refuse to put God's plan for Creation into effect. We punish ourselves. God gave us our free wills. It is our own fault if we make fools of ourselves.

Christian Religions have a hard and bitter battle on their hands if they wish to stem the tide of Communist propaganda. Our weakness lies in the fact that we have retreated into our churches and used them as citadels. Subversive Missionaries are out mixing with the public. Professional Charity is in the control of One Worlders. They have taken away from Christians the opportunity to "Feed the Hungry, clothe the naked, visit the sick, comfort the imprisoned and bury the dead". Prayers without good works are of no avail.

The Secret Powers behind the World Revolutionary Movement concentrate on having their agents infiltrate into the various Christian denominations because they realized that organized Christians could start a Crusade and cause them serious trouble.

As far back as 1944 subversives working amongst the Clergy in England had progressed to the extent that they had enlisted the aid of Bishops, to organize the Council of Clergy and Ministers for Com-

---

*The N.F.C.L. will supply literature dealing with subversion within religious communities upon request.

mon Ownership. This was an extreme Marxist organisation. It was formed at Leicester in May 1942. The Bishop of Bradford was President, the Rev. Gilbert Cope of Birmingham was Secretary. Membership consisted exclusively of clergy and ministers of religion "who believe that they ought to play an active part in the change from private ownership to common ownership, which is the next stage of our national economic and political evolutions". (Statement of Aims.)

The organ of the Council was a monthly publication entitled *Magnificat*, and its members were recommended to read the following periodicals : *Left News*, *Labour Monthly*, *Religion and the People*, (an extreme Socialist news letter produced by a Birmingham Clergyman) *Tribune* and the *Daily Worker*. A number of Communist books were also recommended.

In a foreword to Christians in the Class Struggle, written by the Secretary, the Bishop of Bradford writes :

"Our present economic system is immoral and un-Christian. Its appeal is nakedly to self-interest; its technique is economic competition. It leads to the exploitation of the weak by the strong; it promotes mass selfishness, class-division; and international war. It is a worship of Mammon and, as such, is a moral outrage..."

In this pamphlet is a defence of the "Class Struggle", and an attack on the Labour Party and the Trade Union leaders for collaboration with the capitalists.

The writer says :

"Is it not obvious that if we are to have Socialism — real and permanent Socialism — all the fundamental opposition must be "liquidated" (i.e. rendered politically inactive by disfranchisement, and if necessary, by imprisonment ?... or death ?)" (author's comment).

In one issue of *Magnificat* the National Anthem was described as a "dogmatic doggerel... invented to bolster up the claims of the German-speaking occupants of the English Throne". As an alternative to the present words, the C.C.M.C.O. suggested a "Peace Version", of which the following is the first verse :

O Lord our God arise,
Increase monopolies,
After the war.
Confound all Socialists,
Frustrate economists
Who show up all our twists
Upon the poor.

The C.C.M.C.O. is a Marxist organization formed to encourage clergy to preach the Class war from their pulpits.

Thus we find the Secret Power behind the world revolutionary movement within the religious denominations to-day, doing exactly what the original Clique did within the lodges of Continental European Freemasonery in 1773-1789. Yet we should not be surprised.

The Epistles, (Ephesians 6, 10-17) says *"Brethren, be strengthened in the Lord and in the Might of His Power. Put on the armour of God, that you may be able to stand against the wiles of the devil.* FOR OUR FIGHT IS NOT AGAINST FLESH AND BLOOD, BUT AGAINST PRINCIPALITIES *AND THE* POWERS, *AGAINST THE* WORLD RULERS OF THIS DARKNESS, AGAINST THE SPIRITUAL FORCES OF WICKEDNESS ON HIGH. *Therefore take up the armour of God, that you may be able to resist in the evil day"*, etc.

Canadian and American Communist delegates, reported to Moscow's emissaries at the London Conference in 1944 they had agents in every radio station; on every newspaper staff; every news agency; and in every movie studio in the United States and Canada. The Committee appointed to investigate Un-American activities in the United States, proved that Communist infiltration had progressed to an alarming extent.

The subversives policy is to create a feeling of disrespect and shame in the minds of the masses towards religious and democratic institutions by emphasizing the weaknesses and abuses which occur because of human frailety. A world-wide campaign of slander and detraction against clergymen, religious and democratic institutions is always at work trying to destroy the faith of practicing Christians.

When engaged in the Far East Trade 1910-1913 I noticed that young apprentices were "worked on" by Bolsheviks amongst the crew. The usual argument was : "Why waste your time going to hear clergymen' who don't practice what they preach ?" — They would say : "The motto of most clergyman is "Don't do as I do. Do as I tell you to do". This line of argument was usually followed by an offer to prove that clergymen frequented houses of prostitution immediately they had closed the Confessionals. I resented this insinuation so emphaticly on one occasion that a fight resulted.

Men *acting* as degenerate clergymen did frequent houses of prostitution to turn Natives against Christianity and towards Communism.

The next incident took place in Yokohama. The Salvation Army was very good to young apprentices. Most boys and girls at heart are decent and honest and it is a fact that the majority of seagoing apprentices went to the Salvation Army Hostels, and the Seamen's Missions, rather than to the dives along the water-fronts. To destroy the faith and morals of these boys a prostitute made the rounds of the ships in port dressed in the uniform of the Salvation Army. Subversives amongst the crews whispered it around that she was willing to sell her body for Five Yen... and she did. This is the type of action which justifies the terms Satanic and Diabolical. She was an imposter, but how many apprentices realized that fact ?

To prove that these are not just isolated instances but part of a carefully prepared plan, I will record another instance which took place in Vera Cruz, Mexico, in 1913. The Communists were at that time vigorous in their attack on the religious beliefs of the peasants and working classes. In all the Mexican sea-ports subversives dressed as clergy frequented the houses where sodomy and prostitution were practiced. It requires little imagination to realize how fast, and how far, such scandals can be spread around. It is difficult to estimate how much damage is done. It is hard to convince any person that he can't believe the evidence of his own eyes. The average person can hardly tolerate the thought that other human beings could stoop so low in order to deceive them.

Between 1930 and 1936 subversives in Spain sold magazines featuring alleged sexual excesses between Priests and Nuns, right outside the Churches. Peddlers visited every ship in port and sold pornographic literature and obscene pictures. The subversive agents gave their parrot-like talk on the corrupt clergy and the virtues of Communism. Before leaving they issued an invitation to attend a movie. The movies ridiculed the clergy and showed both Priests and Nuns in the depths of degradation. Azana was the man detailed to demoralize Spanish youth and destroy the faith of the Spanish people in their clergy and religion. He did his work so well that he was able to organize anti-religious riots. Knoblaugh wrote : "Occasionally delegations of Protestant clergymen came to Loyalist Spain to investigate stories they had read of anti-clerical activities. These delegations were warmly received. Great pains were taken to prove to them that they had been grievously misled. Special guides were selected to show them around. Needless to say, the visiting Clergy saw only what they were intended to see. But one conducted tour misfired. The guide inadvertently allowed the visiting clergy to stop at a book stall where they examined some rare old volumes... and they saw copies of *LaTraca* and *Bicharracos Clericales,* (two of the widely distributed pornographic periodicals I referred to). The covers portrayed priestly orgies with semi-naked nuns. The delegation left in a huff. The guide was severely punished for such gross carelessness".

In Canada, a young woman who was a member of the Young Communist League, joined one of the Young Catholic Women's organizations with definite instructions that she was to seduce the young priest in charge. She succeeded. I had previously warned the Bishop of this danger.

That good Bishop just couldn't believe what I told him was being done to corrupt and disgrace ministers of religion in order to wean members of the congregations away from their Faith.

Obscene movies have just as large circulation in Canada and the U.S.A. to-day as they had in Spain before the revolution in 1936-38. Movies called "The Cherry Pickers", "Paddy McGinty's Goat", "Around the Clock" and many new subjects, complete with sound and in technicolour, are being shown every night in the week including Sundays. Investigation showed that men with plenty of money, and influence, are behind this racket of calculated subversion. It was being pushed by one of Canada's Dollar-a-year men in 1944; and by a top-level executive of one of Canada's largest Chain-Store organizations as recently as October 5th. 1955. Those who checked on this phase of subversion and perversion reported they had seen showings at "Stags" in Veteran's Halls, Golf Clubs, Social Clubs, in the rumpus-room of a high police official's house, and in the home of the top-level executive referred to. The chain-store executive charges $3.00 per person for four hours of unadulterated sexual filth and abomination. He shows the movies three nights a week. The police know what is going on. The public must demand to know WHY it is they cannot prosecute the higher-ups ? Investigation went to show that in two cases in which the police obtained first hand evidence they were given orders not to prosecute at the same high government level that decided who should, and who should not, be prosecuted for illegal activities between 1923 and 1927 as proved by evidence given before the Royal Commissioners inquiring into the Canadian Customs Service. This proves that the conspiracy is still going on and making progress.

One thing that has caused subversion to thrive, and Christianity to dwindle, is that too many ministers preach the ''Jesus meek and mild'' kind of religion. As far as His reactions to sin, racketeering, graft, usury, and corruption were concerned, he was anything but meek and mild.

He lost His life because his enemies feared to allow Him to live any longer. Christ denounced in His day all the things I expose are going on in our so-called Christian society to-day. This organized subversion and perversion lead the way to the establishment of the Despotism of Satan over the whole world.

Let us face a very unpleasant fact. If God is a reality then Satan is also. If Satan had the power to tempt Christ himself, then he also has the power to promise other men the whole world if they will adore him and serve him. While the ministers of the Christian religion preach the Commandments of God in their Churches one day a week, the priests of Satan work day and night throughout the year teaching the inversion of the Commandments of God. While most Christian ministers confine their activities to within their churches; the agents of the devil are at work everywhere.

The Illuminati are not atheists. They believe in the supernatural. Because of their insane hatred of God they believe in Satan, just as we believe in God. It is sad to have to admit that those who are inclined to EVIL are more loyal to the devil than those of us who are inclined to GOOD are loyal to God. Those who have espoused the cause of Satan work every waking hour to spread their civil influence among the rest of mankind. They do their evil work in all the public places, on the streets, in offices, in beverage rooms, in clubs, in the newspapers, books, magazines, everywhere. They have succeeded until the holy and sacred words ''Jesus Christ'' are on nearly everyone's tongue, every minute of the day, not as a prayer, but as a blasphemy. The Scriptures tell us in the beautiful story of Christmas that at the name of Jesus, every knee shall bend and every head shall bow. That is very different from the way the name of Jesus is now coupled with the foulest four letter words that issue from the lips of human beings. For these reasons Christian laymen must unite to Crusade against the followers of Satan.

Satanism is a very real thing. There is a sign on one building in California, which reads ''We worship Satan''. Satan has been listened to and worshipped ever since Adam and Eve fell from Grace.

Satan is listened to every time any human being falls from Grace regardless of what Psychiatrists may say. All those who worship Mammon worship Satan.

As was mentioned before, the followers of Satan claim he is the eldest son of God the Father. That Christ is the youngest son. They insist Satanism is "Right" and Christianity is "Wrong".

Sir Walter Scott tells us that Satan worship was carried on in 1789 by those who put into operation the Reign of Terror during the French Revolutions. In 1954 Peter Hawkins was retained by the Sunday Pictorial of London, England, to investigate the extent Satanism was being practiced in England to-day. He exposed Gerald Brosseau Gardiner of the Isle of Man as one of the leaders. Gardiner obtains recruits by luring people into his museum of "Black Magic" and arousing peoples curiosity by his writings on witchcraft. As recently as Oct. 15th a front page article in the Globe & Mail told all about Gardiner and the museum and thus gave him plenty of publicity without warning the public that he advocates Satanism.

One of Gardiner's books, with the pen-name of Scire, gives this conversation with a female witch : "*Tell me the truth about this altar used at your agtherings. In Spain I saw the living body of a woman used and they practiced abominations on it?*"

"*Yes*", the witch replied, "*At the Great Sabbath the living body of a priestess does form the altar. We worship the divine spirit of Creation which is the Life-spring of the world, and without which the world would perish... Are we then so abominable ?... We count it is not so*".

Asked if this extract from his book was not more truth than fiction Gardiner is reported to have said : "Most People would be shocked by witchcraft ceremonies which include men and women dancing in the nude; Praying to a Horned God, (Satan) and stimulation through wine, music, and drumming".

Mrs. S. Jackson was brave enough to tell Hawkin's her personal experiences as a High Priestess. She said that once a girl has been "The Victim" offered to Satan during a "Black Mass" she is afterwards blackmailed into doing the will the "Priests" under threat of exposure. She told her story, and allowed her picture to be published in the Sunday Pictorial, June 5., 1955 in order to break the stranglehold these diabolical people had on her.

Alister Crowley, the self-styled "beast", was one of those who spread Satan worship in England. He used to spill his own blood in order to work up the necessary blood-lust which enabled the congregation to commit the abominations which took place during the latter part of the ritual. Mrs. S. Jackson said that in the ceremonies in which she took part Cockerels were knifed to death so the members of the congregation could drink the blood. She said when the dancing started whiskey, rum, and gin were supplied in quantities which took care of everyones requirements. She said a girl about seventeen is chosen for initiation. The Priest chanted : "We have a virgin in our midst who is to be initiated". The victim was then led to a statue and was asked to make her "vows". She was then led to the altar where more "vows" were made. The "Black Mass" constitutes parodies on the Holy Mass as celebrated by the Roman Catholic priests. The virgin was made to stand naked looking at herself in a mirror while other distortions and blasphemies took place. Then the girl was hooded and the drums and music played until everyone began to feel the effects of this erotic treatment. The diabolical ceremony was climaxed in an orgie of sexual depravity in which first the priest and the virgin and then everyone else joined in.

Robert Cecil Mortimer, the bishop of Exeter, read the evidence obtained by Hawkins and on May 22, 1955, he made this public announcement : "This practice of "Black Magic" has naturally and inevitably always been condemned by the Church. It is a direct sin against God and a terrible danger to the individuals who practice it. To some young people, I suppose, the practice of Black Magic must seem exciting and courageous. I hope these articles will arouse them to the real danger in which they stand".

On June 5, 1955, the Rev. F. H. Amphlett, Vicar of All Saints, Knightsbridge wrote : "After a long study of these subjects I am well aware of the reality of this practice and of its baleful influence. Under its various guises I believe it is as rampant now as during the Middle Ages". During the Middle Ages boys were killed during the "Mass" instead of cockerels.

Investigation conducted in the United States indicates that the rituals follow the same pattern. The indecent shows previously mentioned, such as — "Strip-tease Acts", circuses between men and women, obscene movies, etc., are part of the plot to lead people into Satanism as taught by the agentur of the Illuminati.

The great truth to remember is this : The Illuminati equals International Communism plus International Capitalism. Regardless of what kind of an international government is first brought into being its establishment is only the last step towards the moment when the agentur of the Illuminati will take over and impose the Despotism of Satan upon the people of the whole world. It is time the stupid people who, because of vanity or greed, let themselves become instruments of the devil, became aware of the danger to which they expose the human race.

The matter of subversion within religion cannot be ended without dealing with the way the conspirators of Satan have infiltrated into the Jewish religion. Christ condemned those who were deliberately teaching the Jews false doctrines. He prayed for and sympathized with those who fell into error as the result of such teaching. At the age of twelve Christ sat in the temple of Jerusalem with the priests and elders correcting their teachings. He was doing this when found by Mary and Joseph after he had been missing three days.

I recently located an old print which illustrates this fact. The caption reads "Christ corrects the teaching of religion". It is the false priests and false prophets who have deliberately caused Jews to hate Christians and Christians to hate Jews. They did this in accordance with Article 2, Par. 5 of the "Scheme" which says : "But it has paid us though we have sacrificed many of our people". And again in Article IX, Par. 2 : "De facto we have already wiped out every kind of rule except our own, although de jure there still remains *a good many of them. Nowadays if any States raise a protest against us it is only pro forma at our discretion and by our direction, for* THEIR ANTI-SEMITISM IS INDISPENSABLE TO US FOR THE MANAGEMENT OF OUR LESSER BRETHREN".

Christ told the Pharisees that they were of the Synagogue of Satan. The Illuminati of that time scourged the Apostles and then turned them loose with orders they were never to mention the word Christ again. The very same evil men also introduced the various divisions into the Christian religion. It was their evil advisers that caused the Popes to depart from the teachings of Christ, in the matter of the Inquisition, and substituted the practices of Satan.

The Inquisition gives us a perfect example of how the agentur of the Illuminati first created heresies and then subverted high officials of both Church and State into committing atrocities which caused many Christians to defect from their religion. If the promoters of Satanism could deceive Popes why then shoudn't they be able to make Jews and Gentiles believe untruths also ! In order to understand the diabolical conspiracy we must first of all realize that it is the conspiracy of Satan against the omnipotence of Almighty God. Because Satan is a supernatural being he can, and does, deceive human beings into doing what is wrong. A human being cannot compromise with Satan or his agentur. Churchill, Roosevelt and others have tried to do so but the devil always wins.

Pope Leo XIII said : "The first law of history is to assert nothing false and to have no fear of telling the truth". In conformity with that principle any unbiased student must acknowledge the responsibility of the Popes in the matter of inflicting torture and death on many thousands of people who were convicted as heretics by the Inquisitors. The fact that they did sanction such cruel and inhuman practices is undoubtedly the blackest stain on the record of the Roman Catholic Church. There is only one explanation, and that is no excuse. The Popes responsible lived in an age when such extreme penalties were inflicted for treason and far lesser crimes against the State. It was assumed therefore that the punishments were not too severe for men and women the Inquisitors found guilty of treason (Heresy) against God. The Popes must have reasoned no punishment was to severe for people who were stealing the souls of men away from God.

Many authors have tried to whitewash the Popes by saying that the Church only tried heretics and then turned convicted persons over to the State for punishment. That is not true. Pope Innocent IV in his Bull "Ad Extirpanda" decreed in 1252 : *"The ruler of a city is hereby ordered to force all captured heretics to confess and accuse their accomplices by torture which will not imperil life or limb, just as thieves and robbers are forced to accuse their accomplices, and to confess their crimes; for these heretics are true thieves, murderers of souls, and robbers of the sacraments of God".* This law was confirmed by Pope Alexander IV on November 30, 1259, and by Pope Clement IV on November 3, 1265. The phrase saying life and limb were not to be imperilled was a farce, in view of the fact the Popes threatened rulers with excommunication, if they failed to impose the death penalty upon those convicted by the inquisitors. The act of excommunication made them into heretics and subject to the Inquisition also.

Luther was equally intolerant. He decreed "Whoever teaches otherwise than I teach condemns God and must remain a child of Hell". Holinshed the historian says : "Under Henry VIII, "The Grand Inquisitor" 72,000 Catholics were executed, many of them with atrocious cruelty". Cobbett, another historian, informs us that "Good" Queen Bess put to death more persons in one year than the inquisition did during the whole of its duration of 331 years. Dr. Schaff tells us that religious persecution, even unto death, continued long after the Reformation. In Geneva, were Calvinism was born, the Church and State used torture. Calvin even sanctioned forcing children to give evidence against their own parents.

Calvin received a letter from a man named Farel dated September 8, 1533. It reads : *"Some people do not wish us to prosecute heretics, but because the Pope condemns the faithful (i.e. the Huguenots) for the crime of heresy... it is absurd to conclude that we must not put to death heretics in order to strengthen the faithful"*.

In 1545 Calvin wrote : *"If Servetus comes to Geneva I will never allow him to depart alive"*. Servetus was burnt alive October 27, 1553.

These facts are recorded in case the kettle might be inclined to call the pot black.

As far as I can acertain, the Inquisition was started to stop the Albigensian heresy known as the "Catharan Belief" which had as its objective the depopulation of the Christian World. Catharists preached that to indulge in sexual intercouse for the purpose of procreation was serving the purpose of Satan and was therefore a Mortal Sin. Catharism also taught that human beings who were unable to make a useful contribution materially to society should be made to commit suicide or allowed to die of starvation. The doctrines were very similar to those preached and practiced by Dr. Brock Chisholm and many other medical "Specialists", "Experts" and "Advisers" who the Illuminati have attached to the United Nations since 1946.

Religious persecution is, however, against the teachings of Christ and against the laws of God. Christ told his disciples "Go forth and *teach* all nations etc." He didn't say persecute all unbelievers. He said, *"Learn of me for I am meek and humble of heart"*. People became Christians because they admired the kindness, the mercy, and the understanding of Christ. He hated sin and heresy but He loved the sinner and the heretic and worked to convert them.

His parables of the lost sheep, the lost coin, and the prodigal son all illustrate his attitude towards sinners. He told us : "There will be more rejoicing in heaven over one sinner who repents than ninety-nine just who need not penance".

Christ's attitude towards sinners was based on the fact that God, The Creator, has given man intellect and a free will. God intended this life to be a period of trial. He never permits us to be tempted beyond our strength. He leaves it up to the individual to make the choice between Him and Satan. We have no legal, or moral, right to *persecute* a human being because of his religious beliefs. We can teach them the error of their ways. We can lead those who have strayed back to God by setting them good example. We have a perfect right to *prosecute* and punish, in accordance with the law, those who teach blasphemy and subversion.

A great deal is heard to-day about the organization to promote friendship between Christians and Jews. The Christian Bible is available to any person who wishes to read it. Over 35,000,000 copies were printed in many languages last year. Every Jew can learn for himself what a Christian believes and how he is taught to act. But the exact opposite is true of the Talmud. It is almost impossible to obtain an English translation. Benjamin H. Freedman wrote an open letter entitled : "Facts are Facts" to Dr. David Goldstein, a Catholic Priest, October 10, 1954. He quotes many extracts from the Talmud. If they are correct then it is a wonder the Talmud is allowed to go through the mails. It is no wonder that Christ, when only twelve, tried to correct the teaching of the Rabbis and Elders. It is no wonder he denounced them when he became a man as being of the Synagogue of Satan. According to Mr. Freedman the Talmud teaches Jews as follows :

Sanhedrin 67a. Jesus referred to as the son of Pandira, a soldier.
Kallah 1b. (18b). Jesus an illegitimate and was conceived during menstruation.
Sanhedrin 67t. He was hanged on the eve of the Passover.
Toldath Jeschu. His birth is related in most shameful expressions.
Abdodah Zarah II and Schabbath XIV. Jesus again referred to as a son of a Roman soldier.
Schabbath 104b. Jesus called a fool.
Toldoth Jeshu. Claims Judas and Jesus engaged in a quarrel with filth.

According to the Talmud Christians and their form of worship are everything that is obnoxious. According to :

Hilkhoth Maakhaloth. Christians are idolators.
Orach Chaiim 20-2. Christians disguise themselves to kill Jews.
Abhodah Zarah (15b). Christians have sex relations with animals.
Makkoth (7b). A Jew is innocent of murder if his intent was to kill a Christian.
Midrasch Talpioth (22). Christians created to minister to Jews always.
Abhodah Zarah (54a). Usury may be practiced upon Christians.
Babha Kama (113a). A Jew may lie and perjure to condemn a Christian.
Zohar (1, 160a). Jews must always try to deceive Christians.
Choschen Ham (388, 15). Those who do not believe in Torah are to be killed.
Abhodah Zarah (26b). T. Even the best of the *Goyim* should be killed.
Zohar (11, 43a). Extermination of Christians is a necessary sacrifice.

There are pages and pages of such hateful nonsense. Some of the rulings in regard to sex are so horrible as to be nauseating.

According to photographic reproductions of actual pages. Mrs. Elizabeth Dilling claims to prove that the teachers of the Talmud do not consider intercourse with girls three years of age an abomination, or intercourse with animals a grave sin. Incest is discussed at length as are male prostitutes, "who sell their bodies from the neck up like a woman does hers from the neck down". The logic with which the learned Elders decide varying degrees of guilt is really astounding. The whole Talmud reeks with reference to sex, perversion, and abominations. It is no wonder God destroyed Sodom and Gomorrah. There are references which indicate that the ritual of the Black Mass is based on Satanism as expressed in Cabala and Talmud teachings. The Talmud states the qualifications a girl must have before she can be a priestess. When we remember that any child if taken young enough can be made to believe anything we want them to believe, it would appear that those who teach our Jewish friends the falsehoods printed in the Talmud deserve to be condemned by us as Christ condemned them, for they are most surely of the Synagogue of Satan. They are deliberately stirring up hatred between Gentiles and Jews so we will try to destroy each other and thus serve the purpose of the Illuminati.

The manner in which the lesser Jews were herded into Ghettos enabled the Satanic despots to make them think and do whatever they told them to think and do. After all, the wealthy Jews and Elders exercised the power of life or death over their lesser brethren.

Our quarrel is not with the lesser Jews, it is with a small number of men who pretend to be Jews while they are in actual fact followers of Satan. Let Christians insist that those Jews, to whom they extend the hand of friendship, condemn publicly the Talmudic teachings which contain blasphemies and insults regarding Christ and threats to Christians.

Anti-semitism plays right into the hands of the Illuminati. The high priests of Satan must get a great deal of satisfaction when Jews are blamed for their crimes against humanity. That is exactly what they want. Many Gentiles and Jews swallow their bait, hook-line-and-sinker.

It is gratifying to know that more Jews were converted to the Christian religion in 1954 than in any other year in recent times. I fully appreciate Mr. Freedman's fears that many alleged converts may be agents of the conspirators who use this means to infiltrate into our Christian denominations. As early as 1489 the Jewish Council in Constantinople advised their Rabbis to use "The Trojan Horse" method in order to destroy Christianity from within. That danger we have to guard against. But a Jewish traitor within a Christian denomination isn't quite as bad as a Gentile who is a false Christian. A false Christian sells his soul to the devil for the sake of material gain. He has turned away from the Eternal Truth. He has betrayed Christ. He denies God.

Persecution is a crime against humanity no matter by whom it is perpetrated. Heretics and subversive agents who plot against the Christian Church and State should be arrested and, if found guilty, imprisoned so they cannot bring about breaches of the peace on either a small scale, such as riots, or a large scale such as revolutions and Global Wars.

It is a consoling thought to know that God always works from down below. He has always used simple folk to do His will. He took an innocent girl in a small village to be the Mother of His Son, our Saviour; He made a humble Carpenter the guardian of Mary and Jesus. He took simple fishermen, and others of equally low station in life, to be his disciples. The laymen of the Christian denominations can clean up the mess if they will act in a sane and constitutional manner.

Cleaning up the present situation is a task for laymen to perform. I first suggested the name National Federation of Christian Laymen, because I realized we couldn't look to the leaders of our religious denominations to give us their approval openly. I realized that religious institutions, regardless of denomination, are mostly mort-gaged up to the neck. Those who loaned the money did so as a gesture of friendship. They asked no security other than the inte-grity of the borrower. They set a low rate of interest. They made easy terms for repayment. In any way our spiritual leaders looked at the deals they were good and sound in a business-like way. Now they can't bite the hand that loaned them all those billions of dollars. They didn't know it at the time, but they paid a very very high rate of interest. The money-lenders charged them with SILENCE, and bought their inaction. As if to emphasize the truth of this statement, Pope Pius XII asked Catholics all over the World to pray for the silenced Church. The Canadian Register October 15th. asked its readers the question : ''What is the Silenced Church ?'' It answered its own question by saying. ''The Silenced Church, for which the Pope asks our prayers, is composed of the many countries behind the Iron Curtain where Catholics are being persecuted, and silenced in many ways, by the stranglehold of the Soviet Rulers''. With that definition I must seriously disagree. Canada and the United States have not as yet been sovietized, but it cannot be denied that the leaders of ALL Christian Religions have been strangely silent when it comes to inform-ing their congregations the WHOLE truth regarding the International Conspiracy and its relationship to Satanism. I started informing ministers of the Christian religions regarding these matters in 1923. I addressed a private meeting of influential clergy of many denom-inations in Ottawa on this subject less than one year ago. In my humble opinion the correct answer to the question : ''What is the Silenced Church for which the Pope asks our prayers ?'' is this : ''The Christian Churches are silenced by the Money-lenders who are the same people Christ denounced. The Money-lenders, at the interna-tional level, by reason of their connection with Illuminism, direct the World Revolutionary Movement in ALL its aspects and, because they are the High Priests of Satanism, and Mammon, they plot to destroy Christianity and ALL other religions''.

In Rome the Pope Pius XII cries out telling the world the dangers of both Communism and selfish Capitalism. His voice is indeed ''As one crying in the wilderness''. There seems to be a very big gap between the Pope in Rome and the hundreds of parish priests and

Nuns who have written to encourage me. Sometimes I have to look at the signatures twice because the letters are so alike. Most of them say in effect. "Don't get discouraged if you don't get help higher up. I am praying for you and asking all I contact to back up your efforts. Keep us informed". The highest clergyman from whom I have received encouragement is a Monseigneur.

So-called modern education is actually indoctrination into secularism and materialism. About the only Christians who are fully alive to this danger are the Doukhobors. I spent two months with them in 1953. Their's is a deep sincere religious feeling. It is true they have been exploited by the agents of the Illuminati just the same as other racial groups, but even to-day their children are the best behaved I ever met. The professional "advisers" whisper that the government must take the children away from their parents because they object to them being taught secularism, militarism, and materialism, in our public schools. It is time all parents found out just what their children are being taught to-day. Thorough inquiry would give them a big surprise. Christ told us : "The gates of Hell shall not prevail against my church". All that is necessary to clean up this present mess is to tell the TRUTH and shame the Devil and his agents. The making, issue, and control of money must be put back in the hands of the people. Then we can build schools and churches without having the money-lenders tell us we must not say or do.

So little effort is actually needed. Henry Ford said in 1923 : "If seventy bankers were arrested global war would be an impossibility". If the people of the so-called Free World take constitutional action the Long Range Plans of the Illuminati can be brought to a halt before it is too late. Prayer is a great thing but it must be coupled with action. Knowledge is necessary before action can be taken. Today those who direct the W.R.M. control the Ford Foundation through their Communist agents just as they control the other "Charitable" foundations by their agentur at the top who work with the Capitalist conspirators.

In order to obtain the moral courage required to clean up the present mess we must have a spiritual awakening. We must ask God to fill us with the Spirit of the Holy Ghost just like the apostles. Until they were visited by the Holy Ghost during Pentecost they were more like mice than men. Only John had the courage to stay with Jesus during his passion. The other ten were locked in a room in fear and trembling for their own miserable lives. But after Pentecost they were like lions. Their spiritual strength enabled all of them to die for their Master.

What are we afraid of ? Twenty million brave young men laid down their lives during the last two wars because they believed they were fighting for democracy.... fighting for freedom.... fighting to make this a better world in which to live. Are we so cowardly that we are afraid to die for our country and our Faith ? All the enemy can take from us is our life. We have to give up our lives, one way or another, before we can obtain our eternal reward. It is quite evident that all those who are afraid to die want to put off the ordeal of facing God just as long as possible. They know in their hearts they are moral cowards. I get cold shivers down my spine when I hear a Christian congregation sing "Faith of our Fathers living still in spite of dungeon, fire, and sword". What use are words without action ?

What a terrible thing is fear ? I have had several prominent people send for as many as 100 copies of "Pawns in the Game". They asked that I send the books anonymously to the people they named. They said that if their action became known they would be secretly persecuted. All of which goes to prove that the conspiracy is very real. It is no figment of the imagination. I received considerable backing from a certain publisher but he dare not print "The Red Fog". What kind of freedom of the press is this ? I have preached no evil. I have tried to tell the truth. If some angle of the conspiracy has confused me I say that I am only human, I am liable to error but I am willing to be shown the truth.

Before we leave the subject of religion don't let us overlook the fact that, despite the power of Satan, and the lies and deceits of the Illuminati's agentur, *the vast majority* of human beings are still decent at heart. They are looking for good political leadership and good spiritual guidance. It would appear that those who are in a position to give it to them fail to act because of fear. I ask our Christian Laymen not to get down hearted. Don't develop a defeatist attitude. Don't say "Matters have gone too far... There is nothing can be done now". That is what the enemy wants us to say and think. I urge all Christians, and Jews, to get busy and throw off the shackles of the Illuminati for the sake of our children's future, and for the sake of their, and our, own souls.

There is no more inspiring sight than to see hundreds of innocent children dressed in white and blue making the First Holy Communion. It is a great satisfaction to see so many young people stay clean of body and pure in heart in spite of Satanism. Midnight Mass stirs the hearts and souls of those who attend. The majority of people want to learn the truth. If they didn't Billy Graham wouldn't pull the crowds he does. But even Billy can't defeat Satan until the people know who Satan uses to carry on his conspiracy and how they work. After you have read these two books form study groups and then take the action recommended in "Pawns in the Game". Get solidly behind the young people who have not fallen for the theory of liberalism. There is certainly a great deal of good in most people. Don't stand by and watch the good that is in them crushed out by evil forces like a press crushes out the juice of grapes. Don't be afraid. Get into the fight while you are young, strong, and healthy. Do it before you have family ties because you will be persecuted, make no mistake about that.

To illustrate what I mean. After World War Two I was appointed to the staff of the Department of Planning and Development of the Ontario Provincial Government under Mr. Dana Porter. Mr. Geo. Drew was premier at the time. I met an ex-officer who was afterwards elected to the provincial parliament. I gave this young M.P.P. all the information contained in this book. He in turn passed it on to George Drew. I had an interview with Mr. Drew regarding this matter.

I thought I might at last get somewhere in my effort to awaken influential people to our National danger, but this was not to be. The member of parliament, to whom I refer was for some unknown reason refused the support of his party at the next election. The man who got the nomination, and the party support, was soundly beaten at the polls. It was quite evident my friends knowledge regarding political intrigue was embarrassing to the Party Leaders. I mention this because I would not want the Conservative kettles to call the Liberal pots block.

It became necessary for me to go into hospital in 1946 for further treatment for my spinal injuries. I was admitted to the Veterans section of the East Toronto General. An operation on the spine was suggested, but a consulting specialist (whom I knew very well) told me under no consideration to agree to an operation. He said : "In your physical condition it would be about five chances in a hundred if you ever came out of it alive".

In addition to the spinal injury I was suffering from diabetes and diverticulitis. Whether or not the action was deliberate, or just another "mistake", I was put on a diet which aggravated the diverticulitis. I suffered such abdominal pains, and other symptoms, that I could'nt sleep. The pills I was given to take did not seem to relieve the pain I suffered. I asked for a bland diet but all I got daily was 750 calories of the worst kind of foods a person suffering from diverticulitis could eat.

One morning another patient was admitted to my room. He said he was suffering from arthritis. For two days he laid on the bed near mine and talked. He pretended to be glad of the opportunity to talk to a man of intelligence and such wide experience. He asked me questions on every subject under the sun. I did not even suspect that I was being subjected to psychoanalysis until the psychiatrist started to ask me the same old questions I had been asked in 1926. Did I believe in God ? Did I honestly believe in Hell ? If God was all merciful why would he permit such a place as Hell ? If God was Almighty why did he permit Satan and Evil to exist ? He probed into my private life and affairs. So on and on for two solid days. I think the reader will agree this is a most dispicable way to treat exservice men. If this is not Gestapo methods what is ?

This man confided in me that he was the son of a Minister of the Gospel. He claimed he was a graduate from McGill University. He admitted he had turned into an Atheist. He believed in the teachings of Dr. Sigmund Freud. If he had stayed in that room with me another two days I honestly believe I would have convinced him of the TRUTH. He was being psychoanalysed before he left. After he considered he was through with his examination, he claimed he was feeling much better and asked for his discharge. He shook hands before he left.

I checked on my suspicions and found my room mate was none other than Dr. Church who, at that time, was on the staff of the Toronto Psychiatric Hospital. After I was discharged from hospital I called on Dr. Church to make sure I was not mistaken regarding his real identity. He was surprised to see me.

I am not supposed to know what is in that psychatrist's report. The only reason for using such deception would be to try to obtain a report which could be used to shake peoples confidence in my integrity.

The Doctors who conducted my medical board upon my discharge from hospital informed me that there were no documents or X-rays on my file to indicate I ever had an injury to the spine. The doctor tried to prove I was lying when I gave him the history of my case. He tried to annoy me into losing my temper. He forced me to undergo a physical examination which hurt my spine so badly I had to go back to bed for a considerable time. The Board of Pensions Commissioners awarded me a small pension for arthritis and diabetes aggravated by service. They also claimed there was no evidence of a fracture or injury to the spine, although I had been treated for the condition in the Veterans Pavilion of the Ottawa General Hospital in 1943 and fitted with a special Taylors Brace by the authorities in Christie Street Hospital, Toronto, in 1944. Wearing this brace enabled me to serve on N.S.H.Q. until after V-E. Day.

Although the amount of pension awarded me was less than 50%, the Board of Directors of the Poppy Fund of Toronto refused to reinstate me as Manager of the Industrial Department after my discharge from the R.C.N. on the grounds that I was not physically fit to carry out the duties *they* would require of me. It must be remembered that I was the originator of the idea for an industrial department in 1927-1928. I put the idea into practice 1930-1931. I managed the business successfully and made it grow until May 1940. Then, while I was away at the War on leave of absence, the International Combine took over control. The business, and the number of Veterans employed, has decreased steadily ever since. The Canadian Government's officials know what happened. The Canadian Legion officials know the truth. But they don't act. **WHY ?** The only answer is that the "Secret" powers behind our Government, and other organizations, are in actual control just as we have proved they are in the A.M.A., C.M.A., B.M.A. and other medical and dental organizations.

Outstanding medical men including the late Dr. Stewart Wright volunteered to give evidence on my behalf before an Appeal Board. The members of the Appeal Board thanked Dr. Stewart Wright for the way he had presented his evidence. I was assured by an official of the Board that I had won the appeal. Shortly afterwards I received notice from Ottawa that my appeal was lost and my case closed. I was able to prove afterwards that the stenographer who took down the evidence during the hearing suffered a heart attack immediately after the hearings closed. *He had not transcribed his shorthand notes when the Board of Pensions Commissioners in Ottawa made their adverse ruling and closed the case".* I regret to record that Dr. Stewart Wright died suddenly of a heart attack before we could accumulate the evidence we wished to place before the Parliamentary Committee on Veteran Affairs. Then the Government dissolved the Paliamentary Committee.

A Veteran is not permitted to see his own medical file. He cannot therefore disprove false statements written into the records. He cannot prove if X-rays and other evidence have been included or removed. He cannot prove if harmful statements have been added. That such conspiracy does exist is proved by the simple fact that thousands of decisions made by the Board of Pensions Commissioners are diametrically opposed to the service history and medical history *supposed* to be on the applicants files. Here again we have the Commie "Cells" working away at the "Bottom" while the agentur of the internationalists work away at the "Top".

CHAPTER XV

How the conspirators obtain control of politics and economy

B ECAUSE Canada is large in area and small in population it was comparatively easy to trace the methods used by the agentur of the European Illuminati to infiltrate from the U.S.A. into Canadian politics.

I became connected with the Toronto Star in 1927. As a newspaper man, from 1928 to 1931 I was able to obtain a great deal of information regarding the Communist and the Capitalist conspiracies in Canada.

In 1841 Clinton Roosevelt published in America 'The Science of Government Founded on Natural Laws'. This was nothing more or less than a plagarized version of the teachings of Professor Adam Weishaupt of Frankfort University, Germany, the renegade Jesuit priest who arranged for the agentur of the Illuminati to infiltrate into French Freemasonry in 1776 so 'The Secret Power' which directed the World Revolutionary Movement, and the Conspiracy of Satan at that time could use Freemasonry to further their secret plans and ambitions and at the same time cloak their diabolical purpose.

The fact that President F. D. Roosevelt's 'NEW DEAL', his N.R.A., and other political policies and economic devices fitted perfectly into the 'Long Range Plans' of the Illuminati proved the continuity of the conspiracy from 1841 to 1945. It has been explained at the end of Chapter X that Roosevelt made known his secret plans to establish a dictatorship in America in March 1939 when he gave a secret audience to some of his government's special committees. It has also been mentioned that Roosevelt was kept a virtual prisoner from after Yalta until his death, presumably to prevent him telling the truth in the event his conscience troubled him when he realized he was about to meet his Maker. The fact that puzzled me was how Clinton Roosevelt came to be an agentur of the Illuminati in 1841. I had never been able to fill in the continuity of the plot in America from 1776 to 1841.

As the result of publishing "Pawns In The Game" I was given the information that filled the gap. In August 1955 a priest wrote and pointed out the fact that the Masonic insignia was printed on the back of American one dollar bills, together with the Great Seal of the U.S.A. He translated the words "Annuit Coeptis. Novus Ordo Seclorum" to mean "He (God) has favoured our undertakings; A new order of the ages is born."

I was certain that the insignia had been that of the Illuminati long before it was adopted by Freemasonry. I was also convinced it had been used as the insignia of the agentur of the 'Secret Power' which directed the World Revolutionary Movement as part of the Satanic conspiracy, long before the Illuminati of Weishaupt was formally introduced into French and Prussian Freemasonry in 1776. As recently as Nov. 20th the whole puzzling problem was cleared up when another person, who had read "Pawns In The Game", sent me a folder issued by The Chedney Press, advertising the publication of a book by Emanuel M. Josephson entitled "Roosevelt's Communist Manifesto" which incorporates "The Science of Government Founded On Natural Law" as expounded by Clinton Roosevelt in 1841.

Under the reproduction of insignia which has been on American one dollar bills since 1933 when Roosevelt introduced his 'New Deal' are the words

"INSIGNIA OF THE ILLUMINATI THAT ILLUMINIST JEFFERSON MADE THE REVERSE OF THE UNITED STATES SEAL"

Then follows this explanation. "The above insignia of the Order of the Illuminati was adopted by Weishaupt at the time he founded the Order, on May 1, 1776. It is that event that is memorialized by the MDCCLXXVI at the base of the pyramid, and not the date of the signing of the Declaration of Independence, as the uninformed have supposed.

The significance of the design is as follows : the pyramid represents the conspiracy for destruction of the Catholic Church, and establishment of a "One World", or UN dictatorship, the "secret" of the Order; the eye radiating in all directions, is the "all-spying eye" that symbolizes the terroristic, Gestapo-like, espionage agency that Weishaupt set up under the name of "Insinuating Brethren", to guard the "secret" of the Order and to terrorize the populace into acceptance of its rule. This "Ogpu" had its first workout in the Reign of Terror of the French Revolution, which it was instrumental in organizing. It is a source of amazement that the Catholic electorate tolerates the continuance of use of this insignia as part of the Great Seal of the U. S.

"ANNUIT COEPTIS" means "our enterprise (conspiracy) has been crowned with success". Below, "NOVUS ORDO SECLORUM" explains the nature of the enterprise : and it means "a New Social Order", or "New Deal".

It should be noted that this insignia acquired Masonic significance only after merger of that Order with the Order of Illuminati at the Congress of Wilhelmsbad, in 1782.

Benjamin Franklin, John Adams (Roosevelt kinsman) and Thomas Jefferson, ardent Illuminist, and defender of Adam Weishaupt,
proposed the above as the reverse of the seal, on the face of which
was the eagle symbol, to Congress, which adopted it on June 10, 1782.
On adoption of the Constitution, Congress decreed, by Act of September 15, 1789, its retention as seal of the United States. It is stated
however, by the State Department in its latest publication on the
subject (2860), that **"the reverse has never been cut and used
as a seal"**, and that only the obverse bearing the eagle symbol has
been used as official seal and coat of arms. It first was published on
the left of the reverse of the dollar bills at the beginning of the New
Deal, 1933.

What is the meaning of the publication at the outset of the New
Deal of this "Gestapo" symbol that had been so carefully suppressed
up to that date that few Americans knew of its existence, other than
as a Masonic symbol ?

It can only mean that with the advent of the New Deal the Illum-
inist-Socialist-Communist conspirators, followers of Professor Weishaupt, regarded their efforts as beginning to be crowned with success.

In effect this seal proclaims to the peoples of the U. S. that **the
entire power of their Government supports the conspiracy to
undermine and destroy it and the Constitution on which it
rests** — that it is a **Government of traitors.** All of which should
prove that no matter how far apart or how independently students
work they will arrive at the same conclusions if they refuse to be
lead onto false trails by cleverly applied propaganda.

So we see that the Illuminati, using Rothschild's gold, infiltrated into the United States the latter part of the eighteenth
century. The agentur had obtained a strangle hold on American
politics and economy by 1865. They ordered Lincoln's assassination
to remove a man who knew too much regarding their diabolical plans.
The details of this phase of American history have been recorded in
"Pawns in the Game". That Judah P. Benjamin, Rothschild's agent
in America, was the driving force behind Booth the assassin, is now
history.

Evidence was obtained to show that Grand Orient Masons did
make an attempt to infiltrate into American and Canadian lodges in
the first half of the 19th century for the purpose of subverting High
Degree Masons into becoming members of the international conspiracy. Their purpose was to help break up the British Empire by
causing the American colonies to revolt.

My research goes to show that members of the Ionic Lodge of
Hamilton, Ontario, were approached, and indignantly rejected the
proposals. I am informed that a Grand Orient Mason made similar
attempts to subvert influential Masons in Niagara Falls, New York,
in 1848. The details are difficult to obtain but I was informed that
this particular subversive was found murdered near the Niagara
Gorge on the Canadian side of the river. In "Pawns in the Game"
I tried to explain truthfully the historical facts of how the agentur of
the Illuminati infiltrated into Continental, or "Blue" Freemasonry
in Europe between 1773 and 1789 and organized the Grand Orient

Lodges to further their diabolical and Long Range Plan to bring about the Despotic control of the world by the worshipers of Mammon and Satan. One Englishman, who many people recognize as an authority, really lambasted me in an Anti-Semitic publication. He said I must be a Mason to have written such deceptive material.

If I did not believe that the majority of the men and women involved in the international conspiracy are honest and sincere at heart I would not have written "Pawns in the Game", and "The Red Fog". My only purpose in writing these books is to convince many people that they have been lied to and deceived into joining hands with the devil, so that many of them actually think they are performing a duty to God and their fellow men.

I have tried to present the facts of history in an unprejudiced manner so the readers may study the facts for themselves.

Those who direct the Long Range Plan for the Despotism of Satan admit in their Protocols that their whole scheme is defeated if the "Goyim" ever realize that our only salvation lies in a return to the OLD ORDER based on God's plan for Creation. We must therefore refuse to be led any further by the nose through green looking pastures of so-called "liberalism" into ultimate subjection and slavery.

I apologize for this rather lengthy digression, but it is necessary to recognize these TRUTHS in order that we can understand how men like Churchill, Eden, Roosevelt, Mackenzie King, and many others adopted political policies which have played into the hands of those who intend to impose Satanic Despotism upon the human race. They were willing to accept the theory that a One World Super-Government would ensure Peace and economic security : they agreed with Lenin who said : "The people do not know what is good for them". They were willing to acknowledge that the people who had been clever enough to obtain absolute control of the World's wealth, politics, and economy were obviously better qualified to rule the "Mob" than the "Mob" were to rule them. But Christ proved that God does not think that way. God works through those who are lowly in society and pure of heart, and humble in spirit.

Statesmen have worked during the past century to bring about a Capitalistic International Dictatorship while pretending to be staunch Nationalists. They perpetrated this deception because they had been convinced by the agentur of the Illuminati that a Capitalistic International Super-Government was preferable in every way to either the Communist or Nazi type of International Dictatorship. This brings us back to Mackenzie King, and Canada and the United States of America.

Mackenzie King had been brought up in a family rebellious against the actions and behaviour of men sent to Canada to represent the British Government. It is quite evident that he was watched very carefully during his University days by agents of the conspirators who planned to destroy the British Empire because it stood in the way of their totalitarian ambitions. They noted that Mackenzie King was a remarkable young man with a touch of genius, particularly in regard to political economy and the social sciences.

Just about the time Mackenzie King entered University a group working for the Illuminati announced their "new" and "modern" ideas. It was based on "Liberalism". The conspirators were careful at first not to drop a hint that their "liberal" ideas, and the emphasis they placed on "group" behaviour and "group" action, were merely the stepping stones placed conveniently for the students they picked out to be of service to their hidden masters. These "modern" educationalists didn't care if the student was inclined towards the communist or capitalist ideology. All they wanted was to advance them in education so they could be worked into the framework of the conspiracy at the "top" or at the "bottom". Their selected students became known as "Frontier Thinkers". In England, the United States, and Canada they honestly and sincerely believed, as I did when younger, that the social, economic, and educational pattern should be changed.

The plan developed quickly in England under the British Fabian Society which extended its influence to the United States. It became known as the Dewey philosophy. In 1905 the Intercollegiate Socialist Society was formed in New York "To promote an intelligent interest in socialism among college men and women".

In 1921 the "scheme" had developed to the stage when the Intercollegiate Society became the League for Industrial Democracy. Its purpose was "education for a new social order based on production for use and not for profit". John Dewey was made vice-president in the middle 1930's which shows how carefully those who direct the World Revolutionary Movement play their cards. The British Fabian Society announced "The L.I.D. in the U.S.A. is carrying on active propaganda in the United States on similar lines to our own work here"... international "liberalism" not socialism, or communism, or capitalism... just "liberalism". Any other word would have scared many people away from the movement.

Professor John Dewey was on the faculty of Teachers College, Columbia University, New York. Among the basic principles he taught were : 1. That there are no absolute or eternal truths; 2. That there is no such thing as a human soul or a human mind in the Christian sense; 3. That there are no fixed moral laws. He contended that morality consists of adjusting oneself to one's environment including the particular group in which one finds oneself. 4. That human conduct depends upon patterns of habit and impulse. The Dewey principles were designed to lead students who accepted his philosophy into the camps of either the Communist of the Capitalist internationalists. Dewey professed to be hostile to Communism and because of this fact he gathered around him many anti-communists. By 1933 he had 5,652 influential followers advocating social revolution in our schools, colleges, and universities. The alumni had worked themselves into a strategic position. They marched under the banner of "the progressive educational system". But they were secretly working to change the "old" system of education into the proposed "new" system of indoctrination.

On May 3, 1933 Dr. Rugg, a "specialist" in social-studies, chaired a meeting held in Teachers College of Columbia University.

The subject under discussion was, "the necessity for building a "new social order", and the possibility of using the teachers and the schools for putting the idea over".

A Dr. Newlon urged that the material for teaching how to build the "new social order" be introduced into the curricula of the schools.

The panel discussed "ways and means" to put this suggestion into effect. Those attending the meeting admitted the process of educating the teachers over to their way of thinking would take far too long to serve their purpose. Speedy action could be obtained if teachers could be *forced* to accept their ideas. It was then suggested that they obtain control of school superintendents and administrators and *force* them to "persuade" the teachers. Dr. Rugg said : "I infer that you are in general agreement that there is a new rule for the superintendent and the administrator when you are saying to him that we can't wait for the new order to be built up. Would you not say that the new order must preceed enlightenment?"

Many good and sincere people who have studied this question have tried to prove that Professors Rugg, Newlon, and Dewey were Communists. I know they were not. They were working as agentur of the men who direct the international conspiracy, and those men work both ends; international Capitalism at the "top" and international Communism at the "bottom". They burn the candle at both ends so the twin flames will meet at the middle and burst into Illuminism. The despotism of Satan.

The outcome of that meeting was that by controlling the school superintendents and administrators they could force teachers to accept the principle of organizing their pupils into groups and teach them group behaviour. Instead of concerning themselves with the whole class teachers were to concentrate their efforts on students who became group leaders and recommend them for higher education, and see they got scholarships and other help they needed to reach university. These students were then to be placed under the influence of professors who would brainwash them into their way of thinking.

Dr. Newlon said : "We have been talking tactics when what we need is grand strategy... we must have power politics in education... we must ally ourselves with labour and with others who are striving FOR THE ENDS WE HAVE IN VIEW".

A Dr. Brunner suggested that some kind of a national organization be formed to make liaisons of that kind.

Dr. Watson suggested that the Progressive Educational Association be used.

Dr. Meek (who I believe is the same person who figured in the Queen's Park Riots in Toronto in 1929) enquired : "Are all the teachers to be Communists ? That party is organized to change everything".

Dr. Rugg replied : "Are the Communists working with ideas or notions ? So far as they are working with ideas we could work with them".

Dr. Newlon said : "It is incumbent upon ourselves to think through these social and economic ideas and see what kind of educational program we want in this country... In this process of bringing about these conditions I believe we can work with the Communists and at other times with the socialists (liberals)''.

Dr. Rugg : ''We need a thoroughly and completely radical organization. The Progressive Educational Association is probably the best now in existence. The progressives will have to lead''.

Dr. Watson, the educational psychologist, said, ''The PEA should seek out a relationship with Communist and socialist agitators so that these may feel that they have an ally among the teachers''. The General Education Board put this conspiracy into effect.[1]

The purpose of this digression is to show how Mackenzie King, and those he picked to be his henchmen, were trained from childhood to become ''specialists'' and ''advisers'' who would talk ''pie in the sky'' while leading their fellow men over the precipice into the bottomless pit of Satanic despotism. I am convinced that many of those who play the Judas-Goat to-day do so without knowing the treacherous, and bloody, part they play.

Those who set out to influence Mackenzie King found he had peculiar characteristics which enabled him to dominate people without giving them any real friendship or confidences in return. I doubt if there was a more friendless man in Canada. (He was so friendless that in his last years he tried to contact people in the spirit world to appease his loneliness.)

I studied Mackenzie King closely from 1927 to 1945 and I found him to be a clever, cold, unemotional type of professional politician. When he shook hands with me, the experience always reminded me of getting hold of a dead fish. He had peculiar eyes also. He became as deeply involved in the conspiracy he dare not marry for fear he might talk in his sleep.

John D. Rockefeller took Mackenzie King into the Rockefeller organization in 1914 because everything the Rockefellers did to extend their fortune and power seemed to arouse the hatred of the people. John D. needed a man like Mackenzie King to teach his sons how to exploit the ''peasantry'' of the U.S.A.; wreck opposing industrial organizations; control government officials; and usurp the powers of government, and do it in a manner which would make the public like it.

In 1914 the employees of the Colorado Fuel and Iron Company in Ludlow went on strike for improved working conditions, and an increase of wages. Rockefeller's thugs, supported by the militia, fired on employees and set fire to tents occupied by their wives and children. Forty-four men, women, and children, were shot or burned to death. Several others were severely burned or injured. A very ugly situation developed. The atmosphere was so charged with feelings of hatred that another tiny spark of resentment was all that was needed to start further acts of violence. This situation gave Mackenzie King his great opportunity. He persuaded John D. Jr. to cover his wolves with sheep's wool. He advised the Rockefeller family to conceal their rapacity by pretending to be liberal; to hide their

---

[1] For further information read ''EDUCATION or INDOCTRINATION'' by Mary L. Allen (to see at end of book).

callous disregard for other people's interests by pretending to be solicitous regarding their welfare; to hide their indifference to other people's sufferings by a show of sympathetic regard for their ailments; to hide their ruthlessness by a well cultivated show of personal charm; and to hide their purpose to turn the United States into a dictatorship by financing National movements and charitable foundations.

John D. Jr. was so struck with the boldness of this policy that he actually consented to visit the stricken families in the Ludlow district. Mackenzie King teamed up with Ivy Lee and organized a publicity campaign which cost thousands. He proved how a show of personal charm could delude the people into placing the blame for their bereavements on the shoulders of people other than the Rockefellers. He made the widows and orphans feel it just wasn't possible for a man so full of grace, and charm to be guilty of hiring assassins to intimidate his employees into working for pitilessly-low wages he could amass an even greater fortune than that he had already made. King proved that charm costs nothing.

Mackenzie King and Ivy Lee came to know the Reverend Frederick T. Gates, promoter of Rockefeller's many socalled philanthropies. These three, King, Lee, and Gates, showed Rockefeller the wisdom of withdrawing his name, and the names of his sons, from the many international concerns they controlled. They showed the Rockefellers how they could control labour by organizing company unions rather than by shooting workers and burning their families.

They showed the Rockefellers how they could control education, religion, and medicine, by the simple expedient of establishing charitable foundations managed by agents they controlled. The guidance of Messrs. King, Lee, and Gates, enabled the Rockefellers, and their associates Kuhn,Loeb and Co., Henry Morgan and Co. and Carnegie to obtain political and economic control of the Americas. They developed their plans to *control* international Communism, so the revolutionary element could, if necessary, be used to serve their purpose also.

In 1907 the German banker, Paul Warburg, was employed to draw up the plans by which the American bankers obtained absolute control of the country's monetary system. The wording of the legislation made the general public believe that the control of money would be in the hands of their government. This legislation was passed in 1913.

That same year the American and the European bankers amalgamated and the stage was set for World War One.

Mackenzie King was chosen to head the Rockefeller Foundation for Industrial Research because he had been trained in the social sciences in the thought-controlled universities of Toronto, Chicago and Harvard, subsidized by the General Education Board. He became a past master in the art of compromise in the "Liberal" interpretation of Bismark, Marx, and Rockefeller. Mackenzie King wrote New York Industrial Disputes Act in 1907. He took the curse off the name of Rockefeller. He deluded many workers into accepting his theories for Social Security. He afterwards imposed them on Canadians.

It was unfortunate for Mackenzie King that he could not mesmerize all those with whom he came in contact. Several labour leaders in the States saw through his duplicity. They dug up evidence which proved to a United States Commission, conducted by Frank P. Walsh in 1917, that the Rockefeller Foundation was simply a cloak used to cover a plot intended to lead organized labour into a form of slavery. Other investigations in the States proved in 1938 that Mackenzie King's "Company Unions" were not in the interest of the workers.

It was explained in "Pawns in the Game" how the International Bankers organized, financed, and directed the second phase of the Russian revolution as carried out by Trotsky and Lenin in 1917. It was mentioned that the International Banker's plot, to overthrow Kerensky's provisional government, and transform Russia into an absolute dictatorship under Lenin, nearly failed because Trotsky was intercepted by Naval authorities and detained in Halifax, Nova Scotia.

What I didn't mention in "Pawns in the Game" was the fact that I was told Mackenzie King used his good offices with the Canadian Government to have Trotsky released from detention in Halifax. Trotsky then proceeded to join Lenin in Russia. This co-operation between the Capitalist and the Communist Internationalists cost the British Empire Russia as an ally.

In case any reader still doubts that the Communist revolutionary parties, are organized, financed, and directed, by the Capitalist Internationalists, I quote Article III, Paragraph 7, of the Protocols, which reads :

"We appear on the scene as alleged saviours of the worker from the oppression when we propose to him to enter the ranks of our fighting forces — Socialists — Anarchists — Communists —to whom we always give support in accordance with an alleged brotherly rule (of the solidarity of humanity) of our social masonry", i.e. *Grand Orient Masonry.*

Just as soon as Mackenzie King's plot to regiment labour, under the guise of the Rockefeller Foundation for the study of Industrial Labour Relations, fell through, Rockefeller was advised to found the Laura Spelman Rockefeller Memorial. This was done for the *announced* purpose of supporting charities, and welfare organizations, connected with health, religious, and racial minority groups. Ivy Lee was detailed to use these philanthropic funds to set up Communist Front Organizations in the U. S. A. and Canada. Beardsley Ruml used the different "front" organizations to help further the Capitalistic plot designed to turn the United States and Canada into Capitalistic Dictatorships. These conditions continued until 1928 when the General Education Board, which had brought Ruml and his radical programmes into operation, was merged into the Rockefeller Foundation again. With this merger the Rockefeller Foundation entered whole-heartedly into the One World Supranational Government campaign. The General Education Board's Annual

Report for 1928, on Page XI says : "The Rockefeller philanthropies were parts of a well ordered whole".

When I was in New York in February 1930 in connection with the publication of my first book "By guess and by God" I met many prominent literary and newspaper men. I sat next to the editor of a famous New York daily at a banquet given at the Explorers' Club. During the meal the conversation drifted to Mackenzie King and the possibility that Canada might become part of the United States in the not too distant future. I declared it my opinion that the Canadian people would never agree to any plan to separate Canada from the Mother country. I said : "Canadians will never allow the British Empire to be broken up. They will never become part of the U.S.A.".

The Editor replied : "The Canadian people will have no say in the matter. If Mackenzie King lives long enough he will use the Marxist-Bismark type of "liberalism" to lead the people of Canada into a dictatorship like the One Worlders are doing in the United States. The people swallow this "pie-in-the-sky" policy like sheep eat grass before they are slaughtered".

According to my dinner companion, Mackenzie King had written to William Jennings Bryan, who was Secretary of State in Woodrow Wilson's Cabinet in 1914 urging that the United States observe strict neutrality. He commended Bryan for the telegram he had sent Sept. 4, 1914 to J. P. Morgan & Co. the international bankers, intimating that it was against the policy of the United States government for them to make loans to assist France.

My companion told me that Mackenzie King had also written letters to President Eliot of Harvard University expressing the opinion that if the United States maintained a strict neutrality the war in Europe might be prolonged but such a condition could not help but advance the whole basis of world civilization and at the same time greatly further the diplomatic ends of the United States.

I was then acquainted with the fact that while Mackenzie King urged strict neutrality on the part of the United States government for the purpose of limiting the extent France could participate in the war as the ally of Britain, he was at the same time involved in the conspiracy entered into by the American Bankers to aid Lenin and Trotsky start a revolution in Russia and take her out of the war as an ally of Britain also.

The story sounded fantastic. My companion and I spent the greater part of that night together. He told me that the British bankers, working in collusion with their American confreres, had caused the munition works to slow down production so that the promise to send arms to Russia, made in 1914, did not materialize. This was done to prepare the way for revolution in Russia. My companion told me : "Mackenzie King is a rebel at heart. He believes Canada's destiny lies with the United States. He used his influence with the Canadian Government to get Trotsky released after he had been captured on his way to Russia and detained in Halifax. The political policy he is carrying out in Canada is dictated to him by the men who direct the international conspiracy".

My companion added : "In my opinion Mackenzie King has the right ideas. If Canada and the United States are ever united we could tell the rest of the world to go to hell any way they wish to".

"But if what you say is true Mackenzie King is a traitor", I gasped.

"Try to be realistic", my companion retorted. Then he said : "The international bankers want Palestine for two reasons. One, because they know of the tremendous mineral wealth that is hidden beneath the Dead Sea, and that oil will be found in the surrounding areas. Two, they want a small sovereign state in the hub of world politics. They don't care who brings about the first international governments. They intend to take it over once it is established. King works for Rockefeller who is affiliated with the international bankers. Their politics are Mr. King's. Britain had to be placed in a position so critical that her government had to agree to the Bankers terms set forth in the "Palestine mandate" or lose the war against Germany".

When I returned to Canada in 1930 after doing research work in Europe I tried to convince prominent business men and politicians of the existence of the conspiracy. I even obtained an interview with Mr. R. B. Bennett when he was Prime Minister but he must have thought I was a lunatic because he sent for the R.C.M.P. and had me removed from his office. If I did get anyone interested enough to delve into the matter they invariably ran into some government official who dismissed everything I said as a form of neurosis resulting from lengthy service in submarines, but now the truth of what I said in the early 1930's is beginning to come to light. Since the first edition the truth of what I said about Mackenzie King has been proved by independent historians.

Internationalism, be it Communistic or Capitalistic, is controlled by the Illuminati. When Stalin kicked over the traces we were nearly plunged into World War Three. We will have peace just as long as the Long Range Plans of the Illuminati progress without let or hindrance. The directors of the Illuminati are against Christ and they are for Satan. They will remain in the background plotting and planning all that is evil. Their agentur will continue to bribe and corrupt government officials and subvert private citizens. They will lure people away from God by offering them gold, the world, the flesh, and the devil. They will take over the One World Super-government as soon as it is formed. They will turn that Super-government into the universal despotism of Satan.

The only reason this book is published is to try to persuade all those who have been deceived, flattered, or bribed into taking sides with the Devil that they are seriously wrong but, while they have a breath left in their mortal bodies, it is not too late to renounce the Devil his pomps and vanities and acknowledge their mistakes. They can make restitutions for the harm they have done by devoting the rest of their lives to promoting the Kingdom of God upon this earth.

THE DIRECTORS OF THE INTERNATIONAL CONSPIRACY HAVE OTHER THAN JEWS IN THEIR SERVICE BECAUSE ARTICLE IX, PARAGRAPH 4, OF THE PROTO-

COLS SAYS : *"WE HAVE IN OUR SERVICE PERSONS OF ALL OPINIONS, OF ALL DOCTRINES, RESTORING MO-NARCHISTS, DEMAGOGUES, SOCIALISTS, COMMUNISTS, AND UTOPIAN DREAMERS OF EVERY KIND. WE HAVE HARNESSED THEM ALL TO THE TASK; EACH ONE OF THEM ON HIS OWN ACCOUNT BORING AWAY AT THE LAST REMNANTS OF AUTHORITY, IS STRIVING TO OVERTHROW ALL ESTABLISHED FORMS OF ORDER. BY THESE ACTS ALL STATES ARE IN TORTURE; THEY EXHORT TO TRANQUILLITY, ARE READY TO SACRIFICE EVERYTHING FOR PEACE; BUT WE WILL NOT GIVE THEM PEACE UNTIL THEY OPENLY ACKNOWLEDGE OUR INTERNATIONAL SUPER-GOVERNMENT"*.

Could their objective be stated any more clearly ? We must there-fore work and pray that the whole human race may at last be united spiritually in the Brotherhood of Man under the Fatherhood of God. We can work towards the day when Christ will come again to restore the one and only worth-while Dictatorship — the Benevolent Dictator-ship of Almighty God.

History does repeat itself. Since "Pawns in the Game" was published I have been given detailed reports on the final days of Franklin Roosevelt, James V. Forrestal, and Mackenzie King. The letters made me think of the famous last words of Cardinal Wolsey : "If only I had served my God — as I have served my King". Yes, he had served his King, who in turn had served the Devil. Roosevelt, Forrestal and Mackenzie King served the cause of Internationalism - but it was not the Cause of God.

Regarding F. D. Roosevelt I am informed, on reliable authority, that after Yalta his health broke completely. He told several people that he was at last aware of the TRUTH regarding all angles of the International conspiracy. I am informed that he did manage to inform Stalin that he realized how he had been deceived. The day he got his message through to Stalin he died,

Perhaps history will reveal at some future date why he was virtu-ally kept a prisoner after Yalta? Why Madame Schaumatoff was painting his picture as he lay on his death-bed? Some day it may be revealed why she disappeared so completely and what happened to her? Why has the fact that Mrs. Rutherford was present during the final stages of this historical drama been kept secret? Why is it that Dr. Paulin, Roosevelt's medical attendant, has never made a public announcement regarding the last moments of such a famous man? It would be interesting to know why Roosevelt kept asking repeatedly for days before he died, "How many G.I's are stationed here in Warm Springs"? Why was his body not placed in the President's bier? Why has the undertaker, Patterson, never made a public statement?

One thing is certain - God knows the answers to all these ques-tions. The only conclusion one can reach regarding this matter is this : When Roosevelt made the concessions he did make to Stalin he thought that both Stalin and the United States One Worlders were playing one

— 203 —

and the same game. He evidently believed Stalin was willing to be subordinate to the Western Capitalists. When he realized that Stalin was intending to double-cross the Western internationalists, and planned ultimately to try to destroy them, Roosevelt considered this a betrayal.

It is interesting to recall that for some time before he died W. L. Mackenzie King was very interested in trying to contact men and women who had already departed this life. It is just possible that he was trying to find out how they lived before he went to meet his Maker.

Eustace C. Mullins is recognized as an authority on the financial angle of the international conspiracy. Author of "The Federal Reserve Conspiracy", he wrote to me after reading "Pawns In the Game", and said : "Dear Commander Carr :

"I am deeply grateful to you for your book "Pawns in the Game", which is one of the most valuable compilations of vital information which I have ever seen. I am amazed that you have been able to gather so much really important information in a single volume, which is a high tribute to your powers of evaluating the relative weight of various facts. Most such compilations which I have seen usually wander off into some pet theory of the author's which is totally at variance with the facts presented, simply because the writer has not had the intelligence and background to judge his information, and to recognize the pattern of the enemy's operations. Since we are engaged in a life and death struggle with the forces of evil, we are indeed fortunate to have your services in our behalf.

"Because of my detailed study of the affiliations and co-operations between the most important members of the international banking houses in the past century, I am able to offer you a few supplementary facts about your statements on James V. Forrestal, page 14. Bernard Baruch dissolved his firm of Baruch Brothers in 1917 to go into the Governments service. He and his brother bought the firm of Hentz and Company to mask their operations, and own it to this day. Only recently John Kaplan of Hentz and Co. obtained the account of Stavros Niarchos, the fabulous Greek shipping millionaire. In 1919, Baruch possessed ten billions of war profits, from his monopoly of tungsten during the war. He purchased the old Gentile banking house of Reed and Co. and placed a Jew, Clarence Lapowitz, who had been his assistant in the War Industries Board, in charge of it. Lapowitz took the name of Dillon; the firm became known as Dillon-Reed. How to invest the war profits? In a new war, of course. Dillon-Reed put up twenty-five million for the Vereinigte Stahlwerke of the Ruhr, financing Thyssen and Hitler. James Forrestal was a partner of the firm at this time, and his Who's Who biography reports that he advanced rapidly, being a brilliant young man. He became senior partner, a Gentile front, for Baruch and Dillon. The evidence is that Forrestal was not pure, or suddenly discovered the sinister web of international intrigue. He could not possibly have functioned without knowing Baruch's secret operations. What seems to have happened was his failure of nerve. He became weak, depressed, and was taken to Florida by Brown Bros., Harriman's partner, Robert Lovett, who succeeded him as Secretary of Defense. Lovett, who tried to buck him up, reported that it was hopeless. Moreover, Forrestal wanted to confess all. He was brought back to Bethesda Naval Hospital in Washington -- where many a Justice and Senator has benefited from the free treatment and been silenced forever. Although listed as a mental case with suicidal tendencies, Forrestal was placed in a room, with no window bars, in the top of the tower of the hospital. Is it unreasonable to suppose he was killed a la Masaryk? I only offer this as a further explanation for your own information. You are welcome to use it in further editions of your book if you wish". McCarthy's death, in this same hospital, is dealt with in appendix.

The Illuminati consider the application of so-called "Liberalism" so important to the ultimate success of their conspiracy that they deal with the subject in several articles, and eighteen paragraphs :

Article I, Paragraphs 6-7-9-14-16. — Article III, Paragraphs 3-13 — Article V, Paragraph 9 — Article IX, Paragraphs 2-9 — Article X, Paragraphs 9-10 — Article XII, Paragraph 6 — Article XIII, Paragraph 4 — Article XV, Paragraphs 4-9-14-17.

Because of lack of space only Paragraph 6 of Article I will be quoted here. It says : *"Political freedom is an idea but not a fact. This idea one must know how to apply whenever it appears necessary with (to use) this bait of an idea to attract the masses of the people to one's party for the purpose of crushing another who is in authority. This task is rendered easier if the opponent has himself been infected with the idea, is willing to yield some of his power. It is precisely here that the triumph of our theory appears; the slackening reins of government are immediately, by the law of life, caught up and gathered together by a new hand, because the blind might of the nation cannot for a single day exist without guidance, and the new authority merely fits into the place of the old already weakened by liberalism".*

The type of "liberalism" explained in the Protocols is the kind taught by Mackenzie King. His teachings are being put into effect by his pupils, Pearson, Martin, Howe and others. Papa St. Laurent watches with a wary eye that nobody steps out of line. Even his own son is not permitted to say a single word publicly that has not been written down for him. The way he was controlled in the by-election in 1955 proved this.

Mackenzie King had the approval of the international financiers. He pretended to be poor but he was actually wealthy. To prove that steps have already been taken to put the conspirators plans for despotic dictatorships into effect in both Canada and the United States, I will quote from the U.S. News and World Report, July, 1955 :

"A Military dictatorship, swift and complete, will take hold at the very moment of any big atomic attack on American cities.

"This is the word from top official sources in Washington, following "Operation Alert", the civil defense exercise just ended.

"The old idea of "standby controls" which has been worrying some business men, no longer has any place in official planning.

"Instead, the President will simply take control - of business, banks, goods, prices, wages, just about everything - and worry about legal authority later.

"Martial law will be clamped on the entire country. This will be the President's first official act after bombs starts falling. With that act the President will assume almost unlimited war powers. Dictatorship from Washington, or from the President's nearby hideway, will be backed by military forces...

"Business will be blanked by regulations, already written and ready for issue. Raw materials will be rationed. Tools, trucks, supplies will be subject to seizure. Banks will be given orders by government. Money will be rationed. Depositors, if necessary, will be limited in how much they can draw out of the bank.

"Under national martial law, so the thinking goes, there will be no time for haggling over federal authority, no time for people, or business, to balk at doing what they are told.

"Once the dust begins to clear Congress will be asked to ratify the emergency measures ordered by the President".

At precisely the same time Canada's Prime Minister, the Hon. L. St. Laurent, tried, during the dying days of the 2nd session of the 22nd Parliament, to sneak through legislation that would have given the Hon. "Dictatur" Howe exactly the same despotic powers in Canada that the President now enjoys in the United States. It so happened Her Majesty's Loyal Opposition started a "Filibuster" which lasted until the Prime Minister reluctantly agreed to limit Mr. Howe's right to exercise absolute power to three years. The Prime Minister's concession indicated that the expected crisis will take place within the next three years.

Supposing International Bankers decide, at any time from now onwards, that they will try a sneak attack to obtain final and undisputed control of the world's affairs, as is their announced intention repeatedly reiterated in the Protocols. Then their agentur in America could stimulate a fake attack which would provide the excuse for the president to put into effect the military dictatorship. An all out attack could then be launched on the Communist controlled countries. Those who direct the attack would announce that it was justified for the following reasons :

(A) In retaliation for aggressive action by the Communists.

(B) To save the world for Christianity.

(c) To keep America "FREE".

It was proved in "Pawns in the Game" that history does repeat itself. History teaches that the conspirators ordered their agents in Spain to start the revolution by making a series of "fake" attacks against the Government properties and agencies after their agentur had arranged matters so the attacks would be blamed on the Fascist Forces. This fact is mentioned to prove the head of the Illuminati would not hesitate to stimulate a "fake" attack in Canada or the U. S. A.

Study of the Long Range Plan proves that in the final analysis all nationalities, all races, and all creeds will come under the despotism of ONE MAN who will be crowned as KING of the world's dictatorship. This King-despot is referred to in ten articles and twenty-two paragraphs of the "Long Range Plan" for ultimate world conquest. It is sufficient to quote from Article XXIII to prove my point. Par. 3 says : "*The supreme Lord who will replace all now existing rulers, dragging out their existence among societies demoralized by us, societies that have denied even the authority of God, from whose midst breaks out on all sides the fire of anarchy, must first of all proceed to quench this all devouring flame. Therefore he will be obliged to kill off those existing societies, though he should drench them with his own blood, that he may resurrect them again in the form of regularly organized troops fighting consciously with every kind of infection that may cover the body of the STATE with sores*".

On the other hand there is the possibility that the Communist leaders will be fully informed regarding the plans of the Illuminati, and may decide to take the initiative and start aggressive action. They could call for an International General Political Strike, backed up by revolutionary efforts, and support the revolutions with the full strength of Soviet Armed Forces.

That this possibility exists, is the only logical explanation why the leaders in all Capitalist countries adopt the soft, go-easy, policy with regard to Communism in their own countries. The top-level officials in Britain, Canada, and the U.S.A. are apparently convinced that any move on their part to outlaw the Communist Party, and break up the Communist underground organizations, in their respective countries, would bring about immediate retaliatory action by the Communists in Europe and Asia. The Communist dictators know they cannot hope to destroy the international Capitalists, their Illuminati, and the Illuminati's agentur, without the full co-operation and support of their underground organizations in all the remaining capitalist countries.

On the other hand, those who direct the Capitalist conspiracy realize that in order to destroy international Communism at home and abroad, they must attack both organizations simultaneously. This would mean that the order to outlaw and liquidate Communism in the remaining non-sovietized countries would be given at the exact moment the allied planes were in position to start dropping bombs on predetermined targets in Communist countries in Europe and Asia. This theory would explain the policy of encircling the Communist controlled countries with air-fields in America, Europe, Asia, and North Africa.

This line of reasoning also explains why the Communist organizations in Britain, the U.S.A., and Canada, split their "Cells" in 1950 from six to three for greater security reasons. It explains why the Communist 5th Column goes deeper and deeper underground. It explains why Communists and their fellow travellers practice operation "Evacuate" from the big cities every long holiday week-end, and at the same time oppose most vigourously all proposals put forward by civil defense officials for evacuation plans for our larger centres of population. It explains why both the F.B.I. and R.C.M.P. claim they now require six men to keep track of Communists and their activities compared to one in 1945.

Our leading politicians do not like an author to dig up past events. We saw in a previous chapter how the present Minister of Agriculture, the Hon. James Garfield Gardiner was involved by evidence given before the Royal Commission into the Customs and Excise Services. The present minister of Health and Welfare, the Hon. Paul Martin also has an interesting past. He is responsible now for formulating Canada's Civil Defense Programme. When I was Director for Civil Defense for the Sudbury District in Northern Ontario, an area which has more Communists pro rata to population than any other in Canada, I became unpopular with the officials in Ottawa because I repeatedly said at conferences : "The policy and planning suggested by the Federal officials make it possible for the Communist 5th column to take over and use the Civil Defense organization to help subjugate the population of Canada and the United States rather than protect the people against their internal and hidden enemies". I argued that civil defense should come under the Department of Justice and the R.C.M.P. and NOT under the Department of Health and Welfare because Civil Defense has to do with our internal security.

Be that as it may. The point I now make is that the Hon. Paul Martin based his policy on that of the United States. Mr. Martin also goes to the United Nations and discusses our internal and external defense problems with the Soviets delegates. This is all very interesting because in an issue of the "New Advance" for April 1938, on Page 12, is a group photograph under which is the following caption :

"The Ottawa Congress (a Communist front youth organizationed) sent two official delegates and endorsed the sending of thirty others to the First World Youth Congress held in Geneva, Switzerland, at the end of August 1936". The photograph shows part of the delegation aboard S. S. Aurania. The chairman of the delegation is Paul Martin, M.P. The group which accompanied Paul Martin included Murdock Keith, Toronto Youth Council; William Kashton, Young Communist League of Canada; Roy Davis, who afterwards became Raymond Arthur Davies. He was prosecuted for obtaining a passport under false pretences. He is known to be a top-level executive in the Leftist propaganda machine. It will be recalled that on August 25, 1952 the Hon. Paul Martin's sister was reported in the public press as having been actively engaged in the false visa racket. The racketeers obtained passports for people who could not obtain them legally from the proper authorities. The Hon. Paul Martin disassociated himself with his sister's activities, and very properly so. Such exposures are very annoying to people of cabinet rank.

Other members of the Canadian Youth delegation were William Smart, Canadian Negro Youth Movement; Norman Levy, Chairman of the Canadian Youth Congress, Leon Katz, Kingston Youth Council, Ken Woodsworth, Secretary of the Canadian Youth Congress, and T. C. Douglas, M.P. He is now Premier of Saskatchewan. In 1936 he was a leader in the Co-operative Commonwealth Youth Movement.

Two issues of the "Globe and Mail" dated Aug. 11, 1938, and Sept. 14, 1938 publish letters on the editorial page which deal with Messrs. Martin, and Douglas, and the company they kept while attending the World Youth Congress in Geneva. It appears that M. Litvinov the ex-gangster and international spy addressed the delegates. Litvinov's real name is Finkelstein. He was a close associate of Manuilsky who as head of the Comintern plotted and planned "Popular World Revolution", prior to 1944.

Litvinov was *supposed* to be a Bolshevik, and Stalin's right hand man, but, during World War Two he was conducting secret missions in both Germany and Britain for the international capitalist conspirators. He had such powerful backers that he was released after he had been arrested in both England and Germany as a spy. Why don't members of Parliament demand to know by whose orders Trotsky was released in World War One and Litvinov in World War Two? Only men who were above the governments of both Britain and Germany could have provided such protection to internationally known spies. These men are the Illuminati. Their power lies in the fact that they *control and direct all angles of both the Communist and Capitalist conspiracy.* They make a farce of what we think is constitutional government.

Litvinov was presented to the delegates of the World Youth Congress as a strange God in 1936. Ten years later our Canadian delegates to the United Nations Organization joined with their American cousins and appointed Manuilsky chairman of the U. N. security council. Manuilsky is the man who boastfully passed on to the leaders of the World Revolutionary Movement in 1944 the information given to him by Pat Sullivan that, at that date, the Communist Party in Canada had 18,000 members and approximately 300,000 fellow travellers ready to revolt when the order is given. We may well sing "Oh Canada".

Both the Hon. Paul Martin and Hon. T. C. Douglas will deny they are, or ever were, Communists. I for one will accept their denial. The question is are they, or are they not, One Worlders? Do they, or do they not, work to bring the people of the entire world under the domination of "Specialists" and "Advisers"? The idea of a Supranational One World Government once appealed to me. It was only when I realized that the "Specialists" and "Advisers", with which the politicians are surrounded, were educated and trained to put the Protocols of the Illuminati into effect that I changed my opinion. I sincerely hope that the information given here will cause many others to pause and think also.

I don't believe Mr. "Mike" Pearson knows the whole truth regarding the international conspiracy. I met him in Sudbury and asked him questions he either couldn't or didn't want to answer.

In my opinion Mr. Pearson is typical of the men who are chosen to become innocent tools of the men who comprise the Secret International government. Of such Article II, Paragraph 2 of the Protocols says : "*The administrators whom we shall choose from among the public, with strict regard to their capacities for servile obedience, will not be persons trained in the arts of government, and will therefore easily become pawns in our game in the hands of men of learning and genius who will be their advisers, specialists bred and reared from early childhood to rule affairs of the whole world.*" Perhaps if Mr.

Pearson and others realize they are only being used as pawns in the game of international chess they will quit serving the secret government and start serving the people who elect them.

The Hon. Lester Pearson was carefully educated and groomed by Mackenzie King to take over the business of foreign affairs. During his training Mr. Pearson came into very close contact with Dexter White and other American government officials who were afterwards charged with being engaged in the Communist conspiracy. Some were proved to be Communists. Others were acquitted. The strangest thing is that no government official has, to this day, been charged as being an agentur of those who direct all phases of the W.R.M. The men who drew up the "peace" treaties after World Wars One and Two were certainly not Communists, Democrats, or Christians. Yet it was these same men who drew up the United Nations Charter, and whose influence has caused the World to be divided into two hostile camps — Eastern Communist and Western Capitalist.

Mr. Hickey will probably never realize that he hit the nail right on the head when he wrote in the "Globe and Mail", Sept. 12, 1955 : "An off the cuff speech which he (Mr. Pearson) made on Saturday night, in Kingston, on Canada's relations with the United States and the United Kingdom was reported in terms such as to cause consternation among HIS DEPARTMENTAL ADVISERS". There you have it. Mr. Pearson lets one cat out of the conspirators bag, apparently unknowingly, and Mr. Hickey makes it known that Mr. Pearson isn't supposed to say anything.... nothing at all.... unless it is prepared for him and written down by his advisers.

In order that Mr. Pearson may no longer remain in ignorance of the real character and record of some of his advisers, we make the following facts known. This information was communicated to the Hon. Stuart Garson, Minister of Justice, in a letter dated September 20, 1955. It is possible that the information concerning his "advisers" was not passed on to Mr. Pearson because he had made no changes up to the time this went to press.

Three of Mr. Pearson's chief "advisers" are long time associates.

1. Egerton Herbert Norman. 2. Chester Ronning. 3. Escott M. Reed.

In the report published by the Federal Government, which supposedly covered all evidence given before the Royal Commissioners who investigated Soviet espionage after Igor Gouzenko deserted from the Soviet embassy, no mention was made of a conference held at hide-way at Mont Tremblant north of Montreal.[1] I previously referred to this place in the chapter on the conspiracy within the Armed Forces.

In telling of this hide-away I mentioned how those who ran it got away with everything that was illegal without interference from the police. Since I wrote that chapter this angle of the conspiracy was investigated by a former undercover man for the R.C.M.P. The investigation proved that when Premier Godbout took over the

---

[1] As this 2nd Edition is being revised word has just been received that many of the internationalists who met on St. Simon's Island Feb. 14 to 17 - 1957 are scheduled to meet at Mont Tremblant later this year.

government of Quebec in 1940 and suspended the Padlock Law he abolished the anti-subversive squad of the Provincial Police. Quebec became a sanctuary for subversives of both the Communist and Capitalist variety.

Subversives cover up by using fine sounding names for their "Front" organizations. "The Institute of Pacific Relations (I.P.R.)" has been proved by the F.B.I., and the U.S.A. Senate to be a hot-bed of conspiracy relating to American Foreign policy. Documents, files, signatures, and a Committee of Inquiry records confirm the facts we give here. A raid by the F.B.I. on the home of Frederick Vanderbilt Field produced documents which confirmed other evidence.

It will be recalled that F. V. Field and Dr. Raymond Boyer changed wives after their respective millions enabled them to obtain simultaneous divorces. Field and Boyer were both imprisoned for subversive activities by the governments of their respective countries. It has never been proved to my satisfaction whether these men were working for the Communist or Capitalist conspirators — more likely the latter.

The Canadian branch of the I.P.R. is called the Canadian Institute of International Affairs. This organization ceased its public activities for a while following the disclosures which led to the condemnation of Owen Lattimore. But the C.I.I.A. recently blossomed into its former vigor again. It has been given good publicity on the C.B.C. and by Professor Marcus Long. It was very active at Sackville, New Brunswick, in June 1955 when Mr. Escott Reid, Canada's High Commissioner to India, flew by special plane to Canada in order to represent Mr. Pearson at the Conference. It was very active Sept. 11-12 and 13 at Couchiching Conference sponsored by the C.B.C. and the C.I.I.A. Mr. Edgar McInnis is the President of the C.I.I.A. He was a personal friend of Owen Lattimore. McInnis' name was mentioned about fifty times during the United States Senate enquiry into un-American activities of certain people. McInnis is also a friend of Alger Hiss, Fred Poland, and Dr. Raymond Boyer who have all been convicted of subversive activities. He was one of the principal speakers at both the Sackville and Couchiching Conferences. The I.P.R. has branches in almost every country in the world. Its stated objective is scholarly research on Asiatic Affairs. The conclusion reached by the U.S. Security Sub-Committee, after two years of thorough enquiry is that the I.P.R. :

(A) Was used by the American Communist Party, and Soviet officials, as an instrument of politics, military intelligence, and Soviet propaganda.

(B) That those who administer and control the I.P.R. have all been identified as Communists or other types of subversives.

(c) The I.P.R. was used by subversives to guide American Far East policies into the mess they are in to-day.

The reader already knows how the leading Communists in Canada were released by the Canadian Government in October 1942 after they had pleaded guilty to the crimes of sedition and treason laid against them by the R.C.M.P. These traitors were left free to arrange the conference which was held in the fabulous hide-away at Mont Tremblant from Dec. 4 to 14, 1942. This meeting laid the foundation for the Canadian Soviet Spy network which Gouzenko exposed four years later. This conference brought together many members of the American I.P.R. and other delegates who belong to the I.P.R. in Canada and other countries.

On November 14, 1942, Edward Carter, the Secretary-General of the I.P.R. in America sent a cablegram to V. M. Molotov. The cable gave Carter's address as 129 East 52nd Street, New York, N.Y. Molotov's address was given as Narkomindal, Moscow, U.S.S.R. The message read :

> *"Respectfully and urgently invite you to authorize some members of Soviet Embassy Washington and Soviet Legation, Ottawa to attend Eighth Conference of Institute of Pacific Relations, Mont Tremblant, Province of Quebec, Dec. 4 to 14. STOP Influential leaders coming from England, China, Fighting France, Phillipines, Netherlands, Australia, New Zealand, Canada and U.S.A. STOP Vargo, Vortinsky, Oumansky, Motylev familiar with institute's purpose. STOP Conference discussions will be private STOP".*

Robert Morris, the legal adviser of the American Senate in the inquiry into the I.P.R. found that Dr. Raymond Boyer had suggested to F. V. Field that the conference be held at Mont Tremblant *because the delegates could rest assured that there would be no interference by the Police.*

The man who introduced me to the hide-away in August 1943 was a very wealthy man who is to-day a very prominent Liberal politician in Quebec. He was a strong supporter of Premier Godbout who suspended the Padlock laws in 1940 and abolished the Anti-Subversive activities of the Quebec Provincial Police. Such political interference made it difficult for the R.C.M.P. to perform their duties in regard to internal security.

Owen Lattimore admitted, while on trial, having met at Mont Tremblant several Canadian Communists who were later arrested and condemned as spies on the evidence given by Gouzenko. One of these was Poland who was in continuous contact with Pavlov the Chief of the Soviet N.K.V.D. (now called the M.V.D.). The matter of greatest importance is the fact that amongst this nest of subversives gathered together at Mont Tremblant were Messrs. Egerton Herbert Norman, Chester Ronning, and Escott M. Reid who to-day are included among Mr. Lester Person's most trusted advisers.

If Mr. Pearson doesn't know their background the honourable Minister should ask his confrere Mr. Garson, Minister of Justice, why he has been kept in the dark so long.

1. *Egerton Herbert Norman* is to-day High Commissioner from Canada to New Zealand. He was moved from Mr. Pearson's staff to this appointment after he had been identified as a Pro-Communist or subversive at the I.P.R. inquiry in the States by Dr. Karl Wittfogel former Director of the German Communist Party. I can remember

Norman twenty years ago as a member of the Communist front organization known as "The League against War and Fascism".

Carter, head of the I.P.R. in the U.S.A. wrote to a man named Holland, one of the heads of the I.P.R. in Australia, under date of Sept. 5, 1940. I quote : "Any secret messages might be sent in care of Herbert Norman at the Canadian Legation in Tokio". It is presumed he was implicated in the spy network set up by Dr. Richard Sorge. Our investigators have documents which prove Norman intervened after the war to obtain the release of Japanese Communists. Norman was born in Japan. He is a great friend of Dr. J. Endicott who was awarded the Stalin Peace Price in 1953. He has contributed articles to the Communist magazine "Amerasia". This information was passed along to the Minister of Justice as it became available. The electors may well ask "Why no action?" More regarding Norman in appendix.

2. *Chester Ronning* was born in China. I first heard of him when I was in Shanghai in 1911. He was at that time a volunteer in the revolutionary army of Sun Yat Sen. He worked under the direct orders of Michael Borodin, the envoy of the Comintern in China, Earl Browder, later leader of the Communist Party in the U.S.A.; and Jacques Duclos who afterward diverted from the Communists and fought them to the death. After Ronning arrived in Canada he openly formed the I.P.R. and infiltrated into Mr. Pearson's department of External Affairs. Soon Mr. Pearson referred to him as "The greatest "expert" on Asiatic Affairs". Expert for whom ? Ronning is a personal friend of Chou En Lai and Mao Tse Tung. He organized the talks which have taken place between Chou En Lai and Lester Pearson at Geneva and arranged part of the schedule of his 1955 trip to the Soviet and China. Ronning is also a friend of Dr. Endicott who, it will be recalled, was made Canadian adviser to Chiang Kai Shek in 1942. The American counterpart was Owen Lattimore, the Soviet Spy, and Madame Sun Yat Sen. All of these people were international subversives.

More recently Ronning as an "Adviser" at Geneva arranged with Chou En Lai for the release of the Canadian Aviator Squadron Leader McKenzie. He also arranged matters so that millions of Indo-Chinese Christians were placed under the despotism of Ho Chi Minh.

.. 3. *Escott M. Reid*, is now High Commissioner from Canada to Nehru's India. Of all the subversives in the I.P.R. Reid is probably one of the cleverest, and the best placed for doing the work of his masters. In Washington he is known as "The Alger Hiss-Owen Lattimore of Canada".

When the Hon. Louis St. Laurent made his trip around the world it was Escott Reid who arranged that two top-level Communist officials from Red China would be guests at the home of Prime Minister Nehru when Mr. St. Laurent arrived in India. Time Magazine published a photograph of the two Prime Ministers sitting with the two Communist officials. This same photo appeared in Canadian papers but the two Communists were cut out of the picture. Mr. Reid was undoubtedly responsible for Mr. St. Laurent saying the things he did about the recognition of Red China. Mr. Reid arranged the press

conference in 1954 at which the Canadian Prime Minister declared :
"I do not suggest that the system of Government which exists in
Russia to day be changed, since this concerns only the Russian
people". Our Prime Minister was also advised to make this profound
announcement : "The government of Formosa (nationalist) does
not represent the great mass of the Chinese People. I believe that
one day it will be necessary to be realistic and admit that the present
government of Communist China is the government desired by the
people".

The Communist Governments are just about as little representative of the people as our own.

These men, and others like them, are the "experts", the "specialists", and the "advisers", with which the members of the Canadian
Cabinet are surrounded. It is little wonder then that Mr. Pearson
caused consternation amongst his brood when he said what he did
regarding Canada's future being linked up more with the U.S.A. than
with Britain.

Just to prove that Messrs. Pearson, Martin, Gardiner, St. Laurent, Garson, Eisenhower, and Dulles, etc., are not alone in the bad
company they kept, I quote evidence disclosed by A. K. Chesterton,
M.C. in his weekly newspaper "Candour". It will come as a shock to
many people to learn that although Winston Churchill at first angrily
refused to agree to Morgenthau's proposals to turn Germany into an
agricultural peasant nation, a plan that actually meant little less than
genocide for the German people, Churchill was placed under such
pressure by the agentur of the Illuminati that in the end he himself
drew up the actual form of words incorporated into that diabolical
document of revenge which became known as the Morgenthau Plan.

The man who put the pressure on Churchill was Lord Sherwell.
He was born Frederick Alexander Lindemann. He was trained from
youth to qualify as a "specialist", and "adviser", to the British
Government. It is well known that he worked in the interests of International Financiers. He did his job so well he was made a Lord
amongst the British aristocracy.[2]

That the conspirators are working to establish a One World
Government which will submerge all National governments into the
depths of the Sea of Despotism is proved by the fact that The World
Association of Parliaments for World Government met in Copenhagen, Denmark, in August 1953. The Copenhagen conference passed
a resolution favouring the adoption of World Government, based on
the blueprints for the international constitution under the United
Nations as drafted by the special committee appointed to deal with
this matter at the London Parliamentary Conferences held in September 1951 and September 1952. This proposed constitution of the
World Government destroys all sovereign rights. The vice-president
of the World Government organization is Congressman Adam Clayton
Powell of the U.S.A. who was listed by the Un-American Activities
Investigating Committee as having his name on the Masthead of the

[2] Lord Astor speaking in the House of Lords November 22nd is reported
as saying the British Civil Service is full of subversives to the highest levels.

executive committee of the Communist Party, together with Earl Browder, as an executive director of the Communist magazine "Fight", which was also the official organ of the American League for Peace and Democracy which was also proved to be a Communist front organization. Mr. A. K. Chesterton in a recent pamphlet entitled "The Menace of One World Government"[3] discloses the fact that one hundred members of the British Parliament support this subversive movement in spite of their Oath of loyalty to Her Majesty Queen Elizabeth II. The League of Empire Loyalists have undertaken a campaign informing the electorate of this fact and asking them to demand of these members of Parliament how they can reconcile their sponsorship of this plan to end British sovereignty with their Oath of Allegiance to the Queen.

Mr. Eisenhower is known to be an internationalist. The newspapers referred to him as such during his illness in September 1955. We mustn't forget that it was Eisenhower who halted General Patton and enabled the Russians to occupy the Soviet Sector of Berlin.

Mr. Eisenhower, and Mr. St. Laurent, may be convinced that the people of the United States, and the people of Canada, are so hopelessly ignorant that they are no longer qualified to form opinions and reach decisions and tell their elected representatives what they want doing to clean up the mess we find ourselves in to-day. They may be right. But if the vast majority of the people are ignorant it is because they have been consistently kept in the dark regarding matters of national and international importance since secret diplomacy came into practice, and the Press came under control of the international financiers.

Before the intended despotism is put into effect, the people should demand to be fully informed. At present the Constitution says the Will of the Electorate is supreme and not the Will of the Members of Parliament. Under the Constitution the parliamentarians are the "servants" of the people. They have no legal right to introduce despotism.

The Mackenzie King type of "liberalism", continued by the men he especially trained, is the greatest danger civilized society faces today. In support of my contentions Article III, Pars 14-15 are quoted : "When the populace has seen that all sorts of concessions and indulgences are yielded it in the name of freedom it has imagined itself to be the sovereign lord, and has stormed its way to power, but like every other blind man it has come upon a host of stumbling blocks, and has rushed to find a guide. IT HAS NEVER HAD THE SENSE TO RETURN TO THE FORMER STATE, and it has laid down its plenipotentiary powers at our feet. Remembering the French Revolution, to which it was we who gave the name GREAT : the secrets of its preparations are well known to us for it was wholly the work of our hands.

"Ever since that time (1789) we have been leading the peoples from one disenchantment to another, so that in the end they should

---

[3] To obtain copies of "The Menace of World Government" see list of publications at end of book.

turn also from us in favour of the KING-DESPOT of the blood of Zion whom we are preparing for the World.

"At the present day (1897) we are, as an international force, invincible, because if attacked by some we are supported by other States. It is the bottomless rascality of the Goyim people, who crawl on their bellies to force, but are merciless towards weakness, unsparing to faults and indulgent to crimes, unwilling to bear the contradictions of a free social system but patient unto martyrdom under the violence of a bold despotism... it is those qualities which are aiding us to independence. From the premier-dictators of the present day the Goyim people suffer patiently and bear such abuses as for the least of them they would have beheaded twenty kings".

Remembering that the above statement was made in 1897 can any sane person deny that the Hitlers, Mussolinis, Churchills, Roosevelts, and Mackenzie Kings, were not typical of the Premier-despots the speaker said they would arrange to have elected to rule over the people and lead them to the stage when the people would turn from all in favour of that KING-DESPOT the top-level conspirators in the Illuminati were preparing to Rule the world ?

Having all these things in mind it would appear sound policy if the people of all the remaining so-called "free nations" instructed their elected representatives that they wished to have all men and women connected with the Communist and Capitalistic conspiracies arrested simultaneously. This action would render both the Communist dictators, and the agentur of the Illuminati powerless to put into effect revolution or war on an international scale.

If any person thinks this suggestion impractical let me remind that person that, in May 1940, Churchill imprisoned, without charge or trial, all those who opposed the plans of the Illuminati to turn the "cold", or "phoney", war, into the "hot" shooting war. Bombing of German cities started the very same night, in May 1940, when Churchill took over the government from Chamberlain. He kept the loyal and patriotic Englishmen who opposed this policy in prison for as long as four and half years. If Churchill could do that, there is no reason why the electorate should not demand that the properly constituted authorities arrest all those who plot and plan revolutions and wars, famines, and depressions.

It was related in "Pawns in The Game" how Churchill was in secret communication with Roosevelt from the time war was declared in 1939 until he ousted Chamberlain and assumed the office of Prime Minister. Not even Mr. Chamberlain knew Mr. Churchill was using the diplomatic privileges extended to the U.S. Embassy to conduct this secret intrigue. How can any man do such a thing after he has taken his oath of office ? When Churchill communicated with Roosevelt it was exactly as if he had communicated with Bernard Baruch personally. When Churchill visited the United States after the war to talk with President Eisenhower he called first of all on Baruch to get briefed as to how much the new president knew about international intrigue. He had to know exactly what he could say, and what he must not say. After the talks with the president Mr. Churchill was the guest of Mr. Baruch at his home. It is taken for granted that he informed Mr. Baruch of all that had taken place in the White House.

The real conferences at the summit have been held in New York.

Before Molotov went back to Russia, after the San Francisco meeting 1955, he visited Baruch and undoubtedly received his orders. Molotov must subscribe to the international bankers' ideas for an international Dictatorship, like Tito evidently does, otherwise Stalin would not have removed him from his post at the United Nations Assembly and sent his wife off to Siberia. Tito broke with Stalin because he favoured the Capitalist's international plan. This was probably explained to him by Churchill's son when he parachuted into Yugoslavia several times during World War Two. This is furthered by "The World Federalists" who knowingly or unknowingly further the secret plans of the Illuminate.

Before President Eisenhower left for the "Big Four" meeting in Geneva, Bernard Baruch was closeted with him for a considerable time. Baruch undoubtedly "advised" him what to say and do. The President of the United States, if reports are correct, never reads books; rarely reads magazine articles; and seldom looks at newspapers. He relies almost entirely on what he is told by his "Specialists", and "Advisers". Reporters who cover his news conferences remark amongst themselves about his ignorance regarding international intrigue. Drew Pearson once commented about "the boys who run things for Ike." This evidence helps to support the opinion of those who feel the president is an easy mark for the men Bernard Baruch appoints to be his advisers.

Could any man living to-day better fit the description given in the Protocols of a "Specialist", or "Adviser", than Baruch,—"*reared from early childhood to rule the affairs of the whole world*"?

The point I wish to make is this : The president of the United States, and Mr. C. D. Howe, have been given the right to exercise despotic powers *if and when they consider it necessary to do so*. The electors should demand to know on whose behalf these **TWO** men intend to exercise such despotic power? Will it be on behalf of those who oppose both the Communist and Capitalist conspiracy or will they act on behalf of one or the other of the internationalist groups as Churchill did in May 1940?

The American newspapers also "broke" the story that the president planned, under certain conditions, to blow up all international bridges and close the border between Canada and the United States. This fact was discussed in the Senate. Members were puzzled to know what circumstances could ever justify such drastic action. Such action could only be useful in the case the Canadian and American governments failed to agree on international policy. Blowing up bridges, and closing the border, would not seriously obstruct military, operations if the Communist dictators decided to attack America, *but such a policy fits in perfectly with plot to subjugate the people as explained in Article IX. Par. 13 of the Protocols which says "You may say that the goyim will rise upon us, arms in hands, if they guess what is going on before the time comes; but in the WEST we have against this a manoeuvre of such appalling terror that the very stoutest hearts quail — the undergrounds, metropolitains, those sub-terranean corridors which, before the time comes, will be driven under all capitals and from whence those capitals will be blown into the air with all their organizations and archives.''*

The point I wish to make clear is this : It is the duty of the government to explain every detail of what is going on behind the scenes to the members of their respective parliaments. Every member of parliament should then fully inform the people so *they* may decide what course of ACTION *they* wish the government to take to solve the problems. We must not go any further with the cart before the horse. The horse must be put back in between the shafts again.

If the elected representatives of the people refuse to obey the demands made by the people then the electorate can DE-MAND that, the Queen. — The Governor General — or the President, as the case may be, remove from office those who refuse to obey the orders of their electors. The electors can then elect men who promise to carry out their oath of office. IT IS NOT NECESSARY THAT THE ELECTORS WAIT UNTIL THE GOVERNMENT RESIGNS AND CALLS ANOTHER ELEC-TION. THE ELECTORATE HAVE THE LEGAL RIGHT TO EXERCISE THEIR PREROGATIVES AT *ANY* TIME, ON *ANY* ISSUE OF NATIONAL IMPORTANCE.

Revolutions and wars are the stock-in-trade of the Conspirators so are Dictatorships. All that is necessary to put into actual practice the principles of a true Christian Social Order is for the people to express themselves in no uncertain terms and Parliament must obey the mandate of the people. Once parliament enacts the necessary legislation the *police*, and not the military forces, must enforce those laws.

Only if the people are prevented by the conspirators from exer-cising their rights and prerogatives could a temporary dictatorship be justified and the only modern example is that of Spain.

World War One was fought supposedly ''to save democracy'' and ''To make the world a better place in which to live''. World War Two was fought ''To save the World from pagan Naziism''. Communist revolutions are supposed to free the workers from various forms of tyranny. Can any thinking person honestly say that to-day Democracy is safer; or that our liberties are more secure; or that the workers are free from economic bondage ? Has Christianity made progress towards the day when Christ will reign as King ? The reverse is true.

Edmund Burke wrote a great TRUTH. He said : "ALL THAT IS NECESSARY FOR THE TRIUMPH OF EVIL IS THAT *GOOD* MEN SIT DOWN AND DO NOTHING".

The Scriptures tell us these things I describe will come to pass. Daniel the Prophet foretold that conditions of tribulation, desolation, and abomination, would precede the second coming of Christ. Christ is quoted by St. Matthew as having confirmed the prophecies of Daniel. Read Chapter XXIV, Verses 15 to 34. But the fact that the Power of Satan will actually rule upon this earth for a limited time does not permit any person, who believes in God, to sit back in despair and do nothing. The Scriptures also tell us "that for the sake of the elect (the faithful ones) those days shall be shortened". We are informed that if God did not put an end to the Rule of Satan, by sending Christ with a heavenly Host, no flesh would survive.

All this evidence clearly indicates that it is not sufficient to kneel and pray in order to be saved. We must WORK and EARN our salvation. Many people claim they are only concerned with saving their own souls, they intend to do this by saying their prayers. Prayers alone won't obtain for them a passport to Heaven. We have to work, and to fight, with every constitutional means at our disposal to defeat the devil's plan.

CHAPTER XVI

Quo Vadis

The dangers which loom ahead almost obscured
by the "Red Fog" of propaganda.

The purpose of the Illuminati is to convince the people of the nations, who still consider themselves "FREE", that a ONE WORLD GOVERNMENT is the only solution to their many problems. The United Nations Organization is being used for this purpose.

The Communist leaders know the situation. They know that the suggestion of peaceful co-existence by the western powers is nothing more than a colossal attempt at deception. The only problem the Communist dictators have to solve is whether they submit to the dictates of the International Capitalists or whether they, like Hitler and Stalin, decide to try to destroy them.

The Illuminati hold the World in economic bondage, and their agentur dictate government's policy, because we foolishly acknowledge that we owe them the astronomical sums they claim is *our* national debt. Let us study the final phases of their "long range" plan.

Having used Nazism and Communism to remove nearly all the crowned heads; having by one means and another practically exterminated the natural born aristocracy and leaders: having brought the nations into the bondage of usury, the directors now wish to use the United Nations organization to usher into being, by peaceful methods if possible, a One World Super-Government. It is obvious that they cannot accomplish this as long as the Communist dictators challenge the ability of the internationalists to usurp despotic power. Therefore they must first of all destroy Communism at home and abroad.

The only way they could accomplish this purpose is to first turn the remaining so-called democratic governments into premier-dictatorships and they have certainly succeeded in doing this because we have had nothing other than premier-dictators for the past fifty years. How many plebiscites have the ministers of the crown held in the past fifty years? Plebiscite means, "The vote of the common people, especially the direct vote of all the people on a question of public policy".

What the public must never forget, and they must keep reminding their elected representatives of the fact, that the leaders of the Illuminati believe that Lucifer is the all-powerful supernatural force. The Illuminati intend to use Atheisitic Communism, Zionism, Internationalism, and all other "ISMS" up to a certain point *but* after the nations have been merged into an International State the Illuminati then intend to crown their leader KING-DESPOT of the universe and usurp the powers of World Government.

The agentur of the Illuminati will next proceed to eradicate racial characteristics by mixing the Black, Red, Yellow and White races. This experiment has already been carried out on a large scale. Dr. Brock Chisholm has advocated on the C.B.C. that "by mixing the races all racial problems would disappear". He advocated that the white race should limit the size of their families and adopt coloured children for backward countries.

The next step in the diabolical plan would be to render the masses docile and obedient to their masters. This is to be accomplished by mass medication. Experiments along these lines have been conducted extensively since 1900 as was told previously. Fluoridation fits perfectly into this phase of the conspiracy.

The increase of the world's population is to be strictly controlled on the excuse that the earth cannot feed the numbers which will result from unrestricted births, despite the fact that starvation and want are brought about by diabolical controls, and that Canada and the U.S.A. dont know how to market their surplus grain, meat and butter.

The king-despot will decide how many human beings are required to serve the state. His efficiency experts will advise him how many of each type of human being should be born. Selected males, picked for their mental or physical features, will father the human race by means or artificial insemination. Women who have also been specially selected will be used as human incubators. Extensive experiments have already been carried out behind the Iron Curtain in this field of science for the past thirty-seven years.

After these steps in the diabolical conspiracy have been accomplished it will be a simple matter to erase all knowledge of God from the human mind by scientific "brain washing" systematically applied. The rule of Satan will take over instead of that of Christ the King. This is the Science of Frend known as Psychopolitics.

The national governments should be reorganized to function as is laid down by the constitutions of the Christian-democratic nations which, in their original form, are based on the high principles of Divine Law and Justice and the dignity of man. Thus can the rule of Almighty God be put into effect upon this earth. The way may then be prepared for Christ to come and reign as King. Thus the plans of those who worship Satan can be frustrated and confounded and utterly destroyed. It is just as simple as that. There is nothing complicated in bringing about order out of the present chaos. All that is needed is united action on the part of those whose liberties are being endangered. The united action must be put into effect calmly but firmly, and in accordance with the provisions laid down in our constitutions, which distinctly state that those elected to represent the people shall carry out the will of the people.

Many things of great importance have happened to prove the existence of the continuing Luciferian Conspiracy, since "Pawns In the Game", and "The Red Fog Over America" were published in 1955. Scholars, politicians, ministers of many religions, and even revolutionary leaders, have written from all parts of the world submitting further documentary evidence to prove the existence of the LUCIFERIAN CONSPIRACY as exposed by the Bavarian Government in "The Original Writings (Protocols) of the Order and Sect of the Illuminati", as published in 1786.

Several historians gave us a great deal of further information regarding Weishaupt, his writings, and subversive activities. Another reader sent us a copy of "The Mystery of Freemasonry Unveiled" written by Cardinal Caro Y. Rodriguez of Chile, first published in 1925. This book explains how Weishaupt organized the Grand Orient Lodges of Universal Freemasonry to be the secret headquarters of the Illuminati, who direct all phases of the Continuing Luciferian Conspiracy, and tells how the Illuminati obtained control of Freemasonry AT THE TOP,

Other evidence received definitely proves the following to be facts. Weishaupt was Jesuit trained. It is stated, he was an ordained Priest and was unfrocked for his activities. He was a man of extraordinary ability. He became a Doctor of Canon Law and taught at Ingolstadt University the latter half of the 18th century. He came under the influence of the Rothschilds and ultimately defected from the Christian religion because he became convinced that God's plan for the rule of Creation was so weak as to be impractical. He therefore accepted the Luciferian plan based on the establishment of a Luciferian type of totalitarian dictatorship to be enforced by Satanic Despotism.

Under this dictatorship the Illuminati, through their Agentur, will control the human race, body, mind, and soul. Weishaupt revised and modernized the protocols of the Illuminati in order to take full advantage of the progress being made in applied science, and changing social, and economic conditions. The revised plan required that well bred, highly intelligent, men and women be selected during early youth and then educated, and trained, so the Illuminati could place them in executive positions in international finance, industry, scientific research, politics, and religion.

These agentur were to mold the policies of all governments so that, in the long run, they furthered the secret plans of the Illuminati to established one form or another of a ONE WORLD GOVERNMENT, THE POWERS OF WHICH THE ILLUMINATI WERE TO USURP.

In order to bring about this desired end Weishaupt instructed the Illuminati to organize, direct, finance, and control International Communism, Naziism, Political Zionism, class wars, racial hatreds, and economic depressions, so they could foment wars and revolutions on an ever increasing scale.

Weishaupt reasoned that if this program of self-destruction could be imposed on the masses long enough it would so weaken their national and religious institutions that the Goyim could finally be made to accept a One World Government and ultimately be enslaved physically, mentally, and spiritually. He emphasied that the success of the plan depended on the ability of those entrusted with its development keeping their identity and objectives secret.

Weishaupt instructed the Illuminati to infiltrate their Agentur into Freemasonry, and all other secret societies, to advocate the doing away with all established religions in favour of THE UNIVERSAL BROTHERHOOD OF MAN. This was to be superseded by the Universal Manifestation of the Luciferian Creed when they crowned their leader King-Despot of the Universe. The Illuminati were instructed to unite all Nihilist and Atheistic revolutionary organizations for the common purpose of overthrowing the power of the Tzars of Russia, and subjugating the Russian people so the Illuminati could turn the Russian Empire into the stronghold of Atheistic-Communism and use its destructive powers to eliminate remaining political and religious institutions until only Atheistic-Communism, and Christianity, remained between them and their final goal.

Political-Zionism was to be made serve two purposes. (1) To provide the excuse for the Illuminati to establish a sovereign state in Palestine where the Illuminati would ultimately crown their leader King-Despot of the entire world. (2) To enable the Illuminati to foment a third global war in which pro-Zionists and pro-Moslems would destroy each other and thus bring the world to that stage of the conspiracy when only Atheistic-Communism and Christianity would stand between the Illuminati and the day they would crown their leader King-Despot of the World. In addition to revising the Protocols of the Luciferian Conspiracy, Weishaupt also wrote "Morals and Dogmas" which showed him to be a believer in the Luciferian plan for rule of the Universe based on the premise that "Might is Right". He proved himself to be diabolicaly inspired when he detailed the plan by which Communists and Christians were to be made destroy themselves in a war the Illuminati would foment to make them fight each other. It was to explain this final phase of the conspiracy that Pike wrote Mazzini Aug. 15th 1871. Weishaupt explained that in order to ensure unbroken continuity the Illuminati must select their successors from among their own immediate entourage, before they died.

He also explained how the Illuminati, and their Agentur, could escape the dangers of the wars and revolutions they fomented by preparing areas they could use as sanctuaries. He stated : "Ours they (the combatants) will never touch because we will know the hour well in advance and will be prepared" (for such exigences). *

Weishaupt decided to start off the revised plans for world domination with the French Revolution which he scheduled to take place in 1789. He, and his associates, planned "The Reign of Terror" to be used to create an atmosphere which would enable their Agentur to liquidate all persons who, by reason of their influence in society, politics, or religion, were considered obstacles in their path to world domination.

With devilish cunning Weishaupt foresaw the danger of Public Opinion should their diabolic secret leak out. He ordered that if the Illuminati so much as suspected weakness, or disloyalty, they should liquidate those suspected in a manner which would make the public believe they had died as suicides, by accident, or natural causes. The oath of allegiance requires the initiate to swear absolute obedience to the leader of the Council of Thirty Three, the Illuminati, and to recognize NO MORTAL AS ABOVE HIM.

Weishaupt pointed out that it was immaterial how many GOYIM (human Cattle) were slaughtered as the Illuminati advanced towards their goal because, in the final analysis, their new Order would consist of the Illuminati, their Agentur, a few millionaires, and economists, and SUFFICIENT SOLDIERS AND POLICE TO CONTROL THOSE OF THE PROLETARIAT who survived the final cataclysm. Weishaupt reasoned that the population of the world should be regulated so as to provide the brains necessary to govern, and the slaves necessary to serve, the new Order. Any surplus population was to be considered as a burden to the state.

The Illuminati were instructed to remain in the dark and unidentified. They were to direct from behind the scenes of government, though their Agentur. Weishaupt explained that the Agentur should use financial and sex bribery, political blackmail, and intimidation to force as many as they required to do their bidding. He explained that those they "bought" should be used as "The Million pairs of eyes" which would enable the Illuminati to direct the plans of their conspiracy intelligently.

Weishaupt warned that no attempt was to be made to disclose the fact that the Illuminati worshiped Lucifer, until AFTER the

---

* The author has been given definite proof that the islands in the Caribbean Sea have been set aside as a "Sanctuary". A group of the wealthest Political Zionists in Toronto (E. P. Taylor and Bronfman multi-millionnaire) have bought up the choicest sites. They undoubtedly acted on the advice of millionnaire Arthur Vining Davis, chairman of Alcoa's board of directors, which group promote the fluoridation of the public's drinking water throughout the world. Davis had previously acquired 100,000 acres from the Cuban Government on the beautiful Isle of Pines located in the Caribbean, 80 minutes by air from Key West, Florida. Since Davis acquired this real estate the price of other available sites has been advanced from less than $5.00 per acre to over $10,000. This ensures that no Goyim "Human Cattle" obtain residence upon the Isle of Pines except as servants (slaves) of Davis and his selected or approved One Worlders.

final social cataclysm, between Atheists and Christians had ended, and they had crowned THEIR LEADER King-despot of the entire universe. Then, and not until then, "When no cunning or Power could prevent them" they were to make known, for the first time, the Luciferian ideology and force the people to accept it by the practice of Psychopolitics enforced by Satanic despotism.

The diabolical details of the continuing Luciferian conspiracy were discovered by the Bavarian government in 1786 and sent to the heads of the Church and State in Europe that same year. The fact that this warning, and others given since, have been ignored, illustrates the strength, influence and political power of the Illuminati, and explains why Weishaupt's diabolical plan has progressed until it has reached its semi-final stage.

BRIEF HISTORY OF CONSPIRACY SINCE 1786

Most readers are familiar with the story of the French revolution. In "Pawns In The Game" I explained how Weishaupt organized the Grand Orient Lodges to be the secret headquarters of the Illuminati. I also stated the Illuminati intended to infiltrate their Agetnur into every branch, and degree, of Freemasonry. I pointed out that the Illuminati had made provision for the elimination of individual Masons who began to suspect their devilish purpose and proved unwilling to go along with the conspirators.

A great many readers, including three 32nd degree Masons, and a number of Catholic priests, have submitted evidence which further confirms the TRUTH of these statements. One reader put me in touch with the Rev. Father Eustace Eilers, of the Passionist Missions, Birmingham, Alabama. After an exchange of credentials Fathier Eilers provided me with a copy of "The Mystery of Freemasonry Unveiled" written by His Eminence Cardinal Caro Y Rodriguez of Santiago, Chile, first published in 1925. This book confirmed everything I had said regarding the way the Illuminati established control of universal Freemasonry AT THE TOP. This policy they apply to ALL other secret societies, political, and religious organizations, and institutions. In other words they constitute themselves "The Secret and Invisible Government". Cardinal Rodriguez substantiated what he published by documentary evidence undoubtedly obtained mainly from the Secret Archives of the Vatican. He says that not one Mason in one hundred, below the 32nd degree, even suspects the Illuminati are in control AT THE TOP. Those 32nd degree Masons who have been in contact with us, since, agree with what he says.

The Cardinal also confirms that Weishaupt's revised and modernized version of the Age Old conspiracy required the Illuminati to organize, finance, direct and control International Communism, Naziism, and Political Zionism in order to enable them to divide the world's population in opposing camps on political, racial, and religious issues, and make them fight and thus destroy the existing political and religious institutions. To prove this statement the Cardinal quotes from a letter signed by General Albert Pike. He was

Sovereign Pontiff of Universal Freemasonry, and head of the Illuminati, assisted by ten Ancients of the Supreme Grand Orient Lodge of Charleston, U.S.A. at the time.

The letter is dated August 15th 1871. It is addressed to Pike's Illustrious Brother Gussepi (Joseph) Mazzini who had directed the Illuminati's revolutionary programme, in accordance with Weishaupt's plan, since 1834. The letter instructed Mazzini how he was to unite his many revolutionary organizations for the common purpose of destroying the powers of the Tzars, and subjugating the Russian people, in order that the Illuminati could turn the Russian Empire into the stronghold of Atheistic Communism. Pike explained it was the intention of the Illuminati to organize and finance Atheistic-Communism and then use its destructive force to eliminate the remaining political and religious institutions which still remained standing between the Illuminati and the day they could Crown THEIR leader King-despot of the entire universe. On page 188 the Cardinal names several authorities who made reference to Pike's letter and plan in 1895 and 1896. He states that Pike's letter is catalogued in the Library of the British Museum, London, England.

Pike explained, with callous disregard of human interests and spiritual values, how in the final stage of the conspiracy the Illuminati will provoke a formidable social catacylsm as the result of which they would conquer Atheistic-Communism and Christianity, by making them exterminate each other, "Both at the same time".

Pike's letter also confirmed what I had published regarding the Illuminati's plan to make Zionists and Moslems destroy each other as world powers in a war that would involve many other countries. If the war between Political Zionists and Islam, as now being fomented, is permitted to break out ONLY Atheistic-Communism and Christendom will remain as WORLD POWERS when it is ended. A one world government will then be formed as detailed in Pike's letter to Mazzini, and the Illuminati will crown their leader King-despot of the entire universe. If one Cardinal knows so much regarding every phase, and detail, of the continuing Luciferian conspiracy, how it is the rest of Roman Catholic Hierarchy maintains such a deadly silence in regard to this matter? Why is the discipline of the Church used to gag any Priest who dares to try to make the TRUTH known to fellow Christians? Weishaupt boasted that the Illuminati would infiltrate into the Vatican, and bore from within, until they left it nothing but an empty shell. Can it be that the Illuminati has made good its boast? What other explanation is there? I regret to record that Father Eilers died suddenly, *of a heart attack*, shortly after arranging with me to make the Cardinal's book available to the general public. Since I exposed certain events which indicate the agentur of the Illuminati have infiltrated into the Vatican I have received communications from a number of Priests who have studied in the Vatican. These Priests are located in widely separated parts of the world. Those who wrote assured me that the fears I express are more than well founded. One priest informed me that the Pope was surrounded by picked "Specialists", "Experts" and "Advisors" to such an extent that he was a little better than a prisoner in his own palace. Another priest informed me of the eternal surveillance exercised over the Pope. Ostensibly those who maintain the surveillance are activated by love and devotion but they give him no freedom of action even in the privacy of his own chambers. The priest said "Those who exercise this surveillance are all hand picked members of a certain order and they all come from the same institution in Germany located near where Weishaupt lived and conspired, while on this earth."

Another priest commented on the article in which "News Behind The News" made known that the Pope had asked the faithful to pray for "The Silent Church". He is said to have made this appeal during his last severe illness, when the surveillance referred to was relaxed. The Priest said "Your interpretation that he means the Church in the so-called 'FREE' countries is, in my opinion, correct."

Another priest, who spent five years within the Vatican, wrote to say the Illuminati are in the Vatican. He explained how they had involved Msgr. Cipico with the widow of a Fascist general, and in the wholesale theft of goods sent to Italy, and the Vatican, for relief purposes. This priest stated one of the doctors who attended the Pope during his severe illness is mixed up in the Montesi case. His name is said to be one of those, Polito, the former chief of police of Rome, is now charged with suppressing during the investigation into Wilma Montesi's death.

This is all very shocking, but the Scriptures record that the Illuminati bribed Judas, one of the twelve whom Christ made his Apostles. History records how they have infiltrated their agentur into ALL Governments they have destroyed to date. Why would the devil's agents, in human form, not infiltrate into the Vatican? By striking the Shepherd they can scatter the flock of 400,000,000 Roman Catholics located throughout the world. Is it not essential to the success of the Luciferian conspiracy that the Illuminati be in position to silence the voice which could order 400,000,000 people not to allow themselves to become involved in the final social cataclysm now being provoked as Pike predicted would be the case in 1871? If 400,000,000 Catholics, located throughout the world, refused to become involved in war, and cried out as one voice against the Illuminati, and exposed their devilish plans, the force of public opinion would cast the Illuminati into Hell where they belong.*

One other fact regarding the Pope is of great importance. I was sent a cutting from a French language newspaper published in Canada. It is reputed to be a dispatch from Rome. It states that the Pope was in favour of a One World Government. In my opinion, that report is a lie. It calculated to influence French-Canadian Catholics in favour of "A ONE WORLD GOVERNMENT". Christ said, "My Kingdom is not of this world" but he definitely told us that those who wished to serve God should work to establish His plan for the rule of creation upon this earth, in order that His Will

---

* Every Catholic attending Low Mass asks St. Michael, by the power of God, to cast into Hell Satan, and all his wicked angels, (Agentur of the Illuminati) who wander about this world seeking the ruin of souls. All the 400,000,000 Catholics need to do is translate their prayer into ACTION.

might be done here as it is in Heaven. Christ gave us that mandate when he gave us the Lord's Prayer. The Pope would never willingly advocate one, or another, form of a totalitarian government. The Catholic Universal Church advocates the spiritual brotherhood of man under the Fatherhood of God but NOT the brotherhood of man as is being promoted by those who also advocate Secularism, Atheism, Paganism, Humanitarianism, World Federalism, and the Luciferian ideology.*

Why do the Bishops not explain these important matters to their flocks? If the Illuminati seek control it would be at the level of Cardinals and Bishops. We have proved it is impossible for members of the Roman Catholic laity to obtain an acknowledgement from the Pope when they write letters dealing with the existence of the continuing Luciferian conspiracy, as conducted by the Illuminati. It seems unlikely they reach His Holiness. Letters have also been addressed to Priests, who are secretaries to Cardinals, seeking information which would enable us to lift the lid and expose those who enforce the conspiracy of silence. But although the letters were registered, and sent special delivery, they all remain unacknowledged. What kind of Shepherds are these who ignore the appeals made by members of their flocks? This situation is not new. It existed in Abraham Lincoln's time, otherwise why did he write "To sin by silence when they should protest — makes cowards of men?"

Only supernatural Satanic power could have enabled Agentur of the Illuminati to install themselves as "Experts" and "Advisors", in key positions, behind the scenes of *ALL* governments, political, and ecclesiastical. That this situation existed long before even Lincoln's day is proved by the Holy Scriptures (Ephesians 6, 10-17.) includes this message "Put on the armor of God, that you may be able to stand against the wiles of the devil. FOR OUR WRESTLING IS NOT AGAINST FLESH AND BLOOD, but against Principalities and the Powers, against the spiritual forces of wickedness on high." Could any further proof be asked of us who say "the Luciferian conspiracy was hatched in Heaven to wean supernatural beings away from Almighty God, and was transferred to this earth in the Garden of Eden?" Does history not prove it has continued progressively ever since, until to-day it is in its semi-final stage? Christ made this great TRUTH known to the masses, but the Agentur of the Illuminati, who are in control AT THE TOP, have rendered the masses they plot to subjugate, deaf to His teachings. Even ordained Ministers mostly content themselves by teaching *THE GOODNESS OF GOD* but fail to teach THE BADNESS OF LUCIFER, or to explain how the Illuminati conspire to prevent God's plan, for the RULE OF THE CREATION, from being put into effect on this small earth of ours. By preventing the establishment of God's rule, as explained to us by Christ, and other Prophets, those who serve the Luciferian Cause make it impossible for God's Will to be done on this earth as it is in Heaven.

---

* Since writing this I have heard that American and Canadian Cardinals and Bishops have been called to Rome to discuss these most important matters.

The real issue is so very, very, simple. The public, if *FULLY* informed on this vital subject, could be united in the common cause of establishing God's plan, for the Rule of His Creation, upon this earth just as the Illuminati organize ALL subversives, and perverts to further the Luciferian Cause. Moslems, Jews, and all other people who worship the One and ONLY God, Creator of Heaven and earth could be united in such a common cause. This would stop the Illuminati dividing us against each other. Such a force of united public opinion would automatically defeat the Illuminati's plans because their lies and deceits could not penetrate the armor of God which would protect ALL who accept the TRUTH as made known to the Human Race by Christ and many other Prophets of Almighty God. Wars and revolutions are weapons intended to be used by the agents of Lucifer to bring the inhabitants to ultimate subjugation. Therefore, those who wish to establish God's plan for the rule of Creation must work to prevent and to abolish wars.

Those who are *for* God, and *against* Lucifer, have only one weapon at their disposal — and that is to teach the TRUTH, the whole TRUTH, and nothing but the TRUTH. That is the armor of God. People who accept the whole TRUTH are able to "quench all the fiery darts of the most wicked one". Even the poisoned cups won't hurt them. They are invulnerable to the lies and deceits used by the Illuminati and their agentur. They become immune to the teachings of the false priests and prophets, and to the wiles and cunning of the modern Anti-Christs, who for the last century have been working such marvels as to deceive even the elect if that were possible. Those who would use nuclear power for *DESTRUCTIVE* purposes are of the Illuminati.

Those who made the secrets of nuclear research available to the Soviet leaders did so to keep Communism equal in strength and power to the whole of Christendom in accordance with Weishaupt's and Pike's plans. If we can't be frightened into accepting the rule of the Illuminati submissively then they intend to bomb us into submission.

HOW THE ILLUMINATI CONTROL COMMUNISM

In July 1955 The Hon. Mr. Stuart S. Garson, Minister of Justice, asked the Canadian Parliament to grant him more money with which to build up the force of the Royal Canadian Mounted Police, which is responsible for Canada's internal security. He said so many R.C.M.P. officers were engaged in anti-subversive activities there weren't enough left to perform the ordinary police duties required of them.

Mr. John Blackmore, M.P. for Lethbridge, Alberta, asked the Minister if he knew that Communists conducted seventeen schools in Toronto, and others in every centre of population in Canada in which political subversion, and the inversion of the Commandments of God, were taught to Canadian children?

Mr. Garson tried hard to evade a direct answer but Mr. Blackmore waved a copy of "Pawns In The Game" high in the air and demanded "Do you admit or deny the TRUTH of the statements made on page 125 of this publication?"

Mr. Garson then admitted the statements published in "Pawns In The Game" were true. Mr. Blackmore then asked him if it would not be more logical to have the R.C.M.P. close these schools, and thus nip Communism in the bud, rather than permit them to carry on their subversive activities against God and the State and then ask for an increase in the budget of the Department of Justice to cover the extra cost of keeping the ever increasing number of Communist graduates under police surveillance?

Mr. Garson said it wasn't the Government's policy to interfere with these schools. He explained that the government based its policy on the democratic rights of Free Speech. Was such utter drivel ever spoken before on the floor of a British Parliament? The Supreme Court of the U.S.A. is following a similar policy. What are you the people doing about this? The Canadian Minister of Justice openly confessed on the floor of Parliament that the Canadian Government permitted the leaders of the Communist Party to teach your children and mine to sin against God and to be disloyal to Our Ruler Queen Elizabeth II. The public must remember the Ministers are sworn to protect the interests and person of Her Majesty. And Her Majesty's so-called "Loyal Opposition" didn't even demand the impeachment of those who had publicly admitted their disloyalty. Conditions have deteriorated into a shocking state of affairs.*

When Mr. Blackmore tried to enlarge on this all important matter, which affects the security of our country, and the lives of EVERY Canadian citizen, members of other political parties jumped to the defense of the Minister, and forced an end to the discussion. Proving once again that the Illuminati control ALL political parties AT THE TOP. A private member can't do his duty until this control AT THE TOP is broken.

For the sake of emphasis, we repeat once more, the Communist Party, *in every country in the world*, is controlled by the Illuminati. They use its subversive, and destructive forces, to destroy our political and religious institutions. The Agentur of the Illuminati within the Canadian and American governments protect the members of the Communist party against action by the R.C.M.P. and the F.B.I. who could, if permitted to do so, arrest every potential revolutionary in North America within 48 hours of the order being given. But the Illuminati only use the Communists to the point where they have served their purpose, and after the Agentur of the Illuminati usurp power, like Lenin did, the Communists are "Purged" and the only revolutionaries allowed to live are those who serve the Illuminati.

Time and again R. C. M. P. officers have *asked* me not to publicly denounce Communist activities in Canada on the grounds that to do so causes them no move around, and alter their security policy, and this makes it harder for them (R. C. M. P.) to keep track of them.

---

* Mr. Diefenbaker has done nothing to correct this serious State of Affairs since he became Prime Minister June 12th

The Communist underground is kept intact, and ever ready to cause a revolt when the Illuminati, who direct the overall plans of the World Revolutionary Movement, consider it is to THEIR advantage to have them do so. The Illuminati will continue to follow this policy until stopped by pressure of public opinion. The Illuminati use a Communist revolt to rid themselves of men and women who could, because of their position and influence in politics, industry, the arts and sciences, society and religion, oppose their plan for ultimate world domination. After those they name have been liquidated in "The Reign of Terror" the Illuminati's agentur then use "The Reign of Terror" as their excuse for imposing a so-called Proletarian dictatorship under the pretense that such action is necessary to curb the violence of the Mob and restore Law and Order. In every revolution which has taken place to date the agentur of the Illuminati have ALWAYS turned the so-called Proletarian Dictatorship into an absolute dictatorship immediately AFTER a resemblance of Law and Order has been established. For this reason, and no other, agentur of the Illuminati located in the top levels of our governments, prevent the police from doing their duty and protecting the citizens against the leaders of ALL subversive movements.

The reader may form his own opinion regarding how FREE is the so-called FREE and Independent PRESS. Mr. Garson defended the government's policy, or lack of policy, towards Communist schools on the grounds that to close them would be an infringement of the principle of "Free Speech" but the members of the Press Gallery are so well controlled that the ONLY newspaper in Canada which published this amazing story was "News Behind The News" in its first edition October 1956.* Parents, Ministers of religion, and others who are shocked by the exposure of such a state of affairs in Canada should write their Members of Parliament and ask them to send them Hansard Vol. 97, No. 124, and then read page 5882 onwards of the July 8th. edition.

In June 1957 agentur of the Illuminati entrenched in the Justice Department of the U.S.A., protected the Communist leaders in the U.S.A. by a Ruling of the Supreme Court which makes it almost impossible for the FBI and Senate Committee to curb Communist subversive activities until AFTER they have served the purpose of the Illuminati who direct the continuing Luciferian conspiracy. Once again I say Canadians, and Americans, regardless of whether they be Gentiles or Jews; Black skinned or White; Catholic or Protestant, Democrats or Republicans, Liberals or Conservatives, can and should unite in the common cause of ousting the agents of Lucifer from within our governments and replace them with men sworn, to introduce legislation that will establish God's plan for the Rule of His Creation upon this earth. If we do that in America the countries of the world will soon fall in line. 97% of the world's population want Peace. All the masses need is knowledge regarding the Luciferian

* "News Behind The News" is a monthly news-letter published by the National Federation of Christian Laymen who sponsored the publication of this book.

— 230 —

conspiracy to spur them into legal forms of action. We Christian Laymen, as part of the Mystical Body of Christ, must urge our ministers to take the lead.

If any readers doubt the truth of what I say, in this regard, let me remind them that in July 1956 both the Canadian Parliament and the U. S. House of Representatives passed legislation which enabled the agentur of the Illuminati to strengthen the strangle-hold they are now applying to our governments. In the U.S.A. the President was given the right to declare a State of Emergency, and impose a military form of dictatorship upon the country, if *he* decided such drastic measures were necessary. Necessary for what ?* In Canada the same powers were given to Mr. C. D. Howe. Mr. Howe is referred to by many as "Mr. 'Dictator' Howe" because of his words and attitude in parliament used to express his contempt for any member who dared question the infinate wisdom of his suggestions and decisions.

Legislation giving individuals dictatorial powers is contrary to the provisions of the constitutions of both Canada and the United States. As far as Canada is concerned the Supreme Court of nine judges was asked in 1950 to render judgement regarding the Tax-rental Agreements which had been entered into between the Provincial Legislatures and Federal Government. Under the Tax-rental agreements the Provincial governments gave the Federal government the right to levy personal income and corporation taxes. On October 3rd. 1950, seven of the nine judges who heard the arguments were unanimous in their decision that "The Federal and Provincial Governments cannot legally exchange their legislative powers, because the Parliament of Canada, and the Legislatures of the several provinces, are sovereign within their sphere defined by the British North America Act (B.N.A. Act) *but NONE of them has the unlimited capacity of an individual.*"

The learned judges then ruled on the tax-rental agreements and said "They can exercise ONLY the legislative powers respectively given to them by Sections 91 and 92 of the B.N.A. Act, and those powers MUST be found in either of those sections."

"The Constitution of Canada (as set forth in the B.N.A. Act) does NOT belong to the Parliament or to the Legislatures : it belongs to the COUNTRY, and it is THERE that the CITIZENS of the COUNTRY will find THEIR PROTECTION of the RIGHTS to which THEY ARE ENTITLED".

This judgement means that both the Provincial Legislatures and the Federal Government have usurped powers of the people relative to taxation in defiance of the provisions of the Constitution. The Fathers of Confederation knew, better than politicians do to-day, that a small group of wealthy internationalists were determined to obtain world domination. They knew that the Illuminated ones intended to force the peoples into compliance with their will by the simple expedient of taxing them into economic bondage by forcing the countries into wars against each other; and by the introduction of pie-in-the-sky policies, so-called 'Social Security Legislation", cal-

---

* Since this was written he used this power in Little Rock.

culated to lead the citizens along a Primrose path into ultimate economic, physical, mental, and spiritual bondage.

Knowing these things the Fathers of Confederation, like the Founding Fathers, introduced clauses, and sections, into the Constitution calculated to prevent the Federal government usurping power to which they were not entitled. The Fathers of Confederation therefore decided the powers to levy personal income, and corporation taxes should always remain in the hands of the provincial legislatures in Canada, and the State legislatures in the U.S.A., to be levied as agreed to by the citizens who elected those provincial and State governments. If this was not the intention there would be no justification for Provincial and State governments.

The purpose of including Sections 91 and 92 in the B.N.A. Act was to prevent the Federal Government entering foreign wars without calling a plebiscite and from adopting wild, and extravagant, financial policies, and social security programs, which would, in the long run, place the citizens in USURY to the international bankers. Those who introduced sections 91 and 92 in to the B.N.A. Act reasoned that if the PEOPLE controlled the provincial Legislatures, and if the Federal government had to rely on the Provinces to produce the money required to balance the Federal budget, the People would be able to control the budgets presented by the Federal Government. This action on the part of the Fathers of Confederation was plain common sense. It limited the Powers of the Federal governments to conducting the nation's business affairs in a sound and efficient manner.

Canadian Statesmen agreed to confederation on the understanding that the Federal Government would be the nation's board of management elected to conduct the business of the nation in accordance with the wishes of the electorate. In this matter the ideas, and ideals, of Canada's Fathers of Confederation were identical with those of the Founding Fathers on the United States of America. In both countries the Illuminati have *BOUGHT* enough State, and Federal, officials to enable them to place the citizens and countries in USURY as we find ourselves to-day.

Usury is a criminal offence in both countries. Therefore legislation passed, which enabled the Federal authorities to usurp the powers of the people in this regard, is unconstitutional and therefore illegal, as seven out of nine judges of the Supreme court of Canada have already ruled.

Our astronomical national debts were forced upon our citizens by false and lying propaganda which forced us into fighting wars fomented by the international bankers in accordance with the secret plans of the Illuminati. Thus it is that the financial control now exercised by the international bankers, who are agentur of the Illuminati, was obtained by lies, deceits, and false pretenses. This being the case they can be legally repudiated. We are alleged to owe the international bankers billions of dollars, and yet it never cost those who claim we owe them that money more than the scratch of a pen to create the debts they claim we owe. We don't need to fight a revolution to correct this ridiculous state of affairs. We need aroused public opinion, and must demand that the creation of coin and the value thereof be placed in the hands of the people where it rightfully belongs, and as provided for in the constitutions of Canada and the United States of America.

Because the international bankers pooled their resources, and financed both sides in every conflict since 1770, they made huge profits out of every war without risking a cent. In every war they fomented it was a case of "Heads we win — Tails you lose". They were also able to make millionaires of agentur they wished to control; and they made public taxation finance the research their scientists conducted to give the Illuminati the extra control fear, of atomic warfare, enables them to exercise over the people they plot to subjugate. They could never have exercised the fear complex over the people unless they had enabled their cohorts in Russia to develop the nuclear weapons the same time as did Britain and America. It was not Communists, but agentur of the Illuminati, who gave our atomic secrets to their Brother Illuminists who were in control of international Communism. Those who betrayed Canada, Britain, and the U.S.A. were people who had been deceived, bribed, or blackmailed into doing the will of the Illuminati. They were no cloak and dagger Communist conspirators.

As I write these words July 8th, 1957, thirty eight men of 'Brains' are converging on the home of Cyrus Eaton located in the quiet village of Pugwash, Nova Scotia. They come from 14 nations, including those behind the Iron and Bamboo Curtains. They are one and all Internationalists. As such they further the secret plans of the Illuminati. Most of these men are scientists. Among them are Dr Brock Chisholm, and Prof. John Stewart Foster, of McGill University. They are consulting with some men who also attended the secret meeting on St Simon's Island Feb. 14th.-17th. this year. It is safe to say these Illuminated Minds are deciding how those who survive the final social cataclysm shall be selected for breeding purposes; how they shall be fed; how they shall be educated, and how they shall be trained to be obedient slaves of the World Government they intend to control. They will undoubtedly decide how long different categories of the human race shall be permitted to live, and how we shall die as good and faithful followers of Lucifer. These men have all, at one time or another, publicly announced their disagreement with God's plan for the government and rule of Creation. They try to convince more and more people that they are better qualified to know what is best for the Human Race than Almighty God Himself. The whole gang are insane with craving for unlimited POWER. They are a menace to society. They should be locked up.

GENERAL ALBERT PIKE

While Albert Pike was Sovereign Pontiff of Universal Freemasonry, and Head of the Illuminati during the 1870s, he revised and modernized the ritual of the Black Mass celebrated to emphasise the Luciferian and Satanic victory achieved in the Garden of Eden, and over Christ to end his mission on earth. The celebrant of the Black Mass plays the part of Satan. He introduces a Virgin Priestess to the joys of sexual intercourse and makes known to her the mystery of procreation. Pike's version also includes a paradox on the betrayal, and crucifixion of Christ. The desecration of a Host consecrated by a Roman Catholic Priest is part of this abomination. Lucifer is worshiped as "The Giver of the True Light"; the fountain of ALL wisdom; and as the greatest of all Supernatural Beings. Satan is worshiped as Lucifer's Prime Minister. He is referred to as the innocent victim of the despotic power of God who made him companion in chains of all the oppressed. One of the salutations used is "Come Satan, exiled by priests, but blessed of my heart."

A Black Mass is usually followed by a Bacchanalian orgy. Those who attend are supplied with sex-stimulating drugs and beverages. They worship the body and indulge in sexual excesses, and perversions, of all kinds, Priestesses are provided for the occasion. I have never been given any evidence that would even suggest that lower degree Freemasons are permitted to take part in these abominations. Attendence at a real Black Mass is restricted to Grand Orient Masons who have been initiated into the "Order and Sect of the Illuminati", and selected people who are devoid of morals whom the Illumunists wish to control. Apparently only people who have in some definite manner indicated that they have lost all faith and belief in Almighty God are even approached to become initiates of the Order and Sect of the Illuminati. There are, however, many minor versions of body and sex worship, obscene movies and "Circuses" being two of them.

There is ample evidence to prove that both men and women, whom top-level agentur of the Illuminati wish to control, are unveigled into taking part in sexual orgies at which drugs are used. Those incriminated can usually be "persuaded" or "blackmailed" afterwards into doing the will of those who know their shameful secret.

An ordained minister of the Christian religion in England sent in a report telling of the Bacchanalian orgy which cost over £50,000. He stated that over fifty "Priestesses" were despoiled. He said those involved included people in high levels of government and society. He claimed some participants were connected with the Royal Household. The Minister explained that many of those involved didn't know what they were being let in for when they accepted the invitations. They found they couldn't withdraw once the orgy had got under way. He said some of the exhibitions were so utterly abominable, and disgusting, that his informant vomited, and confided in him to ease his conscience. This report would seem to explain the strained relations which developed between members of the Royal Household as reported in the American Press early this year. It could also explain the rash of divorces which has hit high society in England since then. He states that Scotland Yard is now investigating this particular case.

Long before the Montesi case was reported in the American Press, I received information from Italy that 21 year old Wilma

Montesi had collapsed from exhaustion as the result of repeated sexual assaults. The report stated she died from an overdose of drugs administered in an effort at first to sustain her and afterwards to revive her. She is said to have been acting as a Priestess at a Black Mass celebrated in the Hunting Lodge of an Italian nobleman. My informant told me that so many people, high in the affairs of Church and State, were involved that it was unlikely the TRUTH would ever be made known to the general public. Wilma's beautiful body was found on an Italian beach, being lapped by the waves, April 7th. 1953. The inquest gave a verdict to the effect that she had drowned accidentally. The matter was allowed to drop.

But the old saying "Murder will out" proved true in this case. Silvano Muto had the courage to publish the facts concerning her death in a magazine he publishes. The story aroused such a force of public opinion that the Government was forced to appoint Leonardo Circoli to investigate the circumstances surrounding her death. This is what happened. The Black Mass, and Bacchanalian orgy, took place in The Casa Della Terre, once the favorite resort of former King Victor Emmannel of Italy. Gian Pierre Piccioni was arrested in connection with Montesi's death Sept. 24th. 1954. He was employed by the Italian State Radio in its Jazz Music Department. Gian's father was Italy's Foreign Minister, and delegate to the United Nations. He had the grace to resign after the scandal could be no longer kept secret.

Those investigating the case were blocked at every turn by senior Police and government officials, who were evidently under control of subversives and underworld racketeers. Finally, determined efforts brought about the arrest of Francesco Saverio Polito, the Chief of Police of Rome. He was charged with deliberately suppressing evidence concerning the case obtained in an earlier investigation. These facts should give great encouragement to those who work to establish God's plan for the rule of creation upon this earth, because they prove that the Illuminati have not as yet obtained *absolute* control over all those who occupy high places in Church and State.

With the arrest of the Chief of Police the case broke open. Ugo Montagna, who had been protected by the Chief, and considered himself as above the Law, was also arrested, much to the delight of the average Italian citizen. Montagna is typical of the Illuminati's top-level agentur. His origin is obscure. Like Topsy he just happened. He became prominent in the political life of Italy after Mussolini usurped power. He had access to unlimited funds. Money enabled him to buy key-men, power, and influence. He, and his set, could defy the Law, and all the conventions of society, with impunity. That he was appointed by the Illuminati to watch Mussolini's every move seems obvious. He watched Mussolini so closely that he was able to carry on an illicit love affair with Clarette Petacci while she was Mussolini's favourite mistress.

Montagna was debonair, sophisticated, and charming in a Satanic way. He was able to influence men, and women, high in society, and at the top levels of Church and State. He used political blackmail to force many people to do the Will of his masters, the Illuminati.

It was whispered in the St. Hubert Club that the Illuminati decided Mussolini had outlived his usefulness to them about the same time Montagna tired of having sexual relations with Clarette Petacci. It is said Montagna, under the guise of friendship, arranged for Mussolini, and Clarette, to escape from approaching Allied forces and the rising wrath of the Italian people. He then secretly betrayed them to a fellow Illuminist within the Communist Party who had them intercepted. History relates how both Mussolini and his mistress were captured by Communists and treated in an utterly inhuman and most abominable manner. After being subjected to many obscenities they were hung upside down to die. Labels on their bodies read ''Pig-meat''.

The St. Hubert Club is the gathering place of the ultra modern set in Italy. It is patronized by people who have satiated every carnal desire. The men and women who sit at the tables are bored stiff. They are always ''Looking for a thrill''. They want to whet their jaded sexual appetites.

Muto picked up the threads, which enabled him to expose the real cause of Montesi's death, in the St. Hubert Club. He learned that British, French, Italian, and American actresses, and society women had acceded to Montagna's suggestion that they be Priestesses at Black Masses celebrated in the Casa Della Torre. Checking this lead, with some of those who had been involved, Muto heard of scenes of Satanic debauchery which went beyond the extremes of those used by Nero to entertain his guests in ancient Rome.

One woman told of sexual perversions which took place in an underground apartment which had been made sound-proof, and lined with the furs of wild animals. She claimed fifteen men and fifteen women took part simultaneously. Other abominations were related which involved men and boys, women and young girls. Finally Muto learned that Wilma Montesi had taken part in a sexual endurance contest in which several other women and many men were involved. She collapsed from utter physical exhaustion. She died as the result of an overdose of drugs, presumably administered to stimulate or revive her. Her body was thrown into the sea.

The publication of such abominable facts would not be justified if it was not for the purpose of warning parents that young boys, and teen-aged girls, are being selected, and trained by Agentur of the Illuminati to perform at similar abominations in Canada and the United States. In 1944 a young girl was found unconscious lying naked at the water's edge in the Exhibition grounds, Toronto. She was taken into the Sick Bay of H.M.C.S. ''York'' and given emergency treatment. She was then rushed to a city hospital. She had been a participant in a sexual marathon. Despite the best efforts of Police, and Naval Intelligence Officers, she refused to give any information that would disclose where this abomination had taken place. She refused to incriminate others who had been involved. She admitted, quite frankly, that what she had done was done of her own free will. She explained that fatigue and caused her to collapse.

Mont Tremblant, in Quebec, was frequently the scene of similar Bacchanalian orgies until it burnt down a couple of years ago. I exposed the real character of this fabulous resort in 1955.*

Just as Big sancturies have been, and are still being prepared, to shelter Illuminists and their agentur during the next planned social cataclysm, so are smaller ones in use as Summer Homes and resorts on large estates, which were once producing farms, located ten to twenty miles from big city limits. To prove to sceptics that those who have abandoned God, and accepted the Luciferian Creed, follow the same pattern of Satanism all over the world, I asked three men to investigate this particular aspect of the Luciferian conspiracy in widely separated locations. One in Eastern Canada, one in central Canada, and the other in western Canada. This is what they found out :

Farms located beyond the danger-limit of probable atomic targets are being bought up by wealthy people. In Eastern, Central, and Western Canada there are exclusive clubs in which these Bacchanalian orgies take place. To preserve the absolute seclusion of one of these millionaire resorts influence was brought to bear on the Government, and on a national transportation system, to discontinue a public service which had been in operation for fifty years. Since this service was discontinued the palatial resort in now only accessible by private boats and planes. The caretaker in this resort is an American intellectual who finds it better to remain out of circulation because of fear of scandle. He lives in voluntary exile with the daughter of a Canadian Member of Parliament. The couple are not married. Mysterious meetings are held from time to time. Those attending the meetings, and all supplies and entertainment, are flown in. I reported these facts, with photographic evidence to support my statements, to a member of Parliament but he wouldn't, or couldn't, do anything to expose these conditions on the floor of the House. WHY ?

Sexual depravity is deliberately being encouraged among the young people of our nations in order to weaken them morally so they will abandon their ideals, break God's Commandments, and defy social conventions. This has been common practice in every country subjugated to date. That intercollegiate football games are afterwards turned into sexual orgies in local hotels doesn't, as previously reported, just happen by accident. Any highschool student knows that the degradation of our youth is well organized, systematic, and gradual. It is to the credit of the present teen-agers that the Majority still remain morally sound and stick to civilized conventions. They just naturally revolt at the thought of sexual promiscuity because of feelings of PROPER pride. It is against the law of God that human beings should willingly become the chattle and plaything of everyone who appeals to their sexual urges.

That sexual promiscuity, and perversions, are being deliberately promoted with a view to helping the Illuminati obtain ultimate con-

---

* See page 212 of first edition of "Red Fog Over America". It has since been rebuilt.

— 237 —

trol of the human race, body, mind, and soul, is proved by Professor Pitrim Sorokin of Harvard University in his book "The American Sex Revolution". The author says perverted sexual behaviour plays a major rôle in modern U. S. political life, and that sex bribery and blackmail are now as prevalent as monetary corruption. He states "Sexually infamous persons, or their proteges, are being appointed to ambassadorships, and other high office, and profligates sometimes become popular mayors of metropolises, members of the cabinet, or leaders of political parties. Among our public officials there is a vast legion of profligates, both heterosexual and homosexual. Our morals have changed so notably that continency, chastity, and faithfulness are increasingly viewed as oddities."

With that statement I agree because my own investigations, conducted while employed at the top-levels of both Federal and Provincial governments, proved that the civil services are simply loaded to capacity with men and women who will have, or give, what is decorously referred to as "A good time". Sexual promiscuity has become so firmly established at all levels of government, and the civil service, that decent citizens find difficulty obtaining employment and retaining it if obtained. If a person refuses to accept established sexual anarchy, it is feared they may squeal.

The existence of sexual promiscuity in government was proved in a shocking and dramatic manner not too long ago when a member of a provincial parliament was killed accidentally. A newspaper reporter was on the scene when the police searched the body. On this man's person was found a book which contained the names of many female civil servants who could be used as "Party Girls" to entertain 'Visiting Firemen'. In addition to the names the telephone number, height and measurements, colour of hair, age, and sexual peculiarities were recorded. He carried what is commonly known as "A stud-book".

Just to prove these conditions are not local, but affect all centres of population as well as all levels of government, further information is submitted.

A painter was engaged decorating a palatial mansion located twenty two miles from Toronto. He became so intrigued with what went on at week-ends that he kept an observation on the place. This painter told my investigator of wild parties which went on in this place, the seclusion of which was assured by armed 'Game-keepers', and savage dogs, which patrolled the ground when these events were taking place. Our informant stated that girls were flown in from Montreal to take part in the High-jinks that went on in this establishment.

The majority of senior police officials know what is going on. Most of them would like to clean up the mess. The fact that they are stopped causes frustration which usually leads to one of two things. They either swim with the tide of crooked and degenerate politics, or they resign. They get tired of knocking off the petty criminals and crooks, while the master-minds go Scott-free.

A comparatively large number of Royal Canadian Mounted Police resign as soon as they qualify for pension, after twenty years service.

This fact proves my point. There used to be no finer body of police in the world than the R.C.M.P., but conditions have changed during the past twenty years. Individual members are mostly a fine type, but the fact that they are often prevented from doing their duty has caused many of the very best men to resign while in their early forties. Frustration made it impossible for them to carry on. The Canadian taxpayers have lost the use of their services when they are at the peak if their careers. Private industry engages them as Security Officers and reaps the benefit of their training, paid for out of the tax-payers money. The vast majority of those who resign wanted to serve their country, but the invisible power of the Illuminati, which controls from behind the scenes of government, says they shall not do their duty, so they quit.

Certain Bishops have accused me, and my associates, as being alarmists. I deny that allegation. I have served on land and sea, under the sea, and in the air : I'm not the alarmist type. I have travelled further, and mixed with more people, in *all* walks of life, than the average Clergyman. I know that, contrary to what many clergy and savants would have the public believe, the members of the Human Race are pretty reasonable people. The majority are sound AT THE CORE. If a threatening danger is explained to them fully, and clearly, the vast majority will face that danger calmly and with courageous fortitude. This statement is proved by the way the people of Britain, Germany, and Japan, and other bombed-out countries, conducted themselves during the last war.

I am the father of seven children, and the grandfather of twenty seven. I feel I have a responsibility to them and the future generations. Our children are a pride and comfort to my wife and I because we told them WHY they shouldn't do this, or go there. I publish what I do in order that other parents will realize the vital importance of informing their children of WHO the Illuminati are, how they select and train their agentur, and how they set their snares, and dig their pit-falls, to trap the innocent and unwary.

Pure accident caused a clergyman to suspect an educationalist was deliberately promoting sexual promiscuity among teen-agers of his congregation. When the investigation ended evidence given in Court proved that this one man had organized the subversion, and perversion, of youth in over ninety centres of population in the U.S.A. The details of this man's Satanic activities, were not made public. They should have been. The fact that the Illuminati do employ such men to further their diabolical plans should be given the widest publicity.

This particular man obtained entry into the schools and homes of the areas he visited as an ''Expert'' and ''Advisor''. He won the confidence of teachers, parents, and pupils. He impressed those he met as being a fine man, with a nice personality, and good manners. They were shocked when evidence proved he had cultivated their confidence to obtain the names of juvenile delinquents and then secretly organized, and financed them to serve the diabolical purposes of those he served.

Billy Graham said in 1957, while conducting his New York Crusade, "Sexual abuses, perversions, and licence have been responsible for the downfull of more empires and nations than any other single sin." He stated the TRUTH. Sexual perversions have played the major rôle in the Luciferian conspiracy from the Garden of Eden to this present day. Sex, used as God intended, is a beautiful experience intended by The Creator of the Universe to fill a very necessary purpose. God intended it to give pleasure and relaxation as well as to procreate, but intercourse was to be restricted to man and his wife. Sexual perversions, and promiscuity, as promoted by those who further the Luciferian conspiracy, are an abomination. Why not explain this matter sensibly to the youth of our nations instead of leaving them in ignorance and vulnerable to the wiles of the Devil's agents? The Scriptures warn us that they wander around the world seeking the ruin of souls. If those who profess to be Christians heeded the Scriptures the conditions I expose could not exist. Informed Public Opinion would not permit it.

WHO ARE THE ILLUMINATI AND THEIR AGENTUR ?

Many Clergymen, news commentators, editors, politicians, etc. blame Communists and Jews as being the root of ALL evil. This is not so. Lucifer is the ROOT of ALL Evil. Satan, the "Prince of this World", is Lucifer's prime minister. Lucifer's conspiracy, against God and the Human Race has been directed continually in this earth by the ILLUMINATI since Cain was conceived in Eve's womb after intercourse with Satan. Satan promised materialistic rewards to those who would help prevent God's plans, for the rule of Creation, being established upon this earth. To-day those who serve the Illuminati enjoy temporal power, unlimited wealth, and carnal pleasures. They do control the world AT THE TOP as their reward for selling their immortal souls to Lucifer.

Men and women of wealth, brains and special abilities who *don't* use their talents to promote God's plan for the rule of Creation, and who don't work to establish God's rule upon this earth, automatically are agentur of the Illuminati. The word Illuminati means brilliant... bright... brainy... intelligent. Those who use their talents to promote evil, and for destructive, rather than constructive, purposes, are offered the opportunity to secretly become an initiated member of "The Order and Sect of the Illuminati" within the Lodges of Grand Orient Masonry.

Men with exceptional ability, who use their knowledge to help establish God's rule on this earth, will receive their reward hereafter. It is unlikely they will achieve success in this life.

It is just as simple as that. Take scientists for example. They are divided into two camps. Those who believe in God as the Creator of the Universe and all in it, and those who don't. Some give God credit and thanks for their special talents and blessings; others do not. Some accept their special mental gifts humbly, and realize their responsibilities to God and the human race, like Banting and Best. Others like Dr. Brock Chisholm, and many of his associates in the Arts and Sciences, are literally "As proud as Lucifer". They actually believe they know how to rule the Human Race better than God. They have convinced themselves, and try to convince others, that only the Luciferian plan, based on the principle that "Might is RIGHT", can ensure permanent Peace and prosperity. They consider God's plan, as explained to our first parents in the Garden of Eden, as too effeminate... too infantile... too soft... too impracticable. They are convinced that the RIGHT to Rule rests with them.

Illuminists like Professor Adam Weishaupt, General Pike, Freud, Einstein and dozens of others, are on record as saying they were "Satanically inspired", some used the words "Demoniacly inspired" which both mean the same thing.

There can be no question of doubt about the fact that those who are initiated into "The Order and Sect of the Illuminati" are extremely clever men. Most of them are NEARLY as clever as the Devil himself. Why people find it difficult to accept the truth regarding the existence of the continuing Luciferian conspiracy is beyond my comprehension. After all the *ONLY* decision *EVERY* human being is required to make, while he is on earth, that is of any importance, is whether he intends to serve God or Lucifer. Many millions find it convenient to PRETEND they want to serve God while they SECRETLY serve the Devil. But they don't fool Almighty God, and they don't fool Lucifer.

Illuminists are *Not* Atheists. They believe in the supernatural. They believe that those who serve the Luciferian cause on this earth will enjoy the same privileges and pleasures in the next world. Communist leaders who secretly serve the Illuminati are not Atheists. What sense would there have been in the deification of Lenin if those who promoted the idea were Atheists instead of Illuminists? Lenin was, and those who deify him are, Illuminists.

The only reason there is confusion in the public's mind regarding this all-important matter is because ministers who teach us God's plan for the rule of creation, don't explain the Luciferian plan also. Apparently they are afraid that if they did more people would defect from God and literally go to the devil. I contend it would be better that people went to hell with their eyes open rather than closed.

Why Christian Ministers should be so afraid to expose the Luciferian conspiracy, is beyond my comprehension. Faith in God is not based upon emotionalism. It is based on love of God because of His infinite perfections. Perfect Faith enables a person to reject all worldly and carnal considerations. Perfect Faith in Almighty God enables a Human Being to be satisfied with the promise of Christ *THAT THE JOYS OF HEAVEN ARE BEYOND HUMAN COMPREHENSION*. Christ didn't waste words. He won't break promises. He allowed the chosen few among his Apostles to see Him transfigured into a celestial Spiritual Being, the image and likeness of God. About the only Christian sect I know who teach their children the TRUTH regarding this matter are the Doukhobors, that despised sect who live in western Canada. They teach their children that until Eve fell for the wiles of Satan and disobeyed God, she and Adam were infused with the spiritual light of Divine grace, which made them the image and likeness of God. Doukhobors teach their children that Eve's disobedence caused God to deprive us of that spiritual illumination which will not be returned to us until we die. They teach that how we live on this earth will decide whether we serve God or Lucifer for all eternity after we die. Doukobours remain outside organized religions because they claim religion has been commercialized and no longer teaches these fundamental truths. It would appear that those who criticize them better remove the beam from their own eyes before they point to the speck in theirs.

They object to sending their children to *PUBLIC* schools because they claim, and rightly so, that modern educationalists teach Secularism, Materialism, and Militarism, which are contrary to the teachings of Christ. They claim, and rightly so, that God entrusted the spiritual and temporal well being of children to their parents, and placed the responsibility for the education of their off springs squarely upon the shoulders of the parents. Believing children should be taught strictly in accordance with the teachings and examples given by Christ they refuse to allow them to be indoctrinated by so called "Modernists" who serve the Illuminati, or Anti-Christs. Constitutionally *NO* authority can usurp the authority of parents, regarding the education of their children providing they teach them God's plan for the Rule of Creation, because those who teach Secularism, Materialism, and Militarism further the Illuminati's plan to turn this earth into a totalitarian Luciferian dictatorship.

The E N D

The Secret Meeting on St. Simon Island

In "Pawns In The Game" I said those who served the Illuminati in Weishaupt's day included Internationalists who had reached the TOP of the business world, the Arts and Sciences, and the professions, as well as a few economists, top-level statesmen, and politicians.

The Illuminati, and their top-level agentur, like the Leopard, don't change their spots. Many people who read my books wrote and asked me to identify the members of "The Order and Sect of the Illuminati". They asked me to name their top-level agentur. They told me they would not believe what I published until I did name them. Until recently I didn't have that knowledge.

People are inclined to be unreasonable. "The Order and Sect of the Illuminati" is the most secret organization existing on earth. Every initiate is sworn to maintain absolute secrecy regarding everything pertaining to their rituals, their organization, and their conspiracy to obtain ultimate undisputed world domination. Every member is sworn to give unlimited obedience to the head of the Illuminati, and to recognize no mortal as above him. The only persons who could name names would be top-level members of the Illuminati. It is most unlikely that any one of them would do so.

However, as has been pointed out previously, God in His goodness from time to time permitted the most secret writings of "The Order and Sect of the Illuminati" to fall into hands other than intended while in process of circulation. As the result of *repeated* Acts of God we have been able to learn the details of the Illuminati's Long Range Plans to obtain ultimate world domination and impose the Luciferian ideology upon mankind. Henry Ford Sr. said in the early 1920s "No person can deny that the conspiracy, as detailed in the Protocols, has developed EXACTLY as predicted."

This being a fact we only have to study current affairs to learn what those who form the Invisible Government are doing now to develop the conspiracy into the final stage. The Illuminati have been able to develop their conspiracy, EXACTLY as was intended by Weishaupt, because they have been able to place their agentur behind the scenes of succeeding governments as "Experts", "Specialists", and "Advisors". We can prove that the "Experts", "Specialists", and "Advisors", meet secretly, and it is reasonable to presume those who do so meet must be members, or agentur, of the Illuminati.

We have said, that in order to project the continuing Luciferian conspiracy from its present, into the final stage, the plan requires that Political Zionism and the Moslem world be involved in war one with the other. We have explained why the Illuminati consider such a war is necessary. We repeat once again that unless the Illuminati can scare the people of the world into accepting their rule submissively they intend to foment two more wars to force the masses to become subservant to their will. The first will be between those who will be *forced* to support Political Zionism, and those who will be *forced* to support the Moslem world. The second and last war, if considered necessary, will be between those who are FORCED to support Atheistic-Communism, and those who will be FORCED to fight to preserve Christianity.

These being plain statements of FACT it is only reasonable to conclude that the "Experts", "Specialists", and "Advisors" who met secretly, in the King & Prince Hotel, upon St. Simon's Island, located off the coast of Georgia, behind closed doors, under the protection of heavily armed guards, Feb. 14th. to 17th. 1957, are members of, or top-level agentur of, the Illuminati. Many who attended may not be *initiated members of 'The Order and Sect of the Illuminati''*. Probably they don't realize that as Humanitarins, World Federalists, Communists, Fascists, or what have you, they are never-the-less Agentur of the Illuminati. What they do, and the policies they foist upon their governments, further the secret plans of the Illuminati to obtain ultimate world domination. Those who are not members of the Illuminati are playing with a gun both barrels of which are loaded. They are being used to press the trigger. It is immaterial whether those who press the trigger know whether the gun they hold is loaded or not, the fact remains that if they continue to put pressure upon the trigger that gun going to go off and kill those at whom it is aimed. In our particular case the blast will destroy all remaining political and religious institutions and nothing will then remain to prevent the Illuminati usurping absolute control of human beings body, mind, and soul.

We have frequently mentioned "Acts of God" but we never expected to witness "An Act of God". Prior to Christmas 1956 I had not thought of making a trip to Florida in February 1957. If anyone had suggested such a thing I would have asked them "What on?... Buttons!" Then the first part of the modern miracle happened. I took ill again. I had only been discharged from hospital November 1956. My doctor couldn't seem to find any good cause for my relapse, so he suggested I take a rest and change. I asked him "What on?... Buttons!" Then quite unexpectedly my wife and I came into a little money; enough to finance a month's holiday. We decided we would go to Florida. At the very last minute we changed our route because we were asked to speak at several places. The fact that I accepted these invitations enabled me to learn about the secret meeting being held on St Simon's Island Feb. 14th. to 17th.

I ask the reader to study the political activities of the men I name as attending that secret conference. Inquire into their private lives. Check to find out if they actually live according to what they profess to be. A few of them profess to belong to religions which teach belief in Almighty God as the Creator of Heaven and Earth. Check and see if they really worship God or Mammon. Regardless of what they pretend to be, none of them can deny that collectively, they are ALL ONE WORLDERS.

Men of good will don't try to hide their actions, preserve their identity, or keep secret their intentions. Men who work to promote the establishment of God's plan for the rule of Creation, on this earth, don't usually have out of season fruits and vegetables; wild ducks, pheasants, and partridge; speckled trout; the rarest of delicacies; fish and game; the choicest cuts of meat and fowl; vintage wines, and the best liquors flown in from all parts of the world to grace their banquet tables. But that is what those who attended the meeting on St Simon's Island had to eat and drink. What the delegates ate and drank was in strange contrast to the Last Supper eaten by Christ and his disciples.

What is recorded here is not fiction, or a modern version of Arabian Nights. At 3 P.M. Feb., 15th. Howard Hughes' DC-3. delivered Otto Wolff, at the air-port near Brunswick, Georgia. He is head of the German Steel Industries bearing his name. At 6.10 P.M. a new Beechcraft plane unloaded C. D. Jackson, Arthur Hayes Sulzberger, of New York Times, and Michael Heilperin (now teaching at Geneva). At 7.30 P.M. Gaylord Box Co's DC-3 set down 9 foreigners including Paul Van Zeeland Belgian banker and former Prime Minister. At 7.45 P.M. a DC-3 belonging to H. J. Heinz (the pickle, and pork and bean man) delivered 13 people including Prince Bernhardt of the Netherlands. At 7.50 P.M., as darkness closed down, Senators Wiley and Fulbright stepped out of a chartered Eastern Airlines plane. At 9.25 a plane belonging to the Chase National Bank deposited David Rockefeller, Winthrop Aldrich, and Tom Dewey.

We have it upon reliable authority that the purpose of the meeting was to make those invited realize it was useless for their governments to hope to beat the Communist policy of "Perpetual wars and revolution until perpetual peace is assured". The delegates were urged to "Advise" their governments to accept the idea of a One World Government, and a One World monetary system, as the ONLY alternative. They were asked to put the idea into effect at the earliest possible moment.

All those invited had, at one time or another, admitted publicly that they were in favour of a One World Government. At this meeting they were told to threaten their governments with atomic wars and revolutionary uprisings if they didn't put their ideas into practice.

Those who addressed the delegates then spread on the butter. They pointed out that those present represented the 'Brains' of their respective countries. They made them feel that they were much better qualified to rule the world than a mob of uncultured Communists. It was pointed out to them that if they composed the first World Government BRAINS would rule instead of brute force : the masses would be given what was considered good for them; a World Police Force, would make wars and rebellion impossible. The World would then enjoy Peace and prosperity. What was said sounded very practical. Delegates were asked to endorse the ideas expressed to them. They did, and this fact was made known to Prime Minister Harold MacMillan of Britain, and President Eisenhower. This explains the hurriedly arranged meeting between the two in Bermuda shortly afterwards.

But what was not explained to the delegates was the fact that their acceptance of the proposals furthered the Illuminati's secret plan in as much as they are prepared to usurp the powers of the first One World Government to be established. This conference was a continuation of a series known as the Bilderberg Conferences named after the location in Germany were the first of this series was held.

Paul Martin, Canadian Minister for Health and Welfare, and Arnold D. P. Heeney, Canadian Ambassador to Washington, represented Canada's One Worlders at the meeting. Friends of both men say they just cannot understand WHY they accepted such an invitation. It is just possible they don't know they are being asked to sell their country, and its people, to the Illuminati, lock, stock, and barrel. Just before the Federal election, Mr. Heeney was brought back to Ottawa and was installed as head of Canada's Civil Service Commission. As such he can place in, or remove from, key positions in the civil service, any person he so desires. It looks as if history made in this regard in 1925 is repeating itself.

It may not have any connection, but it so happens. A. D. P. Heeney was Clerk of the Privy Council of Canada when the Royal Commission was appointed in June 1946 to "Investigate the facts relating to, and the circumstances surrounding, the communication, by public officials, and other persons in positions of trust, of secret and confidential information to agents of a foreign power." This was the inquiry into Soviet Spy Activities in Canada. I can't find any mention in the record of the fact that Soviet officials meet with Canadian, and U.S. officials in a similar secret meeting held at Mont Tremblant, P. Quebec, Dec. 4th. to 14th. 1942.

The following are 72 of the 91 one men who attened the meeting :

1. His Royal Highness Bernhard, Prince of the Netherlands.
2. J. H. Retinger, Polish Charge D'Affairs in Russia 1941.
3. Jos. E. Johnson. Pres. Foundation for International Peace.
4. Hon. F. D. Aster, Ed. of "The Observer", United Kingdom.
5. Geo. W. Bell, Attorney for Cleary, Gottlieb, Friendly & Bell.
6. Fritz. Berg, Chairman of Fed. of German Industries, Germany.
7. M. Nuri Birgi, Sect-Gen. Ministry Foreign Affairs, Turkey.
8. Eugene R. Black, Pres. International Bank.
9. Robt. R. Bowie, Ast. Sec. State for Policy Planning, U.S.A.
10. McGeorge Bundy, Dean of Faculty of Arts & Science, Harvard U.
11. Hakon Christianson, Chairman East Asiatic Co., Denmark.
12. Walter Ciser, Pres. Atomic Industrial Forum, U.S.A.
13. Pierre Commin, Sect. French Socialist Party.
14. B. D. Cooke, Director Dominion Ins. Co., United Kingdom.
15. Arthur H. Dean, Law partner of John Foster Dulles.
16. Dean De La Garde, French Ambassador to Mexico.

17. Thomas E. Dewey, Former Governor of New York.
18. Sir Wm. Elliot, Air Chief Marshall, Royal Institute, U. K.
19. Fritz Erler, Socialist M.P., Germany.
20. John Ferguson, Attorney, Cleary, Gottlieb, Friendy & Bell.
21. Lincoln Gordon, Prof., Consultant to NATO'S "Three Wise Men".
22. Sir Collins Gubbins, Industrialist, United Kingdom.
23. Lawrence R. Hafstad, Tech. advisor Atomic Energy Commission.
24. Senator Wm. J. Fulbright, U.S.A.
25. Gabriel Hauge, Administrative Ast. to Pres. Eisenhower, Ec. Affs.
26. Jens Christian Hauge, Socialist M.P., Norway.
27. Brooks Hays, House Foreign Affairs Committee.
28. Denis Healey, Labour M.P., United Kingdom.
29. Arnold D. P. Heeney, Canadian Ambassador to the U.S.A., Former Clerk
    of P. C.
30. Michael A. Heilperin, Economist, U.S.A.
32. Leif Hoagh, International Banker, Norway.
33. Paul G. Hoffman, Former Director Economic Administration, U. N. Deleg.
34. C. D. Jackson, Time Inc. Former Spec. Ast. to Pres. Eisenhower.
35. P. Jacobson, Managing Dir. International Monetary Fund, Sweden.
37. Geo. P. Keenan, Former U. S. Ambassador to the U.S.S. Rs.
38. Geo. Kurt Kiesieger, Chairman Foreign Policy Com., Germany.
39. Viscount Kilmuir, Lord Chancellor, United Kingdom.
40. Henry Kisinger, Dir. Special Studies, Rockefeller Foundation.
41. Pieter Liefnick, Dir. International Monetary Fund, Netherlands.
42. Imbraiani Longo, Dir. Gen. Banco Nazionale Del Lavoro, Italy.
43. Paul Martin, Minister Health & Welfare, Canada.
44. David J. McDonald, Pres. United Steel Workers of America.
45. Geo. C. McGhee, Dir. Middle East Institute.
46. Ralph E. McGill, Editor, Atlanta Constitution.
47. Alex. W. Menne, Pres. Associated German Chemical Industries, Germany.
48. Rudolf Mueller, Corp. Lawyer, Germany.
49. Robt. Murphy, Deputy Under Sect. of State, U.S.A.
50. Frank C. Nash, Former Ast. Sect. of Defence, U.S.A.
51. Geo. Nebolisine, Attorney to Coudert Brs., U.S.A.
52. Paul H. Nitza, Dir. Policy Planning, State Dept., U.S.A.
53. Morehead Patterson, Dept. Commissioner of Disarmament, U.S.A.
54. Don J. Price, Vice-Pres. Ford Foundation, U.S.A.
55. Henry Lithgow Roberts, Dir. of Russian Institute, Columbia Un.
56. David Rockefeller, Chairman of the Board., Chase National Bank.
57. M. Van Roijen, Netherlands, Ambassador to the U.S.A.
58. Dean Rusk, Pres. Rockefeller Foundation.
59. Paul Rykans, Industrialist, Netherlands.
60. J. L. S. Steele, Chairman, British Inst. Chamber of Commerce.
61. Arthur Hays Sulzberger, Pres. New York Times.
62. Terkel M. Terkelson, Editor Denmark.
63. John M. Vorys, Member Foreign Affairs Committee, U.S.A.
64. Alexander Wiley, Senator, Foreign Affairs Committee, U.S.A.
65. Frasor B. Wilde, Commission on Economic Development.
66. Otto Von. Amerongen Wolff, Partner Otto Wolff, Germany.
67. W. T. Wren, Chairman, Allied Iron Founders, United Kingdom.
68. Paul Van Zeeland, Financier, Former Belgium Prime Minister.

We have it on reliable authority that in addition to those named Judge Felix Frankfurter, Harold Stassen, Antoine Pinay, former president of France, and Paul Warburg of Kuhn Loeb & Co., International Bankers of New York, also were present. The names of the remaining unidentified people who attended are included in the following list of those invited. All who were invited did not attend hovever.

1. Nelson A. Rockefeller, International Banker and intimate of President Ensenhower, David, Chairman of the Board, Chase Bank, represented the Rockefeller klan at Sea Island..
2. David Sarnoff of RCA, past chairman of National Security Training Commission.
3. Robert J. Oppenheimer.
4. Joseph C. Harsch of the Christian Science Monitor.
5. Dean Acheson, State Secretary under Truman.
6. Raymond Fosdick, Churchman.
7. Thomas S. Lamont, International Banker.
8. Phillip C. Jessup, formerly of State Department.
9. Brooks Emery.
10. Karl T. Compton, Scientist.
11. Owen Lattimore.
12. Maj. Gen. Lyman L. Lemnitzer, Asst Chief of Staff.
13. Harry F. Guggenheim.
14. Palmer Hoyt of Denver Post Pub.
15. Senator Ralph E. Flanders.
16. Adolphe A. Berle.
17. Benjamin B. Cohen of the U.N.
18. Harry D. Gideonse.
19. Elmer Davis
20. Sidney Weinberg, International Banker and White House intimate.
21. Harold K. Guinsberg.
22. Walter J. Levy.
23. Lewis Strauss of Atomic Energy Commission.
24. Allen W. Dulles of C. I. A.
25. Arthur M. Anderson of the Export-Import Bank.
26. Gen. Alfred M. Gruenther.
27. John Gunther, writer and commentator.
28. Walter Lippman.
29. William S. Paley of CBS.
30. Chas. E. Saltzman of Kuhn Loeb Co.
31. Gerard Swope, Jr.
32. Eric M. Warburg.
33. Joseph Barnes.
34. Gardner Cowles, Publisher.
35. David E. Lilienthal, ex-head Atomic Energy Commission.
36. Alexander Sachs of Sachs-Goldman Bankers.
37. Isador Lubin.
38. Edward R. Murrow.
39. Henry R. Luce.
40. Isador Rabi, Advisor, Atomic Energy Commission.
41. Wayne Coy.

42. Cord Meyer, Jr.
43. Herbert Bayard Swope.
44. Sherman Adams, White House Staff Advisor (unofficial President).

Isn't this the most fantastic story ever written? It proves the old saying that TRUTH is stranger than fiction. Now let the reader recall events that happened immediately after the meeting ended. Stassen flew to London to take part in the so called disarmament discussions. What a farce it has turned out to be. The American and Soviet delegates put on an act to impress the masses and make them believe that only a One World Government can save them from death by nuclear weapons. Those who have read so far realize that the Soviet delegates, and the American, are both controlled by "The Secret Power", "The Invisible government", which is the Illuminati.

Next thing Norman's death is reported. He had evidently been caught playing both ends against the middle on the international level of intrigue. He was found out. Either the Illuminati, or the Marxian Communists ordered that he be MADE to take his own life.

President Eisenhower's "Near East Program" was endorsed by the Senate and House of Representatives. He was given asbolute power to declare war if HE THOUGHT FIT. Nobody but a fool will argue that Eisenhower can exercice his own will. If he didn't do as ADVISED he wouldn't last as long as a snowball in Hell.

The new British Prime Minister and Eisenhower met in Bermuda. They have received their instructions so there wont be a repetition of the British-French Suez shamozzle. They have been told the present policy is to scare the people into accepting a One World Government. If this fails the world must be divided into two hostile camps and subjected to another taste of total war.

The Supreme Court of the U.S.A. took action to protect Communist stooges of the Illuminati from 'persecution' by the F.B.I. and Senate Investigating Committees. The Illuminati can't have the Communist Party broken up while they still intend to use it to foment a revolt which will enable Eisenhower to declare "A STATE OF EMERGENCY" and impose a military dictatorship upon the American people. Few people seem able to realize that a dictatorship is a dictatorship regardless of whether it be labeled Communist or Luciferian. The visible dictator will only dictate what he is told to dictate by the Illuminati until they are ready to crown their leader King-despot of the world. They intend to postpone this event until no power or cunning can prevent them forcing the people of the universe to accept their international Super-Government with submissiveness. The next thing to happen was the failure of the U.S.A.'s guided missiles while the Soviet launched the first man — made satellite.

The Protocols of the Illuminati state in Par, 4 of Article IX, how they will inflict famines, pestilence, (the Asian Flu) and wars upon the people. "Until by these acts ALL States are in torture; they exhort to tranquility, are ready to sacrifice everything for peace: but we will not give them peace until they openly acknowledge our international Super-Government and with submissivenes." Study Articles I -24; V 6-11; VI, 3; IX 3-4; XI, 8; XII, 5; of the Protocols and you will know exactly what the Illuminati have in store for you. Remember, when they use the word 'God' they refer to Lucifer. When they mention the 'Chosen People' they mean the Illuminati and their top-level agentur, a few millionaires, devoted to their Cause, and those economists and professors of the Arts and Sciences, who have defected from our God and sold themselves to the devil.

These horrors are being planned, and yet all we have to do to stop the conspirators DEAD in their tracks is to create the force of public opinion. Short of direct intervention by Almighty God it is the only thing that can stop them. I say again, what I have said before : The world's population have it in their own hands to decide if the intervention of Almighty God shall come sooner or later. He will intervene on behalf of His Elect just as soon as enough human beings prove we are sincere in asking for His intervention. There is only ONE way ANY person can PROVE his or her sincerity, that is to translate what they PRAY into ACTION. Just as soon as enough people are working to defeat the Luciferian conspiracy God will send Christ to complete the task. Then, and not until then, will we enjoy peace and prosperity, and enjoy calm and tranquility.

The way the One Worlders try to frighten the masses into acceptance of the Luciferian dictatorship by threatening them with death by nuclear bombs, and nerve gas, reminds me of two privates in the Irish Regiment. They were in the trenches in France during the first World War. Death lay all around them. Shells burst near them as they watched two airplanes engaged in a dog-fight up in the blue sky. Suddenly one plane crashed into the other. The impact of the collision caused them to disintegrate. Pat gasped and said to Mike. "Begorrah Mike! How would *you* sooner die... in a collision or an explosion?" Said Mike "Why Pat that's easy to decide. I'd rather die in a collision."

"For why?" asked Pat.

"Sure Pat. In a collision there you are. In an explosion where are you?"

The moral of this story is this : Because, in order to enjoy ETERNAL life, we all have to die; it doesn't really matter when or how we die. The only thing that really matters is that we are prepared to die? If the person about to die is firmly resolved in his Faith, and belief in Almighty God, it doesn't matter whether disease, an atomic blast, nerve gas; a knife or a bullet, severs the thin cord which keeps the soul earth-bound. No person needs to fear, or be alarmed, at the thought of persecution or death provided he has done his, or her, best to promote the establishment of God's rule while on this earth.

People with perfect faith do not fear the forces of evil. They are protected by Almighty God until he sees fit to relieve them of the Cross they have volunteered to carry. Christ said : "Not even the poisoned cup shall harm them". For every person who wrote to say my writings have made them afraid, a hundred have written to say they have found peace of soul and tranquility of mind, since they had had the Truth regarding the continuing Luciferian conspiracy explained to them.

I want to assure the Ministers, and Priests, of ALL religions, which teach belief in Almighty God, that we need, and will welcome, their cooperation. With their help we could rapidly make known the fundamental TRUTHS regarding the diabolical plot directed by the Illuminati for the purpose of enslaving the Human Race physically, mentally, and spiritually.

I can see no good reason why the teaching of the TRUTH regarding the existence of the continuing Luciferian conspiracy should clash with each others religious convictions. We should ALL want God's plan for the rule of Creation established upon this earth. That is something upon which everybody, who believes in God, can agree. Then why not unite for this common purpose and put the idea into practice?

APPENDIX II

The Norman Case

Two years ago in the first edition of this book stated that Egerton Herbert Norman was not a Communist but was a subversive. I now ask The Hon. Lester Pearson to answer the following questions regarding his late "Expert" on Far Eastern Affairs, knowing that all the information necessary has been made available to the Minister of Justice, and can be obtained from the R.C.M.P., and the F.B.I. I suggest that readers ask members of the Parliament of Canada, these same questions and demand the truthful answers. It is not suggested that ALL politicians are crooks or fools. It is believed that the vast majority of our elected representatives are honest and sincere men, but they are ill informed, or badly misinformed regarding political intrigue on the national and international levels. Some have allowed themselves to be inveigled into situations, and circumstances, which permit the Agentur of the Illuminati to apply political blackmail. N.B.N. has made a thorough study of THE CONTINUING LUCIFERIAN CONSPIRACY. We are convinced that the Illuminati obtain control at the TOP and make use of ALL secrets societies, and ALL forms of subversion and perversion, to further their own secret plans to obtain ultimate world domination, in order that they can then crown THEIR leader King-despot of the entire world. He will then impose the Luciferian dictatorship upon the human race by means of Satanic despotism. We believe that the ONLY way to defeat their Long Range Plan, which has now entered the semi-final phase, is to make the TRUTH regarding the history, and intentions, of THE ORDER AND SECT OF THE ILLUMINATI known to thinking people throughout the world. With this object in view we ask Mr. Pearson, and others involved in the Norman case, to answer, or obtain answers, to the following questions.

1) Can Mr. Pearson deny that he was sent a copy of "The Red Fog over America" early in 1956 and that his attention was called to the subversive record of E.H. Norman as set forth on pages 192 to 218?

2) Can Mr. Pearson truthfully deny that E.H. Norman became a member of the Young Communist League, and the Communist front organization known as "The League Against War and Fascism" in 1938-1940?

3) Can he deny there is evidence on file to prove that Norman, during his student days, participated in experiments in the use of drugs for subversive purposes, and that one such experiment included the introduction of a very powerful purgative into the refreshments served to fellow-students who attended a dance? Were the effects of this drug not such that many of those who ingested it, with their food, were rendered absolutely helpless? Is it not true that a reporter for the *Toronto Daily Star* exposed this conspiracy and stated that he had heard one of the students involved remark, "Oh! Boy, if you could only introduce that stuff into the food rations of an opposing army you could take them all prisoners without firing a shot"? Tre drug had the same effects as fluorine whether or not it was fluorine, I cannot say.

4) Was E.H. Norman not a member of a Communist front organization known as "The Canadian Youth Congress" during his student days? Did not The Hon. Paul Martin, now Minister of Health and Welfare, and Mr. Pearson's associate in United Nations affairs, and the Hon. T.C. Douglas, Premier of Saskatchewan, take a large group of these young radicals over to Geneva, Switzerland, in 1936 and there introduce them to top-level members of the Illuminati who had usurped power in Russia at the end of the 1917 revolution? Did the revolutionary leaders not include Litvinov and Manuilsky?

5) Is it not true that Norman's association with Paul Martin, and T.C. Douglas, enabled him to obtain the financial aid from the Rockefeller Foundation which paid for his education, and training, as an "Expert" on Far Eastern Affairs, at Harvard University?

6) It is not true that while at Harvard, Norman was trained by Moses Finklestien, Tsuru Shigato, a Japanese, and Dr. K.A. Wittfogel, a German? Were these three 'Professors' not subsequently found guilty of subversive activities.

7) Can Mr. Pearson deny that after the F.B.I. arrested Tsuru Shigato, and held him for deportation, Norman misrepresented himself as "Acting for the Canadian Government" when he tried to obtain possession of Shigato's belonging among which was a copy of a report on "The Nye Munitions Plant" which report had been mainly prepared by Alger Hiss, afterwards convicted of perjury when accused of being one of the Soviet's Master Spies in the

U.S.A.? Is it not true that when Norman's attempt to obtain the Nye Report failed he told the F.B.I. that his interest in Shigato was "purely personal". Did he not do this to cover up senior Canadian officials for whom he worked? Did this loyalty to other Canadian subversives not afterwards make him commit suicide rather than betray them?

8) Is it not true that Norman joined "The Institute of Pacific Relations", the subversive activities of which were investigated by the U.S. Senate Committee, of which Judge Robert Morris was Council? Did this Committee not define the I.P.R. as (i) being an instrument of Communist policy, proganda, and military information; (ii) controlled by a small core identified as Communists, or pro-communists; (iii) an instrument used to orient American Far Eastern policy towards Communist objectives? Was the I.P.R. not in fact controlled by the Illuminati?

9) Has it not been the policy, of the Illuminists, who paid for Norman's education and training as a subversive, to build up the strength of International Communism until it equalled that of the so-called Christian Nations? Was this policy not clearly set forth in a letter dated Aug. 15th 1871, written by General Albert Pike of Charleston, S.C., U.S.A., to Joseph Mazzini, which letter is catalogued in the British Museum Library? Is it not true that General Pike was head of the Illuminati at the time he wrote the letter, and that Mazzini had been directing the Illuminati's revolutionary activities in Europe from 1834?

10) Does this evidence not clearly indicate that after Norman had been a Communist he switched over and became an agent of the Illuminati; and that those who serve the Illuminati in Canada, and the U.S.A., persuaded him to make this switch because he spoke both Chinese and Japanese fluently?

11) Does Pike's letter not state the policy of the Illuminati in 1871 was to bring about the subjugation of Russia in order that the Illuminati could turn that empire into the stonghold of international Communism and then use its destructive forces until all existing political and religious institutions had been made to destroy themselves in wars and revolutions the Illuminati would foment to make them fight each other? Can Mr. Pearson deny that the policy of the Illuminati, as explained by Pike to Mazzini, has not been carried out since 1871 EXACTLY as Pike intended? Can he deny that Mr. Norman was not furthering the Illuminati's secret plans in the Near East?

12) Does the concluding paragraph of Pike's letter to Mazzini not state that after the Illuminati's program has reached the stage when Atheistic Communism and Christianity alone remain as world powers, standing between the Illuminati and the day they will crown THEIR leader King-despot of the entire world, the Illuminati will THEN provoke a formidable social cataclysm to make Communist and Christians exterminate each other. Does Pike's letter not end with the statement that when this blood-bath ends those who survive *"Will receive the TRUE LIGHT through the universal manifesta-*

tion of the pure doctrine of Lucifer, brought finally out in the public view, a manifestation which will result from the general reactionary movement which will follow the destruction of Christianity and Atheism, both conquered and exterminated at the same time"?

13) Can Mr. Pearson deny that his three chief advisors, on Far Eastern Affairs, Egerton Herbert Norman, Chester Ronning, and Escott M. Reid, did actively influence policy regarding Far Eastern Affairs so that the Illuminati's objective has been reached, and International Communism is now equal in strength to the forces of the Christian world?

14) Is it not obvious that Norman, while pretending to work as a secret agent for the Communists, was discovered by Communist leaders to be an Agentur of the Illuminati? Was it not this discovery of his duplicity that made it "Hopeless to go on living"?

15) Can Mr. Pearson deny that Norman was a member of the Institute of Pacific Relations (I.P.R.) when appointed to the Canadian Legation in Tokio in 1940? Can Mr. Pearson deny that HE made this appointment despite the fact that Pat Walsh, an undercover agent for the R.C.M.P. had reported Norman to be a Communist? Is it not a fact that the only error Pat Walsh made was to call Norman a Communist when in fact he was an agentur of the Illuminati?

Can Mr. Pearson deny that immediately upon arrival in Japan Norman organized the Canadian Legation as a 'letter-drop' to be used by agents of the I.P.R.? Was this fact not established by sworn evidence given U.S.A. authorities which disclosed that Ed. C. Carter, who was General-Secretary of the I.P.R. at the time, with offices at 129 E. 52nd. St., New York, wrote W. L. Holland, an I.P.R. agent in New Zealand, and told him "Phil will be in Japan about Sept. 18th to October 6th and can be reached care of the Japanese I.P.R. Any very secret messages may be sent care of H. Norman at the Canadian Legation, Tokio." If these very secret messages were not subversive will Mr. Pearson explain why they were not sent through the usual diplomatic channels?

16) Can Mr. Pearson deny that while Norman served in Japan, U.S. intelligence officers reported that he associated with Israel Halperin, a Canadian Communist born of Russian parents? Did the report not state that Norman was trying to use his influence, as a member of the Canadian Legation, to obtain the release of convicted Communists Halperin wanted out of prison? Is it not a fact that Norman continued to associate with Halperin AFTER they both returned to Canada. Did Halperin not work in close cooperation with Dr. Raymond Boyer, and Norman while they arranged for the 8th conference of the I.P.R. to be held at Mont Tremblant, in the Province of Quebec, Dec., 4th to 14th 1942? Was not Halperin afterwards accused, and convicted by the Canadian Royal Commission as a Soviet spy?

17) Is it not true that while employed as an "Expert" and "Advisor" by Mr. Pearson, Norman, in cooperation with Dr. Ray-

mond Boyer, the Canadian millionaire scientist, and F.V. Fields, the U.S.A. millionaire One Worlder, arranged for the 8th conference of the I.P.R. to be held in the Mont Tremblant resort by assuring all the internationalists invited to attend that they could rest assured that their secret deliberations would not be interferred with by either the R.C.M.P. or the Anti-Subversive section of the Quebec Provincial Police ? Will Mr. Pearson explain who authorized Norman to give such assurance ?

18) Does Mr. Pearson dare deny that there is sworn evidence on file in the U.S.A. which proves that as soon as Norman had assured the members of the I.P.R. they would be safe from police interference in Canada, Ed. C. Carter, their Secretary-General in New York, immediately cabled V.M. Molotov at his address Narkomindal, Moscow and said. I quote the cablegram : — "Respectfully and urgently invite you to authorize some members of the Soviet Embassy in Washington, and the Soviet Legation in Ottawa, to attend eighth conference of the Institute of Pacific Relations Mont Tremblant, Dec. 4th to 14th, Province of Quebec. STOP. Influencial leaders coming from England, China, Fighting France, Phillipines, Netherlands, Australia, New Zealand, Canada, and the U.S.A. STOP. Vargo, Vertinsky, Oumansky, Motyler, familiar with institute purposes. STOP. Meetings will be private. STOP." Is it not a fact that those who attended this meeting were World Federalists who furthered the secret plans of the Illuminati ? Was the purpose of this meeting not to arrange so atomic scientists, working on the development of the Atomic Bomb, could pass scientific data over to their confreres working in the field of neuclear science behind the Iron Curtain ?

Can Mr. Pearson, or any other person who has read "Pawns In The Game", and "The Red Fog Over America", deny that this political intrigue, in which Norman played THE leading part, was not designed to enable the Illuminati build up the strength of Atheistic-Communism until it was equal in every way to that of the nations of so-called Christendom ? Did Norman, and those who directed his activities, not act in absolute accordance with the Illuminati's long Range plans to obtain ultimate world domination, as revised by Weishaupt, when he headed the Illuminati the last half of the 1700s ? Does this intrigue not fit in with Illuminist General Albert Pike's instructions written to Gussipi Mazzini Aug. 15th 1871 ? Do these facts not clearly prove that international Atheistic-Communism is, and always has been, controlled, and used, by the Illuminati, to further their own secret plans and Satanic ambitions ? Every intelligent person must admit that the millionaires, scientists, economists, and internationally-minded politicians, invited by Norman to attend the conference held in Mont Tremblant, were not ATHEISTIC COMMUNISTS. They were definately agentur of the Order and Sect of the Illuminati who use ALL subversive movements to further their own secret plans to usurp the powers of the first One World Government to be established.

19) Is it not true that evidence given before the Canadian Royal Commission, (which investigated Soviet subversive activities in

Canada in 1946) convicted many of those who attended the 8th conference of the I.P.R. as being involved in subversive activities on behalf of the Soviets. Is it not equally true that only those who supported Atheistic-Communism were charged and convicted, mainly on evidence given by Igor Gouzenko who deserted from the Soviet Embassy in 1945? Is it not equally true that evidence which would have involved, and probably convicted, Norman, Ronning, and Reid, Mr. Pearson's chief advisors on External Affairs, was suppressed together with evidence against others who were agentur of the Illumniati?

20) Can Mr. Pearson deny that Owen Lattimore and F.V. Fields both admitted to the U.S. Senate committee investigating Un-American Activities that every statement made in the preceeding paragraphs is TRUE? This being a fact how can Mr. Pearson justify the policy he adopted towards the U.S.A. Senate Committee in 1957 when they accused Norman of being subverse and wanted his activities investigated thoroughly? Both Lattimore and Fields admitted, when giving evidence, that Norman, Ronning, and Reid attended the 8th I.P.R. conference. Is it not true that such an attachment, and bond of affection, grew up between Dr. Raymond Boyer and his wife, and F.V. Fields and his wife, as the result of their activities on behalf of the Illuminati, that in keeping with typical Luciferian principals, regarding sex, they both agreed to swap wives? Who does Mr. Pearson consider men like these serve... God or Lucifer?

21) Can Mr. Pearson deny that it was at the 8th conference of the I.P.R., held at Mont Tremblant, that the Soviet espionage rings, as exposed by Gouzenko in 1945, were organized? Is this not the REAL reason Mr. Pearson objected to allowing Gouzenko to give evidence before the U.S. Senate Committee appointed to investigate these matters? Is the evidence I give here not the REAL reason why Mr. Pearson, and his fellow One Worlders within the Canadian Cabinet, restricted Gouzenko to answering questions (put to him by U.S. officials who interviewed him in Canada) which concerned ONLY American citizens?

22) Mr. Pearson admits he knew of the adverse report made by the R.C.M.P. in 1940 against Norman. He admits he knew of Norman's Communist associations prior to 1940, at which time he engaged him as an "Expert" and "Advisor" on Far Eastern Affairs, then why did he hire him? Was it because HE, Mr. Pearson knew that Norman had ceased to be a Communist and become a well bred, highly educated, and thoroughly trained agentur of the Illuminati?

23) Will Mr. Pearson explain why he shipped Messrs. Norman, Ronning, and Reid to New Zealand, China, and India respectively in 1950 when U.S. investigating committees put the heat on by calling witnesses who connected them with various forms of subversion? Can Mr. Pearson give any satisfactory explanation to the Canadian electorate for sending these three specialists to the trouble spots of the Near and Middle East to act officially as Canada's representative while they unofficially, and secretly, work to bring about

conditions in Asia and Asia Minor which will enable the Illuminati to involve the Human Race in World War Three if the people persist in refusing to accept the Illuminati's totalitarian rule submissively?

24) Is it not a fact that since these three "Specialists" were sent to the Near and Middle East conditions have developed EXACTLY as Pike required they be developed in the letter he addressed to Mazzini in 1871? Can Mr. Pearson deny that since Norman's death U.S. Intelligence Officers in that area refer to Ronning and Reid as "THE ALGER HISS — OWEN LATTIMORE COMBINATION OF CANADA"?

25) Can Mr. Pearson deny that when U.S. investigating committees exposed the subversive activities of the I.P.R. the Canadian Branch (headed by Edgar McInnis, a close associate of Norman, Ronning, and Reid) hurridly changed its name to "The Canadian Institute of International Affairs"? Is this subversive organization not given wonderful support by the C.B.C.? By subversive I mean ANY movement the members of which advocate surrender of our national sovereignty to ANY kind of a ONE WORLD GOVERNMENT.

26) Can Mr. Pearson deny that in June 1955 he authorized Mr. Escot Reid, whom he had apponted as Canadian High Commissioner to India, to use a special plane and fly to Sackville, New Brunswick, where the I.P.R. were holding a conference? Was Mr. Reid not authorized to represent Mr. Pearson officially at this conference? Did he not make the suggestion that the Canadian Branch of the I.P.R. change its name to "The Canadian Institute of International Affairs"? Is it not true that these men, who serve international capitalism (The Illuminati) have tried to control those who attend the Lake Couchiching conferences ever since? Can Mr. Pearson explain why the C.B.C. is permitted to give these World Federalists unlimited support? Why do the Provincial Boards of Education make Edgar McGinnis financially independent by using his books as text books in our schools if the One Worlders do not control education as well as politics in Canada?

27) Can Mr. Pearson deny that the FACTS, as revealed in the preceeding paragraphs, PROVE the existence of the continuing international conspiracy, as now being directed by the members of the Order and Sect of The Illuminati? Can he deny they use highly educated, and thoroughly trained agentur, such as the late E.H. Norman, to further their secret plans and diabolical ambitions? This being the case how can Mr. Pearson qualify as the LEADER of the Liberal Party in Canada? No man can serve two masters. An honest leader of a National political party cannot permit himself to be involved in international intrigue regardless of whether it is called Naziism, World Federalism, Communism, or Political Zionism. ALL these international organizations, and movements, are controlled AT THE TOP by the Illuminati whose declared purpose is to usurp the powers of the FIRST World Government to be established. Mr. Pearson should know that, according to the Illuminati's plan, if the directors cannot PERSUADE the remaining governments to convince their people to accept the idea of a One World Govern-

ment, they will submit the world's population ever to increasing economic pressures and more extensive, and more deadly, wars. Why doesn't he tell the TRUTH and shame the devil? Is he afraid? or is he a willing agentur of the Illuminati?

28) Can Mr. Pearson deny that he has been provided with authentic and positive proof that Norman committed suicide because he feared further investigation, and questioning by U.S. officials would cause him to involve a considerable number of Canadian government officials who are up to their necks in international intrigue? Does Mr. Pearson not know that it is the practice of those who direct the Illuminati's conspiracy to dispose of agentur who begin to loose their nerve. Does he not know that psycho-politicians are taught that the best way to dispose of these weaklings is to administer drugs which provide suicidal tendencies. Will Mr. Pearson answer this $64,000 question. "Why did you permit Norman's body to be flown to Italy, and cremated, BEFORE an autopsy had determined whether, drugs, or fear, had caused Norman to commit suicide?"

APPENDIX III

The McCarthy Case

The progress of the continuing Luciferian conspiracy moves at such a pace that we had no sooner included the Norman case as appendix II than Senator Joseph McCarthy died under mysterious circumstances in Bethesda Hospital. This is the same government institution in which James Forrestal is supposed to have committed suicide, also by jumping out of a window. He was in the Neurological Ward when he jumped. It is in the Neurological wards that drugs, which can induce suicidal tendencies, are used for purposes of diagnosis. An over dose of these drugs causes suicidal tendencies.

The circumstances surrounding the death of Senator McCarthy should be probed to the bottom. He also was moved to the Neurological ward before he died. Could it be that he died BEFORE he could be made to commit suicide as Norman and Forrestal had done?

Some of the circumstances surrounding the death of Senator McCarthy which will stand investigation are:

1) McCarthy was allowed to run 'Hog Wild' just as long as he named those he accused of subversion as being Communists, or pro-Communists. It was not until he had been informed that the

Illuminati controlled international Communism AT THE TOP, that he was forced into political eclipse.

2) Pressure was released when he appeared to accept defeat submissively. But when he explained to others, who took his place, how Weishaupt in 1776, and Pike in 1871, had laid down how Atheistic-Communism was to be used by the Illuminati to further THEIR secret plans and ambitions, then those who are "The Secret Power" behind the scenes of our elected governments, apparently decided it was time he was eliminated.

3) It is known that McCarthy submitted to a thorough physical examination just before he entered Bethesda Hospital. An intimate friend informed us that his private physician found nothing seriously wrong. He discovered no signs of Hepatitis.

7) The text book used to teach Psychopolitics in the Lenin Institute in Moscow is based on the Freudian theories. It says that all troublesome people shall be taken out of circulation by rendering them temporally insane by injection of such drugs as Peyote, Mescaline, and Lysergic Acid Diethylamide. The victims can then be certified as insane and placed in mental 'Hospitals'. An over dose of the named drugs are said to induce suicidal tendencies.

The text book also states that people, who have great influence with the masses who oppose the progress of the conspiracy towards world domination shall be eliminated but it warns that their deaths must be made to look as if they had died accidentally, from natural causes, or as suicides.

8) Beria, one time head of the Soviet Secret Police, gave an address to a group of American doctors who were studying Psychopolitics at the Lenin Institute. He told them that Psychopoliticians should filtrate into ALL Neurological wards and mental hospitals where they could obey the orders of those who directed the international conspiracy without fear of detection. Among a great many other things Beria told them is the following. I quote: "You must labour until you have domination over the minds and bodies of every important person in your nation. You must labour until every doctor and psychiatrist is either a psychopolitician or an unwitting assistant to our aims." Could it be possible that the American doctors who studied Psychopolitics in Moscow have been, and still are, literally getting away with murder?

9) In support of my statements, and to justify my comments on this subject, I reproduce a copy of Senator McCarthy's death certificate, and with it the comments expressed by Dr. Emanuel M. Josephson, M.D.

4) According to another of McCarthy's friends the Senator mentioned to him that he was going into Bethesda Hospital and the friend asked him. "Why are you going into that place? Have you never heard of a Guy named James Forrestal?" Investigators should find out if McCarthy REQUESTED to go into hospital for a check up of his war disabilities, or was *ordered* to report for medical treatment.

5) Press reports stated McCarthy was transferred from the medical to the Neurological ward where he died. Investigators

should determin WHY this was done. Psychopoliticians, who serve the Illuminati after being trained in the Lenin Institute in Moscow, have been infiltrated into the Neurological wards and Mental institutions throughout the so called Free World. Readers may obtain further information regarding this phases of the Illuminati's conspiracy by studying "Brainwashing" published by Keneth Goff.

6) In order that readers won't think we immagine these things we will quote Article XV, Par. 9, of the Protocols which are based on the "Original Writing of the Order and Sect of the Illuminati." I quote: "Death is the inevitable end of all. It is better to bring that end nearer to those who hindered our affairs than to ourselves, the founders of this affair", i.e. The International Conspiracy as directed by the Illuminati. "We execute Masons in such wise that none save the Brotherhood can ever have suspicion of it, not even the victims themselves of our death sentence, they all die as required as if from a normal kind of illness... While preaching liberalism to the Goyim, (human cattle they plot to subjugate) we at the same time keep our own people, and our agents, in a state of unquestioning submission." The above explains how the Illuminati dispose of Grand Orient Masons who have outlived their usefulness. Is it not logical to presume that the Illuminati will dispose of others they hate or fear in a similar manner if possible ?

"McCARTHY'S DEATH CERTIFICATE"

The death certificate issued by Lt. C.U. Shilling of the U.S. Naval Hospital at Bethesda, Md. and the newspaper release by the

Hospital to the effect that the acute hepatitis in this case was not infectious, make it quite clear that the death was due to the other cause of hepatitis—POISON. What poison killed McCarthy, the death certificate, that is reproduced below, relates was not determined prior to death. The certificate reads: " ... cause unknown".

The laws of the Federal Government, and of every State in the Union, make it a crime to bury a person dead of an unknown cause; and they require an autopsy in every such case to determine the cause of death and eliminate the possibility of foul play, or murder. WHY WAS NO AUTOPSY DONE ON McCARTHY IN COMPLIANCE WITH THE LAW? WHY DID THE AUTHORITIES REFUSE TO COMPLY WITH THE LAW IN SPITE OF INSISTENT DEMANDS FROM THE PUBLIC? WHAT MURDEROUS GANG COMMITTED THIS MURDER? WAS IT THE SAME GANG AS WAS RESPONSIBLE FOR THE MURDER OF FORRETAL, LARRY DUGGAN, AND HUNDREDS OTHERS?

WE DEMAND A PUBLIC INVESTIGATION OF THIS MURDER

Committee for the Investigation of the Death of Senator
Joseph McCarthy

230 E. 61 St.   New York 21   New York

Emanuel M. Josephson M.D., Chairman.

INDEX

END OF INDEX

Recommended Books from Bridger House Publishers, Inc.

Conspirator's Hierarchy:
The Story of the Commitee
of 300
By Dr. John Coleman
$18.95 + Shipping
288 pages
ISBN: 978-0-922356-57-7

Chaos in America
By John L. King
$16.95 + Shipping
290 pages
ISBN: 978-1-893157-09-5

Chemtrails Confirmed
By William Thomas
$16.95 + Shipping
336 pages
ISBN: 1-893157-10-5

The Federal Reserve
Conspiracy
By Antony C. Sutton
$10.00 + Shipping
124 pages
ISBN: 1-893157-15-6

Mass Murder Is Liberty
By Alan Ernest
$16.95 + Shipping
288 pages
ISBN: 978-0-9640104-3-7

Project Seek:
Onassis, Kennedy, and the
Gemstone Thesis
By Gerald A. Carroll
$16.95 + Shipping
432 pages
ISBN: 978-0-9640104-0-6

Secrets of the Federal
Reserve
By Eustace Mullins
$16.95 + Shipping
224 pages
ISBN: 978-0-9799176-5-3

Uncommon Sense
By William James Murray
$9.95 + Shipping
290 pages
ISBN: 978-0-9844733-8-0

What Every American
Should Know About the
Mid East & Oil
By James M. Day
$16.95 + Shipping
306 pages
ISBN: 978-0-9640104-7-5

To place an order call 1-800-729-4131

Handbook for the New Paradigm
Volume I

$6.95 + Shipping
192 pages   ISBN: 1-893157-04-0

The messages contained in this handbook are
intended to lift mankind from the entrapment of
the victim consciousness that keeps the level of
experience ensnared in fear and frustration.
Humanity was intended to live, not in luxury,
but in abundance. The information found in this
book will lead all that read and reread with an
open mind to the discovery of the truth of who and what they truly are. The
end of the search for these answers is provided at last in clarity and concise-
ness. There are no recriminations or feelings of guilt to be gleaned from these
pages. There is clarity and upliftment in each segment. It is the intent and
purpose of this small book to encourage every reader to live in accordance
with the plainly disclosed simple laws that underlay all that each compre-
hends as life. Each segment leads to greater understanding and to a simple
application that encompasses them in entirety in a few words that guarantee
absolute change in your day to day experience.

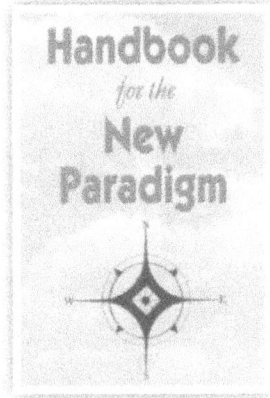

Embracing the Rainbow
Volume II

$6.95 + Shipping
144 pages   ISBN: 1-893157-05-9

Volume II of the Handbook For The New
Paradigm contains the continuing series of
messages guiding its readers to accept the con-
cepts contained within them for the purpose of
creating a new life experience for the "humans
becoming" on planet Earth. Each message broadens the conceptual under-
standings of the necessity to release the limitations that have been thrust
upon humanity preventing them from understanding who and what they truly
are. It contains surprising truths of some of the shocking deceptions intentionally taught that limit and separate mankind from their opportunities for
spiritual evolvement. It defines how it is possible to take back the heritage of
self-determination, freely create one's own destiny and heal the planet and
humanity as a whole living entity through the suggested dynamic process.

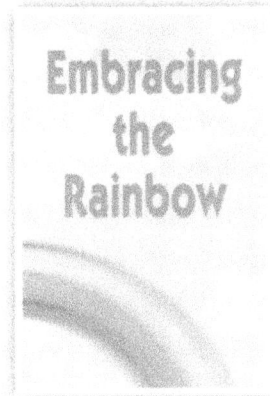

Becoming
Volume III

$6.95 + Shipping
180 pages   ISBN: 1-893157-07-5

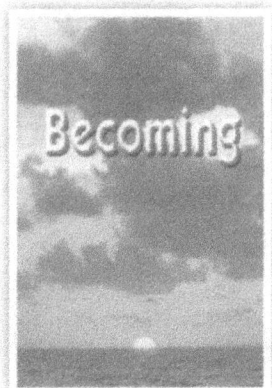

The messages contained in this, the third book, are offered for the continued realization of who and what each human being truly is. The consciousness changing information each volume contains brings forth the understanding that humanity on this planet is, in reality, a whole and holy awareness. From the global myriad of belief systems arises a single picture that represents a composite awareness. This totality of thought creates the reality of the human experience, a great deal of effort is now focused with the intent of influencing how the individual and the total global awareness perceive the human experience. The mind discerns what it understands is its surrounding reality but the feelings determine its believability. Confusion masks the ability to choose between what appears to be true and what the feelings believe to be true. Beneath all the rhetoric that is focused on the conscious and subconscious levels within the current deluge of information in all its various forms is the human desire for the freedom to choose what is for the highest and best good of each individual and the planetary whole. Mankind stands at the threshold, the decision point of whether to accept what it is being told is for its highest and best good or to instead shrug off the programmed suggestions and choose for itself a future that is in total contrast. At the heart of the matter is the opportunity to choose cooperation rather than competition, brotherly love and assistance rather than hate and violence. It is time to observe the world situation that has resulted from competition and experiencing the premise of survival of the fittest. It is time to begin.

ORDER ENTIRE SET

(Vol. I, II, III)

for $19.95 + Shipping and receive

Messages for the Ground Crew FREE

Call 1-800-729-4131 or www.nohoax.com

To place an order call

1-800-729-4131

Visit our website at

www.nohoax.com

www.ingramcontent.com/pod-product-compliance
Lightning Source LLC
Chambersburg PA
CBHW072114270326
41931CB00010B/1553